Intercultural Communication

Preliminary Edition

Edited by Tina Kistler

Santa Barbara City College

cognella®
academic publishing

Bassim Hamadeh, CEO and Publisher
Michael Simpson, Vice President of Acquisitions
Jamie Giganti, Managing Editor
Jess Busch, Graphic Design Supervisor
Jill Helmle, Acquisitions Editor
Brian Fahey, Licensing Associate

cognella
academic publishing

www.cognella.com   800-200-3908

CONTENTS

WHO ARE YOU?
UNDERSTANDING OTHERS

HOW DO WE GET ALONG?
CREATING DIALOGUE

Credits

Where Do I Begin?

Establishing a Theoretical Foundation

Intercultural Communication

By Thomas M. Steinfatt and Diane M. Millette

The study of intercultural communication is important in any society or culture. This is especially true in the United States, which has made *intercultural openness* a central feature of its cultural persona. The United States is currently experiencing the greatest period of immigration in its history. Although the late 19th and early 20th centuries witnessed a greater *proportional* population increase due to immigration, the actual *number* of legal immigrants entering the United States since 1980 was greater per decade than in any previous time in history. When illegal immigration is factored in, the current period of immigration is unsurpassed in American history, yielding a nation whose cultural heritage is changing, and, as a corollary, its communication is changing as well.

COMMUNICATION

Following Langer (1942), we believe that communication in its most fundamental form is intrapersonal. Communication begins as an attempt by human beings to come to know their environment through symbols. This occurs through a gradual recognition by the child that symbols, objects, and ideas, and internal mental representations of them, can be related to each other in a meaningful fashion. To paraphrase Langer, children first use communication to bring objects into their minds, not into their hands. Once children learn that this is possible, then symbol-object-mind relationships are possible. Only after such relationships are learned can communication evolve to a social stage where people recognize that others also make similar symbol-object-mind

 University Readers

COMMUNICATION & MEDIA STUDIES
 COLLECTION™

 Routledge
Taylor & Francis Group

inferences, and that these related networks of inferences can be used to interact with others. At the social stage, communication can be used for social tasks, such as making requests or transmitting cultural information. In all stages of human development, communication involves the assignment of meaning by the individual to external stimuli, including symbolically encoded messages from other persons. Communication is inherently a meaning assignment process within the individual. Since meaning is assigned to messages based on the beliefs, attitudes, and values of the individual, and since persons from different cultures often have different beliefs, attitudes, and values, the normal human misunderstandings which occur in same-culture interactions are often magnified by the wider differences in cultural assumptions and belief systems inherent in cross-cultural interactions.

CULTURE

The diversity of the concept "culture" is illustrated by Kluckhohn's (1949) 12 meanings for the term, from the way of life of a people, their social legacy, pooled learning, way of thinking, feeling, and believing, through their mechanism for normative regulation of behavior and techniques for adjusting to the environment and other people, to theories about the way these people behave. Citing Max Weber as inspiration, Geertz (1973, p. 5) holds that "man is an animal suspended in webs of significance he himself has spun, I take culture to be those webs, and the analysis of it to be therefore not an experimental science in search of law but an interpretative one in search of meaning."

We conceive of culture in its broadest sense as the accumulated knowledge and beliefs of specific portions of humanity. Thus defined, the fundamental nature of culture is phenomenological: culture exists fundamentally in the hearts and minds of people. Cultural artifacts such as paintings, sculpture, machinery, and construction projects are products of the knowledge and beliefs that constitute culture. While cultural artifacts provide clues to culture, culture itself can be passed on to other persons and future generations only through communication. No study of culture's artifacts, no matter how deep or extensive, can describe, explain, predict, or even transmit culture from one person or generation to another without communication about cultural meaning. Intercultural communication involves communication between people from different cultures, leading to several questions: What constitutes a "different" culture? Do intercultural differences necessarily involve different languages? Different ways of thinking? Different world-views? Different beliefs, attitudes, and values?

INTERCULTURAL COMMUNICATION

While there is little disagreement that communication between a Karen hill tribesman in northern Thailand and an American college student involves intercultural differences, we might ask if communication between any two persons with different attitudes, beliefs, and values also involves intercultural differences. For example, while the value system espoused by a given corporation is commonly referred to as corporate culture, does that mean that communication between workers at IBM and Microsoft necessarily involves intercultural differences? Perhaps. Between someone at IBM and a farm worker? Possibly. To study such interactions from an intercultural perspective might raise different questions and produce different answers from those found in a more standard organizational communication analysis. But rather than attempt to give final answers, we prefer to discuss the central thrust of intercultural communication, as opposed to attempting to delineate intercultural communication's absolute boundaries.

Thus, we regard the study of intercultural communication as the study of communication between people with different mind-sets and ways of looking at and perceiving the world that go beyond the differences normally found among people who regard themselves as culturally similar. Since communication occurs through cognitive processing, we might ask whether Eastern and Western ways of thinking are different. Does such a notion imply different cognitive structures or communication processes, or, can the observations which lead people to infer a different way of thinking be explained simply through different content in beliefs, attitudes, and values within the cultures? Though commonly applied to communication between persons who are each embed ded in a different cultural group, intercultural communication also has heuristic utility when applied to the examination of two persons, ostensibly from the same culture, gender, age, ethnic group, and socioeconomic status, whose assumptions about the nature of the world and ways of relating to it are sufficiently divergent to produce the forms of misunderstanding commonly found in intercultural analysis. *The central thrust of intercultural communication is in the analysis of meaning assignment in interactions between persons whose attitudes, beliefs, and values differ due to a corresponding difference in their cultural or co-cultural backgrounds.* These attitudes, beliefs, and values represent, in part, the individual's theories of what others in the same culture believe, as well as how this differentiates persons of that culture from persons of other cultures.

FOUR MAJOR AREAS OF INTERCULTURAL COMMUNICATION STUDY

The term *Intercultural Communication* has both a broad and a narrower referent. The broad sense is that of an encompassing term for four major areas of intercultural communication defined by their intent: I. *Cross-cultural Communication*; II. *International Communication;* III. *Development Communication;* and intercultural communication's narrower referent, IV. *Intercultural Communication proper.* These areas are not fixed and independent. Studies in each area often have relevance to studies in others, and some research traditions, linguistic relativity, for example, might be classified in several different areas. We will spend more time discussing some areas than others.

Cross-Cultural Communication

Borrowing terminology from descriptive linguistics, Pike (1966) developed his *etic* and *emic* distinction from *phonetic* and *phonemic*. He observed that phonetics studies sound and symbol production as observed by others outside the person being studied, while phonemics examines meaning, which is inside the person. Thus *emic* approaches look at a single culture, often from the perspective of a person thinking, communicating, and behaving within that culture—so their idiosyncrasies as cultures may be determined. This is the approach of ethnology and cross-cultural communication. And *etic* approaches to intercultural communication examine cultures from the outside—so their commonalities may be determined. The *etic* approach is that of intercultural communication proper.

Cross-cultural communication concerns the comparison of communication across two or more specific cultures or ethnicities, such as Japanese communication styles compared with U.S. communication styles, or African-American, Hispanic, and Anglo styles within the United States. Studies of linguistic relativity and of ethnography are also forms of cross-cultural communication so defined. Scholars concerned with multicultural education and cultural diversity are often interested in both cross-cultural communication and intercultural communication proper. Many works on cross-cultural communication are heavily weighted in the comparison, focusing on one presumably unfamiliar culture almost to the exclusion of the culture presumed to be familiar. In such cases the cross-cultural study becomes more a uni-cultural study.

Communication Across Cultures and Ethnicities

The single cross-cultural interaction which has generated the most in-depth, book-length communication research concerning intercultural communication with its members is Japanese-American communication. Barnlund (1989), Goldman (1990, 1994), Gudykunst (1993), Gudykunst and Nishida (1994), and Sato (1992) each discuss Japanese-American communication from different perspectives. Goldman (1990) and Sato (1992) focus on Japanese communicating with Americans, while Barnlund (1989), Goldman (1994), and Gudykunst and Nishida (1994) are oriented toward the American perspective in interacting with Japanese. Gudykunst (1993) contrasts the study of communication in Japan with that in the United States, and Stewart and Bennett (1991) discuss the cultural patterns of Americans.

Kim (1986) summarizes research on interethnic communication to the mid-1980s. Hecht, Jackson, and Ribeau (2003) provide an example of research on ethnic styles, delineating African-American communication patterns as contrasted with other common U.S. forms. Other views representative of a multicultural and cultural diversity approach to intercultural communication are provided in Andersen and Collins (1992) and Gonzalez, Houston, and Chen (1994). Central to these essays are concerns with the concepts of racism, sexism, prejudice, self-concept, and power differences which enter into interethnic interactions.

Gannon (2004) provides an introduction to the study of various cultures in his book *Understanding Global Cultures*, which is popular within the business community for persons whose work takes them to unfamiliar cultures. Gannon employs cultural metaphors to help those unfamiliar with a given culture attain a notion of the dominant mind-set found in that country or culture. Whether such dominant unified mind-sets exist, and whether the use of such metaphors actually assists in cross-cultural communication or simply provides comfort to prospective travelers, has not been sufficiently studied.

Linguistic Relativity

Another cross-cultural area is the study of linguistic relativity, which can be traced to Aristotle's speculations on whether doing philosophy while using Greek as a symbol system would make the knowledge discovered different if, say, Latin were the symbol system (Steinfatt,1989). Aristotle's answer was that the language in use would not make a substantial difference in the final result—that any thought could be expressed equally well in any language.

This view held sway until the late 19th century, when Cassirer (1953) suggested that the language used to conduct philosophical analyses could influence the resultant knowledge. Cassirer's work was not widely accepted in philosophy, but a young Yale anthropologist, Edward Sapir, began to write and lecture on topics in linguistic anthropology in the late 1800s. Sapir (1921) suggested that thought was potentially relative to language. Prior to 1920 Benjamin Lee Whorf, an undergraduate student in engineering at MIT who was working his way through college as an inspector for an insurance company, began to study Hopi and Mayan cultures. In the 1920s he lectured extensively on his thesis, developed independently of Sapir's ideas, that the language of thought influences its content. Though not Sapir's student at this point, he had heard of Sapir and attended one of Sapir's lectures at Yale late in that decade, eventually joining Sapir's graduate program in anthropology as a student. From this simple meeting was born what has come to be called the *Sapir–Whorf hypothesis,* that language structures thought. Mandell (1931) presents an early view of linguistic relativity; reviews of experimental research may be found in Gibson and McGarvy (1937), Woodworth (1938), Heidbreder (1948), Johnson (1950), Humphrey (1951), (1951), Diebold (1965), and Steinfatt (1988, 1989). Lee's (1996) *The Whorf Theory Complex: A Critical Reconstruction,* provides an excellent discussion of Whorf's intercultural work.

Sapir (1921), Whorf (1956), and Cassirer (1953) are perhaps the best known advocates of the notion that language influences thought. They treated linguistic relativity as an interlanguage phenomenon, a process attributable to differences between languages.

Sapir and Whorf's thesis involves both "linguistic determinism" and "linguistic relativity." Linguistic determinism holds that language shapes thought, but allows that people who speak different languages could still have the same thoughts and think in similar ways. For example, a counterfactual conditional (e.g., "I would take you if I were going that way but I'm not so I can't") is very difficult to express in Chinese. But while the language makes such thoughts difficult to express, linguistic determinism suggests that such thoughts could occur in Chinese, although they would be difficult. Linguistic relativity, a more radical version of linguistic determinism, holds that different languages actually shape thought differently (Glucksberg & Danks, 1975). Linguistic relativity would argue that speakers of Chinese would have great difficulty thinking in counterfactual conditional terms and that thought processes in Chinese would have to follow the structure of the language.

As initially proposed, the *Weltanschauung*—world *view*—thesis of linguistic relativity was very general and thus almost impossible to test. Greenberg (1956), Lenneberg and Roberts (1956), Henle (1958), Fishman (1960), Osgood and Sebeok (1965), and Slobin (1979) all have suggested different ways of organizing the hypothesis. Steinfatt (1989) proposed that three groups of independent variables—phonological, syntactical, and semantic—are possible causative sets in linguistic relativity as the basis for any proposed differences in thought. At least one variable from at least one of these sets must influence at least one dependent measure in one of three variable sets—the logic of thought itself, the structure of cognition and worldview, or perception and areas of cognition—in order for a linguistic relativity effect to be claimed. Beyond looking at differences between natural languages as a source of linguistic relativity effects, Steinfatt (1989) also suggested that substantial phonological, syntactical, or semantic differences in any natural language would have to be regarded as a potential source of linguistic relativity effects. Thus, dialects such as Black-American English, compound bilingualism, aphasics relearning a language, and the deaf, should provide examples of linguistic relativity effects if such effects actually occur. Linguistic relativity should not be limited to the natural language differences proposed by Whorf (1956) and others. Additionally, Steinfatt (1989) suggested that knowledge of the methods by which language is acquired should provide insight into whether linguistic relativity effects are likely to exist.

Traditional Ethnography

The traditional referent of ethnography is the branch of anthropology dealing with the scientific description of specific human cultures, both the fieldwork and the writing that it engenders. Barfield (2001) defines ethnography as systematic description of a single existing culture that can be observed in the present. In Malinowski's (1922) classic definition, ethnography is the endeavor of describing a culture, "to grasp the native's point of view, his relation to life, to realize *his* vision of *his* world" (1922, p. 25). Kaplan (1964, p. 31) refers to this as the "act meaning," as opposed to the "action meaning" that is taken as data by many social scientists. This apprehension of the act meaning was usually accomplished through personal immersion in the object culture involving a lengthy process of participation, participant observation, and interview, often by a single observer, producing highly detailed and descriptive notes that became the raw data for later analysis. The observation process and note creation were the fundamental method, and were seen as largely devoid of theory, though they were often guided by notions of kinship systems and other important areas and classifications. No specific characteristics of culture were to be defined *a priori,* and the researcher was to ignore all preconceived notions of the culture to be studied. The important characteristics, relationships, and patterns would emerge naturally during the research, so that notes had to be very detailed as the observer would not know what would later emerge as important. This form of ethnography became a well-established method for the study of human cultures in the late 19th and early 20th centuries.

Aside from potential concerns with ethnography regarding validity and reliability—since *one* person from an *outside* culture was to assign meaning producing a single known reality—traditional cultures so described were often viewed in isolation from each other and from the world. The methods of traditional ethnography were also vulnerable to political attack since they were associated from the outset with imperialism and the colonial subordination of non-Western peoples by European powers. The observations of ethnographers necessarily occur within the form of ethnocentricity of the times, and most ethnographers believed it was possible for a single "scientific observer" to create detailed interpretations of other cultures from a detached point of view (Vidich & Lyman, 1994). Little consideration was given to the observer's role as observer, nor to the possible impact of an observer on the research, particularly as an outsider from a ruling power. Nor was consideration given to the need for a diverse set of views from multiple observers, with multiple voices speaking from within the community to be studied, who might be heard differently by different observers.

By the early 1960s these criticisms of the traditional ethnographic method were regularly taught as such in U.S. graduate programs in anthropology. This occurred in most programs, but not in all of them. By the 1970s Geertz's (1973) emphasis on "thick description," influenced by Ryle's (1968) discussion of the meaning of a wink, suggests that the descriptions within ethnography must consider the context of the behaviors described, to the point that the description of the behavior makes the behavior in its context meaningful to an outsider. Thin description results from the outside observation of behaviors with little interpretation, and thick description includes the interpretation of the behavior from the point of view of the cultural actor. Beginning with his 1960s work on Javanese religion, Geertz (1960, 1973, 1983, 1988) was one of ethnography's principal proponents. Wolcott (1994) provides a clear description of the use of ethnography in multiple settings, where researchers are especially interested in studying the ways in which people embedded in a culture make decisions. Gladwin (1989) discusses the use of "decision trees" in this process.

The Variance Within is of the Same Order as the Variance Between

Certainly a note of caution is in order whenever a given culture is being described. When discussing a culture and defining its important communication features, abstraction involves searching for what is central within the culture and ignoring the peripheral. Yet central to any culture is cultural variation often involving the peripheral. When we apply intercultural communication to specific situations as communication between, say, Vietnamese and American cultures, or Black and White cultures within American society, this conceptualization implies a certain unity of culture for Vietnamese, Americans, Whites, and Blacks. The assumption often is that people within a culture are relatively similar and the major differences are to be found between those of one culture and those of another. Naturally, nothing is further from the truth. To employ a statistical analogy from the analysis of variance, we may say that the variation within a given culture is normally of the same order of magnitude as the variation between cultures. There is often as much variation in a given culture between its social classes as there is between that culture and any other culture. In fact, ethnic variations within a given culture can easily be greater than the average variation between that culture and another. Learning how a particular cultural group thinks and communicates does not guarantee that such findings will hold for a specific member of a cultural group, especially when the cultural interaction situation is factored in. At a minimum, if the social class and ethnicity of the specific individuals involved is not considered, knowledge of the culture alone is often of little use in predicting interactional outcomes, though this is not always the case (e.g., Jones, 1979).

Postmodernism

The methods of ethnography came under further attack by postmodernism in the 1980s and beyond, an attack that in large part simply echoed the known criticisms of ethnography, emphasizing some criticisms over others, and attempting to fuse them into a postmodern critique. In general, this attempt was neither coherent and well thought out, nor worth exploring further. The most distinguishing and consistent new features of postmodernist attacks were the invention of a non-existent "modernism," allowing postmodernism's straw man attack on it, and the apparent inability of many of its major proponents to write competently in their native language. Its proponents consider this a strong point.

The New Ethnography

Although ethnography has long been a principal method of social and cultural anthropology, its use has rapidly increased as a method in social psychology and communication over the past decade (Vidich & Lyman, 1994). Ellis and Bochner (1996) provide multiple examples of ways of composing the new ethnography. Most of this ethnography as currently practiced appears to be a literary form, as in novels, short stories, and literary criticism, with standards of evidence and interpretation similar to the personal opinion and experience standards of those genres. We can learn a great deal from such forms, as in Richard Wright's classics such as *Black Boy, Uncle Tom's Children,* and *Native Son.* One problem is that not all writers of ethnography are as observant, accurate, and skillful writers as Wright, and that many such writers believe in obtuse rather than illuminating writing forms, possibly an influence of postmodernism. "It takes skill and effort to introspect in a way that is scientifically useful" (Kaplan, 1964, p. 141).

Traditional ethnography involved an outside observer of a culture, partially on the theory that the observer would not be blinded to the culture by being embedded in it. A fish would be the last one to notice that the environment surrounding it was wet. The new ethnography often employs a culturally embedded observer, which introduces both the fish problem, and in the case of auto-ethnography, the problem that the material to be observed is available first hand, only to that single participant. Additionally, that observer is usually employed as the only interpreter as well as the only observer. Such writings can be very helpful and illuminating of intercultural issues, and can also be descriptions that lead nowhere. We are often good judges of some of our motivations and internal states, particularly physical ones such as hunger and pain, and emotional ones such as whether or not our feelings are hurt. We may be less accurate as judges of how others see us, or of why we may have engaged in a particular communicative behavior. Individual outside observers sometimes know us better than we know ourselves. And multiple outside observers are likely to give better predictions in this regard than individual observers. The question then becomes the extent to which the new ethnography can provide more than the feeling that we now understand something better than we did before. The new ethnology will ultimately be judged not for this quality, but for what it adds to the value of studies that employ it, including its heuristic value. If ultimately we cannot describe, explain, predict, or understand the phenomenon under study in some more insightful or more useful way by using the new ethnology, then it will inevitably fade in the face of a better way of doing that.

Criticisms of Social Science Methods

The increase in the use of new ethnographic methods in intercultural communication is based in part on several criticisms of social science methodology. Specifically, proponents of ethnographic analysis usually hold *first*, that the structure required by social science in the research process emanates from the researcher's cultural assumptions, which limits the chances of finding much which does not fit these preconceived assumptions. A *second* criticism holds that generalizations from controlled to natural settings (i.e., experimental to field) are suspect. *Third*, ethnographic analysis holds that interviews must be combined with observations to understand cultural perspectives. *Fourth*, it suggests that quantification necessarily selects some aspects of what is being studied and ignores others, thus reifying and unduly increasing the importance of the selected, while ignoring the unselected. And, *fifth*, ethnographic analysis holds that quantitative analysis ignores the role of human interaction and human choice in a mechanistic analysis based only on the variables selected by the researcher. Many of these criticisms assume that social science methodology equates to quantification. Rather, the goal of social science is the ability to predict the outcome of unknown events using an explanation based on accurate description. Social science equates understanding with prediction. Ethnography equates understanding with thick description.

Criticisms of Ethnographic Methods

The rather obvious response by social science to the five criticisms is *first*, there is no reason to assume that a researcher's cultural assumptions are any less ethnocentric because the researcher chooses single-person observation and written descriptions rather than social science methods. *Second*, generalizations from writing about single person observations as in ethnography are even more suspect than controlled generalizations. *Third*, observations without social science methods will be at least as poor representations of cultural perspectives since the sampling of perspectives will be haphazard at best without those social science methods. Interviews likely should be combined with observations to understand cultural perspectives, and doing that is a good way of combining the strengths of social science and of ethnography. *Fourth*, ethnographic methods necessarily select some aspects of what is being studied and ignore others, thus reifying and unduly increasing the importance of the selected, while ignoring the unselected. And *fifth*, ethno graphic analysis ignores the role of human interaction and human choice in a literary analysis based only on the observations selected by the researcher. In other words, *the problems of research are equally applicable to social science methods and to ethnographic ones.*

Hammersley (1992) discusses some of these problems and possibilities with the ethnographic approach. Perhaps the most telling criticism is that ethnography depends on realism, the doctrine that there is a reality out there to study, and on constructivism, the notion that individuals construct their own social reality. Some social scientists make these same assumptions, while others do not. Ethnographers suggest that they study observed and constructed reality through observation and interaction and then report what they have learned. The problem is that the story produced by such an approach is constructed from personal observations and interactions, a construction just as subject to the ethnographer's culture and biases as any social science account, and probably much more so. Not only do each of the five criticisms aimed at social science analysis by ethnography apply as a critique of ethnographic analysis, but some ethnographers deny that such criticisms are applicable to ethnology, thus putting ethnography close to a position of nonfalsifiability (Popper, 1968). An analysis which cannot be falsified or criticized, where there is nothing that could occur that if it did occur would invalidate the method, cannot be taken as a serious scholarly analysis. Alasuutari (1995) provides a strong introduction to the use of qualitative methods in intercultural communication and with cultural studies in general.

The Qualitative/Quantitative Distinction

While traditionally viewed as a method of social science, the new ethnography is often discussed as a "qualitative" method, to be distinguished from "quantitative" methods, which are then equated with social science. We believe that the qualitative versus quantitative research distinction is inauthentic, in that it involves multiple continuums rather than a single dichotomy. Yet it is a distinction that appears to have permeated the field. One appropriate continuum is good research versus bad research. Every known research method has examples of good, average, and bad research. Good research uses methods that are driven by the questions being asked, and by the purpose of asking these questions. If the method has the potential to answer these research questions in some useful way that can be reasonably defended by those who employ it, against reasonable attacks, then it is on the path toward good research. Some questions are inherently more quantitative: how many, how much, which is a larger effect, etc. Others are inherently more qualitative: what is the nature of the philosophic differences that exist among cultures that appear to affect intercultural communication? But intercultural communication questions of any importance demand a mix of qualitative and quantitative methods. Ethnography and the more quantitative social science methods both provide certain kinds of insights into intercultural analysis. Students of intercultural communication should learn both, as well as the strengths and weaknesses of each, and should not waste time defending any one method as the only possible approach to a problem. Some intercultural analyses have profitably combined the use of ethnographic methods with social science research. Steinfatt (2002), within a largely "quantitative" analysis, uses ethnographic reports to illustrate and illuminate ideal types representing several large subgroups of female sex workers in Thailand, and employs comparisons of Christianity and Buddhism to discuss the moral rationales for working.

Labeling a study as "quantitative" should not be used as an excuse for failing to provide the thick description needed to understand the meaning, importance, and potential application of the research. Similarly, labeling a study as qualitative or ethnographic should not be used as an excuse for entering quantitative results that would not be accepted as scholarly if they appeared in an article labeled "quantitative." For example, the statement, "According to a 1994 broadcast of *48 hours*, roughly 94% of all mentally retarded people are thought to be victims of sexual abuse," appears in a book of essays represented as blurring the boundaries between social science and the humanities (Ronai, 1996, p. 111). One hopes that this example is not what is meant by blurring these boundaries. In that essay, no reference citation is offered beyond the quotation itself, nor is there a definition of terms, nor a notion of who might be the *source* of the thoughts about sexual abuse: it is left unstated whether this was thought by others who are mentally retarded, or thought by clinical psychologists, or by psychiatrists, or by authors of a competent study of the subject, or simply by someone's wild guess. Standards for scholarly writing should receive equal application across methods.

International Communication

International Communication is the study of both (1) mass mediated communication between countries, often but not always with significantly different cultural worldviews (e.g., media imperialism), and (2) interpersonal communication, mediated or face-to-face, between persons representing different governments—one country's government's view as communicated to another country's government—and the factors, whether intercultural, cross-cultural, mediated, or political that influence both the construction and interpretation of such message exchanges.

Studies of international mass mediated communication include, for example, the pioneering work of Sydney Head (1956, 1961, 1974, 1985) on comparative international broadcasting, as well as studies such as McPhail's (2006) work on global communication. Communication in international relations includes diplomatic messages and exchanges; diplomatic posturing; ciphers and code-breaking; assigning meaning to when, where, how, from whom, and through what chain of sources and channels an official or unofficial message is received in determining its authenticity, significance, initial intent, and ultimate purpose.

Development Communication

Development Communication studies organized efforts that use communication to create social and economic improvements, as seen by the introducing culture, often but not always in developing countries. The initial phase of development communication began during the cold war. It involved organized media and interpersonal communication efforts to create social and economic improvements, usually in developing countries and sponsored by developed countries.

Initially based on the cold war theories of W. W. Rostow (1952, Rostow & Levin, 1953), together with Lerner and Schramm's (1967) belief in the apparent success of U.S. World War II heavily funded propaganda methods, development communication was initially designed to increase consumption, and thus capitalism, in developing nations in order to foster Western capitalist beliefs and keep them safe from communism (Rostow & Hatch, 1955). Heavy funding of development communication efforts from first world governments, combined with direct governmental foreign economic and military aid and World Bank funding of top-down economic development to less developed nations, consistently failed to achieve its goals. Proponents of these failed efforts saw the problems in fostering development as based within the developing nations, having little or nothing to do with international relationships. All development was seen as Westernization, conducted largely through trickle-down economics, which in turn was seen as a necessary prerequisite to a stable economy and a stable world.

Kennedy's Peace Corps began a reversal of this model in the 1960s that reached maturity in the 1970s and beyond, featuring people-to-people bubble-up programs, and a far greater consideration in its training programs and implementation of the culture, language, beliefs, attitudes, and traditions of developing nations and peoples, and a recognition of their general mistrust of "propaganda" efforts by the West. At the same time, Rogers's (1962) compilation of and theorizing about the communication processes involved in the diffusion of innovations during development was one of the first books to integrate intercultural communication considerations with development efforts. It summarized and codified most of the prior research on diffusion from research traditions as diverse as mass communication, education, and rural sociology, into a blueprint for introducing cultural change. Rogers and Shoemaker (1971) updated Rogers's initial conceptualization, and Fischer (1974) and Frey (1974) presented related aspects of the problem. Interpersonal-intercultural communication replaced the over-reliance on television of the earlier model, and the use of radio and community newspapers in the new endeavors often proved more effective than television. The entertainment-education model (Singhal & Rogers, 2004) proved particularly effective when used with radio soap operas. Television succeeded in development communication as an educational tool primarily when development programs on TV were viewed in small groups with a local opinion leader present to introduce them, who then turned off the TV after the viewing period to lead discussions of what the TV content meant.

Diffusion research centers on effective methods of introducing new ways of doing things, and of spreading awareness and adoption of the new concept throughout the culture. While innovations diffuse naturally from cross-cultural interactions, the central question of diffusion and development research concerns identifying manipulable predictor variables which affect the rates of adoption and discontinuance of an innovation. Characteristics of "innovators" and "early adopters," which lead to opinion leadership, are studied and contrasted with those of "later adopters" and "laggards."

Diffusion studies examine the characteristics of the innovation itself, its compatibility with local cultural norms, the role of change agents, types of decision making, and consequences of the decision to adopt.

The majority of the consequences are often unintended, unanticipated, and not infrequently negative. Such consequences lead to the consideration of the ethics for deciding when to intervene in another culture. Ethical systems range from the rampant ethnocentrism of colonialism to the hands-off position of extreme multiculturalists. The concern with ethics is related to the more general problem of the ethics of foreign policy. What are the characteristics of a situation which justify intervention? Who should be allowed to make such a decision? Does the receiving culture have the right of refusal? Does the source culture have a similar right? Neither extreme position is tenable because no culture nor cultural practice is an island unto itself. Nazi culture led to the Holocaust; the world should have intervened sooner and more forcibly. The same might be said of Soviet culture under Stalinism and Cambodian culture under Pol Pot. But some intervention decisions that seem obvious to Western morality in areas such as prostitution, female genital mutilation, the oppression of women, and the control of disease, can lead to cultural upheaval and untold human hardship as a result. The Chinese and other Asian nations argue, for instance, that human rights are an invention of Western culture and simply a further extension of discredited colonialist practices.

What ethical system can be proposed that is not based in the moral norms of one culture over another? The traditional answer of Western philosophy is to dismiss any notion of ethical relativity (e.g., Hatch, 1983), for without set moral standards any action can be justified. Is it possible to devise a multicultural morality that allows us to distinguish the legitimate moral claims of any culture from those that are specious? Yet, if an ethical system does not take into account the fundamental conceptions and world view of all cultures in which it is to be applied, what claim can it make to being a legitimate universal absolute morality?

Intercultural Communication Proper

Intercultural Communication in the narrower sense is that of Gudykunst's (1987) reference to *intercultural communication proper,* the study of generalizations about intercultural communication independent of any specific culture or ethnicity. This is also Pike's (1966) *etic* approach, examining multiple cultures from the outside to determine their commonalities. It includes studies of how humans react to any different culture and its peoples, beliefs, and ways of acting and thinking. In this process it considers theories of intercultural competence, ways of obtaining such competence, and measurements of individuals concerning this competence. Also in this process, it may be the case that nomothetic generalizations may profitably exist hand in hand with idiosyncratic theories of specific cultures and of co-cultural groups within each culture. The combination of both types of knowledge approaches will be needed in practical settings where such laws are to be applied. While knowledge of a culture requires additional knowledge of social class and ethnicity of the specific individuals involved in order to predict and understand an interaction, intercultural communication principals alone are insufficient for dealing with many practical problems in communication between two specific cultures. Just as Hall's (1959) State Department students complained that a knowledge of Navajo culture was of little help to an administrator about to join the diplomatic corps in Paris, specific cultural, ethnicity, and social class knowledge, together with knowledge of intercultural communication principals, is needed in order to make informed practical decisions in real situations.

Foundations

Among the earliest writings on intercultural communication proper may be Durkheim's (1897) classic study of suicide among immigrants. Durkheim used his concept of *anomie,* the feeling of rootlessness, of having no culture, of not belonging to either the old country or to the new, to explain high suicide rates across immigrant populations of the time. By the 1920s, Park and Burgess (1924) and their Chicago School colleagues studied European immigrants' integration into American culture, recognizing the initial social processes of accommodation and assimilation (Rogers, 1994).

The social science approach to the study of communication in general was pioneered by scholars such as Lazarsfeld (1944), Lasswell (1948), Hovland, Janis, and Kelley (1953), and Schramm (1954), partially in response to the Hutchins Commission report (Commission of Freedom of the Press, 1947) which sought, among other goals, to identify variables that predict communication outcomes across multiple cross-cultural interactions. Schramm, who had worked as Educational Director of the U.S. Office of War Information during World War II, received a number of grants from the U.S. government following the war to work on anticommunist communication campaigns (Glander, 1996). These grants led both to the founding of communication research institutes and communication programs at Illinois, Stanford, Hawaii, and Iowa, and to the early funding of these programs and their students. The approach favored by Schramm and the government was one providing a well-grounded empirical and verifiable approach to government goals, seeking theories of intercultural communication by developing an abstract calculus of relationships between and among variables that are observable and measurable. Prior to the late 1950s, the studies of culture shock appearing in *Practical Anthropology,* and of prejudice and ethnic relations scattered throughout scholarly journals in sociology, psychology, and anthropology, formed the basis for early intercultural communication research. Schatzman and Strauss (1955) provide one of the early studies of intracultural communication.

Beginnings

The history of intercultural communication as an area is often ascribed to the 1959 publication of Edward T. Hall's *The Silent Language* (Condon, 1981; Dodd, 1982; Gudykunst, 1985b; Klopf, 1987; Samovar & Porter, 1972; Singer, 1987), in which Hall introduced the term "intercultural communication." Alternately, Leeds-Hurwitz (1990), Rogers (1994), and Rogers and Steinfatt (1999) credit the term and the beginning of intercultural communication research to the decade following World War II in Hall's work training American diplomats through the U.S. Foreign Service Institute. This work produced *The Silent Language* as a handbook for intercultural training. Many current intercultural training areas are derived from Hall's work such as those in cultural diversity, cultural sensitivity, and in student exchange and study abroad programs (Kohls, 1984; Mestenhauser, Marty, & Steglitz, 1988). Brislin and Yoshida (1994) discuss methods of assessment and evaluation of intercultural communication training programs. Applications of intercultural communication research useful in various training programs also may be found in Brislin (1990).

Hall's work also led to a major body of social science oriented communication scholarship. He refocused the study of culture as it was practiced by post-World War II anthropology in a number of ways (see Leeds-Hurwitz, 1990). One of these was a shift from anthropology's emphasis on monadic and dyadic studies of a single culture, or a comparison of two cultures—cross-cultural communication—into intercultural communication proper. Hall's concept of intercultural communication as patterned, learned, and capable of being analyzed across cultures in general, was compatible with the social science notions then taking form in mass and interpersonal communication. His emphasis on generalizations fit with American social science, seeking nomothetic lawlike generalizations, and shunning idiosyncratic knowledge characteristic of *an* individual or *a* culture.

Further, Hall's focus on training at the Foreign Service Institute created the practical need for a generalized training program useful for all American diplomats regardless of their culture of destination. Specific cultures and their features were deemphasized not because their differences were irrelevant, but because of practical considerations about packaging the information to groups of trainees about to embark to various different locations and cultures. Thus Hall concentrated on the features of culture that affected the interpersonal interactions his trainees would encounter: tone of voice, gestures, and conceptions of time and space, largely ignoring those features not directly relevant to intercultural interactions. This decision established him as one of the founders of intercultural communication, and relegated him to secondary status within the field of anthropology. While much of the current research in *intercultural communication proper* is quantitative in nature, this orientation is not derived from Hall. As an anthropologist, Hall was both qualitative and applied; his focus was on training. Rather, attention to quantitative methods has come from communication researchers' quantitative training, many of them having become interested in expanding the study of interpersonal communication into intercultural areas. Leeds-Hurwitz (1990) provides an extended analysis of the role of these factors. The publication of *The Silent Language* (1959), was followed by Hall's *The Hidden Dimension* (1966), and Smith's collection of articles in *Communication and Culture* (1966).

Teaching Intercultural Communication

By 1965, Michigan State University's Department of Communication was offering a course titled "Intercultural Communication" taught by Hideya Kumata. Several years later a similar course was offered at the University of Pittsburg. In July 1972, John Condon and Mitsuko Saito organized the Summer Conference on Intercultural Communication held at International Christian University. The conference attracted scholars from multiple disciplines with over 50 contributors and an attendance of over 2,000. One of the contributors, William S. Howell, established the doctoral program in intercultural communication at the University of Minnesota, the source of many of today's leading scholars in the field of intercultural communication.

Early Texts

In 1972, Condon and Yousef (1974) might have produced the first book written with the title of intercultural communication, but publishers were generally uninterested in publication until 1974 because there was no market for intercultural texts at the time (Kelly, 1999), and thus Con-don and Yousef were second to Harms's (1973) *Intercultural Communication.* These books focused the attention of many students on the study of intercultural communication. Increasing interest in intercultural communication led to the beginning of the *International and Intercultural Communication Annual* in the mid-1970s, where much of the social science oriented research may be found. Asante, Newmark, and Blake (1979) and Asante and Gudykunst (1989) provide a number of summary articles. Theories of intercultural communication are summarized in Gudykunst (1983a), Kim (1988b), and Kim and Gudykunst (1988).

Extensive Research Programs

One of the more influential lines of research was established by Gudykunst and his colleagues who focused on three general areas applied to intercultural communication: uncertainty reduction processes, relationship issues, and communication effectiveness. In 1980, Gudykunst and Halsall generated a series of axioms and propositions synthesizing diverse research findings in various disciplines applicable to intercultural relationships. Gudykunst (1983b), reviewing the concept of *stranger,* derived a descriptive typology of stranger–host relationships that included newly arrived, newcomer, sojourner, stranger, immigrants, intruder, middle-man minority, and the marginal person. Related research focused on ethnic identity and close friendship communication patterns (Ting-Toomey, 1981), perceived similarity and social penetration (Gudykunst, 1985a), patterns of discourse (Sudweeks, Gudykunst, Ting-Toomey, & Nishida, 1990), insider and outsider perspectives (Gudykunst & Nishida, 1986b; Ting-Toomey, 1985), and self-consciousness and self-monitoring (Gudykunst, Yang, & Nishida, 1985).

Two influential articles (Gudykunst, 1988; Gudykunst, Chua, & Gray, 1987) are central in the examination of cultural influence on communication in interpersonal relationships. Early research tested Berger and Calabrese's (1975) uncertainty reduction theory by exploring similarities and differences in initial intracultural and intercultural encounters (Gudykunst, 1983c, 1985c; Gudykunst et al., 1987; Gudykunst & Nishida, 1984). Extension of the original model explored boundary conditions (Gudykunst, 1985a), attribution confidence in high- and low-context cultures (Gudykunst & Nishida, 1986a), influence of language (Gudykunst, Nishida, Koike, & Shiino, 1986), social identity (Gudykunst & Hammer, 1988), group membership (Gudykunst, Nishida, & Schmidt, 1989), and anxiety reduction (Gao & Gudykunst, 1990).

Intercultural Competence

Dimensions of intercultural communication effectiveness have been investigated that tested sojourners' cultural perspectives (Gudykunst, Wiseman, & Hammer, 1977), participation in workshops (Gudykunst, 1979), decision-making style (Stewart, Gudykunst, Ting-Toomey, & Nishida, 1986), and ethnocentrism (Hall & Gudykunst, 1989). Kim (1988a) offered a broad-based perspective that synthesized various disciplinary viewpoints of adaptation including anthropology, communication, psychology, sociology, and sociolinguistics. Regardless of a sojourner's motivation for being in a new culture, all people share common adaptation experiences. Accordingly, as strangers they must cope with high levels of uncertainty and unfamiliarity based on their ambivalent status in the host community. Labels such as acculturation, adjustment, assimilation, and integration emphasize different aspects of the adaptation experience. Adaptation theory assumes that individuals can and do adapt to this new, unfamiliar culture. Consequently, the focus is on how adaptation is accomplished from a General Systems perspective that regards individuals and their host environment as codeterminants engaged in communication activities. Adaptation theory proposes assumptions, axioms, and theorems that increase understanding of, and ability to make predictions of, cross-cultural adaptation.

Studies of intercultural sensitivity and competence may be found in the work of Bennett and Hammer (e.g., Bennett, 1986, 1993; Bennett & Bennett, 2004a,

2004b) on their developmental model of intercultural sensitivity (DMIS), and on measuring intercultural sensitivity through the intercultural development inventory (IDI; Hammer, 1998; Hammer, Bennett, & Wiseman, 2003). This grounded theory approach derives a theory of intercultural development (DMIS) based on observing persons' responses to cultural difference, and the organization of the observations into presumed stages of increasing sensitivity to cultural difference. Six such stages are proposed, three *ethnocentric* and centrally based in the observer's culture: Denial of cultural difference, defense against cultural difference, and minimization of cultural difference. And three are *ethnorelative,* wherein the observer's culture of origin is experienced in the context of other cultures: acceptance of other cultures, adaptation to other cultures, and integration within another culture or cultures with the ability to move readily between cultures. The extent of movement between these six stages for an individual may be measured by Hammer and Bennett's IDI, representing the first five of the six DMIS stages. The IDI consists of 60 paper and pencil items drawn from interview statements. The items are designed to measure cognitive structure indicative of a given DMIS stage. This research represents an extensive group of studies using observation, theorizing, and measurement based on those observations, with the resulting theory and measuring instrument tested and verified by multiple methods. The DIMS and resulting IDI represent an impressive line of research, well founded and useful. Discussions of cultural competence may also be found in Leigh (1998), and in Hampden-Turner (1995).

Ethical Issues

A difficult problem with any research on intercultural competence, particularly but not exclusively in its application outside of the Western world, is how to confront ethical issues in the three ethnorelative stages. While a motorbike speeding down the street to market in Phnom Penh with two dozen live chickens wired to it by their feet may be compared by a person well into the ethnorelative stages with similar animal abuse conditions in a Western slaughterhouse or chicken coop, this may not hold true for attitudes toward cultural treatment of power, status, and sex. A major remaining question in intercultural communication is how to recognize the difference during the acquisition of successive ethnorelative stages in accepting cultural practices that the observing culture finds ethically abhorrent. For example, human trafficking, forced or even voluntary brothel work, FGM, the ritual animal sacrifices of Santeria, dog fighting, cock fighting, or the position of the old cleaning woman who is allowed as much of her pay to sleep under an outside stairwell with the rats and insects. Are these cultural or ethical issues? Clearly these examples involve both ethical and cultural issues, but the extent of emphasis on "culture" compared to that on "ethical" in the decisions made by the observer will result in quite different outcomes. One can and should, for example, point out the folly of applying Western norms to Eastern institutions and vice versa, yet there are major consequences for people and animals involved when the applications are or are not made. Is this the business of intercultural communication? It has to be, yet there are no simple answers to what makes the decision rule in these and similar instances one oriented by culture or by ethics. Whose culture is to rule, and whose ethics, and on what basis?

DOING INTERCULTURAL RESEARCH

How one studies intercultural communication depends on why it is being studied. Some scholars seek to build a theory of intercultural communication based on research grounded in the social sciences. Others seek to understand how people interpret behaviors and how the behaviors come to have meaning within a given culture. Governments and organizations are often concerned with introducing change into a particular culture to reduce a perceived evil, such as disease, lack of education, or the existence of human trafficking. People who must work in multicultural or cross-cultural settings, or who train others to do so, are concerned with providing practical advice for improving intercultural communication and easing the way of the trainee in the unfamiliar cultural setting. Others are concerned with the conflicts and misunderstandings which occur in cross-cultural and multicultural interactions. They seek to reduce prejudice and ethnocentrism and to promote peace and tranquility. Theory construction, cultural meaning, cultural change, practical advice to the sojourner, the reduction of prejudice and conflict between ethnic groups—these different goals of intercultural communication research lead to different research questions and different methods for answering them. No single method is always most appropriate in an intercultural setting. Method is always dependent upon the question being asked. Intercultural research is also complicated by the potential for violation of cultural norms, and by the "Heisenberg effect" of potentially changing the object of study through the means used to study it.

A Sample Study

Intercultural communication does not occur in a vacuum. It occurs in real situations with real people who have goals, desires, and much to gain or lose from the way a series of interconnected human interactions progresses. The nomothetic laws generated by research are ultimately useful if they can be applied to specific social interactions within specific cultural or cross-cultural settings. If they cannot be applied in practice, some may still remain useful heuristically, giving us diverse ways of conceptualizing intercultural communication and suggesting new studies and ways of relating to unlike others. When neither occurs, they remain just so much academic esoterica gathering dust on library shelves and computer hard drives.

One of the more interesting areas of intercultural communication is the struggle within immigrant families between parents and children, especially when an apparently socially liberal society such as the United States is the culture of entry. An inherent conflict exists between the role expectations for children in the old country and those in America. As one example, families in the Sunni Muslim community in Miami often experience conflict between parents and children. Parents complain of lack of respect, lack of obedience, willful disregard for and even ignorance of Muslim law, the Sharia, by their children. These are not the ways of the old country, and the parents are genuinely frightened of the unknown and the physical and moral dangers posed by the larger society.

Elements of the Problem

But the children have teenage friends in junior high or high school who can go unescorted to the mall. This is seen by immigrant parents as both a dangerous temptation inviting immoral activity and far too much freedom to ones so young, especially girls. The children want to go to the mall, to have fun, to be American. Such insolence can lead to punishments that would be regarded as physical abuse by American standards, and certainly by social workers. This introduces the threat of social or even governmental interference into the family's life. The parents may resort to real, verifiable threats to send their children back to the old country if they do not obey.

Male dominance introduces an added problem of husband–wife conflict, which would be accepted as normal in the old country. Some women see the need for control of the children in the old ways, in the face of the dangers posed by the existence of violence and street crime in American society, and also perceive the freedom and potential power granted by this freedom which is offered to both themselves and their children. But this freedom cannot be realized for the woman within the confines of a traditional marriage. The only way to achieve true freedom would be for the woman to leave her husband. But this would mean rejection by her extended family, which she cannot tolerate. She exists only within the nexus of the family. To let the children have their freedom while denying the same to herself seems intolerable. She may decide to sacrifice herself and side with the children allowing them some measure of freedom while denying freedom to herself. But usually she will decide to side with her husband. Once she does, she is more motivated to keep the children within the fold of the family and the old ways: If they stray, the blame will fall on her. She may then lose everything she has in terms of status in the family and in relationship to her husband, in addition to losing her children. She may even suffer the social death sentence of divorce because she could not keep the family together, a sentence which she has sought to avoid at all costs. The cultural norms that would resolve these problems in the old country are not applicable in the United States for both cultural and legal reasons.

A useful study might examine methods of managing such family conflicts in a way that keeps the family together, continues the Muslim beliefs and behaviors, yet allows small and gradual increases in freedom to all the participants and a gradual integration into the surrounding cultural nexus. Such a study would require integrating elements of ethnography, social science research methods, and, ultimately, of the diffusion of innovations, in order to be put into practice. In any applied setting, little advice is likely to be acted on which does not conform to the norms and belief systems of the participants. Rogers (1995) lists the criteria for likelihood of adoption of cross-cultural recommendations. The applied researcher in intercultural communication would be well advised to keep these recommendations in mind. The challenge is to determine a message strategy which both achieves goals and operates within the existing belief system under study.

Preliminary Considerations

A number of factors need to be considered in order to conduct the study. First, who is the client? If the study is applied, someone is paying for it, and for a reason. Second, what is the reason? What is the problem as the client sees it? Failure to understand the reasons and reasoning behind the drive for an applied study can be a major source of problems in conducting, completing, and reporting the results of the study.

Third, is the problem, as seen by the client, a reasonable problem which can be studied in a useful manner? How will other groups involved in the problem perceive the purpose of the research and the research enterprise itself? Will there be persons or groups that are attempting to block the research or failing to cooperate with it? What can be done to phrase or rephrase the purpose and the sponsorship of the research and the way and by whom the participants are approached such that all or most parties involved can perceive ownership of the project and the results? How can this project be conceived in such a way that its results could be acted on in a manner which will help both the client and all other groups involved to achieve their goals in some manner? If questions such as these are not addressed prior to the start of data gathering the likelihood of success of the project will be reduced considerably. The project will be worth its cost only if the people and groups involved have some reasonable probability of acting on its recommendations. This point must be explained to and impressed upon the client prior to agreeing to conduct the study. Unless everyone benefits, the client will not benefit, for the results will probably not be implemented.

Fourth, is there a way that theory-driven questions could be integrated into the study without detracting from it? Applied intercultural research can often be a vehicle for testing portions of intercultural communication theories.

Fifth, what needs to be known in order to conduct the study and to achieve usable results, and, what do we already know? Answering these questions corresponds roughly to the literature review phase of typical academic research. In addition to conducting bibliographic searches for a literature review, a "walking around and looking and talking with people" phase is needed. If this pilot review of the people and situations to be studied is not conducted for at least a short time with a few people prior to the project, then at the end of the project the researchers are likely to find they have conducted a pilot review but with a large group of subjects and at considerable expense. The bibliographic review itself should include, but not be limited to, a search of the bibliographic databases available on the Internet. Both applied and theoretical research efforts need to be informed by past research. This information then needs to be sorted for applicability to the research problem. The research can then be designed and conducted.

Addressing the Issues

Assume that the client is the local Muslim Community Association. Assume further that the problem is phrased as one of how to keep families intact, with the children remaining faithful believers in Islam. The problem is translated to read that the level of overt conflict (Steinfatt & Miller, 1974) in the families needs to be reduced. The perceptions of the parents, the children, and the community at large need to be addressed. The researchers may need to attend local community functions, to talk with the people involved, and to talk privately with the children in addition to talking privately with the parents and elders. They will need to display the proper deference to the proper people, and dress, talk, and behave as though they understood the basic norms of the community. For example, men in the research group may need to eat first, with the men in the community in the dining area, while the women wait and eat later, with the community women in the kitchen. Attempts to force American norms onto the group from the start will indicate a lack of understanding and disrespect. Why should these people listen to the researchers about cultural issues if the researchers are so culturally insensitive?

If the researchers are perceived by any of the groups as either on the "side" of one group, or as aloof and distant, the effort will likely fail. Focus groups conducted as a part of the socializing after an evening community meeting can be especially helpful in this regard. Locating children who have actually left their families and the religion, to learn their perspectives, can also be quite helpful. Questionnaires and procedures giving the appearance of academic research may be more trouble than they are worth in applied efforts. Often the appearance of listening, combined with actual sensitive listening and note taking, can be far more revealing and effective than information produced through questionnaires, though it is usually difficult to convince editorial reviewers of this if later publication is desired. Interviews and focus groups with members of a Muslim group which is geographically removed from the group of interest may provide additional insights and information. But different groups can often have strikingly different problems and no firm conclusions should be drawn from work with these additional Muslim groups. If privacy can be maintained, asking members of a Muslim group which is geographically distant about conclusions and proposed solutions prior to presenting them to the client group may produce useful insights. Use of the IDI with each of the main parties might be considered as a way of measuring progress toward openness to cultural solutions, though repeated measurement with the instrument may introduce questions from the participants as well as additional measurement considerations.

One model useful in most such intercultural conflicts is based on getting the groups to subscribe to the norms of respect for the other's status position and views, and respectful acceptance of the other's right to exist and to differ to an extent, within a predefined context. While everyone will usually agree with respect, and some will agree with acceptance, producing actual respect and actual acceptance through message strategies designed to reduce the conflict and tailored to each of the constituent groups is often the ultimate goal. The strategies themselves may be based on applications of theory according to the results of the focus groups and interviews. The message strategies must be acceptable, workable, and must meet the goals of the client and the other groups involved. Any workable message strategy set will usually have a minimum of two levels. The first level will be the initial strategy, and the second, an analysis of the various fallback positions depending on the response of the other to the initial communication attempt. Small-scale training of innovators might be part of the initial research proposal. Larger scale training proposals need to wait for the acceptance of the proposed solutions by the client and other groups involved. But without larger scale training, diffusion of the proposed solutions will be both less likely to occur and much slower in implementation.

REFERENCES

Alasuutari, P. (1995). *Researching culture: Qualitative method and cultural studies.* Thousand Oaks, CA: Sage.

Andersen, M. L., & Collins, P H. (1992). *Race, class, and gender.* Belmont, CA: Wadsworth.

Asante, M. K., & Gudykunst, W. B. (Eds.). (1989). *The handbook of international and intercultural communication.* Thousand Oaks, CA: Sage.

Asante, M. K., Newmark, E., & Blake, C. A. (Eds.). (1979). *The handbook of intercultural communication.* Thousand Oaks, CA: Sage.

Barfield, T. (Ed.). (2001). *The dictionary of anthropology.* London: Blackwell.

Barnlund, D. C. (1989). *Communicative styles of Japanese and Americans.* Belmont, CA: Wadsworth.

Bennett, M. J. (1986). A developmental approach to training for intercultural sensitivity. *International Journal of Intercultural Relations, 10*(2), 179–95.

Bennett, M. J. (1993). Towards ethnorelativism: A developmental model of intercultural sensitivity. In M. Paige (Ed.), *Education for the intercultural experience.* Yarmouth, ME: Intercultural Press.

Bennett, J. M., & Bennett, M. J. (2004a). *Developing intercultural competence: A reader.* Portland, OR: Intercultural Communication Institute.

Bennett, J. M., & Bennett, M. J. (2004b). Developing intercultural sensitivity: An integrative approach to global and domestic diversity. In D. Landis, J. M. Bennett, & M. J. Bennett (Eds.), *Handbook of intercultural training* (3rd ed., pp. 147–165). Thousand Oaks, CA: Sage.

Berger, C., & Calabrese, R. (1975). Some explorations in initial interactions and beyond: Toward a developmental theory of interpersonal communication. *Human Communication Research, 1,* 99–112.

Brislin, R. (1990). *Applied cross-cultural psychology.* Thousand Oaks, CA: Sage.

Brislin, R., & Yoshida, T (1994). *Intercultural communication training: An introduction.* Thousand Oaks, CA: Sage.

Cassirer, E. (1953). *The philosophy of symbolic forms: Vol. 1. Language* (R. Manheim, Trans.). New Haven, CT: Yale University Press.

Commission of Freedom of the Press. (1947). *A Free and responsible press: A general report on mass communications* (The Hutchins Commission report). Chicago: University of Chicago Press.

Condon, J. (1981). Values and ethics in communication across cultures: Some notes on the North American case. *Communication, 6,* 255–265.

Condon, J., & Yousef, F. S. (1974). *An introduction to intercultural communication.* Indianapolis, Bobbs-Merrill.

Diebold, A. R. (1965). A survey of psycholinguistic research, 1954–1964. In C. E. Osgood & T. A. Sebeok (Eds.), *Psycholinguistics* (pp. 205–291). Bloomington: Indiana University Press.

Dodd, C. H. (1982). *Dynamics of intercultural communication.* Dubuque, IA: William C. Brown.

Durkheim, E. (1897). *Le suicide; é tude de sociologie* [*Suicide: A study in sociology*]. Paris: F. Alcan.

Ellis, C., & Bochner, A. P. (1996). *Composing ethnography: Alternative forms of qualitative writing.* Walnut Creek, CA: AltaMira Press.

Fischer, J. L. (1974). Communication in primitive systems. In I. de Sola Pool, W. Schramm, F. W. Frey, N. Maccoby, & E. B. Parker (Eds.), *Handbook of communication* (pp. 313–336). Chicago: Rand McNally.

Fishman, J. A. (1960). A systematization of the Whorfian hypothesis. *Behavioral Science, 5,* 323–339.

Frey, E. W. (1974). Communication and development. In I. de Sola Pool, W. Schramm, E. W. Frey, N. Maccoby, & E. B. Parker (Eds.), *Handbook of communication* (pp. 337–461). Chicago: Rand McNally.

Gannon, M. J. (2004). *Understanding global cultures: Metaphorical journeys through 28 nations* (3rd ed.). Thousand Oaks, CA: Sage.

Gao, G., & Gudykunst, W. B. (1990). Uncertainty, anxiety, and adaptation. *International Journal of Intercultural Relations, 14,* 301–317.

Geertz, C. (1960). *The religion of Java.* Chicago/London: University of Chicago Press

Geertz, C. (1973). *The interpretation of cultures.* New York: Basic Books.

Geertz, C. (1983). *Local knowledge: Further essays in interpretive anthropology.* New York: Basic Books.

Geertz, C. (1988). *Works and lives: The anthropologist as author.* Stanford, CA: Stanford University Press.

Gibson, E. J., & McGarvy, H. R. (1937). Experimental studies of thought and reasoning. *Psychological Bulletin, 34,* 327–350.

Gladwin, C. H. (1989). *Ethnographic decision tree modeling.* Thousand Oaks, CA: Sage.

Glander, T. (1996). Wilbur Schramm and the Founding of Communication Studies. *Educational Theory, 46*(3), 373–391.

Glucksberg, S., & Danks, J. H. (1975). *Experimental psycholinguistics.* Hillsdale, NJ: Erlbaum.

Goldman, A. (1990). *For Japanese only: Intercultural communication with Americans.* Tokyo: Japan Times.

Goldman, A. (1994). *Doing business with the Japanese: A guide to successful communication, management, and diplomacy.* Albany, NY: State University of New York Press.

Gonzalez, A., Houston, M., & Chen, V. (1994). *Our voices: Essays in culture, ethnicity, and communication.* Los Angeles: Roxbury.

Greenberg, J. H. (1956). Concerning inferences from linguistic to nonlinguistic data. In H. Hoijer (Ed.), *Language in culture* (pp. 3–19). Chicago: University of Chicago Press.

Gudykunst, W. B. (1979). The effects of an intercultural communication workshop on cross-cultural attitudes and interaction. *Communication Education, 28,* 179–187.

Gudykunst, W. B. (1983a). Intercultural communication theory. In *International and intercultural communication annual.* Thousand Oaks, CA: Sage.

Gudykunst, W. B. (1983b). Toward a typology of stranger–host relationships. *International Journal of Intercultural Relations, 7,* 401–413.

Gudykunst, W. B. (1983c). Uncertainty reduction and predictability of behavior in low- and high-context cultures. *Communication Quarterly, 33,* 270–283.

Gudykunst, W. B. (1985a). The influence of cultural similarity, type of relationship, and self-monitoring on uncertainty reduction processes. *Communication Monographs, 52,* 203–217.

Gudykunst, W. B. (1985b). Intercultural communication: Current status and proposed directions. In B. Dervin & M. J. Voigt (Eds.), *Progress in communication sciences* (Vol. 6, pp. 1–46). Norwood, NJ: Ablex.

Gudykunst, W. B. (1985c). A model of uncertainty reduction in intercultural encounters. *Journal of Language and Social Psychology, 4,* 79–98.

Gudykunst, W. B. (1987). Cross-cultural comparisons. In C. R. Berger & S. H. Chaffee (Eds.), *Handbook of communication science* (pp. 847–889). Thousand Oaks, CA: Sage.

Gudykunst, W. B. (1988). Culture and the development of interpersonal relationships. In J. Anderson (Ed.), *Communication yearbook* (Vol. 12, pp. 315–354). Thousand Oaks, CA: Sage.

Gudykunst, W. B. (Ed.). (1993). *Communicating in Japan and in the United States.* Albany, NY: State University of New York Press.

Gudykunst, W. B., Chua, E., & Gray, A. (1987). Cultural dissimilarities and uncertainty reduction processes. In M. McLaughlin (Ed.), *Communication yearbook* (Vol. 10, pp. 456–569). Thousand Oaks, CA: Sage.

Gudykunst, W. B., & Hammer, M. (1988). The influence of social identity and intimacy of interethnic relationships on uncertainty reduction processes. *Human Communication Research, 14,* 569–601.

Gudykunst, W. B., & Nishida, T (1984). Individual and cultural influences on uncertainty reduction. *Communication Monographs, 51,* 23–36.

Gudykunst, W. B., & Nishida, T (1986a). Attributional confidence in low- and high-context cultures. *Human Communication Research, 12,* 525–549.

Gudykunst, W. B., & Nishida, T. (1986b). The influence of cultural variability on perceptions of communication behavior associated with relationship terms. *Human Communication Research, 13,* 147–166.

Gudykunst, W. B., & Nishida, T (1994). *Bridging Japanese/North American differences.* Thousand Oaks, CA: Sage.

Gudykunst, W. B., Nishida, T., Koike, H., & Shiino, N. (1986). The influence of language on uncertainty reduction: An exploratory study of Japanese-Japanese and Japanese-North American interactions. In M. McLaughlin (Ed.), *Communication yearbook* (Vol. 9, pp. 555–575). Thousand Oaks, CA: Sage.

Gudykunst, W. B., Nishida, T., & Schmidt, K. (1989). Cultural, relational, and personality influences on uncertainty reduction processes. *Western Journal of Speech Communication, 53,* 12–29.

Gudykunst, W. B., Wiseman, R., & Hammer, M. (1977). Determinants of a sojourner's attitudinal satisfaction. In B. Ruben (Ed.), *Communication yearbook* (Vol. 1, pp. 415–425). New Brunswick, NJ: Transaction.

Gudykunst, W. B., Yang, S. M., & Nishida, T. (1985). A cross-cultural test of uncertainty reduction theory: Comparisons of acquaintance, friends; and dating relationships in Japan, Korea, and the United States. *Human Communication Research, 11,* 407–454.

Hall, E. T. (1959). *The silent language.* Garden City, NY: Doubleday.

Hall, E. T. (1966). *The hidden dimension,* Garden City, NY: Doubleday.

Hall, P. H., & Gudykunst, W. B. (1989). The relationship of perceived ethnocentrism in corporate cultures to the selection, training, and success of international employees. *International Journal of Intercultural Relations, 13,* 183–201.

Hammer, M. R. (1998). A measure of intercultural sensitivity: The Intercultural Development Inventory. In S. Fowler & M. Fowler (Eds.), *The intercultural sourcebook* (Vol. 2). Yarmouth ME: Intercultural Press.

Hammer, M. R., Bennett, M. J., & Wiseman, R. (2003). Measuring intercultural sensitivity: The Intercultural Development Inventory. In R. M. Paige (Guest Ed.), *Intercultural development* [Special issue]. *International Journal of Intercultural Relations, 27*(4), 421–443.

Hammersley, M. (1992). *What's wrong with ethnography?* New York: Routledge.

Hampden-Turner, C. (1995). *Stages in the development of intercultural sensitivity and the theory of dilemma reconciliation: Milton J. Bennett and Charles Hampden-Turner's approaches contrasted and combined.* Cambridge, UK: Cambridge University, The Judge Institute of Management Studies.

Harms, L. S. (1973). *Intercultural communication.* New York: Harper & Row.

Hatch, E. (1983). *Culture and morality: The relativity of values in anthropology.* New York: Columbia University Press.

Head, S. W. (1956). *Broadcasting in America: A survey of television and radio.* Boston: Houghton Mifflin.

Head, S. W. (1961). *A field experiment in the summertime use of open circuit television instruction to bridge the gap between high school and college.* Coral Gables, FL: University of Miami.

Head, S. W. (1974). *Broadcasting in Africa: A continental survey of radio and television.* Philadelphia: Temple University Press.

Head, S. W. (1985). *World broadcasting systems: A comparative analysis.* Belmont, CA: Wadsworth.

Hecht, M. L., Jackson, R. L., II, & Ribeau, S. A. (2003). *African American communication: Exploring identity and cultural interpretation* (2nd ed.). Mahwah, NJ: Erlbaum.

Heidbreder, E. (1948). Studying human thinking. In T. G. Andrews (Ed.), *Methods of psychology* (pp. 96–123). New York: Wiley.

Henle, P. (1958). Language, thought, and culture. In P. Henle (Ed.), *Language and culture* (pp. 1–24). Ann Arbor: University of Michigan Press.

Hovland, C. I., Janis, I. L., & Kelley, H. H. (1953). *Communications and persuasion: Psychological studies in opinion change,* New Haven, CT: Yale University Press.

Humphrey, G. (1951). *Thinking: An introduction to its experimental psychology.* New York: Wiley.

Johnson, D. M. (1950). Problem solving and symbolic processes. *Annual Review of Psychology, 1,* 297–310.

Jones, S. E. (1979). Integrating etic and emic approaches in the study of intercultural communication. In M. K. Asante, E. Newmark, & C. A. Blake (Eds.), *The handbook of intercultural communication* (pp. 57–74). Thousand Oaks, CA: Sage.

Kaplan, A. (1964). *The conduct of inquiry.* San Francisco: Chandler.

Kelly, W. (1999). Jack Condon's intellectual journey. *The Edge. The E-Journal of Intercultural Relations, 2*(1). http://www.interculturalrelations.com/v2i1Winter1999/w99kellycondon1.htm

Kim, Y. Y. (1986). *Interethnic communication current research.* Thousand Oaks, CA: Sage.

Kim, Y. Y (1988a). *Communication and cross-cultural adaptation.* Philadelphia: Multilingual Matters.

Kim, Y. Y. (1988b). On theorizing intercultural communication. In Y. Y. Kim & W. B. Gudykunst (Eds.), *International and intercultural communication annual* (Vol. 12, pp. 11–21). Thousand Oaks, CA: Sage.

Kim, Y. Y., & Gudykunst, W B. (1988). Theories in intercultural communication: *International and intercultural communication annual* (Vol. 12). Thousand Oaks, CA: Sage.

Klopf, D. W. (1987). *Intercultural encounters: The fundamentals of intercultural communication.* Englewood, NJ: Morton.

Kluckhohn, C. (1949). *Mirror for man: The relation of anthropology to modern life.* New York: Whittlesey House.

Kohls, R. L. (1984). *Survival kit for living overseas.* Yarmouth, ME: Intercultural Press.

Langer, S. K. (1942). *Philosophy in a new key.* Cambridge, MA: Harvard University Press.

Lasswell, H. (1948). The structure and function of communication in society. In L. Bryson (Ed.), *The communication of ideas* (pp. 7–51). New York: Harper.

Lazarsfeld, P. F. (1944). *The people's choice: How the voter makes up his mind in a presidential campaign.* New York: Duell, Sloan & Pearce.

Lee, P. (1996). *The Whorf theory complex: A critical reconstruction.* Philadelphia: J. Benjamins.

Leeds-Hurwitz, W. (1990). Notes in the history of intercultural communication: The Foreign Service Institute and the mandate for intercultural training. *Quarterly Journal of Speech, 76,* 262–281.

Leigh, J.W. (1998). *Communicating for cultural competence.* Boston: Allyn & Bacon.

Lenneberg, E., & Roberts, J. M. (1956). *The language of experience*. Bloomington: Indiana University Publication in Anthropology & Linguistics.

Lerner, D., & Schramm, W. (Eds.). (1967). *Communication and change in the developing countries*. Honolulu, Hawaii: East-West Center Press.

Malinowski, B. (1922). *Argonauts of the Western Pacific: An account of native enterprise and adventure in the archipelagoes of Melanesian New Guinea*. London: Routledge & Kegan Paul.

Mandell, S. (1931). The relation of language to thought. *Quarterly Journal of Speech, 17*, 522–531.

McPhail, T. (2006). *Global communication: Theories, stakeholders and trends* (2nd ed.). Malden, MA: Blackwell.

Mestenhauser, J. A., Marty, G., & Steglitz, I. (Eds.). (1988). *Culture, learning, and the disciplines: Theory and practice in cross-cultural orientation*. Washington, D.C.: National Association of Foreign Student Affairs.

Osgood, C. E., & Sebeok, T A. (1965). *Psycholinguistics*. Bloomington: Indiana University Press.

Park, R. E., & Burgess, E. W. (1924). *Introduction to the science of sociology*. Chicago: University of Chicago Press.

Pike, K. L. (1966). Etic and emic standpoints for the description of behavior. In A. G. Smith (Ed.), *Communication and culture* (pp. 152–163). New York: Holt, Rinehart & Winston.

Popper, K. R. (1968). *The logic of scientific discovery* (3rd ed.). London: Hutchinson.

Rogers, E. M. (1962). *The diffusion of innovations*. New York: Free Press.

Rogers, E. M. (1995). *Diffusion of innovations* (4th ed.). New York: Free Press.

Rogers, E. M. (1994). *A history of communication study: A biographical approach*. New York: Free Press.

Rogers, E. M., & Shoemaker, F. F. (1971). *Communication of innovations: A cross-cultural approach* (2nd ed.). New York: Free Press.

Rogers, E. M., & Steinfatt, T. M. (1999). *Intercultural communication*. Prospect Heights, IL: Waveland Press.

Ronai, C. R. (1996). My mother is mentally retarded. In C. Ellis & A. P. Bochner (Eds.), *Composing ethnography: Alternative forms of qualitative writing* (pp. 109–131). Walnut Creek, CA: AltaMira Press.

Rostow, W. W. (1952). *The process of economic growth*. New York: Norton.

Rostow, W. W., & Hatch, R. W. (1955). *An American policy in Asia*. Cambridge: MIT Technology Press.

Rostow, W. W., & Levin, A. (1953). *The dynamics of Soviet society*. New York: Norton.

Ryle, G. (1968). *The thinking of thoughts: What is "Le Penseur" doing?* (University Lectures, no.18). University of Saskatchewan. http://lucy.ukc.ac.uk/CSACSIA/Vol14/Papers/ryle_1.html

Samovar, L. A., & Porter, R. E. (1972, 1994). *Intercultural communication: A reader*. Belmont, CA: Wadsworth.

Sapir, E. (1921). *Language: An introduction to the study of speech*. New York: Harcourt, Brace, & World.

Sato, A. (1992). *Understanding Japanese communication*. Tokyo: Japan Times.

Schatzman, L., & Strauss, A. (1955). Social class and modes of communication. *American Journal of Sociology, 60*, 329–338.

Schramm, Wilbur L. (1954). *The process and effects of mass communication*. Urbana: University of Illinois Press.

Singer, M. R. (1987). *Intercultural communication: A perceptual approach*. Englewood Cliffs, NJ: Prentice-Hall.

Singhal, A., & Rogers, E. M. (2004). The status of entertainment-education worldwide. In A. Singhal, M. J. Cody, E. M. Rogers, & M. Sabido (Eds.), *Entertainment-education and social change* (pp. 3–20). Mahwah, NJ: Erlbaum

Slobin, D. T (1979). *Psycholinguistics.* Glenview, IL: Scott Foresman.

Smith, A. G. (Ed.). (1966). *Communication and culture.* New York: Holt.

Steinfatt, T. M. (1988, November). *Language and intercultural differences: Linguistic relativity.* "Top Three" paper, Intercultural Communication Division, Speech Communication Association, New Orleans, LA.

Steinfatt, T. M. (1989). Linguistic relativity: Toward a broader view. In S. Ting-Toomey & F. Korzenny (Eds.), *International and intercultural communication annual: Vol. 13. Language, communication and culture* (pp. 35–75). Thousand Oaks, CA: Sage.

Steinfatt, T. M. (2002). *Working at the bar: Sex work and health communication in Thailand.* Westport, CT: Greenwood.

Steinfatt, T., & Miller, G. R. (1974). Communication in game theoretic models of conflict. In G. R. Miller & H. W Simons (Eds.), *Perspectives on communication in social conflict* (pp. 14–75). Englewood Cliffs, NJ: Prentice-Hall.

Stewart, E. C., & Bennett, M. J. (1991). *American cultural patterns: A cross-cultural perspective.* Yarmouth, ME: Intercultural.

Stewart, L. P., Gudykunst, W. B., Ting-Toomey, S., & Nishida, T. (1986). The effects of decision-making style on openness and satisfaction within Japanese organizations. *Communication Monographs, 53,* 236–251.

Sudweeks, S., Gudykunst, W. B., Ting-Toomey, S., & Nishida, T. (1990). Developmental themes in Jap-anese-North American interpersonal relationships. *International Journal of Intercultural Relations, 14,* 207–233.

Ting-Toomey, S. (1981). Ethnic identity and close friendship in Chinese-American college students [Suppl.]. *International Journal of Intercultural Relations, 27,* S383–S406.

Ting-Toomey, S. (1985). Toward a theory of conflict and culture. In W. Gudykunst, L. Stewart, & S. Ting-Toomey (Eds.), *Communication, culture, and organizational processes* (pp. 71–86). Thousand Oaks, CA: Sage.

Vidich, A. J., & Lyman, S. M. (1994). Qualitative methods: Their history in sociology and anthropology. In N. K. Denzin & Y. S. Lincoln (Eds.), *Handbook of qualitative research* (pp. 23–59). Thousand Oaks, CA: Sage.

Vinacke, W. E. (1951). The investigation of concept formation. *Psychological Bulletin, 48,* 1–31.

Whorf, B. L. (1956). *Language, thought, and reality.* Cambridge, MA: MIT Press.

Wolcott, H. F. (1994). *Transforming qualitative data.* Thousand Oaks, CA: Sage.

Woodworth, R. S. (1938). *Experimental psychology.* New York: Holt.

SUGGESTED READINGS

Bennett, J. M., & Bennett, M. J. (2004a). *Developing intercultural competence: A reader*. Portland, OR: Intercultural Communication Institute.

Bennett, J. M., & Bennett, M. J. (2004b). Developing intercultural sensitivity: An integrative approach to global and domestic diversity. In D. Landis, J. M. Bennett, & M. J. Bennett (Eds.), *Handbook of intercultural training* (3rd ed., pp. 147–165). Thousand Oaks, CA: Sage.

Gudykunst, W. B. (1988). Culture and the development of interpersonal relationships. In J. Anderson (Ed.), *Communication yearbook* (Vol. 12, pp. 315–354). Thousand Oaks, CA: Sage.

Gudykunst, W. B., Chua, E., & Gray, A. (1987). Cultural dissimilarities and uncertainty reduction processes. In M. McLaughlin (Ed.), *Communication yearbook* (Vol. 10, pp. 456–569). Thousand Oaks, CA: Sage.

Hall, E. T. (1959). *The silent language*. Garden City, NY: Doubleday.

Hammer, M. R. (1998). A measure of intercultural sensitivity: The Intercultural Development Inventory. In

S. Fowler & M. Fowler (Eds.), *The intercultural sourcebook* (Vol. 2). Yarmouth ME: Intercultural Press.

Hammer, M. R., Bennett, M. J., & Wiseman, R. (2003). Measuring intercultural sensitivity: The Intercultural Development Inventory. In R. M. Paige (Guest Ed.), *Intercultural Development* [Special issue] *International Journal of Intercultural Relations, 27*(4), 421–443.

Kim, Y. Y., & Gudykunst, W. B. (1988). *Theories in intercultural communication: International and intercultural communication annual* (Vol. 12). Thousand Oaks, CA: Sage.

Lee, P. (1996). *The Whorf theory complex: A critical reconstruction*. Philadelphia: J. Benjamins.

Leeds-Hurwitz, W. (1990). Notes in the history of intercultural communication: The Foreign Service Institute and the mandate for intercultural training. *Quarterly Journal of Speech, 76*, 262–281.

Pike, K. L. (1966). Etic and emic standpoints for the description of behavior. In A. G. Smith (Ed.), *Communication and culture* (pp. 152–163). New York: Holt, Rinehart & Winston.

Rogers, E. M. (1995). *Diffusion of innovations* (4th ed.). New York: Free Press.

Rogers, E. M., & Steinfatt, T. M. (1999). *Intercultural communication*. Prospect Heights, IL: Waveland Press.

Steinfatt, T. M. (1989). Linguistic relativity: Toward a broader view. In S. Ting-Toomey & F. Korzenny (Eds.), *International and intercultural communication annual: Vol. 13 Language, communication and culture* (pp. 35–75). Thousand Oaks, CA: Sage..

Steinfatt, T. M. (2002). *Working at the bar: Sex work and health communication in Thailand*. Westport, CT: Greenwood.

Whorf, B. L. (1956). *Language, thought, and reality*. Cambridge, MA: MIT Press.

Tides in the Ocean: A Layered Approach to Communication and Culture

By Sandra L. Faulkner and Michael L. Hecht

Culture is a lens for viewing the connections and relationships that define the human experience. Just as physics has become more and more focused on the connections and relationships among energy and matter, so too have the human sciences come to focus on these sources of connectivity. We believe that the construct of "culture" provides a means for understanding and explaining the connections among people as well as between people and their environment. At the same time, it helps explain how people's various identities come together to create the self. We consider culture to be like a "lens" because it focuses us on these connections, helping us see more clearly something that, while containing material objects, is actually symbolic.

In this chapter we will attempt to describe and explain the lens of culture, and show you how it can be used to understand everyday occurrences as well as the more complex and enduring patterns of human experience. We hope to demonstrate how something can be both abstract and concrete, complex and simple. We invite you to look into our chapter through your own lens of culture and hope that the following will help you interpret this lens while lending understanding to those used by others.

But lenses are not passive or benign pointers. Rather, they may change the observation itself by bringing it closer or moving it further away, and by clarifying or distorting an image. Think of a camera lens that zooms in and out. Think also of what we mean by getting a camera lens "in focus"—we see more clearly what is in the middle of the picture while the edges or borders are fuzzy. In this way, the lens of culture calls our

attention to parts of our experience, putting those parts in the foreground and center of our world picture. And what do we see most clearly through the lens of culture? We believe that culture highlights most clearly three concepts: *code, conversation,* and *community*. Culture helps us understand the codes of conduct and thought, the ways in people converse and interact, and the communities in which they live.

Gerry Philipsen (1987) was among the first to point out these three unifying concepts of culture. We use his approach as a starting point and offer definitions of cultural codes, conversations, and communities as well as discuss what it means to define culture as a code, conversation, and community. We will use Michael's culture to illustrate these concepts. Michael is of Eastern European Jewish American descent and was raised in New York City.

CULTURAL CODE

A *code* is a system of symbols, rules, meanings, beliefs, values, and images of the ideal. It is a world view or source of order. Geertz (1973) described culture as "webs of significance" (p. 5) and goes on to discuss the patterns of meanings and symbolic forms. Similarly, Carbaugh (1985) discussed culture as "a system of meaning or process of sense making" (p. 32), while Gudykunst and Kim (1992) referred to it as "a unified set of symbolic ideas" (p. 4). There are many ways to see these codes. One way is to examine the types of ceremonies that different cultures perform. These ceremonies reflect what is valued, and each has its own rules and customs. Think about the ceremonies you attend (e.g., weddings, funerals, graduation). What does a funeral mean to you? How do you behave at one? What clothing do you wear for it? In some cultures (e.g., Japan) white is preferred to show respect for death, and others (e.g., United States) prefer dark colors. Think about the rules for job interviewing. When starting a new job, what codes will you need to master to succeed as an employee? Cultures teach us about how to interpret events; how to behave; how to be. This is what we mean when we say, culture is a code.

Jewish American Code: Hebrew/Yiddish, Knowledge, Religion

Michael was encouraged to speak Hebrew, the language of the Jewish Bible when growing up. As eastern Europeans, his grand parents spoke Yiddish, a language combining Hebrew and German that had been used by previous generations of immigrants to assimilate to German culture. His parents, aunts, and uncles spoke this language, though all but the eldest of the next generation were discouraged from its use because of the belief it would interfere with learning Hebrew and would mark them as lower class and foreign.

But this marks only the "language code" of the culture. Remember, that in our definition we discussed code as meaning and values. One of the unifying values in this culture is knowledge—the quest for information and wisdom through study. Historically, Jewish culture has emphasized knowledge, reserving the Sabbath for study.

Finally, Judaism invokes a religious code. This more formal system is cataloged in the Jewish Testament, though it is not used as a rigid set of laws as much as a set of guidelines for life within Michael's cultural group.

CULTURE AS CONVERSATION

Conversation involves patterns of verbal and nonverbal interactions. Borman (1983) talked about culture as "the sum total of ways of living, organizing, and communing" (p. 100), while E. T. Hall and Hall (1989) described it as a program for behavior. Hymes (1974) thought of culture as a speech community, in a sense combining culture as conversation with culture as community. For example, Black English represents a distinctive language code (Hecht, Jackson, & Ribeau, 2003). Culture tells us how to interact with others. Think about traveling to another culture as a salesperson. Who would you contact at a company to make the sale? How should you start the conversation? Now think about meeting people in another culture. Can you ask about personal topics? How quickly is it appropriate to invite someone to your home? Our cultures give us the answers to these questions about how to carry on a conversation.

Jewish American Conversation: Expressive, Aggressive, Political

The conversational style that Michael's culture invokes is a highly expressive and aggressive one. Conversations are animated and issues are engaged in a direct and sometimes provocative manner. Often, these discussions turn to political issues. Michael remembers family dinners becoming debates about the issues of the day, often between him and his elder sister with his father moderating. Just as Jewish religion and biblical interpretations are debated in religious practice, so to is this style of interaction pervasive in the group's cultural conversation.

CULTURE AS COMMUNITY

A *community* represents a group, shared identities, a sense of membership, who "we" are and the way people organize themselves. Linton (1955) defined culture as an organized group, and Winkelman (1993) talked about it as the people who share the culture. Carbaugh (1989) wrote extensively about "personhood"—what we consider a person to be and how they constitute part of a group. For instance, what does it mean to be a student and how does a student become part of a university student body? Many writers refer to culture as a "way of life," clearly implicating the community or collectivity. Nations are perhaps the most common way of thinking about a culture. Nations have a sense of place but, more importantly, are a group of people. We talk about the French culture, the Russian culture and the Chinese culture.

Jewish American Community: Temple, Other Jews

Being a Jewish American means feeling part of a group or community. This community is often defined locally around the Temple or Synagogue but more broadly includes all Jews. However, within Judaism there are sects or denominations (Orthodox, Conservative, Reform, and, recently, Reconstruction), and these may define the boundaries of group membership for some. Clearly, non-Jews are defined as outsiders and the pervasiveness of Yiddish words that mark this status is a clear sign of the importance of distinguishing Jews from non-Jews.

Your Cultural Code, Conversation, and Community

Stop for a moment and think about your own cultural group membership(s). Do you feel aligned with a particular group? Or, perhaps, more than one? Choose a group and see if you can describe its code, conversation, and community. In our college classes, students sometimes describe their fraternity or sorority as a culture, or even the entire university (e.g., Here at Penn State there are people who consider themselves "Penn Staters"). Others choose their ethnic or racial group, religious group, or nationality. Still others define their group by sexual orientation.

USING THE CULTURAL LENS

Thus far, we have described culture as a lens for viewing the human experience and explained that the lens focuses us on code, conversation and community. We noted, however, that in addition to focusing on a particular picture (e.g, codes or conversations or communities) the lens also provides a perspective on the content—in a sense zooming us in on the details or zooming us out to see the overview.

We approach this issue from a layered perspective—that is, we assume that culture exists on different layers or levels. Some people define culture as only the group (e.g., African Americans) ignoring individuals. We believe that culture is present in individuals as well as shared by collectivities and communities. Philipsen (1987) commented that we need to understand how people manage the tension between the pull of communal life and the impulse of individuals to be free, and that we need a definition of culture that addresses this dynamic push and pull (or "dialectic" as Baxter and Braithwaite explained).

Examining culture from this perspective allows one to consider the polarities and contradictions in social life, rather than viewing culture as simply the group or the individual, or even as existing at some point along a continuum from one to the other (Hecht, 1993). Using a layer metaphor lets us see that polarities are present in all interaction, and it broadens the view of contradictions as polar opposites between two elements (e.g., individual and society). This seems especially relevant to the examination of culture given that culture exists and is expressed on multiple levels. Culture is not only a characteristic of the individual or society; it is a characteristic of both the individual and society as well as the interrelationships between the two. The notion of layering is a metaphor used to represent people's experiences and how they understand their experiences. We experience our social worlds in many ways including behaviorally, emotionally, spiritually, physiologically, experientially, and cognitively. These various realms are like "tides in the ocean, each integrated into the whole ocean (i.e., human experience) and yet each with identifiable characteristics (i.e., a separable realm of the experience)" (Hecht, 1993, p. 77). Thus, the final characteristic of the cultural lens is to identify layers or levels at which culture can be viewed.

THE LAYERS OF CULTURE

The Layered Approach (Baldwin & Hecht, 1995, 2000; Hecht, 1993; Hecht & Baldwin, 1998; Hecht, Jackson, Lindsley, Strauss, & Johnson, 2001) identifies four layers of culture: the personal, enacted, relational, and communal.

The *personal layer* examines one's self-concept or spiritual sense of well-being. Culture can be conceptualized as a characteristic of a person—who they think they are and how they see themselves (self-concept). Above, we illustrated code, conversation, and community by-showing how Michael saw himself, his personal take on his culture.

But culture is also expressed in the way people communicate. This is called the *enacted layer* and focuses on how messages express culture. There are both direct and indirect ways of expressing culture. For example, you telling someone directly you are Morman or you can mention specific Morman people who you know to express it indirectly. In addition, culture is enacted through specific practices such as putting up a Christmas tree, singing the National Anthem, fasting during Ramadan, or wearing a dashiki. Not all communication is about expressing identity, but much in what we say and do expresses who we are.

The *relational layer* refers to how one's culture is *formed* through one's relationships, is *invested* in one's relationship to other people, and *exists* in relation to one's other identities. We learn about culture through our families and teachers—through our relationships. We practice our culture with other people (e.g., religious and cultural celebrations, national holidays). Sometimes we even define ourselves in terms of our relationships (e.g., as someone's relational partner, someone's father, someone's friend). Often our cultural groupings are defined in terms of others, a process labeled ingroup or outgroup distinction. These group distinctions are commonly evoked in intercultural communication. Dividing the world into ingroups and outgroups or us versus them is a natural phenomenon and thus, necessary to consider in intercultural research and practice. In fact, this is one of the key concepts in intercultural communication theory. The "intergroup perspective" has been developed by authors such as Tajfel, Giles, and others, and focuses on how people make distinctions between groups in which they feel memberships and those in which they do not, as well as how people communicate' across group lines. Our national cultures, for example, are often contrasted with other groups, particularly if they are traditional enemies and rivals (e.g., England and France). Other examples of ingroups include professions, families, religions, and social clubs. Among adolescents, they can include distinctions based on interests, like the skaters versus the jocks, or based on musical interests. Consider all of the world conflict that results from religious differences. These ingroup and outgroup distinctions play a major role in intergroup relations and underlie some of the most serious problems the world faces today (e.g., in the Middle East and the Balkans-Eastern Europe). At times, just the act of categorizing people into two groups fosters intergroup discrimination (Tajfel, 1981).

What determines the nature of intergroup conflict? Intergroup threats are present when individuals experience anxiety about interacting with outgroups (Tajfel, 1981). Individuals tend to experience high levels of anxiety if there has been little prior contact with or knowledge about outgroup members. Conversely, anxiety also results from a history of intergroup hostility and competition, especially if one group has been in a minority or low-status position. This is evident in recent international conflicts (e.g., Bosnia, Middle East) as well as interracial relations in the United States. Anxiety about interaction also is related to ethnocentricity. Being able to only see your own country or groups' point of view is ethnocentrism. When people want to show solidarity with an ingroup, communication tends to converge and when differences between ingroups and outgroups are being expressed, communication tends to diverge (Giles & Coupland, 1991). Research by Hecht et al. (2003) revealed that satisfaction in ingroup conversations depends on feeling you have some power or control over the conversation as well as the establishment of relational solidarity; satisfaction with outgroup conversations is contingent on establishing common ground through the communication of acceptance, shared world view, not stereotyping, and understanding.

Finally, the *communal layer* focuses on how a group of people or some particular community shares an identity, such as being Jewish or Gay. A community possesses its own identity and shared visions of personhood. This is perhaps the most common way to see culture—as a group of people. When we talk about "Japanese culture" we are not focusing on individual Japanese people but, instead, talking about the collective or group as a whole. This notion of collectivity or community is certainly important to how culture is defined and should not be neglected. In fact, the communal layer is probably the most common way of thinking about culture. Unfortunately, focusing on culture as communal can also be the source of problems because if you assume that members of the culture automatically share common characteristics, you will have stereotyped them. That's why it is important to remember that most of the time when we talk about culture we are talking about characteristics of the community or collectivity, not the individuals.

Connections Among Layers

These four levels, or layers, can work individually, in pairs, or in any combination. For example, you might ask about the values of a specific cultural group (communal level). Or, you might wonder how an individual's view of herself (personal level) effects how she interacts with members of the outgroup (relational level).

In addition, the layers may be in conflict with each other such as a person who feels pride in his or her own religious identity, yet does not wish to participate in religious practices. Another conflict may be a couple who come from two differing groups' (e.g., Muslim and Christian)—they see themselves as possessing a relationship or relational culture of their own (relational level), though the larger collectivity (communal level) may not approve.

Moreover, the layers are considered to be interpenetrating, that is they can be found within each other. For example, relationships help shape personal understandings while at the same time relationships are formed out of a person's culture. Thus, the relational layer is in the personal layer and the personal is in the relationship.

When these four layers are considered, culture can be seen as a *negotiation* among the individual, the enacted, the relational, and the communal layers, or any combination of the four. For example, think of how a gay Jew in a committed relationship with a non-Jew negotiates identity and culture at these various levels.

This ends our discussion about conceptualizing culture. Certainly, there are many other factors to consider. Culture is intergenerationally transmitted (e.g, handed down from generation to generation; Murphy, 1986); it is the human-made part of the environment (Triandis, 1990); it encompasses our practices and behaviors that signal our differences (Fiske, 1992). Some would argue that the most important aspect of culture are the power relations and hierarchies it creates (Hall 1986). However, for our purposes the concepts of code, conversation, and community considered at personal, enacted, relational and communal levels is adequate for understanding of culture.

In the remainder of this chapter we will consider a theory of culture at each of the four layers. We hope this review will provide you with some idea about how culture and communication have been conceptualized (although it is not meant to be exhaustive). It should be clear that culture and communication are inseparable. There can be no culture without communication that constitutes and creates the code, is the conversation, and binds and organizes the community. Similarly, communication requires a code to give it meaning and is a set of cultural practices engaged in within and between communities.

Personal Layer

A number of writers have talked about how culture shapes or creates the individual or self. For instance, Hofstede (1991) focused on cultural values. While he was interested in describing the values of entire cultures, other writers have shown how individuals in cultures use these values and are influenced by them (e.g., Triandis, 1994). Communal values influence individual's (e.g., being Japanese in a collectivistic country) self-concepts and behavior. Space precludes a discussion of all such values, so here we focus on *Individualism/ Collectivism* and *Gender* as cultural characteristics of individuals.

Individualism/Collectivism. Individualism versus collectivism is one of the most basic cultural dimensions. According to Tomkins (1984), an individual's psychological makeup is the result of this cultural dimension. For example, he reported that human beings in Western Civilization have tended toward positive or negative self-celebration, and in Asian thought harmony between humans and nature is another alternative that is represented. Whether people live alone, in families, or tribes depends on the degree of individualism-collectivism in a culture (Anderson, 1985). An emphasis on community, shared interests, harmony, tradition, the public good, and maintaining face characterize collectivistic cultures. Collectivism "pertains to societies in which people from birth onwards are integrated into strong, cohesive ingroups, which throughout people's lifetime continue to protect them in exchange for unquestioning loyalty" (Hofstede, 1991, p.51). Societies in which people look after themselves and those in their immediate families and where ties are loose characterize individualistic cultures (Hofstede, 1991).

In individualistic Western cultures, people rely on personal judgments (Triandis, 1994), whereas an emphasis on harmony among people, between people and nature, and on collective judgement can be seen in people from Eastern cultures (Gudykunst et al., 1996). People living in the United States, for example, tend to place a very high value on individualism (Bellah, Madsen, Sullivan, Swidler, & Tipson, 1985; Kim, 1994). More traditional and collectivist cultures place value on the interdependence among individuals and conforming to social roles and norms whereas individualistic and less traditional cultures stress independence in the pursuit of personal goals and interests and self expression. The best and worst in U.S. culture can be attributed to individualism. If we think of some of the positive elements, we may consider individualism as the basis of freedom, creativity, and economic incentive. The majority of Americans believe "that a man [or woman] by following his [or her] own interest, rightly understood, will be led to do what is just and good" (Tocqueville, 1945, p. 409).

On the other hand, individual consciousness may disrupt the systemic nature of life on earth by pulling humans out of their ecological niche, that is separating humans from nature with the increasing isolation and industrialization (Bateson, 1972). The downside of individualism includes alienation, loneliness, materialism and difficulty interacting with those from less individualistic cultures (Condon & Yousef, 1983; Hofstede, 1991). Thus, our individualism leads us to value creative ways of expressing ourselves (e.g., the person who is the "life of the party") but may challenge our ability to work together as a team (e.g., sacrifice for the common good).

Even though the United States is the most individualistic country (Hofstede, 1984/1990), certain ethnic groups and geographic regions vary in their degrees of individualism. For instance, African Americans place a great deal of emphasis on individualism (Collier, Ribeau, & Hecht, 1986; Hecht et al., 2003; Hecht & Ribeau, 1984: Kochman, 1981), whereas Mexican Americans place greater emphasis on relational solidarity and their families (Hecht & Ribeau, 1984; Hecht, Ribeau, & Sedano, 1990). This translates into a general tendency for African Americans to "tell it like it is" in conversations in order to preserve authenticity and Mexican Americans to focus on the relational with others in conversations, sometimes avoiding negative information in the process. There is a tendency to relay on *simpatia*, a preference for harmony in interpersonal, relations such that negative comments may be ignored in a conversation.

Of course, the very notion of individualism suggests that a person's own values may transcend his or her cultural group membership. In fact, there is evidence that personal individualism may transcend cultural differences for certain variables. Singelis (1996) urged us to examine the connection between context and individual variables. Schmidt (1983), for example, compared the effects of crowding on people from the United States (an individualistic culture) and Singapore (a collectivist culture). Schmidt hypothesized that similar psychological variables would underlie people's stress and annoyance responses to crowding. He studied students at a U.S. university bookstore during the first 3 days of the quarter (a typically crowded time) and Singaporean high school students in their places of residence and found similar perceptions for both cultures on the relationships among personal control on annoyance and stress about environmental crowding. What we conclude is that no culture or individual is completely individualistic or collectivistic. All have some conception of the person as well as the group. What differs is the relative value placed on each and how people work out the competing pressures (e.g., the role of sacrifice).

Gender. Although gender is typically thought of (and investigated as) as an individual characteristic, it has been neglected as a cultural dimension. We conceptualize this dimension of culture as the rigidity and definition of gender roles. Cultures that are more rigid expect members to act within a narrow range of gender-related behaviors and stress traditional gender-role identification. Hofstede (1984/1990) described masculine traits within such a world view typically as attributes such as strength, assertiveness, competitiveness, achievement, and ambitiousness, whereas feminine traits are attributes such as affection, compassion, nurturance, and emotionality. More rigid societies prescribe masculine behavior for men and feminine behavior for women, although there is a tendency for women in masculine societies to be "tougher" than women in feminine societies (Hofstede, 1998). "The masculinity-femininity dimension relates to people's self-concept: Who I am and what is my task in life" (Hofstede, 1984/1990, p. 84). A cross-cultural study comparing advertisements from Japan, Russia, Sweden, and the United States suggests that countries can be characterized along these masculine feminine dimensions. Milner and Collins (2000) discovered that television advertisements from feminine countries (Sweden, Russia) compared with more masculine countries (Japan, United States) contained more depictions of relationships for male and female characters. They conclude that a feminine country's dominant orientation is reflected in media, specifically television advertising and the depiction of characters in relationships.

Cross-cultural research shows that while young girls are expected to be more nurturant than boys though there is considerable variation from country to country (E. T. Hall, 1984). An important area to explore are the kinds of goals individuals value in their lives. Hofstede's (1984/1990) work examined the degree to which people of both sexes in a culture endorse primarily masculine or feminine goals. Goals such as competitiveness, assertiveness, ambitiousness, and a focus on material success are considered masculine, whereas nurturance, compassion, modesty, and a focus on the quality of life are considered feminine goals (Hofstede, 1998). A cross-cultural study with male and female Israeli Arab students (more traditional collectivist culture) and male and female Israeli Jewish students (more individualistic less traditional culture) demonstrated the role that culture plays in discriminatory behavior (Lobel, Mashraki-Pedhatzur, Mantzur, & Libby, 2000). Lobel et al. (2000) presented students with candidates for class representative, one male with traditional feminine interests (ballet) and characteristics (slight build) and one male with masculine interests (football) and characteristics (broad-shouldered build). The study revealed that all participants discriminated against the feminine male, but the Arab students discriminate more explicitly. They were less likely to elect him, to believe that others would freely choose him, and to think that he should be elected. Additionally, they liked him less than the masculine candidate and compared with the masculine candidate were less likely to report engaging in activities with him. The authors conclude that any transgression against gender norms in Arab culture is looked upon more harshly because of the collectivist tradition while more individualistic Israeli Jews are judged less critically for deviating from gender norms.

Given all of the differences we have described, what goals should we adopt? Research suggests that androgyny (combinations of both feminine and masculine goals) results in more self-esteem, social competence, success, and intellectual development for both men and women. In other words, it is actually healthier for both male and females to adopt more androgynous patterns of behavior. For instance, males may harm their health by internalizing emotions rather than externalizing them as women are usually apt to do (Buck, 1984). It would be helpful for those used to a "masculine" style to express their emotions. Being concerned with both the task (traditionally "masculine" qualities) and emotional issues (traditionally "feminine" pursuits) is important in our intimate relationships. Inman's (1996) research on men's same sex friendships showed that self-disclosure and expressivity were as vital to men's friendships as "continuity, perceived support and dependability, shared understandings, and perceived compatibility" (p. 100). Self-disclosure and expressivity benefit friendships, both male and female (Jones & Dembo, 1989). Furthermore, over time romantic partners are more less satisfied if partners adhere to stereotyped gender role expectations (Ickes, 1993). Quakenbush (1990) discovered that in dating and sexual relationships, androgynous men compared with men with masculine and undifferentiated gender roles, reported the most comfort.

Jackson (1997) provided yet another argument for the advantageousness of androgyny when he speaks of the cultural crossroads Black masculinity occupies. Black men alternate between embracing and rejecting the more rigid gender roles of American mainstream culture and the more androgynous and interdependent gender roles with their own culture. He believes that androgyny is an approach that should be taken given the difficulty of separating masculine and feminine characteristics. Individuals need all characteristics to get a sense of a cultural self and to foster a strong community (Jackson & Dangerfield, 2003).

In short, we discussed the dimensions of individualism-collectivism and gender as part of how culture shapes or creates the individual or self. Individualism refers to cultures where individuals are more loosely connected and focus on personal achievement whereas collectivism references cultures were strong and cohesive groups are the norm. However, all cultures display characteristics of both. Similarly, we argue that displaying masculine and feminine qualities is advantageous, even though cultures can be characterized broadly as masculine and feminine and gender roles vary to a great extent.

Relational Layer

The relational level focuses on relationships between different elements of a culture (e.g., how it balances individualism and collectivism), how a culture defines relationships between people, and on the relationships between people that are culturally based (i.e., intergroup relations; relations between members of different cultural groups). For example, Hecht et al. (1993) talked about how African Americans attempt to balance the desire for sharing or commonality with the group and the value placed on individuality (i.e., the relationship between different elements of the culture). Gaines and his colleagues (1996; Gaines & Ickes, 1997) studied interethnic romantic relations, concluding that people in these types of relationships are often more romantic (i.e., relationships between people that are culturally based). Others have been concerned with prejudice and discrimination between groups (Hecht, 1998), that is how a culture defines relationships between people. Thus, the relational level can focus us on the relationships between individual members of groups or between and among the groups themselves. *Co-Cultural Communication Theory* is one example of a relational layer approach that focuses on the relationships between groups and their members. *The Dialectical Approach* (see chap. 15, this volume) focuses on how elements of a particular culture relate to each other (e.g., how competing values are balanced) as well as how the balances struck among the elements within one culture (e.g., individualism and collectivism) relate to the balance in a second culture.

Co-Cultural Communication Theory. Co-Cultural Communication Theory examines an assortment of domestic co-cultures in the United States in terms of elements such as age, class, sex, education, ethnicity, religion, abilities, affection or sexual orientation. Orbe (1996, 1998a, 1998b) described this perspective as an examination of how those traditionally without societal power communicate "within oppressive dominant structures" (Orbe, 1998a, p. 1). The term co-culture is used in order to avoid negative connotations from terms that have been employed to describe the many cultures within the United States. The connotations of "subculture" and "minority communication" suggest that less importance is attached to a group member's communication among the variety of co-cultures that exist in our society (e.g., people of color, women, gays/lesbians/bisexuals). Orbe preferred co-culture "to signify that no one culture in our society is inherently superior over other co-existing cultures" (Orbe, 1998a, p. 2).

Co-Cultural Theory is predicated on the belief that some co-cultures have gained dominance in major social institutions over time. As a result, these co-cultural groups (e.g., European Americans and men) figure centrally in predominant social structures such as religion, corporations, and legal entities rendering other co-cultural groups marginal. Co-Cultural Communication Theory examines how dominant and underrepresented group members interact with each other and across groups and is based on the assumption that some co-cultural groups (e.g., people of color) have developed communication orientations in the United States to survive because of their marginalized positions. Orbe (1998a) identified two premises of the theory:

1. Although representing a widely diverse array of lived experiences, co-cultural group members including women, people of color, gays/lesbians/bisexuals, people with disabilities, and those from a lower socioeconomic status will share

similar societal positioning that renders them marginalized and underrepresented within dominant structures, and;

2. To confront oppressive dominant structures and achieve any measure of success, co-cultural group members adopt certain communication orientations when functioning within the confines of public communicative structures. These communication strategies will be addressed later in the chapter.

These premises recognize the similarities in co-cultural group members' experiences of sexism, racism, heterosexism, ableism (i.e., discrimination against those who are not able-bodied), and classism, while acknowledging different experiences in the daily lives of co-cultural group members. For example, two women can both be African American, but one could also be lesbian and experience homophobia in addition to racism. Co-cultural group members may overhear racist and sexist comments in the workplace (e.g., "Since we hired more women, there has been more gossip around here." "You know how lazy Mexicans are ... ") and use an avoidance strategy with co-workers.

Dialectical Approach. A Dialectical Approach, while not a theory, highlights another aspect of the relational nature of intercultural communication. Whereas, Co-Cultural Communication Theory is concerned with how members of groups as well as the groups themselves relate to each other, the Dialectical Approach focuses us on how the elements of culture are related. How does one cultural value relate to another value? For example, a fraternity may value good grades but also see itself as a "party" group. How does a member balance the need to study for an important exam with the pressure to party that night? A school may be trying to develop a strong sense of community that includes responsibility to the group at the same time it wants its students to be creative. How does a student balance the individuality needed for creativity with the need to be part of the collective whole?

Drawing on previous theory, Baxter and colleagues suggested that the elements of communication are dialectically related to each other (for a summary of this approach to communication and relationships, see Baxter & Montgomery, 1996; Rawlins, 1992). This means that concepts like academics and partying, and creativity and community are not separate from each other. That is, we don't focus on one or the other, or even a fixed combination of each. Instead, they are competing or opposite pressures that work at the same time. If the culture values both we are unlikely to escape their influence. In fact, one would not want to, from a dialectical perspective, because we are interested in multiple points of view that affect each other. Rather than looking for a resolution in a middle ground or compromise, the Dialectical Approach highlights the continuing need to balance and rebalance competing forces. In fact, these forces are seen as part of the same whole or entity rather than as separate and inconsistent with each other.

Thus, the dialectics or contradictions cause tension in relationships and cultures, but this tension is necessary and not necessarily antagonistic (Werner & Baxter, 1994). For example, individual autonomy and interdependence with another person defines any relationship. A person desires to be an individual while at the same time establishing a connection with another person. Both elements are necessary even though they are in opposition.

The Dialectical Approach has been applied to the study of culture by a number of authors (e.g., Carbaugh, 1989; Hecht et al, 2003; Martin, Nakayama, & Flores, 1998). We can identify at least two additional implications for the study of communication and culture that the Dialectical Approach gives us. First, it implies that both culture and the members of the culture change are in process. When we communicate with others, we can not assume that if a person belongs to a particular culture he or she will have certain characteristics. Individuals change during their lifetime, as does the cultural environment in which they live. For instance, the United States in the 1980s is not the same as the United States in the 21st century.

Second, dialectics places an emphasis on the relational rather than individual characteristics of people and culture. Looking at culture dialectically means that we look at the holistic relationships, that we focus attention between the aspects of intercultural communication, individuals and individuals in relationship to other groups. Martin et al. (1998) asked "Can we understand culture without understanding communication and vice versa (p. 6)?" They provide an example of the former Yugoslavia by asking "Can we understand the conflict in the former Yugoslavia by only looking at the Serbian experience" (p. 6)?

Cultural studies have described a number of specific dialectics. Some of these are characteristic of a particular culture (e.g., the dialectic between sharing and individuality with African American culture described above), while others tend to be present in most, perhaps all cultures. We will discuss more of the general dialectics in greater detail.

The first of these is the *cultural-individual* dialectic which refers to the idea that intercultural communication contains elements of both culture and individuals, that is individuals may have behaviors that are not shared by anyone else (e.g., a certain, idiosyncratic way of using language), and they may share communication patterns with others whom they share cultural practices (e.g., family members). For instance, your younger brother may call a lemon a neebee, but he may also call your Aunt, Tante, like everyone else in your family. A second dialectic, that of *present-future/history-past*, represents the need to balance our past with the present and future. What is the relationship between past, present and future? Does the culture value one more than the other? Or does the culture value the flow from one to another? For some, the past is viewed through the present. Think about the Israeli-Palestinian conflict. Both Israelis and Palestinians share an important tie to Jerusalem, their holy city. To understand the conflict, we need to know the history of each people, yet the current view of the conflict depends on the context of what occurs today.

The relational elements are also emphasized in the final two dialectics: personal-social and privilege-disadvantaged. The *personal-social* dialectic emphasizes the connection between an individual's social roles and his or her personal characteristics. When a police officer talks about certain topics he or she may be interpreted in certain ways depending on the context. Imagine how differently you would interpret what the officer was saying if it were uttered while writing a ticket versus while relaxing with you at a local pizza pub. The final dialectic, *privilege-disadvantage*, involves the role of power in intercultural communication. We have different types of privilege and power (e.g., social position and political preference) as individuals, which we carry with us into interactions. For instance, the intercultural interactions of a U.S. tourist in Africa will be influenced by economic power and this establishes a different relationship with the citizens of the country than if the visitor was a worker who came from a poor nation in Southeast Asia.

Enacted Layer

It is important to understand that culture is not merely an abstract way of understanding the world. Rather, an important element of culture are the ways it is enacted—that is, how it is expressed by behavior, particularly communication, and how these behaviors are themselves cultural practices. So, our messages can announce our culture to others. But at the same time, culture cannot exist without its being expressed. So when we communicate we create and recreate our culture. *Communication Accommodation Theory*, described in another chapter, provides an excellent example of culture as enactment. It examines the process of how identity may affect communication and references how individuals are motivated to move towards or away from others through language and nonverbal communication. In addition, *Co-Cultural Communication Theory*, introduced in the previous section, not only talks about the relationships between groups but also how these relationships get enacted in communication. We continue our discussion of this theory below and link it to research on ethnic similarities and differences in communication.

Orbe (1996, 1998a, 1998b) revealed six factors that influence how co-cultural group members communicate within dominant social structures by examining oral narratives of individuals possessing a wide variety of co-cultural experiences. These factors include preferred outcome, communication approach, abilities, perceived costs and reward, field of experiences, and situational context. The six interrelated factors affect the communication and communication orientation group members possess. Each of these factors is intimately connected to the others. *Preferred outcome* refers to the goal that a person has for an interaction and may affect the *communication approach* an individual adopts, that is the voice that a person uses which can be assertive, aggressive, or nonassertive. "Each person asks herself or himself the following question, 'What communication behavior will lead to the effect that I desire'" (Orbe, 1998a, p. 5)? Consciously or unconsciously, co-cultural group members answer this question about how their communication behavior affects the relationship between themselves and dominant group members. Nonassertive behavior describes actions where a co-cultural member puts others' needs before his or her own by being inhibited and nonconfrontational. Aggressive communication includes hurtfully expressive actions that are self-promoting and controlling (Orbe, 1998a). Somewhere in the middle of these two is assertive behavior that is characterized by expressive communication that enhances the self and takes others into consideration. Orbe (1996) described 12 strategies that co-cultural group members use when communicating with dominant group members. These include:

1. Avoidance is maintaining a distance with others, not getting involved, and only communicating with people that are different from yourself when necessary. A young gay man described this:

> "I don't get involved too much … They will have these conversations … but I don't get involved because I don't want to lead them on one way or the other (concerning his closeted identity). I just communicate what has to be done" (p. 163)

2. Idealized communication refers to no change in communication when conversing with others different from yourself. The idea that "people are people," means a person emphasizes individuals' similarities and ignores differences.

3. Mirroring is like assimilation. This strategy is used when a person wants "to make their co-cultural identities less visible while adopting those behaviors of the dominant culture" (p. 163). This is when a person "talks white" and avoids the use of slang and ethnic idioms.

4. Respectful communication is marked by graciousness, being less threatening and less assertive, and the use of formal titles. When talking to male supervisors, a 20 year-old woman stated "I am very aware of their expectations of me and try to follow them."

5. Self-censorship occurs when a person says nothing and "swallows it." A person could be afraid of another's reaction to an open and honest response, so they "blow it off" and say nothing.

6. Extensive preparation entails cognitive rehearsal and research. An African American man talked about how he prepared talking with European American

men so that "I am much more through and pointed" (p. 165). Before an encounter with someone outside of your group, you extensively prepare.

7. Countering stereotypes refers to the negation of existing stereotypes. "I guess you can say that I make more of an effort to be a positive person so that people can see that those qualities [black, lesbian, woman] are not negative ones" (p. 165). A person tries to set a positive examples through their behavior without debating dominant group members about stereotypical beliefs.

8. Manipulating stereotypes is a reaction to dominant's cultures stereotypes by con forming to these stereotypes for personal gain. For instance, crying, flirting, or sweet-talking to "manipulate men."

9. Self-assured communication occurs when a person simply is themselves. This means exhibiting positive self-esteem. "I let my accomplishments and personality speak for me," said a Mexican American man (p. 166).

10. Increased visibility means increasing other people's awareness of the self. Things such as wearing signs of your background and occupying space where others can see you are ways to increase visibility.

11. Utilization of liaisons is using other individuals when interacting with those from the dominant culture. Liaisons include friends, advisors, colleagues, and empathetic supervisors.

12. Confrontational tactics are using direct and belligerent "in your face" methods when interacting with the dominant culture. A European American gay man discussed how he liked confronting heterosexuals with his homosexuality, "Flaming was not the word for me, I mean I wanted everyone to know and deal with it" (p. 167).

Assimilation, accommodation, and separation are three major outcomes of these interactions. If a person "adopts" mainstream culture and eliminates cultural differences to fit in with dominant society, this is assimilation. On the other hand, if a person, rejects the idea of forming a common bond with dominant groups or even other co-cultural groups and limits the amount of interaction with "outsiders," the outcome is separation. Accommodation falls in the middle and refers to an insistence that the dominant cultural rules change to incorporate the life experiences of co-cultural group members. Orbe (1998a, 1998b) crossed the three outcomes with the three communication approaches described earlier to arrive at nine general communication strategies co-cultural members use shown in Table 20.1.

Research by Hecht and colleagues (e.g., Hecht et al, 2003; Hecht et al, 1990) focuses attention on what some co-cultural members, specifically Mexican Americans and African Americans, find to be satisfying communication with European Americans and with one another. Their work provides examples of what a co-cultural perspective would call preferred outcome. They (Hecht & Ribeau, 1984; Hecht et al., 1990) found that Mexican American's preferred a comfortable communication climate developed by both parties where individuals could honestly express themselves without fear of retaliation, judgment, or rejection. Work with African Americans revealed similar themes; acceptance, emotional expressiveness, understanding, authenticity, achieving desired outcomes, and not feeling controlled and manipulated were important (Hecht et al., 2003).

We do need to recognize that individuals will have different *abilities* to establish and enact strategies that work for their goals. A person may not have the skill to surmount a nonassertive orientation to communication in an organization, for example, when a more assertive approach may be warranted for success in promotions (Orbe, 1998b).

Individuals may consider the *costs and rewards* of different communicative practices before they engage in them. For instance, Orbe's (1998b) work in organizations shows that taking an assertive assimilation stance may bring benefits to co-cultural group members in the form of social approval and salary increases. These costs and rewards are often determined by *field of experiences* which are the sum of a person's lived experiences. Past experience helps individuals recognize the consequences and efficacy of certain strategies in different situations. Orbe (1998b) quoted a young Mexican American man who believes that "my father's influence and general background has a lot to do with the way I act in public" (p. 250). Finally, given that situations influence how an individual decides on communication choices, the notion of *situational context* plays a central role in co-cultural theory. The number of other co-cultural members present in a situation, for instance, may affect whether a person manipulates stereotypes in the work place.

Communal Layer

Finally, we come to the communal layer, the layer probably most commonly thought about as culture. Communities, or collectivities, are the groups that share a common culture. Culture can be defined as these groupings, although we prefer to see the community as one way of viewing culture in order to avoid defining culture exclusively as people rather than as codes, enactments, and relationships discussed above. The *Ethnography of Communication* approach provides an excellent example of the communal layer.

The ethnography of communication provides us with a useful way of describing the place of speaking for people from different cultures and misunderstandings that can arise when people from different social groups interact (Carbaugh, 1985, 1989, 1993; Fitch, 1998; Philipsen, 1975, 1987, 1998). This method focuses on collecting and analyzing information about how social meaning is conveyed. More specifically, it illuminates how distinct cultural groups instill styles of communication among themselves and interpret others' communication (Saville-Troike, 1989). "The ethnography

TABLE 20.1
Nine General Co-Cultural Communication Orientations

Strategy	Examples
Nonassertive assimilation	Emphasize similarities
	Develop positive face
	Self-censorship
	Avert controversy
Assertive assimilation	Bargaining
	Manipulating stereotypes
	Overcompensating
	Extensive preparation
Aggressive assimilation	Dissociating
	Mirroring
	Strategic distancing
	Self-ridicule
Nonassertive accommodation	Increasing visibility
	Dispelling stereotypes
Assertive accommodation	Communicating self
	Intergroup networking
	Using liaisons
	Educating others
Aggressive accommodation	Confronting tactics
	Power moves
Nonassertive separation	Avoidance
	Maintaining interpersonal barriers
Assertive separation	Communicating self
	Intragroup networking
	Exemplify strengths
	Embrace stereotypes
Aggressive separation	Exert personal power
	Verbal attacking
	Sabotaging dominant group efforts

Note. Adapted from Orbe (1998a, 1998b).

of communication takes language first and foremost as a socially situated cultural form, while recognizing the necessity to analyze the code itself and the cognitive process of its speakers and hearers" (Saville-Troike, 1989, p. 3). The ethnography of communication would be useful for exploring the interactions of ethnic groups that use the same language such as English-speaking Cuban Americans and European Americans. It would also prove beneficial for the exploration of groups that share the same language (e.g., African and European Americans) but have different speech codes (Orbe & Harris, 2001). We can compare communication styles within groups as well as across groups.

The idea of a speech community is central to the ethnography of communication. A group of people is considered to be a speech community when they share goals and styles of communication in ways not like those outside of the group (Philipsen, 1998; Saville-Troike, 1989). There are four assumptions that ground the ethnography of communication (Philipsen. 1998). One is that meaning is created and shared among members of cultural communities. The differences in groups can be defined by geography and language and also by less visible boundaries such as class. Second, because speech codes are guided by a system or some order, those in a cultural group need to coordinate their actions, that is members of a group must share an understanding of what behavior means. Third, individual groups have particular meanings and actions, and fourth, the assignment of meaning is determined by each cultural groups' distinct resources.

Work by Philipsen (1975) and Carbaugh (1998) demonstrated these assumptions by showing how cultural orientations relate to living. For instance, Carbaugh (1998) found that silence in Blackfoot culture is considered to be a listener-active mode of nonverbal presence important for "communicating with animals and spirits." Silence allows one to maintain interconnectedness, a valued event in Blackfoot culture, while public speaking threatens to disrupt the harmony and is, therefore, considered risky. Philipsen's work in a community he called Teamsterville also demonstrated the importance of examining cultural meaning about the value and importance of talk from the participant's point of view. He found that a sense of place in terms of "marking a place for speech" was different from many other communities; front porches and street comers represented proper places for people to interact. "In Teamsterville it is the presence of such identity-matched personae in a location traditionally set aside for sociability among them, to the exclusion of others, that marks a place for speaking" (p. 224).

When we look at the four assumptions posited by Philipsen (1998), we can see how misunderstanding may arise, particularly when individuals fail to recognize that what they consider to be appropriate use of language or what people should and should not say may not be considered the same in another speech community. For instance, Carbaugh's (1993) analysis of a series of 1987 Phil Donahue talk shows from the former Soviet Union demonstrated that public discussion of sexual matters was not preferable. According to Carbaugh, Donahue brought a private, matter to a public forum when he discussed sex in a rational, technical, and individual way. However, in Russian culture public talk with outsiders should be reserved, while private talk shows a greater expressiveness among insiders. This is in contrast to the values expressed in the United States, particularly on television talk shows.

The end result of the ethnography of communication are descriptions of how diverse communities use speech and other channels of communication. Hymes (1974) wrote that "One needs fresh lands of data, one needs to investigate directly the use of language in contexts of situation, so to discern patterns of proper speech activity" (p. 3). The methods of inquiry include the ethnographic tradition of participant observation where a researcher spends extended periods of time observing and studying a community. What researchers strive to accomplish is a holistic picture of communication behavior in the context of the community or network, "so that any use of channel and code takes it place as part of the resources upon which the members draw" (Hymes, 1974, p. 4).

The idea here is to examine all facets of life that may impact communication behavior such as social institutions, roles and responsibilities, cultural values and beliefs, and the history of a community. "The starting point is the ethnographic analysis of the communicative conduct of a community" (Hymes, 1974, p. 9). This includes paying attention to the participants, the topics of conversation, the setting, and the event.

One goal of the ethnography of communication is communicative competence, skills that a speaker needs to know in order to communicate appropriately within a given speech community (Saville-Troike, 1989). To be successful an individual needs to know the rules of interaction, as well as the cultural rules that dictate the content and context of interaction. That is, what should be said to whom, when, and how. One simple question that a researcher can ask is, "What is being communicated" (Saville-Troike, 1989)? The ethnography of communication makes an important contribution in its focus on what a person needs to know to communicate appropriately in various contexts and the sanctions that may occur for violations of communicative competence in a speech community.

CONCLUSION

In summary, we began our discussion of culture by highlighting three key concepts, *code, conversation*, and *community*. A code referenced the rules, meanings, beliefs, values, and images of the ideal, such as an appreciation for knowledge in the Jewish culture. We wrote about conversation as verbal and nonverbal interaction, for example a highly expressive and aggressive communication style. Community is a shared identity and a sense of membership (e.g., European Americans). Next, we used a layered approach to describe some intercultural theories that operate at each of the four layers, personal, relational, enacted, and communal; at the personal level we discussed *Individualism/Collectivism* and *Gender*, at the relational level Dialectics was introduced, we referenced *Co-Cultural Theory* at the enacted layer, and the *Ethnography of Communication* at the communal layer.

Theories of communication and culture are a rich and diverse area. There is much more to say about communication and culture. Recent work has used the construct of *identity* as an explanatory mechanism (Hecht, 1993). People have identities—senses of who they are— some of which are group based. Complete the following sentences:

I am _____

I am _____

I am _____

I am _____

I am _____

I am _____

Now look at your answers—do any of them mention a group (e.g., religion, race or ethnicity, gender, nation, occupation, school)? If so, then it is a group-based or cultural identity. These new approaches are concerned with how our identities affect communication and relationships (Hecht et al, 2003; Jackson, 1999; Tajfel & Turner, 1986), and help us understand how cultures function and how problems in intercultural relations emerge. Some have suggested that we use the more general term, *intergroup*, to describe these processes.

We have tried to show how important culture is by presenting theories about the wide range of experiences it affects. Culture tells us who we are (at least in part) by shaping our values, perceptions, beliefs, and interpretations. It also defines our society and defines us in relation to our society. It guides our communication and relationships. Of course, a chapter like this is just a beginning. Like culture itself, it is a "never ending story."

REFERENCES

Anderson, P. A. (1985). Nonverbal immediacy in interpersonal communication. In A. W. Siegman & S. Feldstein (Eds.), Multichannel integrations of nonverbal behavior (pp. 1–36). Hillsdale, NJ: Lawrence Erlbaum Associates, Inc.

Baldwin, J. R., & Hecht, M. L. (1995). The layered perspective of cultural (in)tolerance(s): The roots of a multidisci-plinary approach. In R. Wiseman (Ed.), Intercultural communication theory (pp. 59–91). Thousand Oaks, CA: Sage.

Baldwin, J. R., & Hecht, M. L. (2000). The social construction of race. Studies in International Relations, 20, 85–115.

Bateson, G. (1972). Steps to an ecology of mind. New York: Ballantine.

Baxter, L. A., & Montgomery, B. M. (1996). Relating: Dialogues and dialectics. New York: Guilford.

Bellah, R., Madsen, R., Sullivan, W., Swidler, A., & Tipson, S. (1985). Habits of the heart: Individualism and commitment in American life. Berkeley: University of California Press.

Borman, E. (1983). Symbolic convergence: Organizational communication and culture. In L. Putnam & M. Pacanowsky (Eds.), Communication and organizations: An interpretive approach (pp. 99–122). Newbury Park, CA: Sage.

Buck, R. (1984). The communication of emotion. New York: Guilford.

Carbaugh, D. (1985). Culture communication and organizing. International and Intercultural Communication Annual, 8, 30–47.

Carbaugh, D. (1989). Talking American: Cultural discourses on Donahue. Norwood, NJ: Ablex.

Carbaugh, D. (1993). "Soul" and "self: Soviet and American cultures in conversation. Quarterly Journal of Speech, 79, 182–200.

Carbuagh, D. (1998). "I can't do that! But I can actually see around corners": American Indian students and the study of "public communication." In J. N. Martin, T. K. Nakayama, & L. A. Flores (Eds.), Readings in cultural contexts (p. 160–172). Mountain View, CA: Mayfield.

Collier, M. J., Ribeau, S. A., & Hecht, M. L. (1986). Intracultural communication rules and outcomes within three domestic cultural groups. International Journal of Intercultural Relations, 10, 439–457.

Condon, J. C, & Yousef, F. (1983). An introduction to intercultural communication. Indianapolis, IN: Bobbs-Merrill.

Fiske, J. (1992). Cultural studies and the culture of everyday life. In L. Grossberg, C. Nelson, & P. Treichler (Eds.), Cultural studies (pp. 154–173). New York: Routledge.

Fitch, K. L. (1998). Speaking relationally: Culture, communication, and interpersonal communication. New York: Guilford.

Gaines, S. O., Jr., & Ickes, W. (1997). Perspectives on interracial relationships. In S. Duck (Ed.), Handbook of personal relationships (2nd ed., pp. 197–220). Chichester, England: Wiley.

Gaines, S. O., Jr., Rios, D. L, Granrose, C, Bledsoe, K., Farris, K., Page, M. S., et al. (1996, January). Romanticism and resource exchange among interethnic/interracial couples. Paper presented at the annual meeting of the Social Psychologists in Texas, Arlington.

Geertz, C. (1973). The interpretation of cultures. New York: Basic Books.

Giles, H., & Coupland, N. (1991). Language: Contexts and. consequences. Pacific Grove, CA: Brooks/ Cole.

Gudykunst, W. B., & Kim, Y. Y. (1992). Communicating with strangers: An approach to intercultural communication. New York: McGraw Hill.

Gudykunst, W. B., Matsumoto, Y, Ting-Toomey, S., Nishida, T., Kim, K., & Heyman, S. (1996). Influence of cultural individualism-collectivism, self-construals, and individual values on communication styles across cultures. Human Communication Research, 22, 510–543.

Hall, E. T. (1984). The dance of life: The other dimension of time. Garden City, NY: Anchor.

Hall, E. T., & Hall, M. R. (1989). Understanding cultural differences. Yarmouth, ME: Intercultural Press.

Hall, S. (1986). Gramsci's relevance for the study of race and ethnicity. Journal of Communication Inquiry, 10, 5–27. Hecht, M. L. (1993). 2002: A research odyssey Toward the development of a communication theory of identity. Communication Monographs, 60, 76–82.

Hecht, M. L. (1998). Communicating prejudice. Thousand Oaks, CA: Sage.

Hecht, M. L., & Baldwin, J. R. (1998). Layers and holograms: A new look at prejudice. In M. L. Hecht (Ed.), Communicating prejudice (pp. 57–84). Thousand Oaks, CA: Sage.

Hecht, M. L., Jackson, R. L., & Ribeau, S. (2003). African American communication: Exploring identity and culture (2nd ed.). Mahwah NJ: Lawrence Erlbaum Associates.

Hecht, M. L., & Ribeau, S. (1984). Ethnic communication: A comparative analysis of satisfying communication. International Journal of Intercultural Relations, 8, 135–151.

Hecht, M. L., Ribeau, S., & Sedano, M. V. (1990). A Mexican American perspective on interethnic communication. International Journal of Intercultural Relations, 14, 31–55.

Hecht, M., Jackson, R. L., Lindsley, S., Strauss, S., & Johnson, K.E. (2001). A layered approach to ethnicity, language and communication. In H. Giles & W. P. Robinson (Eds.), Handbook of language and social psychology (pp. 429–450). New York: Wiley.

Hofstede, G. (1984/1990). Culture's consequences. Beverly Hills, CA: Sage.

Hofstede, G. (1991). Cultures and organizations. London: McGraw-Hill.

Hofstede, G. (1998). Masculinity/femininity as a dimension of culture. In G. Hofstede (Ed.), Masculinity and femininity: The taboo dimension of national cultures, (pp. 3–28). Thousand Oaks, CA: Sage.

Hymes, D. (1974). Foundations in sociolinguistics: An ethnographic approach. Philadelphia: University of Pennsylvania.

Ickes, W. (1993). Traditional gender roles: Do they make, and then break, our relationships? Journal of Social Issues, 49, 71–83.

Inman, C. (1996). Friendships among men: Closeness in the doing. In J. T. Wood (Ed.), Gendered relationships (pp. 95–110). Mountain View, CA: Mayfield.

Jackson, R. L. (1997). Black "manhood" as xenophobe: An ontological exploration of the Heglian dialectic. Journal of Black Studies, 27, 731–750.

Jackson, R. L. (1999). The negotiation of cultural identity: Perceptions of European Americans and African Americans. Westport, CT: Praeger.

Jackson, R. L., & Dangerfield, C. (in press). Defining black masculinity as cultural property: An identity negotiation paradigm. In L. Samovar & R. Porter (Eds.), Intercultural communication: A reader (10th ed., pp. 120–131). Belmont, CA: Wadsworth.

Jones, G. P., & Dembo, M. H. (1989). Age and sex role differences in intimate friendships during childhood and adolescence. Merrill-Palmer Quarterly, 35, 445–462.

Kim, U. (1994). Individualism and collectivism: Conceptual clarification and elaboration. In U. Kim, H. C. Triandis, K. Cigdem, C. Sang-Chin., & G. Yoon, (Eds.), Individualism and collectivism: Theory, methods, and applications (pp. 19–40). Thousand Oaks, CA: Sage.

Kochman, T. (1981). Black and White styles in conflict. Chicago: University of Chicago Press.

Linton, R. (1955). The tree of culture. New York: Alfred. A. Knopf.

Lobel, T. E., Mashraki-Pedhatzur, S., Mantzur, A., & Libby, S. (2000). Gender discrimination as a function of stereo-typic and counterstereotypic behavior: A cross-cultural study. Sex Roles, 43, 395–406.

Martin, J. N., Nakayama, T. K., & Flores, L. A. (1998). A dialectical approach to intercultural communication. In J. N. Martin, T. K. Nakayama, & L. A. Flores (Eds.), Readings in cultural contexts (pp. 5–15). Mountain View, CA: Mayfield.

Milner, L. M., & Collins, J. M. (2000). Sex-role portrayals and the gender of nations. Journal of Advertising, 29, 67–79.

Murphy, R. F. (1986). Cultural and social anthropology: An overview. Englewood Cliffs, NJ: Prentice-Hall.

Orbe, M. P. (1996). Laying the foundation for co-cultural communication theory: An inductive approach to studying "non-dominant" communication strategies and the factors that influence them. Communication Studies, 47, 157–176.

Orbe, M. P. (1998a). From the standpoint of traditionally muted groups: Explicating a co-cultural communication theoretical model. Communication Theory, 8, 1–26.

Orbe, M. P. (1998b). An outsider within perspective to organizational communication: Explicating the communicative practices of co-cultural group members. Management Communication Quarterly, 12, 230–279.

Orbe, M. P., & Harris, T. M. (2001). Interracial communication: Theory into practice. Belmont, CA: Wadsworth.

Philipsen, G. (1975). Speaking like a man in teamsterville: Culture patterns of role enactment in an urban neighborhood. Quarterly Journal of Speech, 61, 13–22.

Philipsen, G. (1987). The prospect for cultural communication. In L. Kinckaid (Ed.), Communication theory: Eastern and Western perspectives (pp. 245–253). New York: Academic.

Philipsen, G. (1998). Places for speaking in teamsterville. In J. N. Martin, T. K. Nakayama, & L. A. Flores (Eds.), Readings in cultural contexts (pp. 217–226). Mountain View, CA: Mayfield.

Quackenbush, R. L. (1990). Sex roles and social-sexual effectiveness. Social Behavior and Personality, 18, 35–39.

Rawlins, W. K. (1992). Friendship matters: Communication, dialectics, and the life course. New York: Aldine de Gruyter.

Saville-Troike, M. (1989). The ethnography of communication: An introduction. New York: Basil Blackwell.

Schmidt, D. E. (1983). Personal control and crowding stress: A test of similarity in two cultures. Journal of Cross-Cultural Psychology, 14, 221–239.

Singelis, T. M. (1996). The context of intergroup communication. Journal of Language and Social Psychology, 15, 360–371.

Tajfel, H. (Ed.). (1981), Human categories and social groups. Cambridge, England: Cambridge University Press.

Tajfel, H., & Turner, J. C. (1986). The social identity theory of intergroup relations. In S. Worchel & W. Austin (Eds.), The social psychology of intergroup relations (pp. 33–47). Monterey, CA: Brooks/Cole.

Tomkins, S. S. (1984). Affect theory. In K. R. Scherer & P Ekman (Eds.), Approaches to emotion (pp. 163–195). Hillsdale, NJ: Lawrence Erlbaum Associates, Inc.

Tocqueville, A. D. (1945). Democracy in America (Vol. 1, Bradley, Trans.). New York: Random House.

Triandis, H. C. (1990). Theoretical concepts that are applicable to the analysis of ethnocentrism. In R. W. Brislin (Ed.), Applied cross-cultural psychology (pp. 34–55). Newbury Park, CA: Sage.

Triandis. H. C. (1994). Theoretical and methodological approaches to the study of individualism and collectivism. In U. Kim, H. C. Triandis, K. Cigdem, C. Sang-Chin., & G. Yoon, (Eds.), Individualism and collectivism: Theory, methods, and applications (pp. 41–51). Thousand Oaks, CA: Sage.

Werner, C. M., & Baxter, L. A. (1994). Temporal qualities of relationships: Organismic, transactional, and dialectical views. In M. L. Knapp & G. R. Miller (Eds.), Handbook of interpersonal communication (2nd ed., pp. 323–379). Newbury Park, CA: Sage.

Winkelman, M. (1993). Ethnic relations in the U.S. St Paul, MN: West.

QUESTIONS TO PONDER

1. We say that "culture is enacted through specific practices such as putting up a Christmas tree, singing the National Anthem, fasting during Ramadan, or wearing a dashiki." What happens when someone whom you would not typically identify as a member of a culture enacts the practices of that culture? For example, what do you think of white people who wear dashikis? Non-Christians who put up Christmas trees?

2. Think about your own cultural values and choices. If your family was having a reunion or celebrating a holiday together at the same time you were planning a great vacation or had a concert to attend, what would you do? What your family say?

3. Some people reading about Co-Cultural Communication Theory will dismiss it as "political correctness." First, consider how this charge might have some validity. For example, is it useful to assume that all white males are empowered? Are there situations in which a particular white male might not be in power? What assumptions of the theory might distort his experience? Conversely, can you see how U.S. culture has historically favored this group? If a white male got into a certain college (e.g., Yale) because previous members of his family did at a time when the college was exclusively white and male (and probably Christian), does this give him an advantage? What does this tell us about being "PC" as a cultural lens?

4. Choose on approach to culture discussed in this chapter. What does this approach tell you about communicating effectively with members of other cultures?

5. Apply the ethnography of communication to prejudice and hate speech. What would using this approach offer? How would this approach illuminate these problems?

Who Am I?

Understanding the "Self"

Culture: A Web of
Self and Others

The concept of culture fundamentally affects how we conduct a cultural study. It shapes our research questions, our sources of data, our analysis/interpretation, and our writing. So it is appropriate to begin this research guidebook with a discussion of the concept of culture. Since anthropologists invented the notion of culture, innumerable definitions and concepts have entered the literature of anthropology. My intention in this chapter is not to provide a comprehensive list of definitions, but to focus on concepts of culture that address people as interactive agents. After introducing various perspectives on the locus of culture—where culture resides—I shift my focus of discussion to "self," and then "others," both vital agents and participants in culture.

The Concepts of Culture

"I'm a typical American just like everyone else in this room," a student of mine proclaimed with an air of certainty in her voice. Without flinching, another student declared that her "individual culture" represents who she is. These are common statements that I hear from students of multicultural education when they are asked to define themselves culturally. Whether these statements accurately convey the meaning of "culture" will be discussed later. These statements represent two perspectives on culture. The first student's view associates culture with a group of people, in this case, Americans. Her statement implies that there is a definable American culture that she shares with other "Americans" who are identified by clear boundaries. Typical assumed boundaries for culture include nationality, ethnicity, language, and geography. In this case, she selected nationality and geographic boundaries to define her own people as "everyone else in this [American college class] room."

On the other hand, the second student considers culture from an individual's point of view. To her, the definition of culture begins with her. Her belief, behaviors, and perspective define who she is. She does not articulate how her "individual culture" overlaps with others and how different her individual culture is from others. Despite her lack of attention to relationships with others in the society, her focus on individuals draws our attention to the fact that people are neither blind followers of a predefined set of social norms, cultural clones of their previous generations, nor copycats of their cultural contemporaries. Rather, her perspective implies that individuals have autonomy to interpret and alter cultural knowledge and skills acquired from others and to develop their own version of culture while staying in touch with social expectations.

These two different perspectives of culture pursue answers to the same question that anthropologists have asked for over a century: "Where is culture located?" De Munck (2000) expands the question: Is culture located "out there, in the public world" or "in here, in the private sphere of the self"? The question of cultural locus may inadvertently associate culture with something tangible to locate. This association is not intended at all. Although defining culture is a tricky business in our contemporary, complex society, as Agar (2006) agonizes, I do not relegate culture to the physical realm of cultural artifacts. Before delving into what I mean by culture, however, I will discuss how anthropologists have tried to answer this locus question because their answers have important implications for the later discussion of autoethnography.

Symbiosis of Culture and People

First, I need to establish a nonnegotiable premise: the concept of culture is inherently group-oriented, because culture results from human interactions with each other. The notion of "individual culture" does not, and should not, imply that culture is about the psychological workings of an isolated individual; rather, it refers to individual versions of group cultures that are formed, shared, retained, altered, and sometimes shed through human interactions. These interactions may take place in "local communities of practice" in which "what particular persons do [is] in mutual influence upon one another as they associate regularly together" (Erickson, 2004, p. 38). Gajjala (2004) would argue that face-to-face interactions are not a prerequisite to the creation of culture in a highly globalized digital age when interactions can be facilitated by digital means of communication—such as e-mail, telephone, and the Internet. Her cyber-ethnographic study of listservs for South Asian professional women demonstrates that a cyber cultural community can be formed and undergo a transformation into something that is similar to a local cultural community. Whether interactions are conventional or alternative, the fundamental premise that culture has something to do with human interactions within a group is not challenged.

De Munck (2000) expresses the symbiotic relationship between culture and people as follows:

> Obviously, one does not exist as a psyche—a self—outside of culture; nor does culture exist independently of its bearers. . . . Culture would cease to exist without the individuals who make it up. . . . Culture requires our presence as individuals. With this symbiosis, self and culture together make each other up and, in that process, make meaning. (pp. 1–2)

Resonating with this perspective, Rosaldo (1984) declares that we "are not individuals first but social persons" (p. 151).

Although the premise that culture and people are intertwined may be indisputable, it does not produce an equally unequivocal answer to the question: "Where is culture located?" This question has been entertained since the beginning of anthropology as an academic discipline, and answers are divided into two groups: one argues that culture is located outside of individuals, and the other that culture is located inside people's minds. These two different orientations produce different implications as to how we treat the concept of culture.

Culture Outside Individuals

The first orientation—culture outside individuals—considers culture as a bounded whole, with which a group of people is defined and characterized. Individual differences are minimized at the expense of a coherent picture for the whole, and culture is seen to be observable and presentable as a public façade of a group. This view stems from the initial anthropological interest of studying other cultures by looking in from outside and is integrated into Kroeber and Kluckhohn's classic definition of culture originally published in 1952. The added italics accentuate this perspective of culture:

> Culture consists of patterns, explicit and implicit, of and for behavior, acquired and transmitted by symbols constituting the distinctive achievement of human groups, *including their embodiment in artifacts*; the essential core of culture consists of traditional (i.e., historically derived and selected) ideas and especially their attached values; *culture systems may, on the one hand, be considered as products of action*, on the other as conditioning elements of further action. (1966, p. 357)

This "looking-in-from-outside" perspective assumes that other cultures are observable. It creates the distance between anthropologists and local natives and, in turn, engenders the acute sense of difference and of clear boundaries between these two parties. As a result, anthropologists end up developing a sometimes essentialist and often exotic profile of culture to describe a bounded group of people, focusing on observable differences in custom, social structure, language, religion, art, and other material and nonmaterial characteristics. The oft-cited definition by Sir Edward Burnett Tylor (1871), who is characterized as "the founder of academic anthropology in the English-speaking world and the author of the first general anthropology textbook" (Harris, 1975, p. 144), also presents culture as a "complex whole" binding a group of people:

> Culture . . . taken in its wide ethnographic sense is that complex whole which includes knowledge, belief, art, morals, law, custom, and any other capabilities and habits acquired by man as a member of society. (Tylor, p. 1)

Tylor's definition illustrates the very point of this perspective, associating culture with an entire group of people.

De Munck (2000) identifies three versions of this culture-outside-individuals perspective: (1) "Culture is superorganic," (2) "Culture is public," and (3) "The size, position, and strength of social networks" affect the culture of a group (pp. 8–17). The first perspective, superorganic culture, still popular nowadays, postulates that a set group of people is identified with a culture and that culture has a life of its own, dictating, regulating, and controlling people to maintain inner-group "homogeneity." This perspective is illustrated by Benedict's two renowned works. In *Patterns of Culture* (1934) she classified cultures by two types—the orderly and calm "Apollonian" type and the emotional and passionate "Dionysian" type—and characterized Pueblo cultures of the American Southwest as the former and the Native American cultures of the Great Plains as the latter. Her notion of culture as a representation of a whole group also came through clearly in her discussion of Japanese "national culture" in *The Chrysanthemum and the Sword* (1946). My first student's notion of "American" culture is not far from this perspective of superorganic culture. So is Spring's notion of the U.S. "general" culture that is expected to consist of "behaviors, beliefs, and experiences common to most citizens" (2004, p. 4).

The second version of the culture-outside-individuals perspective is argued by Geertz, who sees culture forming in the process of people's interactive communication and meaning-making. Geertz (1973) holds that "culture is public because meaning is. . . . [C]ulture consists of socially established structures of meaning in terms of which people do such things as signal conspiracies and join them or perceive insults and answer them. . ." (pp. 12–13). For him, a person's behaviors cannot be appropriately understood and responded to unless these behaviors are publicly exhibited and others correctly interpret their meanings using the standards familiar to both parties.

The third version of the culture-outside-individuals perspective is apparent in Thompson's work, according to De Munck (2000). Thompson argues that "ensembles" of social relations, created by "social roles, statuses, and norms," affect the culture within a social organization (p. 12). This perspective postulates that culture is associated with the structure transcending individual distinctiveness. The "structure of any entity," including a society, refers to "the more-or-less enduring relationships among its parts" (Kaplan & Manners, 1972, p. 101) and "the continuing arrangement of persons in relationships defined or controlled by institutions" in Radcliffe-Brown's words (1958, p. 177). This social structure "contains" culture according to this view of culture outside individuals.

When this perspective of culture outside individuals swings to the extreme, it is in danger of presenting culture in a form of a lifeless, rigid mannequin—exaggerated, oversimplified, inflexible, and simply artificial—without reflecting real people associated with it or in a form of a self-propelled entity independent of people. In these cases the concept of culture intends to represent something, yet actually says little about people because it is so distanced from them.

Culture in People's Minds

In contrast to the first perspective, the second perspective locates culture in people's minds. In this case, human beings are regarded not only as bearers of culture but also as active agents who create, transmit, transform, and sometimes discard certain cultural traits. According to De Munck (2000), three versions constitute this perspective: (1) the "psychoanalytic and 'human nature' thesis of culture," (2) "personal and public symbols," and (3) cognitively distributed culture.

The first version is supported by Spiro, who rejects cultural determinism—the claim that a societal culture determines the personality of its members and shapes national personality. Instead, he argues that psychological similarities and differences between members of a culture also exist in other cultures. For him, "cultures are systems that function to meet the psychological and biological requirements of human beings as members of society" (De Munck, 2000, p. 19). Since basic human psychology and biology are similar as well as different from society to society, Spiro's observation that "the surface variations in cultures mask underlying similarities" puts this perspective in diametric opposition to the "superorganic culture" perspective that postulates distinctive cultural differences between groups. Erickson's classification of culture "as motive and emotion" is also aligned with this perspective of culture in that people's emotions and motives in their minds are driving forces in their social customs and actions (2004, p. 36).

De Munck (2000) associates Obeyesekere with the second version—"personal and public symbols." According to him, Obeyesekere vacillates "between asserting that culture is in or outside the body," like most contemporary psychoanalytical anthropologists (p. 19). In this version, culture is sometimes viewed as a passive set of ideas located inside meaning-makers and other times as an active agent organizing the society outside individuals. This version recognizes the complex dialectical relationship between culture and people. Erickson's classification of culture as "symbol system" is aligned with this view of culture in that culture is considered as "a more limited set of large chunks of knowledge . . . that frame or constitute what is taken as 'reality' by members of a social group" (2004, p. 36). The members use the knowledge to communicate with each other and regulate each other's behaviors. In this perspective, the knowledge (symbols) exists outside individuals until it is utilized by people; then it enters their minds.

The third version of the culture-in-people's-minds perspective is advocated strongly among cognitive anthropologists who assert that culture consists of cognitive schemas or standards that shape and define people's social experiences and interactions with others. Goodenough (1981) defines culture as "standards for perceiving, evaluating, believing, and doing" (p. 78). When individuals develop their versions of group culture, the individual versions become their "propriospects" in Goodenough's term and "idioverses" in Schwartz's (1978) term.

The view of culture inside people's mind helps people see themselves as active agents of culture. At the same time, when the role of individuals is excessively elevated in culture-making, this perspective is in danger of neglecting the collectivistic nature of "culture." When this happens, the division of psychology and anthropology is likely to be blurred.

A Work-in-Progress Concept of Culture

Acknowledging the potential shortcomings of both perspectives on the locus of culture, here I propose a work-in-progress concept of culture for this book, which is founded on seven premises.

Individuals are cultural agents, but culture is not at all about individuality. Culture is inherently collectivistic, not individualistic. Culture needs the individual "self" as well as others to exist. Therefore, the notion of "individual culture" connoting individual uniqueness defies the core of the concept of culture.

Individuals are not prisoners of culture. Rather, they exercise a certain level of autonomy when acquiring, transmitting, altering, creating, and shedding cultural traits while interacting with others. This individual autonomy is the foundation of inner-group diversity.

Despite inner-group diversity, a certain level of sharedness, common understanding, and/or repeated interactions is needed to bind people together as a group. A formal and official, even intentional, process is not always required to obtain membership of a cultural group. However, a degree of actual and imaginary connection with other members would be needed for them to become part of a collective culture and to claim an identity with the cultural group.

Individuals can become members of multiple social organizations concurrently. In Thompson's terms (1994), some organizations are "egocentric" (with micro-level structures where individuals are more intimately involved) and others "sociocentric" (with macro-level structures such as nations). Some memberships such as race or gender are more likely to be ascribed early in life and others can be achieved later by social or educational affiliations. So, one can be an American citizen, African American, female, graduate of Yale Law School, civil rights activist, and child advocate all at the same time, as in the case of Edelman (1999).

Each membership contributes to the cultural makeup of individuals with varying degrees of influence. Individuals develop varied levels of affinity and identity with different groups of people. The strength of affinity and identity with certain memberships fluctuates, depending on life circumstances. Agar (2006) illustrated this point well with his example of Catholic identity:

> I grew up in a parish with an old Irish priest, so we got that un-enlightened 1950s rural-Irish-gloom-and-doom-and-then-off-to-hell-you-go version. By high school, I thought of myself as an ex-Catholic. When I was about 30, I realized I'd never be ex. Nowadays, Mother Church is mostly a source of stories and jokes, except for the days when I feel like a defrocked Jesuit. The way that my religious culture comes and goes and fits or aggravates the flow of the moment changes from year to year, or even from moment to moment.

Other identities also vacillate, depending on the context in which people are placed. Some people have stronger ethnic identity than others; others have a stronger affinity with their primary groups than with nations. Over time, their primary identities—with the strongest sense of affinity—can shift as life circumstances change. For example, Crane's (2000) interview-based research revealed that during Nazi rule in Germany, female children of Christian-Jewish mixed marriages, who had been integrated into the mainstream German society, became much more cognizant of their Jewish roots and voluntarily and involuntarily took on a strong Jewish identity; this newly acquired identity ended up outliving the Nazi era.

Individuals can discard a membership of a cultural group with or without "shedding" their cultural traits. The effect of certain cultural memberships on people's day-to-day operation can be varied even long after they cease to associate intimately with members of cultural communities. For example, immigrants who change citizenship do not often abandon their native culture and language upon naturalization into their host country. The official abandonment of their original nationality may be refashioned in strict observation of certain cultural practices.

Without securing official memberships in certain cultural groups, obvious traits of membership, or members' approvals, outsiders can acquire cultural traits and claim cultural affiliations with other cultural groups. For example, Olson (1993), a self-ordained Christian missionary, went to Motilone Indian territory in Colombia and Venezuela, learned their language and customs, and became an advocate of the group to the outside world. Without an innate membership, he gained cultural and linguistic knowledge—"languaculture" in Agar's term (2006)—for access to people in the society, which eventually led him to an "affiliate" membership.

The Concepts of Self

Building on these seven premises of culture, I depart from cultural determinism (culture determines group personality) or cultural essentialism (identifiable cultural distinctiveness is relegated to a certain culture). Rather, I see culture as a product of interactions between self and others in a community of practice. In my thinking, an individual becomes a basic unit of culture. From this individual's point of view, self is the starting point for cultural acquisition and transmission. For this reason, scholars of culture pay a great deal of attention to the concept of self. Interestingly, the concept of self varies at different times and in different cultures.

Historical Concepts of Self

Interest in the concept of self has a long history in the Western scholarly tradition. From early Greek philosophers such as Socrates, to early Christian theologians such as St. Augustine (1999, Trans.), to contemporary postmodern scholars such as Gergen (1991), to contemporary psychologists such as Vitz (1977), the discussion of self has been rich and prolific. According to De Munck (2000), the term "self" was not always used in a positive light as it is in contemporary U.S. society. In its first appearance, around the 1300s, it was "used as a noun that packaged sin with the self" (p. 31). So, self was to be denied:

neither to be indulged nor celebrated, but rather to be shunned and ignored. Vitz's notion of "selfism" describes the undesired indulgence of self. This view of self has transformed over time.

Gergen (1991) surveys the changes in the concept of self from the romantic perspective of the 19th century, through the modern one of the 20th century, to the postmodern view of the contemporary era. He characterizes the 19th-century romantic view of self as "one that attributes to each person characteristics of personal depth: passion, soul, creativity, and moral fiber" (p. 6). From this perspective, a person's emotion, feeling, and intuition are considered integral to selfhood. In contrast to the romantic view, modernists deemphasize the affective and intuitive attributes of self and highlight the characteristics of the self residing "in our ability to reason—in our beliefs, opinions, and conscious intentions" (p. 6). With the scientific advances of the 20th century, a person's reason and objectivity are far more valued. However, contemporary postmodernists are skeptics of this modernist sense of a rational, orderly self. Gergen claims, "Selves as possessors of real and identifiable characteristics—such as rationality, emotion, inspiration, and will—are dismantled" in the postmodern view (p. 7). The modern belief in "moral imperatives" and autonomous self (Grenz, 1996; Taylor, 1989) is replaced by the postmodernists' recognition of a "saturated" self that is overcommitted to often divergent pulling forces and demands of surroundings, and a "protean self," in Lifton's term, that constantly adjusts to "turbulent, dislocating, and often violent global forces and conditions" (De Munck, 2000, p. 44).

Although the postmodern view of self might have deprived us of a hope for a self-sufficient, independent, and directional self, it invites us to look at self as a "fragile" and interdependent being. Gergen (1991) articulates the reality of interdependency thus: "[O]ne's sense of individual autonomy gives way to a reality of immersed inter-dependence, in which it is relationship that constructs the self" (p. 147). The attention to community is another contribution of postmodernism to the scholarship of self: "the continued existence of humankind is dependent on a new attitude of cooperation rather than conquest" vis-à-vis community (p. 7). The recognition of self in relation to commu-nity is one of the four insights we could gain from the postmodern perspective according to Hjorkbergen (cited in Meneses, 2000).

The postmodern recognition that human beings are not truly independent and autonomous is ironically aligned with the Christian assessment of humanity. While some Christian scholars criticize the postmodern notion of the directionless self lost in moral relativism, they may easily embrace the notion of the fragile self in need of re-lationships with the Creator and other human beings. As Apostle Paul reminds us, "so in Christ [the incarnated Creator] we who are many form one body, and each member belongs to all the other" (Romans 12:5, New International Version). Although Christianity has provided a foundation for Western thought, its notion of self is different from the Western modern secular view of the self-confident, self-reliant, and independent self. Rather, the Christian self, before and after St. Augustine, does not deny its reliance upon others, whether God or other human beings.

Cross-Cultural Concepts of Self

The concept of self has evolved not only historically but also is cross-culturally varied. Gergen's discussion of the romantic, modern, and postmodern self draws upon the Western secular view of self as "a bounded, unique, more or less integrated motivational and cognitive universe, a dynamic center of awareness, emotion, judgment, and action..." (Geertz, 1984, p. 126). Geertz warns that such a view of self is "a rather peculiar idea within the context of the world's culture." Thus it is entirely possible to view self as something other than a unique, separate, and autonomous being to be distinguished from others and to be elevated as the center of the universe above a community. Comparing the Western view of self with that of the Wintu (Lee, 1959) and the Oglala (Lee, 1986), Lee acknowledges that the sense of self in these Native Americans does not rest on the contradiction between self and other; instead, self and other are viewed as mutually inclusive. For Oglala, "the self contains some of the other, participates in the other, and is in part contained within the other.... [I]n respecting the other, the self is simultaneously respected" (1986, p. 12). Hoffman (1996) also criticizes the fact that "individual uniqueness" is overemphasized as the tenet of self in the Western scholarship of multicultural education because in many non-Western cultural contexts celebration of the individual self is not always valued and self does not always take precedence over others in the decision-making process.

Collectivism,[1] illustrated in the aforementioned Native American cultures, is not always a non-Western ethos. Valuing a community over individuals was apparent in the first-century Mediterranean culture that permeates the New Testament writings. Malina (1993) uses the term "dyadism," in lieu of "collectivism," to describe the "strong group orientation," manifested in the New Testament culture, in which "persons always considered themselves as inextricably embedded . . . conceive[d] of themselves as always interrelated with other persons while occupying a distinct social position both horizontally . . . and vertically" and "live[d] out the expectations of others" (p. 67). In such a culture, selfhood is understood only in relation to others within a community.

Autoethnography benefits greatly from the thought that self is an extension of a community rather than that it is an independent, self-sufficient being, because the possibility of cultural self-analysis rests on an understanding that self is part of a cultural community.

The Concepts of Others

The recognition of varying dynamics between self and others allows us to segue into a discussion of "others." The scholarly interest in "othering" has increased in the society of cultural diversity (Asher, 2001; Canales, 2000; Luke, 1994). Human beings have always developed mental and social mechanisms to differentiate "us" from "them." In the process, they develop criteria for others.

The Typology of Others

The term "others" generally refers to existentially different human beings—those who are other than self. The differences that separate self from others "often shift with time, distance, and perspective" (Canales, 2000, p. 16). Not all existential others pose the same level of strangeness to self. Those who belong to the same community as self are likely to be seen as comrades who share similar standards and values. These are *others of similarity*. On the other hand, others from a different community are likely to be distinguished as strangers who possess and operate by different frames of reference. In identifying others of difference, the perception of difference may play just as powerful a role as actual differences. When differences in behaviors, beliefs, or customs are deemed to be not only irreconcilable but also threatening to the very existence of self and others of similarity, the others are regarded as *others of opposition*, namely "enemies" to their neighborhood, interest group, school, professional organization, or nation. The typology of others—of similarity, difference, and opposition—is helpful in understanding self and its interconnectedness with others, especially as a framework for the autoethnographic data analysis and interpretation that will be discussed in Chapter 9.

Cultural Verstehen of Others

I have already postulated that culture is intertwined with people. This implies that cultural understanding of others begins with genuine encounters with them through which insider perspectives are gained. A genuine relationship develops from an "I–Thou" encounter, as opposed to an "I–It" encounter, according to Martin Buber (Panko, 1976). In this I–Thou encounter, people acknowledge human dignity in each other (Pohl, 1999) and are engaged in genuine dialogue "as a person to a person, as a subject to a subject" (Panko, p. 48). The opposite of the I–Thou interaction is the I–It encounter in which one treats others as objects. Buber does not deny the value of the I–It encounter as a realm in which "we are able to examine all things critically and verify or disapprove what we have experienced" (p. 54), yet he acknowledges that the I–Thou encounter is the only realm where those engaged in dialogue can experience each other's whole being. Neither pretense nor insincerity has a place in this relationship.

In addition to genuine encounters, a true understanding of others also requires empathic understanding—"*verstehen*," in German sociologist-philosopher Max Weber's term. Empathic understanding is an act of putting aside one's own framework and "seeing [others'] experiences within the framework of their own" (Geertz, 1984, p. 126). Although perfect *verstehen* is beyond our human capacity, attempts to empathize can reduce incorrect judgments about others and enhance rich understanding of strangers. This empathic understanding is, in a Malinowskian–Geertzian sense, understanding "from the native's point of view," on which a rich contextual understanding of others' culture is grounded. These steps of understanding are equally helpful in understanding others of both similarity and difference.

Yet understanding others of similarity and difference requires a different course of action on the part of self. To continue the discussion we need to revisit the concept of self as a relational being. This concept of self presupposes the existence of relational partners. In other words, self cannot exist alone in the context of culture. Others from the primary community (e.g., family or religious community) and the secondary community (e.g., professional or interest organization) participate in the production of self in the enculturation or socialization process.[2] Self learns values, norms, and customs from others to become a proper member of the community. Self contributes to the continuity of the community as well. In this give-and-take process, self is invariably bound with others within the cultural group. Consequently, self becomes mirrored in others, and others become an extension of self.

Cultural presuppositions shared by self and others are the foundation of homogeneity, unity, and congruity within the community. In a culturally "congruent"[3] society, relating to others may not be such a daunting task. Others are merely others of similarity; thus, understanding others may easily begin with knowing and affirming self.

When "others" refers to members of other communities—others of difference—self and others are not organically interconnected; rather, such interconnectivity must be intentionally desired and achieved. In a diverse society composed of others from different ethnic, racial, religious, gender-orientation, ability, age, socioeconomic status, profession, civic orientation, or interest groups, relating to and understanding others requires a different course of action from merely affirming self as in a relatively homogeneous cultural context. Self may need to start with "denying self" by putting aside its own standards, crossing its own cultural boundaries, and "immersing" self in others' cultures (Lingenfelder, 1996). Totally breaking away from one's own culture is almost impossible and not desirable when attempting to achieve a healthy balance between affirming self and learning from others. Yet, leaving one's standards momentarily and observing and analyzing differences between self and others from a distance are helpful practices in understanding others of difference. In the process, self may learn from others and take in a part of others. The genuine effort to "*verstehen*" others' culture often engenders cultural crossing between self and others.

Expanding Cultural Boundaries

The product of genuine and thoughtful cultural crossing is known as an "edgewalker" according to Kreb (1999). Edgewalkers have significant "lived" experiences with different cultural communities through which they develop solid cross-cultural competence while maintaining a healthy understanding of self. They exhibit the following qualities:

> 1) comfort, if not identification, with a particular ethnic, spiritual or cultural group, 2) competence thriving in mainstream culture, 3) the capacity to move between cultures in a way that an individual can discuss with some clarity, 4) the ability to generalize from personal experience to that of people from other groups without being trapped in the uniqueness of a particular culture. . . . (p. 1)

Blending old and new cultural competence, edgewalkers constantly turn their former others of difference into others of similarity by reducing strangeness in others and expanding their cultural boundaries. They also engage others in the mutually transformational process because genuine cross-cultural pollination affects both parties. As a result, both self and others end up expanding their cultural boundaries to include each other.

The notion of cross-cultural expansion can be applied at the societal level. Through genuine dialogues with others, a community can also expand its boundaries to include others of difference. Greene (2000) refers to such an inclusive community as an "extended community." This community is characterized as "attentive to difference, open to the idea of plurality" (p. 44), and grounded on "the desire to extend the reference of 'us' as far as we can" (p. 45). The extended community redefines the division of "us and them" and expands the boundaries to treat former others of difference as new others of similarity. In this case the notion of community is no longer founded on mere common characteristics among members, but on the shared ideology of democracy and inclusive wills (Thayer-Bacon & Bacon, 1998).

Summary

So far I have introduced three interconnecting concepts: culture, self, and others. The concept of culture, inherently group-oriented, was examined from two perspectives: culture outside individuals and culture in people's minds. Self, as a basic unit of culture, was also discussed from historical and cross-cultural perspectives. Although self has been viewed differently in different time periods and cultures, I argue that self is consistently connected to others in the realm of culture. The others refer to other human beings differently regarded by self: some are seen as others of similarity (friends to self), as others of difference (strangers to self), or as others of opposition (enemies to self). The view of others is not fixed in people's lives. Rather, the positionality of self to others is socially constructed and transformable as the self develops its relationship to others—especially strangers and enemies—and reframes its views of others. Understanding the relationship between self and others is one of the tasks that autoethnographers may undertake. In this sense, these three concepts are vital building blocks to the discussion of autoethnography, the primary focus of this book.

Self-Narratives

Telling stories is an ancient practice, perhaps as old as human history. Imagine a family clan sitting around a fire pit on a starry night to listen to the family's migration history. Or picture a grandmother rocking in a chair with her grandchildren on her lap, telling her childhood memories. As in these cases, stories can easily contain the autobiographical components of storytellers, even when the stories feature the storytellers' ancestors, families, relatives, neighbors, or communities. This autobiographical storytelling, also called self-narration, sometimes produces written narratives. Self-narratives, "personal narratives" in Gornick's (2001) term, refer to stories "written by people who, in essence, are imagining only themselves: in relation to the subject in hand" (p. 6).

Writings focusing on self have increased significantly in volume in recent decades, representing various genres, authorship, thematic focus, and writing styles. They have come in the form of autobiography, memoir, journal, diary, personal essay, or letter. Some organize autobiographical facts in chronological fashion; others assemble authors' personal reflections around various themes. Some use a more descriptive mode of storytelling like memoirs; yet others use autobiographical facts in "scholarly personal narratives" (Nash, 2004) or in autoethnography (Reed-Danahay, 1997), which tend to be more analytical and interpretive. In this chapter, I first discuss the value of self-narratives in cultural understanding of self and others and later expound on the variety of self-narratives with selected examples.

Growing Interest in Self-Narratives

Gornick (2001) notes the increasing popularity of self-narrative writing: "Thirty years ago people who thought they had a story to tell sat down to write a novel. Today they sit down to write a memoir" (p. 89). A search of the Library of Congress catalogs for the keywords of autobiography and memoir turned up 10,000 entries for each keyword. Lavery (1999) also compiled an extensive list of autobiographies. The growing popularity of contemporary self-narratives rides on the back of postmodernism that values voices of common people, defying the conventional authoritative elitism of autobiography (Wall, 2006). Ordinary authors with no political clout or literary credentials have gained courage to speak their stories.

Recently I came upon a memoir by Plourde (2005) prominently displayed in a university bookstore. Currently a university student, the author accounts her life-changing encounter with a cruel rape by a stranger, subsequent pregnancy, and a dilemma of deciding between abortion and pregnancy as a pro-lifer during her high school days. Obviously such a self-writing is publishable and readily available to readers.

The explosion of self-narratives has enriched the study of this type of writing but makes it an intimidating task to select examples to share because for every selected item many more are left unmentioned. An exhaustive literature review of self-narratives is beyond the scope of this chapter. With help of my graduate assistant Judy Ha, I have made a modest attempt to select and classify over 70 book-length self-narratives and anthologies into seven categories: (1) autoethnographies; (2) memoirs and autobiographies (MA)—racial, ethnic, and language issues; (3) MA—gender issues; (4) MA—religious issues; (5) MA—politics, social conflicts, and wars; (6) MA—childhood memories, family relations, and growing up; and (7) MA—disability, illness, and death. Appendix A presents a bibliography of self-narratives. In this chapter I simply share some examples of this vast genre.

An interest in studying self-narratives, as part of a broader trend of "narrative inquiry," has grown both in humanities and social sciences (Clandinin & Connelly, 2000; Ellis & Bochner, 2000). Memoir writing by literary writers has long dominated the scene of self-narratives in the humanities (Allende, 2003; Angelou, 1969; Baker, 1982;

Baldwin, 1963; De Beauvoir, 2005; Dillard, 1987; Hurston, 1984; Lamott, 2000 & 2005; Momaday, 1976; Rodriguez, 1982). Notable is social scientists' growing interest in self as a subject of academic inquiry (Burnier, 2006). The widespread interest in self-narratives has been demonstrated by scholars in anthropology (Anderson, 2000; Angrosino, 2007; Bateson, 1994 & 1995; Mead, 1972; Reed-Danahay, 1997), sociology (Denzin, 1997; Lucal, 1999; Richardson, 1992), communication (Ellis, 1995; Ellis & Bochner, 1996 & 2000), education (Florio-Ruane, 2001; Gallas, 1998; Obidah & Teel, 2001; Romo, 2004), medicine (Kübler-Ross & Gold, 1997), nursing (Foster, McAllister, & O'Brien, 2005), psychiatry (Jamison, 1996), and psychology (Schafer, 1992).

Ellis and Bochner (2000) note that social scientists' interest in self-narratives falls in one of the four categories: (1) "reflexive ethnographies" in which "authors use their own experiences in the culture reflexively to bend back on self and look more deeply at self–other interaction"; (2) "texts by complete-member researchers" who "explore groups of which they already are members or in which . . . they have become full members with complete identification and acceptance"; (3) "personal narratives" written by social scientists about "some aspect of their experience in daily life"; and (4) "literary autoethnography" written by an autobiographical writer who "focuses as much on examining self autobiographically as on interpreting a culture for a nonnative audience" (p. 740). The common theme underlying all these diverse labels is self-focus.

Although self-narratives focus on the author, self-stories often contain more than self. The irony of self-narratives is that they are of self but not self alone. Others often enter self-narratives as persons intimately and remotely connected to self. As a relational being, the self is invariably connected to others in the family, local and national community, and world, "a series of overlapping, concentric circles with others" in Nash's (2002, p. 26) terms. Friends, acquaintances, and even strangers from the circles are interwoven in self-narratives. Therefore, studying and writing of self-narratives is an extremely valuable activity in understanding self and others connected to self.

Self-Narratives for Understanding Self and Others

Reading and studying others' self-narratives is hardly a one-sided activity that results only in understanding others. Studying others invariably invites readers to compare and contrast themselves with others in the cultural texts they read and study, in turn discovering new dimensions of their own lives.

Florio-Ruane (2001) observed the value of using autobiographies, specifically written by writers of color, in her graduate multicultural education course. She argues that reading these self-narratives for discussion helped her education students, predominantly White middle-class females, learn about different cultures presented by the autobiographers of Asian, Hispanic, African American, and Native American cultural backgrounds while they examined their own cultural assumptions through self-reflection.

Expanding from reading self-narratives, Brunner (1994) advocates inservice teachers' utilizing a variety of texts—not only books but also film or television scripts and musical lyrics—created by others to evoke self-reflection and self-analysis. She argues, "As students are called on to explore their own personal histories, their social, political, economic, and cultural realities through a curriculum of multiple voices, their predispositions tend to become more apparent" (p. 235). For both Florio-Ruane (2001) and Brunner (1994), self-reflection evoked by reading of others is a means to self-discovery.

Self-discovery in a cultural sense is intimately related to understanding others. If "others" refers to members of one's own community (others of similarity), the self is reflected in others in a general sense. Values and standards upheld by the community are likely shared between self and others. Although people do not practice the values and standards of their community in minute detail, the knowledge of the values and standards helps them understand others of similarity from their own community. Therefore, understanding others could smooth the transition to understanding self. If "others" refers to members of other communities (others of difference), understanding the similarity between self and others captures only a portion of understanding others. What is beneficial in this case is studying others thoroughly through comparing and contrasting, which inevitably brings differences to light.

Studying others has a value in itself. However, Hall (1973) and Noel (2000) consider that it has a greater purpose of helping to understand self. Hall unapologetically argues that "the real job" of studying another culture is "not to understand foreign culture but to understand our own . . . to learn more about how one's own system works" (p. 30). Noel chimes in: "the study of [other] culture is the study of our own lives, of our own ways of thinking and living" (p. 81). Whether seeing self through others or against others, the study of self-narratives through self-reflection is beneficial to cultural understanding.

The Variety of Self-Narratives

["Self-narratives" cover a wide range of writings whose primary focus rests on self. Besides the commonality, they vary in genre, authorship, thematic focus, and writing style.]Although the purpose of this chapter is not to provide a full-scale literature review of self-narratives, the variety of self-narratives will be discussed here to provide a context for the discussion of autoethnography that follows in the next chapter.

Genres

All writings are in some ways autobiographical because they reflect authors' perspectives and preferences in their choices of topic, writing style, direction, and conclusion. However, in this genre study of self-narratives, I will discuss only writings that demonstrate an author's explicit intention of bringing self to the surface as an object of description, analysis, and/or interpretation.

With the intentionality of self-exposure in mind, scholars of self-narratives consider St. Augustine's *Confessions* (1999) from the 4th century CE as "something of a model for the memoirist," in which "Augustine tells the tale of his conversion to Christianity" (Gornick, 2001, p. 13). This tradition of confession continued in the spiritual account of a 15th-century English mystic Margery Kempe (2000); spiritual journals of 17th-century Puritan New Englanders such as Sarah Osborn, Susanna Anthony, Harriett Newell, Fanny Woodbury, and Abigail Bailey (Taves, 1992); and Daniel Shea (Mason, 1992). Contemporary spiritual self-narratives in the United States are not limited to Protestantism (Carter, 1996; Lamott, 2000, 2005; Lewis, 1956; Olson, 1993) or Catholicism (Armstrong, 2005; Breyer, 2000; Crossan, 2000; Donofrio, 2000; Hathaway, 1992; Merton, 1999; Norris, 1996), but embrace other faiths or spiritual traditions such as Islam (Ahmedi & Ansary, 2005), Zen Buddhism (Brooks, 2000; Goldberg, 1993), Judaism (Dubner, 1999), and feminine spirituality (Kidd, 2002).

The tradition of self-accounts did not stop in the religious realm. Self-narratives have been broadly adopted in contemporary secular literature in the form of autobiography, memoir, journal, personal essay, and letter. Autobiography is probably the most well-known format of self-narratives. Autobiography tends, chronologically and comprehensively, to depict lives of authors, who are often distinguished as public figures such as the first female Secretary of State, Madeleine Albright (2003), U.S. President Jimmy Carter (1996), U.S.

President Bill Clinton (2004), First Lady Hillary Rodham Clinton (2004), abolitionist and suffragist Frederick Douglass (1995), Indian political activist Mahatma Gandhi (1957), South African President Nelson Mandela (1994), civil rights activist Rosa Parks (1992), First Lady Eleanor Roosevelt (1984), and civil rights activist Malcolm X (Haley & Malcolm X, 1996). The social importance of autobiographers often adds formality to this genre of self-narratives.

Memoir has become a more common option for contemporary writers because this format allows a thematic approach to one's life story but with moderation in scope. Memoirs tend to focus on fragments of memoirists' lives, not the whole life. Phifer (2002) differentiates memoirs from autobiographies in terms of the focus of time:

> Autobiographies present broad overviews, while memoirs focus on only the hours and minutes that are keen in our lives—the times when we are most alive, when experiences penetrate to the quick. In these moments we define ourselves; the ways we respond reveal our souls. (p. 4)

Memoirs tend to follow themes around which memoirists gather autobiographical stories. For example, Ann Lamott's *Traveling Mercies* (2000) focuses on the author's spiritual conversion and development; and Jane Tompkins (1996) narrates the story of her involvement in education as a student and later as a professor in *A Life in School*.

Memoirs are also different from journals. According to Phifer (2002), memoirs are more "selective," with a focus on "the most significant experiences in their lives and then [organizing] their chapters in a sequence that tells a story," while journals "tend to be logs or records of daily growth, musings, and insights" and may feel more "fragmentary" than memoirs (p. 4). Nevertheless, journal writing commonly engages in self-reflection and self-description. Similarly, diaries are used to record daily happenings; they tend to be more chronological and descriptive of the happenings. Both journals and diaries are usually written for the authors themselves, although some end up being published for broader audiences. These formats are valuable to self-narratives because the content often reveals less self-censored behavior and thought. Anthropologists' field journals, and travel journals, war diaries, and spiritual journals, to name a few, exemplify this genre. Anderson's (2000) reflections on her fieldworks and Malinowski's (1967) field diary fall in this category.

The personal essay is another genre of self-narrative. It does not chronicle an author's life per se. It contains personal insights in response to the author's environment. Gornick (2001) argues that a personal essay combines "personal journalism . . . [and] social criticism" and should fall into "the pit of confessionalism or therapy on the page or naked self-absorption" (p. 9). Nevertheless, personal essays have a potential to be self-narratives when they fully expose the authors' perspectives. Letters can also have self-narrative quality when they contain descriptions of the behaviors and thoughts of their authors. Abigail Adams's letters to her husband, John Adams, during the Revolutionary War also became famous as documents revealing her political thoughts on roles of women (Sinopoli, 1997).

Despite the differences in formality, scope, and format, all genres of self-narrative share the common activities of memory search, self-revelation through personal stories, and self-reflection in the process.

Authorship

Conventionally, socially distinguished individuals were considered worthy authors for autobiography or memoir. However, the authorship of self-narratives has become noticeably diversified during the last three decades, to include more historically underrepresented populations, such as people of color (Angelou, 1969), women (Halverson, 2004; McKay, 1998; Sands, 1992), gays and lesbians (Bepko, 1997), and people with disabilities (Fries, 1997).

Self-narratives are generally penned by the "owners" of stories. That is to say, storytellers are identical to authors. In some cases, however, narrators tell their stories to writers who transcribe and edit the stories to varying degrees. Although the narrators still ensure the authority of the stories, the writers are often nevertheless credited. *Narrative of Sojourner Truth* (Gilbert with Sojourner Truth, 1997), *The Autobiography of Malcolm X* (Haley with Malcolm X, 1996), and *Sun Chief: The Autobiography of a Hopi Indian* (edited by Simmons, 1942) are products of such collaboration between socially distinguished figures and professional writers. North American slave narratives took a similar course of documentation when writers and journalists between 1936 and 1938 interviewed over 2,300 former slaves from across the American South to record their lives as slaves. Although most slave narrators have not been elevated to the status of the aforementioned authors, the process of self-narration and documentation was similar.

Thematic Focus

Self-narratives can also be varied depending on the themes they adopt. Themes adopted by self-narrators are as diverse as the authorship is widespread. In this section, I provide just a few examples so that readers may gain the sense of open-endedness in the thematic focus of self-narratives. Some examples include education (Adams, 2007), professorship (Nash, 2002), politics (Albright, 2003), biraciality (Lazarre, 1996; McBride, 1996; Walker, 2001), Mexican-American ethnicity (Rodriguez, 1982; Romo, 2004), religion (Olson, 1993), sexual orientation (Bepko, 1997), disability (Dubus, 1998), love, AIDS, and death of a husband (Peterson, 2003), father-son relationship (Ackerley, 1975; Lott, 1997), and mother-daughter relationship (Corse, 2004).

The thematic focus of some self-narratives is singular in that the entire writing centers on one theme. Richard Rodriguez' (1982) memoir, *Hunger of Memory*, illustrates a singular themed self-narrative in which he describes his assimilating educational experience growing up as a son of a Mexican immigrant in California. His singular focus is contrasted with the multi-faceted memoir of Colin Powell (with Persico, 1995), another child of an immigrant from Jamaica. However, Powell's memoir addresses many other aspects of his life, from education and family to military and political career.

One thematic focus that may interest educators is teaching. As self-reflection for educational practitioners is strongly advocated in teacher education, more educators are engaging in self-reflective narration in the form of cultural autobiography (Chang, 1999; Kennett, 1999) and teacher autobiography (Brookfield, 1995; Clausen & Cruickshank, 1991; Nieto, 2003; Powell, Zehm, & Garcia, 1996; Tiedt & Tiedt, 2005). Others have engaged in teacher research in which they self-observe their teaching practices, examine their relationship with students, and reflect on their teaching philosophy. Obidah and Teel (2001) discuss their professional and Black-White cross-racial relationship as teaching colleagues in a mentoring relationship; Gallas (1998) analyzes her observation of and response to the relationship between boys and girls in her elementary classroom. These teacher research pieces reveal not only the authors' teaching practices but also the cultural assumptions they bring to self-examination. As teachers face increasing cultural diversity in the classroom, their interest in using self-narratives as cultural texts to analyze themselves and others will only grow.

Writing Styles

Self-narratives employ various writing styles such as descriptive/self-affirmative, analytical/interpretive, and confessional/self-critical/self-evaluative. Although different styles may be mixed in a particular self-narrative, one particular style of writing may be pronounced in a narrative depending on the intent of the narrator. The descriptive style of writing tends to be prominent in literary memoirs, in which stories themselves are of high value. An excerpt from Maya Angelou's (1969) first volume of autobiography, *I Know Why the Caged Bird Sings,* illustrates descriptive/self-affirmative writing. She describes her grandmother ("Momma"), one of the most important figures in her early development, who led her to become a confident African American woman:

> We lived with our grandmother and uncle in the rear of the Store (it was always spoken of with a capital*s*), which she had owned some twenty-five years.
>
> Early in the century, Momma (we soon stopped calling her Grand-mother) sold lunches to the sawmen in the lumberyard (east Stamps) and the seedmen at the cotton gin (west Stamps). Her crisp meat pies and cool lemonade, when joined to her miraculous ability to be in two places at the same time, assured her business success. From being a mobile lunch counter, she set up a stand between the two points of fiscal interest and supplied the workers' needs for a few years. Then she had the Store built in the heart of the Negro area. Over the years it became the lay center of activities in town. On Saturdays, barbers sat their customers in the shade on the porch of the Store, and troubadours on their ceaseless crawlings through the South leaned across its benches and sang their sad songs of The Brazos while they played juice harps and cigar-box guitars. (p. 7)

Her grandmother is here depicted as a smart businesswoman who glued the local African American community together. Acknowledgment of her grandmother's strength, intelligence, and caring simultaneously affirms where the narrator came from and who she is. Through stories like this, Angelou also affirms the inherent value of her own life experiences as an African American woman.

Differing from this descriptive writing style, an analytical and interpretive style tends to dominate anthropological and sociological scholarly writings in which autobiographical stories are treated as materials to analyze rather than as a centerpiece to appreciate. Azoulay's (1997) personal story of Black-Jewish interracial heritage is adopted for such a purpose.

> I was born and raised in the United States and am of Jewish and West Indian descent. As a child, my mother escaped Nazi Austria, where Jews were listed as a *racial* category. My father emigrated to the United States as a young boy. His ancestral genealogy includes ancestors from Cuba and Scotland and relatives, by marriage, of Chinese descent. My 1952 New York City birth certificate classified my father's "Race" as "Negro" and my mother as "White," thus designating me a Negro—by law. I lived in Israel for twenty-one years, and my Israel identity card registers only my "Nationality," as Jewish. This background informs my perspective, influences my opinions, and shapes the manner in which I have engaged with the people I have interviewed. (p. 19)

As it is written, it may appear quite similar to Angelou's descriptive writing. However, the reader would soon find out that this personal story serves only as a thematic anchor for Azoulay's book, *Black, Jewish, and Interracial*. She offers no other personal stories of significance besides this description of her racial identity. This story provides an entry point to many stories of other Black-Jewish interracials. She analyzes and interprets in an autoethnographic manner the stories of others who share the same racial identity with her. This approach to her personal story allows her to keep a distance from her own and others' similar stories to analyze and interpret the racial discourse of the United States.

Confessional/self-critical/self-evaluative writing tends to expose self—inequities, problems, or troubles—providing a vehicle through which self-narrators work to come to resolution or self-learning. Spiritual memoirs, personal journals, and diaries may be friendly to this type of writing. Lamott's narration of her imperfect past, an encounter with God's grace, conversion from atheism to faith, and transformation in her relationship with others illustrates this writing style. The following excerpt describes her conversion experience after her long downward-spiral experiences with alcoholism, drug abuse, heavy smoking, and abortion:

> And I was appalled. I thought about my life and my brilliant hilarious progressive friends, I thought about what everyone would think of me if I became a Christian, and it seemed an utterly

impossible thing that simply could not be allowed to happen. I turned to the wall and said out loud, "I would rather die."

I felt him just sitting there on his haunches in the corner of my sleeping loft, watching me with patience and love and I squinted my eyes shut, but that didn't help because that's not what I was seeing him with. . . . And one week later, when I went back to church, I was so hungover that I couldn't stand up for the songs, and this time I stayed for the sermon. . . . I began to cry and left before the benediction, and I raced home and felt the little cat running along at my heels. . . . I opened the door to my houseboat, and I stood there a minute, and then I hung my head and said, ". . . I quit." I took a long deep breath and said out loud, "All right, you can come in."

So this was my beautiful moment of conversion. (pp. 49–50)

Classifying the multitude of self-narratives by these three writing styles is challenging because an entire self-narrative is rarely fixed by one writing style. By understanding the typology of writing styles, however, self-narrators will be able to match writing styles with writing purposes.

Summary

Self-narratives refer to a wide range of written accounts of self, representing diverse genres, authorship, themes, and writing styles. They not only record personal stories of self-narrators but also embrace the sociocultural contexts of the stories. Therefore, writing one's own self-narratives and studying other self-narratives are valuable in learning about self and others, particularly in a cultural sense. The writing process evokes self-reflection and self-analysis through which self-discovery becomes a possibility. The study of other self-narratives helps readers compare and contrast their lives with those of self-narrators. This cognitive activity of compare and contrast engenders self-examination and self-learning. The variety of self-narratives only attests to their increased recognition in humanities and social sciences. In the next chapter I provide an in-depth discussion of autoethnography, a form of self-narrative adopted in the social sciences.

Culture-Gram: Charting Cultural Membership and Identity

Your name: _Leah Yuhyun_   Date of Recording: _2/26/14_

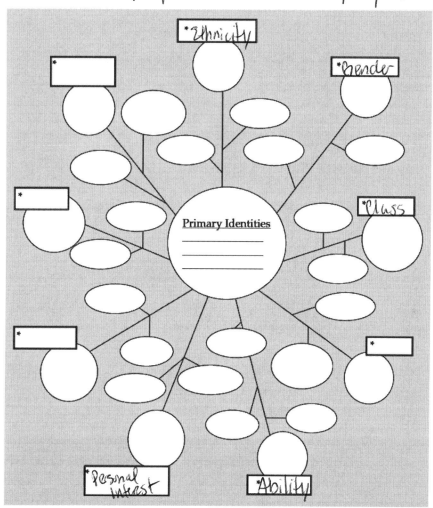

* Consider categories such as race, ethnicity, language, gender, class, religion, ability, profession, and personal interest. You may modify or expand the categories to serve your purpose.

© 2006 Chang

3

Language and Culture

The nature of the relationship between language and culture was under consideration long before anthropology became recognized as a scholarly field in its own right. Wilhelm von Humboldt (1767–1835), a well-known German diplomat and scholar, was one of those who had very definite thoughts on the subject. He wrote, "The spiritual traits and the structure of the language of a people are so intimately blended that, given either of the two, one should be able to derive the other from it to the fullest extent. . . . Language is the outward manifestation of the spirit of people: their language is their spirit, and their spirit is their language; it is difficult to imagine any two things more identical."

In the past, language, culture, and race were often lumped together as though any one of them automatically implied the other two. Modern anthropologists find Humboldt's statement unacceptable in the form in which it was made. One of the tasks and accomplishments of anthropology has been to demonstrate that culture, race, and language are historically separable. Although it is true that human culture in its great complexity could not have developed and is unthinkable without the aid of language, no correlation has yet been established between cultures of a certain type and a certain type of language. In fact, there were and still are areas in the world where societies share a very similar cultural orientation yet speak languages that are not only mutually unintelligible but completely unrelated and structurally different. Such was the case, for example, of the North American Indians of the Great Plains, who possessed many of the same or very similar cultural characteristics but whose languages belonged to at least six different language families: Algonquian (for example, Arapaho and Cheyenne), Siouan (for example, Crow and Dakota), Uto-Aztecan (for example, Shoshone and

Comanche), Athapaskan (Sarcee and Kiowa Apache), Caddoan (Wichita and Pawnee), and Kiowa-Tanoan (Kiowa). The opposite may also hold true: Estonians and Lapps speak related languages (both belong to the Finnic branch of the Finno-Ugric subfamily of the Uralic family of languages), but their cultures are quite different. The absence of any intrinsic (inherent) relationship among a people's physical type, culture, and language was repeatedly declared by Franz Boas, particularly in his eighty-page introduction to the first volume of *Handbook of American Indian Languages* (1911).

The subject of language-culture relationship was also prominent in the work of Edward Sapir. Although Sapir was convinced, just as Boas had been earlier, that "language and culture are not intrinsically associated," he nevertheless believed that "language and our thought-grooves are inextricably interwoven, [and] are, in a sense, one and the same" (Sapir 1921:228, 232). If the distinction between Boas's view and Sapir's contention, as cited, sounds like hairsplitting, let me try to clarify the difference. Both Boas and Sapir had no doubt that the association of a particular culture, physical type ("race"), and language was not given by nature but was a historical coincidence. If this were not so, how could it happen that peoples of different physical types speak the same language or closely related languages and that peoples of the same or similar physical type speak a variety of different and completely unrelated languages? The same sort of random association holds true for language and culture as well as for language and physical type. However, both Boas and Sapir believed that inasmuch as each particular language serves a particular society and is instrumental in helping the youngest members learn to operate within the society's culture, some relationship between the language and the culture could be expected to develop.

Because Sapir's writings aroused a great deal of interest in the question of how languages influence the culture of their speakers, it is important to take up the recent history of this subject in more detail and also to examine it from the perspective of contemporary anthropology.

The Stimulus of Sapir's Writings

Sapir, who had come to the United States at the age of five, became acquainted with Boas at Columbia University while doing graduate work. Impressed by Boas's breadth of knowledge and field experience, he switched from Germanic studies to anthropology. From that time on, most of his energies were devoted to the study of Native American languages. He published prolifically, his book *Language* (1921) remaining a classic to the present day.

In *Time Perspective in Aboriginal American Culture* (1916), Sapir discussed various methods that can be employed to develop cultural chronologies for aboriginal America whenever native testimonies and historical or archaeological records are either lacking or of little or no help. Sapir observed that compared with changes in culture, linguistic changes come about more slowly and evenly, and that language is far more compact and self-contained than culture taken as a whole and therefore is largely free of conscious rationalization on the part of its speakers. Major revolutions, whether violent or not, usually change profoundly the structure of the societies in which they occur, yet languages remain unchanged except for relatively minor adjustments in vocabulary.

Two examples from the many given by Sapir illustrate his use of language as a key to the cultural past of a society. Mount Shasta in northern California was visible to a number of Native American tribes. Among these, members of the Hupa tribe referred to the mountain by the descriptive term *nın-nıs-ʔan łak-gai* 'white mountain,' whereas the Yana name for it was *ωa'galu·*, a word no longer translatable or analyzable. According to Sapir, the Yana word is therefore undoubtedly much older, and one may assume that the country dominated by Mount Shasta was home to the Yana long before the Hupa came to the region. For the Northwest Coast, Sapir considered the Nootka word *tło·kwıa·na,* which refers to the wolf ceremonial complex of the tribe. Because Nootka words characteristically consist of one syllable (made up of a consonant-vowel-consonant sequence) rather than three syllables, the form of the term suggests that it, along with the ceremony, may have been borrowed from another tribe. And indeed the neighboring Kwakiutl people have a wolf dance to which they refer by a term that appears to be the source of the Nootka word. Linguistic data in this case indicate not only that at least some aspects of a culture complex may have been borrowed by another tribe but also which tribe was the likely source of the influence.

What caught the imagination of a great many scholars and inspired active research for several decades, however, was a particular paragraph of a paper Sapir read in 1928 at a scholarly meeting in New York attended by both linguists and anthropologists:

> In a sense, the network of cultural patterns of a civilization is indexed in the language which expresses that civilization. . . . Language is a guide to "social reality." Though language is not ordinarily thought of as of essential interest to the students of social science, it powerfully conditions all our thinking about social problems and processes. Human beings do not live in the objective world alone, nor alone in the world of social activity as ordinarily understood, but are very much at the mercy of the particular language which has become the medium of expression for their society. . . . The fact of the matter is that the "real world" is to a large extent unconsciously built up on the language habits of the group. No two languages are ever sufficiently similar to be considered as representing the same social reality. The worlds in which different societies live are distinct worlds, not merely the same world with different labels attached. (Sapir 1929:209)

The most provocative statement was the assertion that humans are at the mercy of the language they happen to speak.

The Whorf Hypothesis of Linguistic Relativity and Linguistic Determinism

Whereas Boas's and Sapir's ideas concerning the relationship between language and culture primarily influenced only their students and other scholars, the writings of Benjamin Lee Whorf (1897–1941) caught the attention of the educated public. Whorf, a chemical engineer by training, was a fire prevention inspector and later an executive of a New England fire insurance company. Although he continued to work for the company until his untimely death, in 1931 he enrolled in a course at Yale University in order to do graduate study under Sapir, who had just been awarded a professorship at Yale. Among Whorf's numerous subsequent publications, the best known are those in which he expounded on what some have referred to as the Sapir-Whorf hypothesis (see Box 3.1).

BOX 3.1   HOW WORDS AFFECT BEHAVIOR

It was in the course of my professional work for a fire insurance company, in which I undertood the task of analyzing many hundreds of reports of circumstances surrounding the start of fires, and in some cases, of explosions. My analysis was directed toward purely physical conditions, such as defective wiring, presence or lack of air spaces between metal flues and woodwork, etc., and the results were presented in these terms....But in due course it became evident that not only a physical situation *qua* physics, but the meaning of that situation to people, was sometimes a factor, through the behavior of the people, in the start of the fire. And this factor of meaning was clearest when it was a LINGUISTIC MEANING, residing in the name or the linguistic description commonly applied to the situation. Thus, around a storage of what are called "gasoline drums," behavior will tend to a certain type, that is, great care will be exercised; while around a storage of what are called "empty gasoline drums," it will tend to be different—careless, with little repression of smoking or of tossing cigarette stubs about. Yet the "empty" drums are perhaps the more dangerous, since they contain explosive vapor. Physically the situation is hazardous, but the linguistic analysis according to regular analogy must employ the word "empty," which inevitably suggests lack of hazard.

from Benjamin Lee Whorf, *Language, Thought, and Reality* (1956), 135

Expanding on Sapir's ideas, Whorf wrote that

the background linguistic system (in other words, the grammar) of each language is not merely a reproducing instrument for voicing ideas but rather is itself the shaper of ideas. . . . We dissect nature along lines laid down by our native languages . . . organize it into concepts, and ascribe significances as we do, largely because we are parties to an agreement to organize it in this way—an agreement that holds throughout our speech community and is codified in the patterns of our language. . . . [Not] all observers are . . . led by the same physical evidence to the same picture of the universe, unless their linguistic backgrounds are similar. (Whorf 1940a:231)

He further asserted that "users of markedly different grammars are pointed by their grammars toward different types of observations . . . and hence are not equivalent as observers but must arrive at somewhat different views of the world" (Whorf 1940b:61). In these passages Whorf set forth a double principle: the principle of **linguistic determinism**, namely, that the way one thinks is determined by the language one speaks, and the principle of **linguistic relativity**, that differences among languages must therefore be reflected in the differences in the worldviews of their speakers.

Many of the examples Whorf used to support his contention came from Hopi, a language spoken by Native Americans in the pueblos of northeastern Arizona. Although Whorf briefly visited the Hopi villages in 1938, the data for his grammatical sketch of the language (1946) were obtained from a native speaker of Hopi who lived in New York City. In an article dealing with grammatical aspects of Hopi verbs, Whorf put forth the claim that the Hopi "have a language better equipped to deal with such vibratile phenomena [that is, phenomena characterized by vibration] than is our latest [English] scientific terminology" (1936:131). Among his examples are the verb forms *wa´la* 'it (a liquid) makes a wave, gives a slosh,' *ti´ri* 'he gives a sudden start,' and *ʔi´mi* 'it explodes, goes off like a gun.' These and others can be changed from their punctual aspect (a term used to refer to a verb action concentrated into a very short period of time) to the segmentative aspect by repeating (reduplicating) their last two sounds and adding the ending *-ta* to produce the forms *wala´lata* 'it is tossing in waves,' *tiri´rita* 'he is quivering, trembling,' and *ʔimi´mita* 'it is thundering.' Whereas in English the difference between something happening once briefly and something occurring repeatedly over time may call for different phrases (for example, "it explodes" as against "it is thundering," or "it makes a wave" as against "it is tossing in waves"), the Hopi express it by the use of a simple grammatical device. In Whorf's words, the example illustrates "how the Hopi language maps out a certain terrain of what might be termed primitive physics . . . with very thorough consistency and not a little true scientific precision" and "how language produces an organization of experience" (1936:130–131).

In another article, written in the mid-1930s but not published until nine years after Whorf's death, the author stated that "the Hopi language is seen to contain no words, grammatical forms, constructions or expressions that refer directly to what we call TIME, or to past, present, or future . . . or that even refer to space in such a way as to exclude that element of extension or existence that we call TIME" (1950:67). Instead, the grand coordinates of the universe for the Hopi are manifest, objective experience and the unfolding, subjective realm of human existence.

Whorf illustrated his notion of linguistic relativity by using as an example the Apache equivalent of the English utterance "It is a dripping spring" (referring to a source of water): "Apache erects the statement on a verb *ga:* 'be white (including clear, uncolored, and so on).' With a prefix *nō-* the meaning of downward motion enters: 'whiteness moves downward.' Then *tó*, meaning both 'water' and 'spring,' is prefixed. The result corresponds to our 'dripping spring,' but synthetically it is: 'as water, or springs, whiteness moves downward.' How utterly unlike our way of thinking!" (Whorf 1941a:266, 268).

Following up on the hypothesis that a language and the culture it serves mirror each other, Whorf compared the Hopi language with western European languages (labeled SAE for "Standard Average European"). According to him, the differences in linguistic structure between Hopi and SAE are reflected in "habitual thought" and "habitual behavior." For example, "the Hopi microcosm seems to have analyzed reality largely in terms of *events* (or better[,] 'eventing'), referred to in two ways, objective and subjective" (1941b:84); the emphasis is on being in accord, by means of thoughtful participation, with the unfolding forces of nature. Speakers of SAE, in contrast, conceive of the universe largely in terms of things and of time in terms of schedules. SAE languages use tense to mark the time at which an action takes place (as in the past, present, future, or, even more specifically, as in "I had eaten," to express the completion of an action before a specific past time). No wonder, then, that speakers of western European languages tend to be preoccupied with "records, diaries, book-keeping, accounting . . . calendars, chronology . . . annals, histories . . . [and] budgets" (1941b:88).

The implications of Whorf's ideas concerning linguistic relativity and determinism are quite serious. If the worldview and behavior of a people are significantly affected by the structure of the language they speak, and if languages differ in structure, then cross-cultural communication and understanding are likely to be noticeably impaired, if not impossible to achieve. This is why Whorf's ideas received a great deal of attention and stimulated much discussion for a number of years after World War II. From a contemporary standpoint, however, it appears that Whorf overstated his case. Let us next consider how.

Language, Culture, and Worldview:
A Relationship Reconsidered

Critical comments on Whorf's writings were soon to appear. Eric H. Lenneberg pointed out that "a demonstration that certain languages differ from each other suggests but does not prove that the speakers of these languages differ from each other as a group in their psychological potentialities" (1953:463), his comment on Whorf's well-known example of "empty drums": "Clearly, English is capable of distinguishing between a drum filled with an explosive vapor, one that contains only air, and one which is void of any matter. . . . The person who caused the fire could have replaced the word *empty* by *filled with explosive vapor.*"

Others decided to put the principle of relativity to the test, among them Brent Berlin and Paul Kay. According to them, "the prevailing doctrine of American linguists and anthropologists has . . . been that of extreme linguistic relativity," meaning that "each language is semantically arbitrary relative to every other language . . . [and] the search for semantic universals is [therefore] fruitless in principle" (Berlin and Kay 1969:1–2). Their research during the late 1960s, based on the examination of ninety-eight languages from all parts of the world, came up with some unexpected findings.

1. There is a universal inventory of eleven basic color categories from among which the basic color terms in different languages are drawn: These categories are white, black, red, green, yellow, blue, brown, purple, pink, orange, and gray.

2. If a language encodes fewer than the eleven basic color categories, then there is a sequence in which the color terms are encoded: All languages contain terms for white and black; the third term is for red; the fourth term is for either green or yellow; the fifth term is for the other of the previous two; the sixth term is for blue; the seventh is for brown; and the remaining four terms are for the remaining color categories or some combination thereof. (A basic color term consists of one morpheme, is not included in any other color term, and is a general term; accordingly, the English color terms *bluish, crimson,* and *blond* would be excluded by definition.)

The second major conclusion of Berlin and Kay is that "there appears to be a fixed sequence of evolutionary stages through which a language must pass as its basic color vocabulary increases" (1969:14). In addition, a positive correlation appears to exist between the complexity of the color vocabulary and cultural complexity.

Berlin and Kay's findings should not be taken as a total refutation of the concept of linguistic relativity but only of its extreme form. What their conclusions point to, though, is that when it comes to the domains of color vocabulary, there does exist a semantic feature that is universal, or at least nearly universal.

For the purposes of further discussion concerning the relationship between language and culture, the two terms must be carefully defined. The term *language,* as we have already seen, refers to the complex of universally human potentialities for vocal communication or, simply, to the gift of speech. By contrast, **a language** refers to any one of the several thousand systems of oral communication used by different human societies. Language is a part of human genetic endowment, whereas *a* (particular) language must be learned during childhood along with the many nonverbal facets of the particular culture. In a sense, then, *a* language is just as culture-bound as are the traditional habits and value orientations characteristic of the society whose members use it. Furthermore, when discussing particular languages in this context, it is convenient to distinguish between at least two aspects of any language—its *lexicon* (or vocabulary) and its *structure* (conventionally referred to as grammar).

The term *culture* also is all-inclusive. Taken comprehensively, it is understood to refer to the total pattern of human learned behavior transmitted from generation to generation. When one talks about **a culture**, however, the explicit mention of language is, strictly speaking, redundant because any particular language is a form (even though autonomous) of learned behavior and therefore a part of the culture. A solution to this terminological overlap would be to distinguish between a *nonverbal culture* and the corresponding language. Nonverbal culture can be further divided into *mental culture* (for example, worldview or value orientations), *behavioral culture* (for example, wiping one's feet before entering a house or performing a heart transplant), and—according to some anthropologists—*material culture,* that is, the material products of behavior (for example, a pull-open beer can or a radio telescope). Items of material culture are usually the result of the application of behavioral (manual skills) and mental culture (knowledge).

If it is true that all languages, regardless of the superficial differences among them, share some universal features—or in other words, if the structure of language is in some way determined by the structure of the human brain—then one could envision the possibility of a common organization of human experience. In such case, on a deep level the question of the relationship between language and culture would cease to exist.

According to a strong version of this proposition, grammatical categories of a language determine how its speakers perceive the world around them. According to a weak version, there is simply some sort of correlation between a language and its speakers' worldview (the philosophical dimension of a society's culture).

There is no question that the lexicon of any language mirrors whatever the nonverbal culture emphasizes; that is, those aspects of culture that are important for the members of a society are correspondingly highlighted in the vocabulary. For example, words conveying the various characteristics of camels (age, breed, gender, function, condition, and so on) are undoubtedly more plentiful in a language spoken by bedouins who depend on camels than they are in English; the vocabulary of American English, for its part, is replete with the names of makes and models of automobiles, with new names of models of the various makes being added every year. In Pintupi, one of the aboriginal languages of Australia, there are at least ten words designating various kinds of holes found in nature or in manufactured objects: *mutara* is a special hole in a spear, *pulpa* is a rabbit burrow, *makarnpa* is a burrow of a monitor lizard, *katarta* is the hole left by a monitor lizard after it has broken the surface after hibernation, and so on. This example also shows that even though a language may not have a one-word equivalent for a word of another language, it is possible to provide an adequate translation by a descriptive phrase (which in the case of *katarta* may take as many as fifteen English words). To avoid wordiness or the use of borrowed words, many languages coin new words. Some years ago an American anthropologist thought a kinship term was needed to include the meanings of both *nephew* and *niece* and coined the word *nibling,* using the word *sibling* (brother or sister) as a model. However, to conclude that the absence of equivalent terms between different vocabularies must always be associated with a different perception of the world would be far-fetched.

Whorf's examples from Hopi also call for comment. According to Charles F. Voegelin, Florence M. Voegelin, and LaVerne Masayesva Jeanne (1979), the relationship between the punctual and segmentative aspects is not as straightforward as Whorf described it: For example, not all nonreduplicated (not doubled) stems without the ending -*ta* can be said to express the punctual aspect. Furthermore, although speakers of Hopi make little of the division between future and nonfuture, they do indicate tense by temporal adverbs, the suffix -*ni* (future), and the gnomic suffix -*ŋʷi* (meaning that something is generally true).

Whorf claimed that the Apache way of thinking is "utterly unlike" that of speakers of English because the utterance "It is a dripping spring" translates literally from Apache into English as "As water, or springs, whiteness moves downward." But suppose that speakers of a foreign language were to interpret literally *breakfast* as "breaking the fast (abstinence from food)," *bonfire* as "a fire of bones, bone fire," and *spinster* as "a woman whose occupation is spinning" and as a result saw a profound difference between their own way of thinking and that of English-speaking people.

Certain lexical differences between languages may, though, have as a consequence different categorizations of the corresponding part of the environment. Speakers of English use the personal pronoun *you* whether they are addressing one or several children, adults, old persons, subordinates, or individuals much superior to themselves in rank. Only when addressing God in prayer or in certain very limited contexts—for example, in the language of the Friends (the Quakers) or in poetry—does one use the pronoun *thou* (which is singular only). The typical situation in other languages, including most of those spoken in Europe, is more complex. When addressing someone, speakers of Dutch, French, German, Italian, Russian, Spanish, and other languages must choose between the "familiar" personal pronoun (T form) and the "polite" personal pronoun (V form) and/or the corresponding verb form. (The symbols T and V are derived from the French *tu* and *vous,* the familiar and polite second-person pronouns, respectively.) In Czech, for example, to address an individual who is closely related, someone socially close and of long acquaintance, or a child below the age of puberty, one commonly uses the personal pronoun *ty.* But in addressing a casual acquaintance, a stranger, or a person deserving respect, one uses the pronoun *vy,* which also serves as the plural of *ty.* A speaker may occasionally wonder, for example, which of the two forms to use when addressing an adult whom the speaker knew as a child and referred to repeatedly as *ty.* A translation from Czech into English, or vice versa, that involves these pronouns (and/or the corresponding verb forms) is therefore not equivalent.

The Czech phrases *"ty a já"* and *"vy a já"* both translate into English as "you and I," even though the first one makes use of the informal, familiar—even intimate—pronoun and would not be used in situations in which the formal, polite pronoun of the second phrase would be appropriate. The English translation, then, can only be approximate, as it cannot fully convey the nature of the relationship between the speaker and the addressee.

Let us consider another example, one with more significant consequences. Among the Arapaho, a Native American tribe of the Great Plains, the term for "my mother" is *néínoo*. This Arapaho term for "my mother" also applies to ego's mother's sister, a person referred to in the American kinship system as "my aunt" (ego is the person of reference to whom others are shown to be related). However, the term by which ego calls his mother's brother is *nési,* roughly equivalent to "my uncle." Similarly, the term for "my father," *neisónoo,* also refers to ego's father's brother, whereas father's sister is referred to as *nehéi,* roughly equivalent to "my aunt." Now if ego's father's brother is termed *neisónoo,* as is also ego's father, it follows that father's brother's wife would be referred to by the same term as ego's father's wife, that is, *néínoo.* And by the same token, ego's mother's sister's husband is referred to in Arapaho as *neisónoo* 'my father.' Whereas in the American kinship terminology biological parents are distinguished from uncles and aunts, the Arapaho and many other peoples lump together lineal relatives with some of their collateral relatives—the biological mother, her sister, and father's brother's wife on the one hand, and the biological father, his brother, and mother's sister's husband on the other (see Figure 3.1). It follows, then, that anyone who calls some relatives of the parental generation by terms that apply to the biological mother and father is in turn called by all these relatives by terms that apply to biological sons and daughters.

Is one to conclude from the Arapaho kinship terminology that the Arapaho are unaware of the difference between a biological mother (or father) and her sister (or his brother)? Of course not. What it means is that the extension of the Arapaho kinship terms *neisónoo* and *néínoo* from ego's biological parents to additional relatives is paralleled by an extension of ego's behavior toward his or her biological father and mother to all those relatives who are referred to by the same kinship terms. All Arapaho terminological "fathers" and "mothers" have the same obligations toward their terminological "sons" and "daughters," and vice versa, even though opportunities to fulfill them may sometimes be limited by circumstances. Among those "parents" and "children" whose interaction is limited by distance, the emphasis is on extending the relevant attitudes rather than behavior. It is clear that the kinship terminology by which one classifies relatives also governs the type of behavior patterns and attitudes applied to them.

Do grammatical features have any influence on how speakers of a language perceive and categorize the world around them? In some instances they do, at least to some extent. In others the influence is negligible, if any at all. In English the word *teacher* refers to a person who teaches, whether it is a woman or a man. From a pupil's remark "Our teacher is too strict," there is no indication of the teacher's gender, though in subsequent conversation gender may be disclosed by the use of the teacher's name or the gender-specific personal pronoun (*she* or *he*). Such ambiguity is not so likely to occur, for example, in German, which distinguishes between the masculine form of *teacher* (*Lehrer*) and the feminine form (*Lehrerin*). Similarly, the suffix *-in* in German changes *Arzt* 'male physician' to *Ärztin* 'female physician' and *Professor* 'male professor' to *Professorin* 'female professor.' English clearly differs from German in that what is optional in the former is obligatory in the latter. But the claim that this and similar distinctions between the two languages have an influence on the outlook of their speakers would be hard to prove; no one would argue, for example, that sexism is more or less common in countries that speak German, in which the marking of gender is more common (but in these and most other languages, the feminine form is derived from the masculine, as in *lioness* from *lion*, and *Löwin* 'lioness' from *Löwe* 'lion' in German).

Like some other Indo-European languages, German has three genders—masculine, feminine, and neuter—that for the most part have nothing to do with maleness, femaleness, or absence of sexual characteristics. In German, for example, window (*das Fenster*) is of neuter gender, as are girl (*das Mädchen*) and woman (*das Weib*); blackboard (*die Tafel*) is feminine, as is crowbar (*die Brechstange*); and bosom (*der Busen*) is masculine, as are the season of spring (*der Frühling*) and skirt (*der Rock*). Do German-speaking people believe that crowbars and blackboards are feminine in the same way as mother (*die Mutter*) or a woman with whom someone is in love (*die Geliebte*) is? I invite the reader to guess.

With only very few exceptions, in English the plural forms of nouns differ from the corresponding singular forms, as in *child* and *children, mouse* and *mice, horse* and *horses, book* and *books,* and *pen* and *pens.* There is no such distinction in many languages and dialects spoken in the People's Republic of China: The same form of a noun stands for both the singular and the plural. Yet the lack of marked grammatical number in nouns and hence no need to differentiate between one or more entities have obviously not prevented the Chinese from making achievements in mathematics and science. In some languages, however, in addition to singular and plural there is also dual, and in a relatively few languages trial and even quadrual, referring respectively to two, three, or four. For the most part, societies whose languages mark these additional distinctions in the grammatical category of number make little use of mathematics.

Still, several studies do indicate that grammatical features may have some influence on nonverbal behavior. Among the best-known studies of this type is the report on an experiment administered to Navajo and white American children by John B. Carroll and Joseph B. Casagrande (1915–1982). A speaker of Navajo must choose from among several forms of Navajo verbs of handling according to the shape or some other characteristic of the object being handled—for example, solid roundish (rock), slender and flexible (rope), flat and flexible (cloth), slender and stiff (stick), noncompact (wool), and so on. Even though the use of the appropriate forms is obligatory, the selection operates below the level of conscious awareness on the part of the speakers, and even children as young as three or four make no errors. (In a somewhat similar fashion, in English one *shrugs* one's shoulders and *nods* one's head, and no native speaker would ever use one term for the other.) One of the hypotheses of the investigators was that this feature of Navajo affects the perception of objects and consequently the behavior of speakers.

Ten pairs of objects were used, each pair significantly differing in two characteristics. The 135 Navajo children who took part in the experiment included some who spoke only Navajo, some who were more proficient in Navajo than in English, some who were balanced bilinguals, some who spoke predominantly English, and some who spoke only English. Each of these children was presented with one of the pairs of objects, shown a third object similar to each member of the pair in one characteristic only (for example, a pair represented by a yellow stick and a piece of blue rope of comparable length, with a yellow rope as the third object), and then asked to match one of the paired objects with the third. The matching on the part of the Navajo-dominant children was predominantly on the basis of shape rather than color, this tendency increasing with the age of the child. Among the English-dominant Navajo children, color appeared to be more important among the youngest, but by the age of ten the two groups had almost converged, with the selection dominated by shape.

The performance of white children in the Boston area was more similar to that of the Navajo-dominant than the English-dominant Navajo children. According to the two investigators, this result may be due at least in part to the early and continued play of white children with toys of the form-board variety, stressing form and size rather than color. On the basis of the difference between the Navajo-dominant and English-dominant groups of Navajo children, the investigators concluded:

> The tendency of a child to match objects on the basis of form or material rather than size or color increases with age and may be enhanced by . . . learning to speak a language, like Navaho, which because of the central role played by form and material in its grammatical structure, requires the learner to make certain discriminations of form and material in the earlier stages of language learning in order to make himself understood at all. (Carroll and Casagrande 1958:31)

The Navajo are among the most extensively studied Native American peoples, and the depth of our understanding of Navajo culture is due in large measure to those individuals who were exposed to the culture for an extended period of time. One such person is the anthropologist Gary Witherspoon, who made the Navajo country his home for over ten years. Prior to his academic career, he worked for Navajo communities and local boards of education and became an interested and concerned participant in the life of the local communities. He learned the Navajo language by listening to Navajos and talking with them.

In *Language and Art in the Navajo Universe* (1977), Witherspoon shared some of the results of his unique experience with the Navajo language and culture. "In the Navajo view of the world," noted Witherspoon (1977:34), "language is not a mirror of reality; reality is a mirror of language." Ritual language in Navajo culture is powerful, its primary purpose being to maintain or restore *hózhǫ́* (the symbol [´] marks high tone; ǫ is nasalized *o*). Although this word refers to the central theme of Navajo worldview and religious thinking, its use is not restricted to ritual contexts—the word is heard frequently in everyday speech. What is *hózhǫ́*? The stem *-zhǫ́* refers to a state characterized by goodness, peace, order, happiness, blessedness, health, beauty (of the natural surroundings), satisfaction, perfection, well-being, deliberation, care, success, and harmony in one's relations with others (the list is not exhaustive but should serve). The form therefore refers not only to aesthetic but also to moral, emotional, and intellectual qualities, and it is difficult to translate into English by a single word or even a phrase. The verbal prefix *hó-*, which is part of *hózhǫ́*, adds to the meaning of the stem the idea of "total environment"—the whole, the general, the abstract, the indefinite, the infinite. As Witherspoon put it, "Navajo life and culture are based on a unity of experience, and the goal of Navajo life—the creation, maintenance, and restoration of *hózhǫ́*—expresses that unity of experience" (Witherspoon 1977:154).

For the second illustration I let Witherspoon speak for himself (see Box 3.2).

The next example is from Japanese. According to Agnes M. Niyekawa-Howard (1968), the Japanese passive consists of two different constructions. One of these, the ordinary passive, is neutral in meaning. The other, referred to as adversative passive, implies that the grammatical subject of a sentence has been adversely affected, that is, subjected to something undesirable. When the adversative passive is combined with the causative, the resulting connotation is that the subject of the sentence is not responsible for what happened because he or she was "caused" to take the action expressed by the main verb. This connotation is not one that speakers of Japanese are usually conscious of.

The first part of the study consisted of the examination of all passive constructions in about twenty Japanese short stories translated into English by native speakers of English, and twenty English short stories translated into Japanese by native speakers of Japanese. As hypothesized, the connotation of the adversative passive tended to be lost in the translations into English, but it appeared in the translations into Japanese, the Japanese translators having read it into the English original.

The second part of the study compared the interpretations by Japanese and Americans of cartoons depicting situations of interpersonal conflict. As hypothesized, the Japanese were found to attribute responsibility for the

BOX 3.2   CLASSIFYING INTERACTION
THROUGH LANGUAGE

The sentence 'the girl drank the water'

At'ééd	tó	yoodlą́ą́'
(girl)	(water)	(it-it-drank)

is acceptable, but the sentence 'the water was drunk by the girl'

Tó	at'ééd	boodlą́ą́'
(water)	(girl)	(it-it-drank)

is unacceptable and absurd in the Navajo view of the world....

It is rather evident... that we need some nonlinguistic data or information in order to interpret these rather unusual linguistic patterns properly. They are not generated by a set of operations at the deep structural level of Navajo grammar; they are generated by a set of cultural rules which are ultimately derived from more fundamental metaphysical propositions which the Navajo take to be axiomatic.

Taking a cultural approach to the explanation of this pattern in Navajo syntax, some years ago I asked my wife why it was so absurd to say *tó at'ééd boodlą́ą́'* 'the water was drunk by the girl.' She thought long and hard about this matter, unable to see why it was not absurd to me. Finally, she said, "The sentence attributes more intelligence to the water than it does to the girl, and anyone [even you—was the implication] ought to know that human beings are smater than water." Therein I had a lead to solve this riddle, but I was not sure what to make of it. She went on to say that the water does not think, so how could it have the girl drink it. But, I insisted, the water was not acting or thinking, it just got drunk. She countered by saying that the way I had constructed the sentence made it appear that the water was the cause of the drinking action, not the girl.

From the discussion above I later surmised that maybe the sentence should be translated 'the water caused the girl to drink it.' I tried this translation out on several Navajos who knew English. They said it was much closer to the Navajo meaning of the sentence than 'the water was drunk by the girl' but they were still a little uncomfortable with it. After some further thought and discussion, we came up with the translation 'the water let the girl drink it.' Therein we had captured in English not just the covert meaning of the Navajo sentence but the overt absurdity that the meaning expressed.

from Gary Witherspoon, *Language and Art in the Navajo Universe*
(1977), 65–67

negative outcome of events to others to a greater extent than did Americans. Could such an attitude have derived support from the traditionally authoritarian Japanese culture rather than from the structure of the Japanese language? To answer this question, Niyekawa-Howard tested a sample of Germans, another group with a tradition of authoritarianism. Their responses differed from those of the Japanese but were very close to those of the Americans. The study indicated, therefore, that a particular grammatical feature can at least significantly contribute to the reinforcement of a perceptual habit or cultural outlook.

In general, those examining the relationship between language and culture in recent years have advocated more experimental vigor. They have argued that research concerning this relationship must be comparative, that is, contrast two or more languages, preferably widely differing; that it must use some "external nonlinguistic reality" (stimulus) as a standard for determining by comparison the content of linguistic and cognitive categories; that it must contrast the languages of the respective speech communities to determine how they differ in understanding a common stimulus; and that it must make plain the implication of differences in language for differences in thought between the members of these speech communities (summarized from Lucy 1992).

John A. Lucy applied these four components that he considered requisite for adequate empirical research to Yucatec (a Mayan language) and American English. The focus of his study has been on the marking of the grammatical category of number (for example, the pluralization of nouns): Is there any correspondence between the grammatical treatment of number and the habitual thought (cognition) of the speakers of Yucatec on the one hand and those of American English on the other?

For example, in English the marking of the plural is obligatory for a very large number of "thing" nouns, or countables, such as *child, horse,* or *chair;* the only exceptions in nontechnical contexts are mass and abstract nouns, or uncountables, such as *sand, water, butter,* and *honesty.* By contrast, speakers of Yucatec mark plural optionally and for a relatively small number of nouns. The two languages also differ fundamentally in the use of numerals. In English, numerals modify a noun, as in *one candle* and *two baskets.* In Yucatec, numerals must be accompanied by a special piece of structure, a classifier, that identifies the counted object as to its material properties, as in *un-tz'íit kib'* 'one long thin wax,' referring to a candle.

In nonverbal experimental tasks, speakers of both English and Yucatec were responsive to the number of objects presented to them according to how the objects were treated grammatically in the respective language. Speakers of English were aware of the number of animate entities and objects but not of the substances represented by mass nouns; speakers of Yucatec were sensitive to number only for animate entities. In classifying three test objects as to which two of the three were more similar (a small cardboard box, a plastic box similar in form, and a piece of cardboard), speakers of English preferred to classify them according to shape (selecting the cardboard box and the plastic box), whereas the speakers of Yucatec preferred to classify them according to material (selecting the cardboard box and the small piece of cardboard). Although Lucy considered his study exploratory in nature, his findings suggest that "language patterns do affect cognitive performance" or, in other words, that "there is good preliminary evidence that diverse language forms bear a relationship to characteristic cognitive responses in speakers" (Lucy 1992:156, 158).

Some assumptions—for example, that notions of space (that is, a three-dimensional area in which events and objects occur and have relative direction and position) are universal—need to be reexamined. Stephen C. Levinson (1996:353) showed that "systems of spatial reckoning and description can in fact be quite divergent across cultures, linguistic differences correlating with distinct cognitive tendencies." More specifically, languages vary in their use of spatial concepts and in some instances determine the cognitive categories relating to space concepts; also, the speakers of a number of languages do not use spatial terms corresponding to the bodily coordinates of left-right and front-back. One example comes from the Tenejapa Tzeltal of Mexico: Their language uses no relative frame of reference and therefore has no terms for spatial reference that would correspond to *left, right, front,* and *back.* Although terms exist for *left hand*

and *right hand,* they do not extend to other parts of the body or to areas external to it (Levinson 1996).

The fairly general agreement currently appears to be that differences in thought that are responsive to differences in grammatical structure exist but tend to be superficial. However, the field-worker engaged in ethnography or linguistic anthropology must always remember that "language, culture, and meaning have inextricably contaminated each other" (Hill and Mannheim 1992:382–383). (For yet another comment on linguistic relativity, see Box 3.3.)

Ethnoscience

Whorf's interest in the relationship between language and culture was responsible for the development in the 1950s of several closely related analytical approaches to the study of culture. However, Whorf's main focus seems to have been on grammatical categories, whereas the new approaches have focused on lexical classification of the social and physical environments of speakers of a language by means of its word-stock (lexicon). Discussed here under the widely used term ***ethnoscience***, these new approaches include cognitive anthropology, componential analysis, ethnosemantics, folk taxonomy, and the so-called new ethnography. Ward H. Goodenough had these approaches in mind when he wrote in 1957, "We learn much of a culture when we learn the system of meanings for which its linguistic forms stand. Much descriptive ethnography is inescapably an exercise in descriptive semantics. . . . Relatively little [systematic] attention is devoted . . . to isolating the concepts or forms in terms of which the members of a society deal with one another and the world around them, and many of which are signified lexically in their language" (Goodenough 1964:39).

The term *ethnoscience* can easily be misinterpreted. It does not imply that alternative approaches to the study of culture are necessarily unscientific, nor does it suggest that folk classifications—that is, classifications by members of a particular culture—are more scientific than those developed by Western science. Rather, the term refers to a method of studying parts (domains) of a culture primarily on the basis of how they are lexically encoded by native speakers. The assumption is that as a rule what is culturally discriminable is also lexically differentiated.

What ethnoscience is about was neatly illustrated by William C. Sturtevant in one of the earliest surveys of ethnoscientific research, in which he referred to a book published in 1897 by Walter E. Roth, a Victorian ethnologist.

BOX 3.3   CARROLL ON LINGUISTIC RELATIVITY

The speakers of one language...may tend to ignore differences which are regularly noticed by the speakers of another language. This is not to say that they *always* ignore them, for these differences can indeed be recognized and talked about in any language, but they are differences which are not always salient in their experiences. The effect of any one language category is to lead language users to assume, perhaps mistakenly, that there is uniformity of some sort within the category....For example, historians have pointed out that the use of the term "the Middle Ages" may lead to the false impression that the period between the fall of Rome and the Italian Renaissance was in truth a distinct historical period which had uniform characteristics, throughout its length, which set it apart from other periods....

Let us now analyze a simple cross-linguistic example. In English, it is possible to report about someone, "He went to town." Nothing is said about his mode of travel: he might have walked, run, rode a horse, driven a car, or taken a bus or even a boat or a helicopter. It is well known that in German one would have to specify at least a minimum of information about the mode of travel. Use of the verb *gehen* (as a cognate of *go,* apparently the most direct translation) would imply walking or some other form of self-propelled movement; use of *fahren* would imply going in a vehicle; of *reiten,* going on horseback; etc. Russian, and, it so happens, Navaho, could use an even longer list of verbs to distinguish modes of transportation. Thus, in English, it is possible to focus attention on the mere fact of someone's having departed in the direction of town, even though the speaker of English can be more specific if he wants to: *walked, ran, drove, rode, flew, bicycled, rowed, helicoptered* could be substituted for *went* in the sentence indicated.... As compared with German speakers, English speakers are sometimes benefited, sometimes disadvantaged by the possible lack of specificity in the meaning of the English term *go.*

from John B. Carroll, "Linguistic Relativity, Contrastive Linguistics, and Language Learning" (1963), 12–13

According to Sturtevant, Roth "titled the last chapter of his monograph on Queensland aboriginal culture 'ethno-pornography,' warned that 'the following chapter is not suitable for perusal by the general reader,' and described under this heading such topics as marriage, pregnancy and childbirth, menstruation, 'foul language,' and especially genital mutilations and their social and ceremonial significance" (Sturtevant 1964:100). Sturtevant's point is not so much that what today is considered pornography in the United States and other complex societies has changed drastically from what it was a century ago but that the aboriginal Queenslanders, and for that matter many other societies, may not have a concept corresponding to pornography at all, or if they do, it is likely to be somewhat or even quite different from that of the anthropologist's own culture. Consequently, in the opinion of the proponents of ethnoscience, describing other societies in terms of categories not applicable to them is likely to lead to serious distortions.

A good example of viewing a domain of another culture with the help of native categories is the discussion by Charles O. Frake concerning how disease is diagnosed among the Eastern Subanun, slash-and-burn farmers of western Mindanao in the Philippines (Frake 1961). Sickness is one of the most frequent subjects of conversation among these people, and consequently their language has many terms related to disease. Frake's paper is a partial analysis of 186 disease names, one of the numerically more modest terminological sets in Subanun. (The following English labels briefly explain but do not define Subanun terms.) Among the names of human diseases Frake recorded, some were descriptive phrases such as *meŋebag gatay* 'swollen liver,' but most of the disease names were expressed by a single Subanun word. Let us consider the term *nuka* 'skin disease,' which contrasts with, for example, *samad* 'wound,' and *pasuʔ* 'burn.' There are several varieties of *nuka: pugu* 'rash,' *meŋebag* 'inflammation,' *beldut* 'sore,' *buni* 'ringworm,' and others. A *beldut* 'sore' is further classified according to depth (shallow as against deep), distance from the point of origin or attachment (away from, or distal, as against close to, or proximal), severity (severe as against mild), and spread (single as against multiple), with each of the existing varieties referred to by a Subanun term—for example, *telemaw glai* 'shallow distal ulcer (considered severe),' *selimbunut* 'multiple sore,' and the like. The diagnosis of any particular disease may require advice from different people who judge, among other things, whether a particular *bagaʔ* 'proximal ulcer' is shallow (*bagaʔ*) or deep (*begwak*). But proper diagnosis is not an end in itself; it is a pivotal cognitive step in the selection of culturally appropriate responses to illness by the Subanun [and] bears directly on the selection of ordinary, botanically-derived, medicinal remedies from 724 recorded alternatives. The results of this selection . . . influence efforts to reach prognostic and etiological decisions [decisions having to do with the causes of a disease and the prospect of recovery], which, in their turn, govern the possible therapeutic need for a variant of one of 61 basic, named types of propitiatory offerings. (Frake 1961:131)

To sum up: To diagnose and classify Subanun diseases from the vantage point of Western medicine may be appropriate for an article to be published in a medical journal. However, for an anthropologist such a description would fail to reveal or at least would obscure the linkages that the Subanun believe to exist between the method of diagnosing diseases and the application of remedies to them. This is so because the final diagnosis and choice of appropriate treatment have important social and economic consequences in Subanun society.

One of the methods of semantic analysis the so-called New Ethnographers have used is componential analysis. It is a technique applied to a set of terms (lexical items) that belong to a highly patterned and well-defined cultural domain (color terms, disease names, kin terms, terms for daily meals or for liquids taken in by humans, and the like); the aim is to discover the semantic distinctions that make these terms contrast with one another, and this aim is accomplished by analyzing lexical items into their component parts (a lexical decomposition of sorts). The value of a semantic dimension (range of meaning) may be represented by means of binary contrast—that is, the presence (+) or absence (−) of a feature—or simply by opposite characteristics of a dimension. Accordingly, if gender and relative age were among the semantic dimensions selected to analyze kinship terms, grandmother would be female + and old +, whereas grandson would be female − and old − (or, alternatively, grandson would be male + and young +, whereas grandmother would be male − and young −), or the two kin terms would be contrasted simply as female against male and old against young.

Some anthropologists who employ componential analysis seek to discover psychological reality—that is, their descriptions are intended to reflect the folk taxonomies used by the members of the society being studied.

Frake took essentially this approach in his account of the diagnosis of disease among the Subanun. Other anthropologists are more concerned with producing the most efficient and elegant formal account possible rather than trying to discover the cognitive world of the people they study. Fred W. Householder Jr. (1913–1994) referred to a somewhat parallel difference in attitudes toward linguistic analysis as the "God's truth" position and the "hocus-pocus" position, depending on whether the linguist (or, by extension, the anthropologist) believes that the task is to discover the inherent structure in a language or a culture (God's truth position) or that the task is only to impose on the mass of available information some kind of structure that does not conflict with the data at hand (hocus-pocus position; Householder 1952:260).

To discuss the method of componential analysis in detail is beyond the scope of this book, but a few examples are in order. In American kinship terminology, the gender (or sex) of the speaker is never a distinctive variable (component). Whether male or female, the speaker refers to individual kin as *my sister, my brother, my nephew, my niece,* and the like. By contrast, in the kinship terminology of the Arapaho, the gender of the speaker is a distinctive variable in the case of certain kin: The term *neíhʔe* 'my son' is used by a man to refer not only to his own son but also to his brother's son and to certain other kinsmen, but not to his sister's son, who is instead referred to as *néθeʔéθe* 'my nephew.' In contrast, *neíhʔe* 'my son' is used by a woman to refer not only to her own son but also to her sister's son and to certain other kinsmen, but not to her brother's son, who is referred to as *néθeʔéθe* 'my nephew.' Similarly, *neyóo* 'my brother-in-law' is used only by men and *notóʔu* 'my sister-in-law' only by women, and the term *neiθébi,* used by both women and men, is best glossed in English as 'my sibling-in-law of the opposite gender,' that is, as 'my sister-in-law' when used by a man and as 'my brother-in-law' when used by a woman.

Another example: In American kinship terminology, on the one hand, the term *cousin,* whether it refers to the child of one's uncle or aunt or someone descended from a grandparent or more distant relative, is used regardless of whether the individual spoken of is male or female. In other words, gender is not a distinctive component of cousin terminology in English. In Czech kinship terminology, on the other hand, a female cousin is terminologically distinguished from a male cousin, the former being referred to as *sestřenice* and the latter as *bratranec.*

Applying componential analysis to an English terminological set may reveal little if anything that native speakers do not already know, at least implicitly. But to discover the underlying semantic differences among the terms of domains from other cultures helps anthropologists determine what is culturally significant in those societies and how their members structure their experience linguistically.

It would be incorrect to think that ethnoscientists (or New Ethnographers) were the first cultural anthropologists to insist on the importance of discovering how a culture is seen from the perspective of the society's members. Such a view has had a long tradition in American anthropology. Nevertheless, the practitioners of these recent approaches have made some valuable contributions to the study of culture; they have elicited helpful data by making the language of those they study a rich source of information rather than merely the means of communicating. At the same time, however, it must be mentioned that the peak of ethnoscientific research was reached in the 1960s. The main shortcoming of the ethnoscientific method is that its emphasis on understanding culture through language results in the neglect of nonverbal behavior and those aspects of culture that lie outside the domains accessible through terminological sets.

Summary and Conclusions

There is no question that languages differ—if only superficially, as contemporary linguists would add. They differ in sounds, in structure (grammar), and in the ways their vocabularies classify the conceptual world of those who speak them. But despite the differences among the lexical systems of different languages, most linguists would agree that any nontechnical utterance can be expressed with reasonable accuracy in any language, although usually not on a word-by-word basis. When it comes to technical subjects, some languages have highly specialized terminologies that may be lacking in others—one could hardly expect to give a report on quantum chromodynamics in, say, Hopi. Yet Hopi has specialized areas in its lexicon that are not matched in English. In general, those aspects of any culture that are worked out in some detail receive corresponding attention in the vocabulary of the language in order for the speakers of the language to be able to discuss them with ease and accuracy.

Whorf concerned himself with the important question of language-culture dependency in several of his papers, but he overstated his case. Some of his evidence is anecdotal, that is, short and amusing but not necessarily representative of a specific language taken as a whole. One may also wonder how reliable for the purposes of Whorf's illustrations was his Hopi informant, who resided in New York City and must have been nearly or fully bilingual: If the perception of one's environment is affected by the particular language one speaks, then fluency in both Hopi and English might obscure the contrast between the two. According to Whorf, "the Hopi language contains no reference to TIME, either explicit or implicit" (Whorf 1950:67). Hopi may indeed not have tenses in the same sense that English has (as in *I go, I went, I will go, I had gone,* and so on), but speakers of Hopi are able to refer to the time at or during which an action takes place by using morphemes or words that pertain to such time references as "today, late morning, noon, last night, towards evening, yesterday, tomorrow, day after day, once in a while, from tomorrow on until the next day" and "next year" (Voegelin and Voegelin 1957:24).

Noting that speakers of a particular language might neglect objects or events that speakers of another language normally take into account, John B. Carroll restated the hypothesis of linguistic relativity and determinism in a more modest but acceptable form: "Insofar as languages differ in the ways they encode objective experience, language users tend to sort out and distinguish experiences differently according to the categories provided by their respective languages. These cognitions will tend to have certain effects on behavior" (Carroll 1963:12; for his examples, see Box 3.3).

The relationship between language and culture has been put to methodological use by the proponents of cognitive anthropology, who believe that even minute structural distinctions in a culture are likely to be encoded in the vocabulary of the corresponding language. No one questions the contribution these ethnoscientists have made to a better understanding of the peoples they have studied, but their insightful research has invariably been limited to particular domains of culture.

Nonverbal Communication

By Walid A. Afifi
Pennsylvania State University

Sayings that attest to the importance of nonverbal communication in our lives vary from "A picture is a worth 1,000 words" to "Appearances are deceiving." But what are we talking about when discussing nonverbal elements of communication? Many people think of "body language" when discussing nonverbal messages. However, thinking of nonverbal only as body language ignores several important elements. For our purposes, nonverbal communication will be defined as "those behaviors other than words themselves that form a socially shared coding system" (Burgoon, 1994, p. 231). Two primary aspects of this definition are worth noting: First, it includes a wide variety of behaviors besides "body language." Second, it assumes people recognize the meaning of these behaviors within their social or cultural setting. These two aspects of nonverbal will become very clear by the end of this selection.

Scholars often claim that nonverbal messages are more important than verbal ones (see Burgoon, Buller, & Woodall, 1996). Their claim is based on several arguments. First, studies suggest that nonverbal messages make up a majority of the meaning of a message (see Andersen, 1999). Think of the times you've watched people from a distance, not being able to hear what they're saying but being able to see them. Based only on their nonverbal messages, you are able to understand a lot about their relationship and their interaction. You may be able to determine whether they are friends or dating partners, whether they are having a pleasant or unpleasant interaction, and whether they are in a hurry or not; all these interpretations occur without hearing a word. Although the importance of nonverbal messages for the meaning of an interaction varies, they play

COMMUNICATION & MEDIA STUDIES
COLLECTION

at least some role in every interaction. Second, nonverbal communication is omnipresent. In other words, every communication act includes a nonverbal component; nonverbal behavior is part of every communicative message. From how we say something to what we do and how we look when saying it, nonverbal messages are constant influences on our interpretation of what others are communicating to us. Third, there are nonverbal signals that are understood cross-culturally. Unlike verbal messages, which carry meaning strictly within the relevant language culture, nonverbal messages can be used as a communication tool among individuals from vastly different language cultures. For example, individuals from a wide variety of cultures recognize smiles to indicate happiness or recognize hunger from the act of putting fingers to your mouth. Finally, nonverbal messages are trusted over verbal, messages when those two channels of information conflict. Because we (somewhat erroneously) believe that nonverbal actions are more subconscious than verbal messages, we tend to believe the nonverbal over the verbal. All these arguments for the importance of nonverbal messages will be defended by the end of this selection.

In part because nonverbal behaviors are an important aspect of every communication message, this selection will be organized somewhat differently than some others in this book. Rather than focus on one theory or one concept, the primary goal of this selection is to make you aware of the many aspects of our behavior that fall under the rubric of nonverbal communication. As part, of that goal, several theories will be briefly reviewed when they seem to apply particularly well to a type or function of nonverbal behavior. However, it is important to keep in mind that all theories described in this book are behaviorally represented through nonverbal messages; the theories noted in this selection are simply a small sampling of the many theories that could be used as illustrations of nonverbal messages "in action."

The selection is divided into roughly two sections. The first section overviews the various types of nonverbal messages (i.e., codes), starting with body movements (i.e., kinesics) and ending with physical aspects of the environment that affect behavior (i.e., artifacts). You should have a good sense for the breadth and importance of nonverbal communication by the end of that section. The next part of the selection overviews the ways we use nonverbal messages (i.e., functions). Nonverbal messages can be used to accomplish a wide variety of outcomes, from allowing the smooth flow of an interaction to deceiving others. Theories will be applied throughout the selection but will be concentrated in the discussion of functions.

NONVERBAL CODES

As noted earlier, nonverbal behaviors include a lot more than "body language." Although scholars disagree on the exact number, there are seven codes (or categories) of nonverbal behavior that will be reviewed in this selection: kinesics, haptics, proxemics, physical appearance, vocalics, chronemics, and artifacts. I will define each code in turn and discuss some of the associated behaviors.

Kinesics

What do you think of when you ponder nonverbal behavior? If you're like many people who have not studied nonverbal communication, you think of gestures, body movements, eye contact and the like. In other words, you think of only one of the seven codes that exist to describe nonverbal behavior. The kinesic code includes almost all behaviors that most people believe make up nonverbal ways of expression, including gestures, eye contact, and body position. Burgoon et al. (1996) defined kinesics as referring to "all forms of body movement, excluding physical contact with another" (p. 41). As you can imagine, these movements number in the hundreds of thousands, but there are classifications of kinesic activity that help us better place the movements into discrete categories. Perhaps the most, widely used is Ekman and Friesen's (1969) distinction among emblems, illustrators, regulators, affect displays, and adaptors. This typology describes kinesic behaviors according to their intended purpose.

Emblems are body movements that carry meaning in and of themselves. Emblems stand alone, without verbal accompaniment, and still convey a clear message to the recipients. Common examples of emblems include a thumbs-up gesture, "flipping someone the bird," using the thumb and index finger to signal "OK," and moving two fingers across your throat to signal someone to stop. In fact, sports are often an arena where celebratory emblems are displayed or become a part of our cultural fabric. An example is the "raise the roof" signal, an emblem signaling celebration that quickly caught on among sports players and is now understood relatively widely in this culture. The historical development of emblem form and meaning is fascinating and varies dramatically from culture to culture. Certain cultures (e.g., Italy, France, Egypt) rely on emblems for the delivery of meaning much more so than other cultures, but all cultures include emblems as part of their communication channel.

Unlike emblems, *illustrators* do not carry meaning without verbal accompaniment. Instead, illustrators are body movements that help receivers interpret and better attend to what is being said verbally. The sort of "nonsense" hand gestures that often accompany a person's speech, especially when speaking publicly, are one form of illustrators. Yet these "nonsense" gestures actually serve important functions: They help focus the receiver's attention on what is being said, they help the sender emphasize a part of his or her speech, they help the sender clarify what is being said, and so on. A father who scolds his child may accentuate the seriousness of the message by waving a finger in the youngster's face, or a traveler may clarify a description of her lost luggage by drawing a "picture" of its shape in the air as she describes it; these are simply two examples of how we use illustrators to assist the verbal component.

Regulators are body movements that are employed to help guide conversations. They may be used to help signal a desire to speak, or a desire not to be called on, or to communicate to the speaker that you are or are not listening. Perhaps the most common example of a regulator is the head nod. We consistently use head nods during conversation to signal to speakers that we are listening, a sign that encourages them to continue. Other behaviors that function as regulators of our conversation include maintaining eye contact, turning our bodies toward or away from the speaker, and looking at our watch.

Adaptors are body movements that "satisfy physical or psychological needs" (Burgoon et al., 1996, p. 42). These movements are rarely intended to communicate anything, but they are good signals of the sender's physiological and psychological state. There are three categories of adaptors: self-adaptors, alter-directed adaptors, and object adaptors. *Self-*adaptors are movements that people direct toward themselves or their bodies; examples include biting fingernails, sucking on a thumb, repeatedly tapping a foot, adjusting a collar, and vigorously rubbing an arm to increase warmth. *Alter-directed* adaptors include the same sorts of behaviors found among self-adaptors except that they are movements people direct to the bodies of others; examples include scratching a friend's back itch, caressing a partner's hair, adjusting a partner's collar, or dusting off a friend's rarely worn jacket. Alter-directed adaptors often signal to the target person or to the audience the level of attachment between the individuals in the exchange. *Object* adaptors are movements that involve attention to an object; common examples include biting on a pen, holding a (sometimes unlit) cigar, or circling the edge of a cup with a finger.

Finally, *affect* displays are body movements that express emotion without the use of touch. Like emblems, affect displays often do not require verbal accompaniment for understanding. In fact, several studies have shown that people across cultures understand certain nonverbal facial expressions as reflective of particular emotions (see Ekman & Oster, 1979; Izard, 1977). By manipulating three facial regions (the eyes and eyelids, the eyebrows and forehead, and the mouth and cheeks), people can create affect displays that are recognizable world wide. For example, sadness is expressed by somewhat constricting the eyes and forehead region, while flattening the cheeks and displaying a slight downward curvature of the mouth.

Although Ekman and Friesen's category system captures most gestural movements, it doesn't describe all kinesic behaviors. Perhaps most importantly, it gives short shrift to the types and functions of eye contact. A popular saying exults that "the eyes are the window to the soul" Research on eye behavior supports these beliefs. Eye contact has been shown to vary dramatically in form and to differ significantly in function (for review, see Gramet, 1983). It clearly occupies a central place as a channel for message transmission and will emerge in studies reviewed throughout the selection.

One concept that captures several aspects of our kinesic activity and has received considerable research attention is *immediacy*. Included as part of the cluster of immediacy behaviors are the kinesic behaviors of eye contact, body orientation (i.e., the degree to which the interactant's body is oriented toward or away from the other), body lean (i.e., the degree to which the person's body is leaning forward or back), head nods, interpersonal distance (part of the proxemic code), and touch (part of the haptic code). Together, this set of behaviors communicates the degree to which an individual is involved in the interaction. Studies have shown that changes in immediacy behavior strongly affect the outcome of interactions, from having important consequences for the success of job interviews to influencing the attentiveness of patients during interactions with physicians (Buller & Street, 1992; Forbes & Jackson, 1980).

Haptics

A second general category of nonverbal behavior is labeled haptics and refers to all aspects of touch. Perhaps no other code has stronger communicative potential than does touch. Research has shown that individuals place considerable weight on the meaning of touch and that touch has important developmental benefits (see Jones & Yarbrough, 1985). In fact, several studies have found that the absence of touch from parents has serious consequences for children's growth (for review, see Montagu, 1978). Close, physical contact with the caregiver seems to give children the critical sense of protection and security that cannot be attained in other ways. As such, it is not surprising that holding babies is often the behavior that can best calm them and that physicians spend some time explaining baby-holding techniques to new parents.

Touch does not only play an important role during early childhood, it is a critical part of our life as we age as well (see Barnard & Brazelton, 1990). Indeed, the elderly may be most affected by the harmful consequences of touch deprivation (see Montagu, 1978). When lifelong partners pass away, the elderly often lose the one source of affectionate touch on which they have relied for much of their lives. Although certain associations (e.g., long-time neighbors, family members) may help alleviate some potential for loneliness, it is unlikely that their needs for touch will be fully satisfied by these connections.

As with kinesics, haptic behaviors may be classified in multiple ways, some focused on type and others focused on function. Among the type of haptics discussed, scholars have distinguished between the form of touch and its qualities. On the one hand, the form of the touch sends an important communicative message. For example, we could easily separate nuzzles from kisses, rubs from hugs, pokes from hits, pushes from punches, and so on. In fact, Morris (1971) observed 457 different types of touch that seemed to signal the presence of a relationship between the parties. He then categorized the touches into 14 categories of what he labeled tie signs. Among these tie signs are hand-holding, patting, arm-linking, several types of embraces, and kissing. Afifi and Johnson (1999) compared dating partners and male–female friends in their use of these tie signs in college bars. Interestingly, they found more similarities than differences in the frequency that the tie signs were used across the two relationship types. Specifically, all types of tie signs were used in both dating relationships and friendships. However, daters were more likely than friends to lean against one another, use shoulder and waist embraces, and to kiss. Given the relative similarity between daters and friends of the opposite sex in their use of tie signs in bars, it is no wonder that young adults often report confusion about the status of their cross-sex friendships (see Monsour, 2002). Although not assessed by Afifi and Johnson, qualities of the touch, such as the duration and intensity (e.g., amount of pressure) undoubtedly play an important role in their meaning. Both friends and daters may exchange kisses, but a "peck" is different from a longer and more intense kiss. Similarly, a hug can differ dramatically in duration and intensity, aspects that are much more meaningful than simply recognizing that a hug occurred. In other words, both the type of touch and its characteristics serve to define its meaning and affect its outcome.

A final way that touches have been categorized is by their intended purpose. Heslin (as cited in Andersen, 1999) differentiated between five purposes of touch, each increasing in intimacy. *Functional/professional* touches have a specific task-related purpose. They are considered the least intimate forms of touch. Although the type and quality of touch may be considered intimate in other contexts, the receiver of the touch recognizes the function of the touch as being necessary for the task at hand. For example, physicians sometimes touch us in highly intimate areas, but the touch is not considered an intimate one because its function is recognized as being part of the required task of health maintenance. The next function of touch is labeled *Social/polite* and is characterized by relatively formal touches that accompany greetings and departures. A common example of social/polite touches is the handshake. Although other cultures utilize more intimate sorts of greetings (e.g., kisses), the context again defines the otherwise intimate touch as functioning as a polite expression rather than an intimate one. *Friendship/warmth* touches are the sort typically exchanged between friends. The formality of social/polite touches is gone and replaced with qualities of touch that signal increased bondedness. Examples of friendship/warmth touches include partial embraces, full embraces, and pats. *Love/intimacy* touches function to signal elevated closeness and are less likely to be enacted publicly. Touches such as a kiss or a prolonged embrace may serve the love/intimacy function. Finally, touches that function to increase sexual arousal are the most intimate types of touch. The sort of touch that occurs during sexual activity is the most common example of this function. In sum, rather than consider touches as differing by type, this category scheme focuses on their function. The same type of touch (e.g., a backrub) may serve a functional/professional purpose when conducted by a masseuse or sports therapist but act to increase sexual arousal when conducted by a romantic partner. Unfortunately, the existing categorization schemes do not adequately capture the many types of more harmful touches or the more negative purposes of touch (e.g., to harm, to intimidate).

Proxemics

The proxemic category of nonverbal behavior captures the way we use space. From analyses of overpopulation in certain nations, to the impact of small dorm room space, to overcrowding in prisons, studies consistently show harmful, effects of limited space. Although cultures differ dramatically in the amount of space that is typically given, we are all born with at least minimum needs for space. Threatening those space needs, especially for prolonged periods, produces high stress that, in turn, affects our psyche and behavior dramatically (see Edwards, Fuller, Vorakitphokatorn, & Sermsri, 1994). It is not surprising then, that confinement in a very small and dark room is commonly used as a method of torture (www.amnesty.org) and that such torture has devastating psychological impact. Indeed, Lester (1990) found an increase in suicide rates associated with overcrowding in prisons. Donoghue (1992) reported overcrowding as a factor contributing to stress among teenagers in the Virgin Islands. Curiously, he noted that sexual activity (sometimes leading to pregnancy) was one of consequences. Also, Gress and Heft (1998) showed that, the number of roommates in college dorms negatively affected the residents both emotionally and behaviorally. One way in which this need for space is expressed is through our behavior around territories.

Territories are physically fixed areas that one or more individuals defend as their own (Altman, 1975). To maintain the spatial needs provided by these territories, we set up markers so that others know the territory's boundaries (Buslig, 1999). For example, students may put books on the seat next to them to ensure that the seat is not taken, or spread their belongings across a wide area of a table to indicate the area as their own. Fences around property, "Keep Away" and "Do Not Disturb" signs, and markers around beach blankets are other common examples of signaling territory. Interestingly, locations where space is limited are particularly prone to markers of territory. Roommates often send very clear signals about the boundaries of their territory by hanging unique posters or signs that mark the area as their own. The importance of these territories to our well being is evident in the way individuals react to their violation. Intrusions into territory have been shown to produce elevated stress, and behavioral responses varying from withdrawal to confrontation (for review, see Lyman & Scott, 1967).

Unlike territories, which are fixed physical entities, *personal space* is a proxemic-based need that moves along with the individual. It is an "invisible bubble" that expands and shrinks according to context, but follows each individual, protecting him or her from physical threats (Hall, 1966). Violation of that personal space bubble produces responses similar to those found for the violation of territory. In North America, typical personal space has a circumference of approximately 3 ft, but the size of that space varies dramatically and is influenced by a variety of factors, from the target of your conversation to its location (see Burgoon et al., 1996). For example, you would likely feel much more uncomfortable standing 2 ft away from someone in a relatively empty elevator than in a crowded elevator. We recognize that certain contexts necessitate the temporary violation of our personal space, but we also keenly anticipate extracting ourselves from that context and restoring the security that comes with maintaining those personal space needs. A behavior that is commonly used both to violate personal space and restore it is eye contact. Have you ever felt that your personal space has been violated by someone simply staring at you, even from a distance? Many people report such a sensation. Have you ever looked away from someone who got too close physically? That sort of behavior is a common response to the violation of personal space in elevators, for example (see Rivano-Fischer, 1988).

Physical Appearance

The physical appearance category of nonverbal behavior includes all aspects related to the way we look, from our body type, to body adornments (e.g., tattoos, rings), to what we wear. Perhaps no other category of nonverbal behavior has a stronger effect on initial impressions than our physical appearance. The two general types of physical appearance that will be addressed in this selection are body type and attire.

Researchers have identified three general body types: ectomorphs, mesomorphs, and endomorphs (see Burgoon et al., 1996). *Ectomorphic* bodies are characterized by thin bone structures and lean bodies, *mesomorphic* bodies have strong bone structures, are typically muscular and athletic, and *endomorphic* bodies have large bone structures, and are typically heavy-set and somewhat rounded. An individual's body type is partly based on genetic elements such as bone structures and partly based on other elements such as diet and levels of activity. Regardless of the source of one's body structure or the degree to which it has any actual effect on behavior, research has clearly shown that people have strong impressions of others based on their body type. Specifically, ectomorphs are perceived to be timid, clumsy, and anxious, but also intelligent; mesomorphs are seen as outgoing, social, and strong; and endomorphs are considered lazy, jolly, and relatively unintelligent (Burgoon et al., 1996). Some factors may affect these perceptions. For example, women ectomorphs and male mesomorphs may be perceived more favorably than their other-sex counterparts. Unfortunately, research has not sufficiently addressed these possibilities. However, one pattern that has been well documented is that, regardless of actual body size, women are more likely than men to perceive their bodies negatively (for review, see Cash & Pruzinsky, 1990). Such "body image disturbances" have devastating consequences, affecting self-esteem, leading to eating disorders, and even increasing suicide rates (e.g., Phillips, 1999; Stice, Hayward,

Cameron, Killen, & Taylor, 2000). Why do many women have such dislike for their bodies? Although the answer to this question is not at all simple, it is undoubtedly based, at least in part, on a cultural obsession with images of overly thin women (see Botta, 1999).

However, body shape is not the only aspect of physical appearance that has been shown to affect people's perceptions of us. Another strong influence on perceptions is height. Taller men and women are more likely to be seen as competent, dominant, and intelligent (see Boyson, Pryor, & Butler, 1999). Interestingly, however, the advantage of height does not extend to perceptions of women's attractiveness. Instead, shorter women are perceived as more attractive and date more frequently than taller women (Sheppard & Strathman, 1989). Men and women who fall well above or below this preferred standard encounter lifelong difficulties, including a diminished likelihood of relational success and struggles with perceptions of credibility across a wide range of evaluative contexts (see Martel & Biller, 1987). To combat these perceptions, .short people sometimes change their environment to hide their height. For example, Robert Reich, who served on three presidential administrations and is under 5 ft tall, would speak behind a podium and use a step stool, making media viewers unaware of his short stature.

One explanation for the strong perceptions associated with body type and height comes from Evolutionary Theory. Evolutionary theorists (otherwise called sociobiologists) argue that our attraction to others is based in large part on our perceptions of their genetic makeup (see Buss, 1994). They suggest that, much like other mammals, the strongest members of our species receive the greatest attention and are considered the most attractive. For us, signs of health, wealth, and intelligence are the primary determinants of "strength." As such, it is not surprising to these scholars that people's body type (which may be associated with health) and height (which often translates to physical superiority) affect their life success.

Finally, the clothes we wear are a part of our physical appearance that also affects people's perceptions of us. The clothes we wear strongly influence perceptions of credibility, status, attractiveness, competence, and likability (e.g., Kaiser, 1997). This should come as no surprise to anyone who has seen students proudly display their *Abercrombie & Fitch* shirts, observed the respect often afforded to those wearing their military uniforms, or shook their head in frustration at someone who leaves for an interview in completely disheveled clothes. Indeed, individuals wearing formal clothes are seen as more credible and more persuasive than those wearing informal clothes, affecting their success across a range of interaction contexts, from job interviews to dates. Other aspects of physical appearance that relate to people's judgments include tattoos, rings, and hair styles, in sum, studies unequivocally demonstrate that physical appearance, both things under individuals' control (e.g., attire) and those not (e.g., height), strongly influence perceptions.

Vocalics

Vocalics, a category that people sometimes have difficulty recognizing as a nonverbal component, reflect all aspects of the voice, including loudness, pitch, accent, rate of speech, length of pauses between speech, and tone, among many others. Vocalic elements carry much of the meaning of a message and communicate a lot about the sender. Its importance can be reflected by a simple exercise. Try saying the same words (e.g., "Come over here") with slightly different vocalic qualities. Depending on how we say these words, we could communicate anger, passion, sadness, love, or a variety of other emotions. Indeed, studies have shown that we make relatively accurate judgments about a person's sex, age, height, and cultural background based on vocal cues alone (see Argyle, 1988). Like many of the codes discussed so far, vocalic elements also affect perceptions of attractiveness and competence (Semic, 1999). Deeper voices among men, like that of Barry White for example, are considered sexual and romantic, whereas high-pitched voices among men are considered feminine and weak. Other vocal qualities such as accent and speech rate are also associated with intelligence. For example, certain accents (e.g., British accents) may be considered sophisticated whereas others may not (e.g., thick Boston accents). This difference in the attractiveness of accents is illustrated in the movie *My Fair Lady* which is based on the premise that individuals sometimes must change their accent to affect judgments of their credibility.

One theory that has been applied to understand vocalic shifts is Communication Accommodation Theory (CAA, see chap. 16, this volume). Central to CAA is the belief that we converge our speech toward the style of individuals with whom we want to be associated and diverge away from that of individuals with whom we do not want association (see Giles, Mulac. Bradac, & Johnson, 1987). Examples of this behavior can be found across a wide range of contexts, including interactions between individuals of different ages (e.g., adults and the elderly), individuals from different cultures, individuals with different levels of status, even individuals of different sexes (see Gallois, Giles, Jones, Cargile, & Ota, 1995). So, if you were from the eastern United States and were to spend considerable time in the South, you would likely develop somewhat of a Southern accent, at least when around your friends from the South. That accent accommodation is a way of signaling connectedness with the South. Not surprisingly, the degree to which you are willing to accommodate others in your language has also been shown to significantly affect their perceptions of you. Failure to accommodate your vocalic patterns to others implicitly signals to them that you are not interested in joining their cultural group. On the other hand, a willingness to accommodate communicates attraction.

Chronemics and Artifacts

Chronemics and artifacts are the last two categories of nonverbal behavior that we will discuss in this selection. Rarely considered when discussing nonverbal messages, these codes nevertheless play a strong role in our interactions. The chronemic code captures our use and perception of time, including (among other things) our perception of the "appropriate" duration of an event, the number of things we do at once, the importance of punctuality, our use of time in our language, and the desired sequencing of events (Andersen, 1999). The North American culture is preoccupied with the notion of time; life is fast-paced and individuals are seemingly always struggling against time constraints. Two hours seems to be the maximum time that one expects to allot for entertainment or food events; movies are typically 2 hr or less, plays may go 3 hr but will have a prolonged recess to affect the perception of time, and quests often start getting anxious when meals take longer than 2 hr. Other countries differ dramatically from this North American norm. Although we rarely think of these time norms, they become very evident when we visit other countries. For example, Mediterranean countries often take 3 to 4 hr for a meal, making it as much as a social event as it is time for nourishment. This selection will focus on three chronemic elements: duration, punctuality, and the distinction between polychronism and monochronism.

The expectations surrounding event duration are captured in part by the example provided previously. For every event or interaction, we have culturally and socially based expectations about its duration (Gonzalez & Zimbardo, 1999). Whether it be the amount of time a professor spends in an office meeting with a student, the amount of time set aside for a lunch date, or the amount of time before contact is made following a successful first date, these expectations strongly affect our perceptions of others' competence or attractiveness. Imagine if you had strong expectations that someone not call you back until 2 or 3 days after a first date but the person calls you within minutes after dropping you off. That violation of your chronemic expectations would undoubtedly affect your perceptions of him or her. In a similar vein, perceptions associated with punctuality vary according to the context and have important consequences. Punctuality is held with relatively high esteem in the North American culture, especially for more formal engagements. Arriving late to an interview, even if 5 min, is considered inexcusable, but 5 min late for a lunch date may be acceptable. However, even informal occasions have relatively strict punctuality expectations; arriving 30 min late for a lunch date is not appropriate, for example. In other cultures, however, there is a recognition that the time set for an appointment is rarely adhered to, and expectations are that the appointment may begin 30 to 45 min following the originally set appointment time. Failing to meet these culturally and contextually driven expectations have important implications for assessments of individuals (see Burgoon & Hale, 1988).

A final concept related to chronemics that will be considered in this selection is the distinction between polychronism and monochronism (Hall & Hall 1999). Polychronism reflects the act of doing multiple activities at once, whereas monochronism characterizes a focus on one activity at a time. For example, interacting with someone while you are cleaning your apartment, or watching TV while talking to someone reflects polychronistic behavior. Although sometimes necessary, such behavior is often considered a reflection of (dis)interest in the conversation. Of course, certain careers (e.g., secretarial work, CEOs) require that individuals are adept at polychronistic activity, and some cultures consider polychronism a sign of importance, so monochronism is not universally preferred.

The final nonverbal code is *artifacts,* a category that includes "the physical objects and environmental attributes that communicate directly, define the communication context, or guide social behavior in some way" (Burgoon et al., 1996, p. 109). Hall (1966) classified artifacts into two main types: fixed-feature elements and semifixed-feature elements. Fixed features include aspects of our surroundings that are not easily movable and are unlikely to change. Among these features is the structure of our surroundings, including the architectural style, the number and size of windows, and the amount of space available. Studies have shown that such architectural features directly impact the sort of communication that occurs (see Sundstrom, Bell, Busby, & Asmus, 1996). For instance, people who work in small cubicles are much less productive and less satisfied than people who work in their own office space, especially when the office space includes windows. Semifixed features are defined as aspects of our surroundings that are somewhat easily movable. Examples include rugs, paintings, wall color, the amount of lighting, and the temperature, among others. Considerable evidence suggests that these features also strongly affect both psychological health and communication outcome (for review; see Sundstrom et al., 1996). For example, research has shown that the semifixed aspects of a hospital affect the speed of patient recovery (Gross, Sasson, Zarhy, & Zohar, 1998).

In sum, nonverbal messages affect our interactions in hundreds of ways, from movement in our face, to our body posture, our gestures, the space between us, the ways we touch, the intonations in our voice, the way we use time, and the surroundings in which we find ourselves. Together, these nonverbal features inescapably guide the way we act and the outcome of our interactions. However, noting the population of nonverbal message types is only part of the equation. Each of these nonverbal behaviors can serve a variety of functions or purposes.

FUNCTIONS OF NONVERBAL CODES

There are three assumptions about nonverbal behavior that shape the research reviewed in the remainder of this selection (for review, see Cappella & Street, 1985). First, all behavior is motivated by particular goals. In other words, all behavior is functional in some way. You gesture to someone with a specific purpose in mind, you look at someone to get his attention, you touch someone to let her know you're here, you yell at someone to communicate your anger, and so on. Second, each function or purpose can be achieved in multiple ways. For instance, you are not limited to only one way that you can show affection to people. You may hug them, kiss them, hold their hand, or take them out to a fancy restaurant. The third assumption related to this perspective on nonverbal messages is that a single behavior can serve multiple functions. For example, a hug can show someone you care, while simultaneously signaling to others that you and the recipient of the hug are in a committed relationship. These three assumptions are an inherent part of almost all studies of nonverbal communication and guide our understanding of nonverbal messages and their use.

Although scholars disagree on the exact number of functions served by nonverbal behaviors, there are six functions that seem to emerge in most discussions on this issue and that will be highlighted in this selection. These six functions are (a) structuring and regulating interaction, (b) creating and managing identities, (c) communicating emotions, (d) defining and managing relationships, (e) influencing others, and (f) deceiving others.

Structuring and Regulating Interaction

Each of the nonverbal codes serves to shape the quality of the interactions in which we find ourselves. By so doing, they structure and regulate these encounters. For example, Robinson's (1998) analysis of physician–patient interaction reveals the way in which the kinesic behaviors of eye gaze and body orientation signal to patients the physician's willingness to begin the interaction. Patients learn to stay silent until the physician kinesically signals that he or she is ready to start the interaction. Indeed, as noted earlier, many studies of immediacy reach similar conclusions, with varying levels of nonverbal involvement strongly affecting the quality of the interaction. Research on our use of vocalics also demonstrates the many ways that we nonverbally structure interactions. Conversations are typically considered a series of turns at talk. Each turn is requested, given, and ended in subtle, but clearly understood, nonverbal ways. For example, turns at talk are requested by such behaviors as establishing eye contact with the speaker, abruptly and noticeably inhaling a short breath, and starting to gesture toward the speaker (Wiemann & Knapp, 1975). In contrast, we communicate that our turn is ending by subtly changing the rhythm, loudness, and pitch of our voice (Boomer, 1978). In another interesting study on the potential of nonverbal message to structure interactions, Eaves and Leathers (1991) compared the physical layouts of McDonald's and Burger King to determine whether they affected interactions. Their study demonstrated that customers at McDonalds showed considerably higher levels of nonverbal involvement than did Burger King customers. Given these differences within two relatively similar fast-food chains, you can imagine how more noticeable differences in the level of restaurant formality affect our interactions.

One of the clearest signs that nonverbal behavior serves to structure the flow of interactions comes from examining how people adapt behavior during interaction.

Indeed, a long history of research has shown that we react and adapt to one another's nonverbal expressions during interaction (for review, see Burgoon, Stem, & Dillman, 1995). Interaction Adaptation Theory (Burgoon, Stern, & Dillman, 1995) argues that people carry certain nonverbal needs for affiliation, recognize societal expectations for levels of affiliation, and have preferences for particular levels of affiliation from each interaction partner. The levels of these components differ in each context. For example, you may be may upset 1 day and feel the *need* for some autonomy. You *expect* your roommate to greet you and welcome you home. But, your *preference* is that your roommate not interact with you at all for the next few hours. The combination of these three elements produces what is called the *Interaction Position,* a concept that reflects the amount of distance you anticipate from your roommate. The argument in this theory is that your needs and preferences act together with your general social expectations to affect what behavior you anticipate from your interaction partner (i.e., the interaction position, the IP). In the previous example, the IP may be that your roommate will greet you but recognize your mood and give you some space. This IP is then compared to the actual behavior you receive (A). The theory argues that the comparison between your IP and the A determines how you will nonverbally adapt. If the actual behavior (i.e., the A) is better than you anticipated (i.e., the IP) you will converge toward the person's behavior, but if the actual behavior is worse than you anticipated, you will diverge away from that behavior. This "dance" is perhaps the greatest example of concerning the effect of nonverbal behavior on the structure of interactions.

Creating and Managing Identities and impressions

Another general function of nonverbal messages is to communicate to others the groups to which we belong and to convey particular impressions of ourselves to others. I will review two theoretical frameworks that apply this function. Social Identity Theory (Tajfel & Turner, 1979) focuses on our identity as group members, whereas theoretical work on self-presentation (e.g., Goffman, 1959) focuses on our identity as individuals. Together, these theories help explain the way in which we use nonverbal behavior to achieve the function of creating and managing identities and impressions.

Communicating Group Identities. The main premise of Social Identity Theory is that we develop and maintain our self-concept in large part from the social groups with which we affiliate or to which we belong (e.g., ethnicity, sports team, club membership, department, organizational unit).The importance of these group memberships vary according to context (e.g., the importance of your status as a member of a particular fraternity decreases when with your parents), but each group has specific ways through which membership is communicated to others. So, when group membership becomes relevant, we act in ways that convey to others that we are a part of that group, while also letting people who are not in that group become more aware of their out-group status. Not surprisingly, the primary method of communicating these group memberships is nonverbal.

Take membership in a high school clique, for example. Members of a particular clique are. likely to dress in relatively similar ways (physical appearance), and often have specific gestures they use to greet one another or that they use during conversation (kinesics). Individuals can indicate group membership by standing close to one another or by sitting next to each other at the lunch table (proxemics). Group members may spend a significant portion of their day with others in their clique (chronemics), place indicators of affiliation (signs, letters, etc.) on their lockers (artifacts), and may whisper to one another in the presence of an outgroup member (vocalics). Given the importance of group membership (Worschel & Austin, 1986), it is not surprising that we go to such lengths to identify with groups that we consider enhancing to our self concept.

It is also the case that we distance ourselves nonverbally from groups with which we want to remain independent. A look around college campuses shows a lot of the ways that people accomplish this distancing. Individuals often make little effort to include members of ethnic groups other than their own in their conversations. Eder's (1985) study of behavior among midadolescent females showed that group members communicated distance from group outsiders by avoiding interaction, body contact, or eye contact with nonmembers. Although these are examples of interpersonal ways in which we send group-related identity messages, there are ways in which societies or cultures communicate outgroup status to entire groups. Certainly laws discriminating against where particular cultural groups can gather—let alone eat, sit, or stand—are examples of such societal messages that become translated through nonverbal means. Everything from kinesics gestures (e.g., lack of eye contact) to proxemic decisions (e.g., maintaining large distances) to artifacts (e.g., signs indicating that entrance is prohibited to certain groups) communicate exclusion. For example, laws prohibiting the homeless from loitering in certain parks or communities are violations of public territorial rights that reflect one of many ways through which the homeless are shown their status as a societal "outgroup."

Communicating Individual Identities. Besides communicating our identity as members of particular groups, we also send nonverbal messages that are intended to convey our individual identities. Several theories have been advanced to capture this aspect of our behavior. The labels of these frameworks include Politeness Theory (Brown & Levinson, 1987), the Theory of Self-Identification (Schlenker, Britt, & Pennington, 1996), and Facework (Tracy, 1990). Within each of these theories are such concepts as self presentation, impression management, and identity management. In general, they all refer to the idea that we are motivated by a desire to maintain a positive impression of ourselves in the eyes of others. In other words, we generally want others to see us in a positive light. DePaulo (1992) defined *self-presentation* as "a matter of regulating one's own behavior to create a particular impression on others, of communicating a particular image of oneself to others, or of showing oneself to be a particular kind of person" (p. 205). For many reasons, we often manage our impression in front of others nonverbally (see DePaulo, 1992). For example, Albas and Albas (1988) examined ways in which students reacted after receiving graded exams. They found that individuals who received good grades smiled (kinesics), displayed an open body posture (kinesics), and left their exams open with the grade showing, whereas those who received poor grades displayed a closed body posture (kinesics) and left immediately following the class (chronemics).

The use of nonverbal methods to manage impressions is obviously not limited to students' reactions to exam scores; evidence for other applications can be found across a whole host of contexts. Daly, Hogg, Sacks, Smith, and Zimring (1983) reported that people in early stages of relationships spend more time adjusting their clothes, fixing their hair, and attending to their physical appearance than those in later stages. In a similar vein, Montepare and Vega (1988) showed that women's vocalic cues communicated greater approachability and sincerity, among other characteristics, when talking over the phone with men with whom they had an intimate relationship, as compared to those with whom they had no relationship. Finally, Blanck, Rosenthal, and Cordell (1985) reported that judges were more likely to display nonverbal cues associated with warmth, professionalism, and fairness when facing older, more educated jurors than younger, less educated jurors. In sum, the function of creating and managing identities is a common purpose of our nonverbal activity and involves actions from all codes.

Communicating Emotions

Another common purpose of nonverbal behavior is to communicate emotion. In fact, as noted earlier, the majority of emotion messages are communicated through facial cues (i.e., kinesically). Particularly impressive is the evidence that some of these expressions are recognized cross-culturally. The argument underlying the Universality Hypothesis on emotion expression is that humans are innately equipped to decode certain expressions of emotion (for review, see Ekman, 1978), leading to cross-cultural recognition of these emotions. Initially, several studies supported that claim (e.g., Ekman, 1973; Izard, 1977). However, when researchers improved their studies, they found dramatic differences in individuals" nonverbal responses. To reconcile the differences in the research and to help account for both cultural-specific and universal patterns of expression, Ekman and colleagues developed the Neurocultural Theory of emotion expression (Ekman & Friesen, 1969). The theory argues that there is an element of biological innateness in our expression of emotion that accounts for the consistency across cultures in recognition of emotion expressions. For example, an experience of joy produces an upward curvature of the mouth and lips. However, differences in actual expression of emotion occur across cultures due to (a) cultural differences in the association between events and the experience of particular emotions and (b) culturally learned and context-based rules about the appropriateness of expressing particular emotions (labeled *display rules).* The first of these two factors makes sense once you consider the way that cultures shapes the emotions we experience (for review, see Nussbaum, 2000). For instance, some cultures emphasize individuality and are likely to encourage intense emotional responses to events that threaten individuality, whereas other cultures emphasize the collective and are likely to shape emotional responses accordingly. In other words, the same events are unlikely to produce the same emotions across cultures. However, researchers have devoted much more energy toward understanding the second of these factors: display rules. *Display rules* are defined as "socially learned habits regarding the control of facial appearance that act to intensify, deintensify, mask, or qualify a universal expression of emotion depending on the social circumstance" (Kupperbusch et al., 1999, p. 21).

Studies have shown that infants' emotional expressions abide by cultural, gender, and familial display rules before their first birthday (e.g., Malatesta & Haviland, 1982). These rules are communicated by parents from infancy but reinforced throughout life by the media, family members, peers, and even strangers. Common examples of these display rules are those generally discouraging overt public displays of affection, or those directing people on appropriate methods of emotional expression in movie theatres, funeral homes, classrooms, concerts, and so on. Display rules also direct people regarding the appropriateness of emotion expression in close relationships. Considerable evidence demonstrates that "negative" emotions (e.g., anger, jealousy) are considered inappropriate to express in early stages of relationships (for review, see Aune, 1997). Moreover, studies show the way that these display rules affect our expression of emotion even in our most intimate relationships. For example, Cloven and Roloff (1994) found that one fifth of relational irritations were not expressed in couples at the most advanced relational stages, and Aune, Buller, and Aune (1996) found that positive emotions were considered more appropriate to express than negative emotions, regardless of relationship stage.

Defining and Managing Relationships

Another important function of nonverbal messages is to help people negotiate and express the quality or status of the relationship they have with others. These relational messages vary along five dimensions (see Burgoon & Hale, 1987). Labeled the topoi (themes) of relational communication, the five dimensions along which nonverbal messages can differentially communicate relational qualities are (a) the amount of dominance, (b) the level of intimacy, (c) the degree of composure or arousal, (d) the level of formality, and (e) the degree to which the interaction is focused on task or social elements. Evidence associated with how each of these dimensions is communicated nonverbally will be briefly summarized.

Dominance. Nonverbal messages help indicate the degree to which one member of the interaction is powerful dominant, and controlling. The way in which men and women communicate power nonverbally has been examined frequently, most notably by Henley (1977). Behavior from each nonverbal code can be applied to study how dominance is conveyed (see Burgoon et al., 1996). For example, people communicate dominance by refusing to engage in eye contact (kinesics), by initiating touch (haptics), by arriving late for a meeting (chronemics), by having access to large office space or by displaying awards (artifacts), by demanding large personal space needs or unilaterally changing the amount of space between themselves and their interactants (proxemics), by speaking loudly and in a lower pitch (vocalics), and by emphasizing their body size or dressing in formal attire (physical appearance).

Intimacy: Nonverbal messages help communicate the amount of affection, inclusion, involvement, depth, trust, and similarity there is between interactants. As noted earlier in this selection, several studies have shown the benefits of expressing nonverbal involvement in interactions. Displays such as gestural activity, direct body orientation, forward body lean, and close (but socially acceptable) conversational distance increase the success of job interviews, increase liking, and produce perceptions of personality warmth (Burgoon et al., 1996). Whereas expressing involvement is one method of communicating relational intimacy and interest, more intimate messages are communicated in other ways, such as the use of tie signs and an increase in the frequency and intimacy of touch. Interestingly, the eyes are often the best indicator of attraction (Grumet, 1983). Establishing eye contact is typically the first way individuals communicate attraction and people who are attracted to one another look into each other's eyes more than others do. Also, our pupils involuntarily increase in size when we are talking to someone to whom we are attracted, a fact that, in turn, subconsciously seems to make us more attractive to others (Hess, 1975). In sum, the nonverbal methods for communicating intimacy are numerous.

Composure and Arousal. The degree to which individuals are relaxed and calm in an interaction has also been shown to communicate qualities of their relationship. As a general rule, people in close relationships are more likely to be relaxed around one-another than acquaintances. In fact, people sometimes manipulate their levels of composure to send messages about their comfort in the interaction or the relationship. For example, job candidates or people on first dates usually do their best to hide the amount of anxiety being felt in part because they want to show a level of relational comfort. In other words, we make efforts to appear composed in certainty situations precisely because we know what anxiety communicates about relationships.

Formality. Another way in which individuals can communicate qualities of the relationship is through the degree of casualness conveyed in their nonverbal behavior. Although relatively few studies have examined it, the level of formality, like other dimensions of relationship quality, can be communicated in many different ways. Three common methods of indicating the formality of the relationship are through the formality of the attire, through kinesic rigidity, and through conversational distance (Burgoon, 1991; Burgoon et al., 1996). The more casual the clothing, the more relaxed the body posture, the more frequent the hand gesturing, and the greater the distance between interactants, the greater the perception that the interaction is an informal one. Not surprisingly, studies have shown that the likelihood of communicating formality differs across status and that these differences affect people's perceptions. For example, Lamude and Scudder (1991) reported that upper level managers are more likely to be formal than lower or middle-level managers. Interestingly, research has also shown that college teachers are perceived as more effective when they dress informally (Butler, & Roesel, 1991; Lukavski, Butler, & Harden, 1995), whereas physicians and interview candidates are perceived as less effective when behaving or dressing informally (Burgoon et al., 1987; Gifford Ng, & Wilkinson, 1985).

Task or Social Orientation. Nonverbal messages reflecting the degree to which the interaction is one focused on a task constitute the final dimension through which people communicate qualities of their relationships nonverbally. This dimension is typically communicated through the chronemic code and, again, the desirability of communicating a focus on task is strongly affected by context. On the one hand, managers who focus on task, to the exclusion of relational maintenance behaviors, receive the lowest ratings of satisfaction by subordinates (Lamude, Daniels, & Smilowitz, 1995). On the other hand, teachers whose in-class behavior focuses on task produce better student outcomes (Harris, Rosenthal, & Snodgrass, 1986). In general, the communication of a task orientation has been shown to convey lower levels of relational connectedness than socially oriented messages (Burgoon & Hale, 1987).

Influencing Others

A long history of research has examined the methods we use to attempt to change someone's attitudes or behavior or to strengthen already established attitudes or behaviors (see O'Keefe, 1990). In general studies find that we are most influenced by people who we find attractive (i.e., likeable), credible, or powerful (see O'Keefe, 1990).

Social Attractiveness or Liking. Scholars have shown many ways in which individuals can increase their attractiveness to others. For example, studies demonstrate that establishing eye contact increases the likelihood of influencing others in a wide variety of situations including persuading strangers to give a dime for a phone call, donate to a charity, take pamphlets, or pick up a hitchhiker (for review, see Segrin, 1999). Also, light touching is linked to bigger tips, an increase in petition signings, and a greater willingness to sign up for volunteer work (e.g., Goldman, Kiyohara, & Pfannensteil, 1985). Physical appearance cues also strongly affect perceived attractiveness and the potential to influence others. In one study, a confederate gave the same speech to two different audiences but varied her physical appearance through differences in the messiness of her hair and the fit of her clothes (Mills & Aronson, 1965). Results showed that she was more convincing when she was dressed more neatly. In a similar vein, physically attractive political candidates are more likely to get elected for office and physically attractive defendants are less likely to be found guilty (Mazzella & Feingold, 1994; Sigelman, Thomas, Sigelman, & Ribich, 1986). However, other studies suggest that the advantage of physical attractiveness depends at least somewhat on context. Juhnke, Barmann, Cunningham, and Smith (1987) found that strangers were more willing to give detailed directions to college students who were poorly dressed and asking about the location of a lower status location (i.e., a thrift shop) than students who were well dressed or asking for directions to a higher status location (e.g., the Gap). In sum, physical appearance has repeatedly been shown to be a nonverbal signal that functions to increase or decrease the success of social influence attempts.

Credibility. Besides physical attractiveness, research has shown that our perceptions of someone's credibility affect the degree to which they influence us. The notion of credibility refers to "the judgments made by a perceiver (e.g., a message recipient) concerning the believability of a communicator" (O'Keefe, 1990, pp. 130–131). Kinesic behaviors that are related to perceptions of credibility include eye contact, moderate amounts of gesturing, use of supportive head nods, facial expressiveness, and moderately forward leans, all indicators of conversational immediacy (see Burgoon, Birk, & Pfau, 1990). For example, Badzinski and Pettus (1994) showed that jurors determined a judge's credibility by attending to his or her kinesic behavior. Equipped with this knowledge, many lawyers approach the bench of jurors during opening and closing remarks, establish eye contact with each juror, and use other kinesic behaviors that are known to increase credibility ratings.

Besides kinesic elements, vocalic cues also affect perceptions of credibility. Among the most common findings is that nonfluencies in speech strongly decrease credibility ratings and the potential for successful persuasion. Nonfluencies include pauses in speech (e.g., "Auh," "Aummm"), repetition of "nonsense" words (e.g. "like"), and difficulty in articulation (O'Keefe. 1990). Besides the absence of nonfluencies, credible speakers use more varied intonation, speak more loudly and with more intensity, and talk faster (see Burgoon et al., 1996). But perhaps no other nonverbal code has received more attention for its effect on perceptions of credibility than physical appearance. For example, studies have shown that women who have specific eye shapes, short hair, appear older (although not elderly), wear a moderate amount of makeup, and are conservatively dressed were rated as more credible than their counterparts (Dellinger & Williams, 1997; Rosenberg, Kahn. & Tran, 1991). The final aspect known to increase persuadability is the perceived power of the speaker.

Power, Power will be defined in this selection as a perception that the speaker holds a position of authority. Like most assessments, this perception of authority is primarily established through nonverbal means. Again, perhaps the most common method of affecting perceptions of power is through physical appearance. Attire and physical size go a long way toward establishing a speaker's authority. For example, individuals wearing suits or uniforms, and those standing tall, as opposed to those with a slumped posture, are immediately afforded greater perceptions of power than their counterparts (see Andersen & Bowman, 1999). An extreme example of the effect of physical appearance on the success of influence came from Milgram's (1974) research program on obedience. In his studies, he showed that individuals dressed in lab coats were able to convince research participants to administer what participants believed to be fatal levels of electric shock to others. The result of Milgram's research program starkly demonstrated the degree to which people will obey others who they perceive to hold power positions, a perception primarily guided by nonverbal cues.

Deceiving Others

The last purpose of nonverbal messages that will be reviewed in this selection is to deceive others. Deception is defined as "a message knowingly transmitted by a sender to foster a false belief or conclusion by a receiver" (Buller & Burgoon, 1996, p. 205). Although people assume that most interactions involve truth-telling, some studies suggest that a majority actually involve some element of deception (e.g., O'Hair & Cody, 1994). So, how is it that we get away with so much deception and when is it that we're likely to be caught? The answer to both questions lies in our manipulation of nonverbal behavior.

Interpersonal Deception Theory (Buller & Burgoon, 1996) is a framework that, combines several perspectives to help explain the process of deception in interactions. Although the theory is quite complex, it relies primarily on the idea that deception is an interactive activity and that its detection is a process affected by the behavior of both sender and receiver, as well as contextual and relational factors. In other words, whether you are successful at lying is partly based on your nonverbal cues, but it is also affected by the receiver's behavior, the relationship you have with him or her, and the context surrounding the interaction, among other elements. Given the emphasis of this selection, I will focus on the nonverbal behaviors that have been shown to affect the success of the deceiver.

Research suggests that successful liars are those who maintain eye contact, display a forward body lean, smile, and orient their bodies toward the other person (for review, see Buller & Burgoon, 1994). That is, people who can display elevated levels of immediacy are more likely to get away with a lie (Burgoon, Buller, Dillman, & Walther. 1995). Burgoon and colleagues offer at least two explanations for this finding. First, the high immediacy by receivers may produce an adaptational response by the deceiver—increased immediacy. That response, in turn, makes the deceiver appear honest. So, the receiver's immediacy "pulls" the liar into that behavioral pattern and causes him or her look more honest. Another possibility is that the receiver's immediacy makes the deceiver feel better about the success of his or her deception and lessens the anxiety cues that often "leak" from deceivers. In addition to the previously noted cues, successful liars display vocalic fluency and kinesic composure, while also being generally expressive nonverbally and avoiding extended pause rates during conversation. In contrast, unsuccessful liars "leak" their anxiety nonverbally through heightened pitch, greater nonfluencies, negative expressions, nervous behaviors, and generally lowered immediacy levels (for review, see Burgoon, Buller, & Guerrero, 1995).

Although the research on deception is vast and includes much more detailed analysis of factors affecting deception success and failure, among other aspects of the deception episode, the previously noted cues seem to capture some of the essential elements of deceiver behavior.

CONCLUSION

The research reviewed in this selection leaves no doubt as to the impact of nonverbal messages on our lives. To summarize, nonverbal actions are often considered more important than verbal messages for determining message meaning. One reason for their importance is that they are omnipresent—an inherent part of every communication act. Indeed, there are seven codes of nonverbal behavior that could be simultaneously sending messages. For example, one could be communicating attraction by dressing nicely (physical appearance), maintaining eye contact (kinesics), interacting at a close distance (proxemics), lightly touching the other (haptics), varying vocal intonation (vocalics), extending the conversation (chronemics), and setting up the interaction to be in an intimate setting (artifacts). Relatedly, many of these cues could be serving multiple functions, from interaction management to emotion expression to relational management to influence. As such, it is important to keep nonverbal behaviors in mind when assessing the application of all communication theories; they undoubtedly play a critical role in explaining interaction outcomes.

ADDITIONAL READING

Given the breadth of the research on nonverbal communication, it is difficult to summarize the literature well. Nevertheless, there are very good texts available. Textbooks that do an exceptional job of summarizing the research in the area include Burgoon et al. (1996) and Andersen (1999). Another resource for interested readers is Guerrero, DeVito, and Hecht (1999), an edited volume that includes excellent readings from across the spectrum of non-verbal research, each written by some of the best scholars in the area.

Recommended readings within specific areas of nonverbal messages include Burgoon, Stern, et al. (1995) for nonverbal adaptation, DePaulo (1992) for research on nonverbal self-presentation strategies, and Henley (1977) for an extended discussion of dominance and sex differences in the use of touch.

REFERENCES

Afifi, W. A.. & Johnson, M. L. (1999). The use and interpretation of tie signs in a public setting: Relationship and sex differences. *Journal of Social and Personal Relationships, 16,* 9–38.

Albas. D., & Albas. C. (1988). Acers and bombers: Post-exam impression management strategies of students. *Symbolic Interaction, 2,* 289–302.

Altman, I. (1975). *The environment and social behavior.* Monterey, CA: Brooks/Cole.

Andersen, P. A. (1999). *Nonverbal communication: Forms and functions.* Mountain View, CA: Mayfield.

Andersen, P. A., & Bowman, L. L. (1999). Positions of power: Nonverbal influence in organizational communication. In L. K. Guerrero, J. A. DeVito, & M. L. Hecht (Eds.), *The nonverbal communication reader: Classic and contemporary readings* (2nd ed., pp. 317–334). Prospect Heights, IL: Waveland.

Argyle, M. (1988). *Bodily communication* (2nd ed.). London: Methuen.

Aune, K. S. (1997). Self and partner perceptions of the appropriateness of emotions. *Communication Reports, 10,* 133–142.

Aune. K. S., Buller, D. B., & Aune, R. K. (1996). Display rule development in romantic relationships: Emotion management and perceived appropriateness of emotions across relationship stages. *Human Communication Research, 23,* 115–145.

Badzinski, D. M., & Pettus, A. B. (1994). Nonverbal involvement and sex: Effects on jury decisions making. *Journal of Applied Communication Research, 22,* 309–321.

Barnard, K. E. & Brazelton, T. B. (Eds.). (1990). *Touch: The foundation of experience.* Madison, CT: International Universities Press.

Blanck, P. D., Rosenthal, R., & Cordell, L. H. (1985). The appearance of justice: Judges' verbal and nonverbal behavior in criminal jury trials. *Stanford Law Review, 38,* 89–164.

Botta. R. A. (1999). Televised images and adolescent girls' body image disturbance. *Journal of Communication, 49,* 22–41.

Boomer, D. S. (1978). The phonemic clause: Speech unit in human communication. In A. W. Siegman & S. Feldstein (Eds.), *Nonverbal behavior and communication* (pp. 245–262). Hillsdale, NJ: Lawrence Erlbaum Associates, Inc.

Boyson. A. R., Pryor, B., & Butler, J. (1999). Height as power in women. *North American Journal of Psychology, 1,* 109–114.

Brown, P., & Levinson, S. (1987). *Universals in language usage: Politeness phenomena.* Cambridge, England: Cambridge University Press.

Buller, D. B., & Burgoon, J. K. (1994). Deception: Strategic and nonstrategic communication. In J. A. Daly & J. M. Wiemann (Eds.), *Strategic interpersonal communication* (pp. 191–223). Hillsdale, NJ: Lawrence Erlbaum Associates, Inc.

Buller, D. B., & Burgoon. J. K. (1996). Interpersonal Deception Theory. *Communication Theory, 6,* 203–242.

Buller, D. B., & Street, R. L., Jr. (1992). Physician-patient relationships. In R. S. Feldman (Ed.), *Applications of nonverbal theories and research* (pp. 119–141). Hillsdale, NJ: Lawrence Erlbaum Associates, Inc.

Burgoon, J. K. (1991). Relational messages interpretations of touch, conversational distance, and posture. *Journal of Nonverbal Behavior, 15,* 233–259.

Burgoon, J. K. (1994). Nonverbal signals. In M. L. Knapp & G. R. Miller (Eds.), *Handbook of interpersonal communication* (2nd ed., pp. 229–285). Thousand Oaks, CA: Sage.

Burgoon, J. K., Birk, T., & Pfau, M. (1990). Nonverbal behaviors, persuasion, and credibility. *Human Communication Research, 17,* 140–169.

Burgoon, J. K., Buller, D. B., Dillman, L., & Walther, J. B. (1995). Interpersonal deception: IV. Effects of suspicion on perceived communication and nonverbal behavior dynamics. *Human Communication Research, 22,* 163–196.

Burgoon, J. K., Buller, D. B., & Guerrero, L. K. (1995). Interpersonal deception: IX. Effects of social skill and nonverbal communication on deception success and detection accuracy. *Journal of Language and Social Psychology, 14,* 289–311.

Burgoon, J. K., Buller, D. B., & Woodall, W. G. (1996). *Nonverbal communication: The unspoken dialogue* (2nd ed.). New York: McGraw-Hill.

Burgoon, J. K., & Hale, J. L. (1987). Validation and measurement of the fundamental themes of relational communication. *Communication Monographs, 54,* 19–41.

Burgoon, J. K..& Hale, J. L. (1988). Nonverbal expectancy violations: Model elaboration and application to immediacy behaviors. *Communication Monographs, 55,* 58–79.

Burgoon, J. K., Pfau, M., Parrott, R.. Birk, T., Coker, R., & Burgoon, M. (1987). Relational communication, satisfaction, compliance-gaining strategies, and compliance in communication between physicians and patients. *Communication Monographs, 54,* 307–324.

Burgoon, J. K., Stern, L. A., & Dillman, L. (1995). *Interpersonal adaptation: Dyadic interaction patterns.* Cambridge, England: Cambridge University Press.

Buslig, A. L. S. (1999). 'Stop' signs: Regulating privacy with environmental features. In L. K. Guerrero, J. A. DeVito. & M. L. Hecht (Eds.), *The nonverbal communication reader: Classic and contemporary readings* (2nd ed., pp. 241–249). Prospect Heights, IL: Waveland.

Buss, D. M. (1994). *The evolution of desire.* New York: Basic Books.

Butler, S., & Roesel, K. (1991). Students perceptions of male teachers: Effects of teachers' dress and students' characteristics. *Perceptual and Motor Skills, 73,* 943–951.

Cappella, J. N., & Street, R. L. (1985). A functional approach to the structure of communicative behavior. In R. L. Street & J. N. Cappelia (Eds.), *Sequence and pattern in communicative behavior* (pp. 1–29). London: Edward Arnold.

Cash. T. E, & Pruzinsky, T. (Eds.). (1990). *Body images: Development, deviance, and change.* New York: Guilford.

Cloven, D. H., & Roloff, M. E. (1994). A developmental model of decisions to withhold relational irritations in romantic relationships. *Personal Relationships, 1,* 143–164.

Daly, J. A., Hogg, E., Sacks, D., Smith, M., & Zimring, L. (1983). Sex and relationship affect social self-grooming. *Journal of Nonverbal Behavior, 7,* 183–189.

Dellinger, K., & Williams, C. L. (1997). Makeup at work: Negotiating appearance rules in the workplace. *Gender and Society, 11,* 151–177.

DePaulo, B. M. (1992). Nonverbal behavior and self-presentation. *Psychological Bulletin, 111,* 203–243.

Donoghue, E. (1992). Sociopsychological correlates of teenage pregnancy in the United States Virgin Islands. *International Journal of Mental Health, 21,* 39–49.

Eaves, M. H., & Leathers, D. G. (1991). Context as communication: McDonald's vs. Burger King. *Journal of Applied Communication, 19,* 263–289.

Eder, D. (1985). The cycle of popularity: Interpersonal relations among female adolescents. *Sociology of Education, 58,* 154–165.

Edwards, J. N., Fuller, T. D., Vorakitphokatorn, S., & Sermsri, S. (1994). *Household crowing and its consequences.* Boulder, CO: Westview.

Ekman, P. (1973). *Darwin and facial expression: A century of research in review.* New York: Academic.

Ekman, P. (1978). Facial expression. In A. W. Siegman & S. Feldstein (Eds.). *Nonverbal behavior and communication* (pp. 96–116). Hillsdale, NJ: Lawrence Erlbaum Associates, Inc.

Ekman, P.. & Friesen, W. V. (1969). The repertoire of nonverbal behavior: Categories, origins, usage, and coding. *Semiotica, 1,* 49–98.

Ekman, P., & Oster, H. (1979). Facial expression of emotion. *Annual Review of Psychology, 30,* 527–554.

Forbes, R. J., & Jackson, P. R. (1980). Nonverbal behavior and the outcome of selection interviews. *Journal of Occupational Psychology, 53,* 67–72.

Gallois, C, Giles, EL Jones, E., Cargile, A. C, & Ota, H. (1995). Accommodating intercultural encounters: Elaborations and extensions. *International and Intercultural Communication Annual, 19,* 115–147.

Gifford, R., Ng, C. R, Wilkinson, M. (1985). Nonverbal cues in the employment interview: Links between applicant qualities and interviewer judgments. *Journal of Applied Psychology, 70,* 729–736.

Giles, H., Mulac, A., Bradac, J. J.. & Johnson. P. (1987). Speech Accommodation Theory: The first decade and beyond. In M. IVlcLaughlin (Ed.), *Communication Yearbook* (Vol. 10, pp. 13–48). Newbury Park, CA: Sage.

Goffman, E. (1959). *The presentation of self in everyday life.* Garden City. NY: Doubleday.

Goldman, M., Kiyohara, O., & Pfannensteil, D. A. (1985). Interpersonal touch, social labeling, and the foot-in-the-door effect. *Journal of Social Psychology, 125,* 143–147.

Gonzalez, A., & Zimbardo. P. G. (1999). Time in perspective. In L. K. Guerrero. J. A. DeVito, & M. L. Hecht (Eds.), *The nonverbal communication reader: Classic and. contemporary readings* (2nd ed., pp. 227–236). Prospect Heights, IL: Waveland.

Gress, J. E., & Heft, H. (1998). Do territorial actions attenuate the effects of high density? A field study. In J. Sanford & B. R. Connell (Eds.), *People, places, and public policy* (pp. 47–52). Edmond, OK: Environmental Design Research Association.

Gross, R., Sasson, Y., Zarhy, M., & Zohar, J. (1998). Healing environment in psychiatric hospitals. *General Hospital Psychiatry, 20,* 108–114.

Grumet, G. W. (1983). Eye contact: The core of interpersonal relatedness. *Psychiatry, 48,* 172–180.

Guerrero, L. K., Devito, J. A., & Hecht, M. L. (Eds.). (1999). *The nonverbal communication reader: Classic and contemporary readings* (2nd ed.). Prospect Heights, IL: Waveland.

Hall, E. T. (1966). *The hidden dimension* (2nd ed.). Garden City, NY: Anchor/Doubleday.

Hall E. T., & Hall. M. R. (1999). Monochrome and polychrome time. In L. K. Guerrero, J. A. DeVito, & M. L. Hecht (Eds.), *The nonverbal communication reader: Classic and contemporary readings* (2nd ed., pp. 237–240). Prospect Heights. IL: Waveland.

Harris, M. J.. Rosenthal, R., & Snodgrass, S. E. (1986). The effects of teacher expectations, gender, and behavior on pupil academic performance and self-concept. *Journal of Educational Research, 79,* 173–179.

Henley, N. M. (1977). *Body politics: Power, sex, and nonverbal communication.* Englewood Cliffs, NJ: Prentice-Hall.

Hess, E. H. (1975). The role of pupil size in communication. *Scientific American, 233,* 110–119.

Izard, C. E. (1977). *Human emotions.* New York: Plenum.

Jones, S. E., & Yarbrough, A. E. (1985). A naturallistic study of the meanings of touch. *Communication Monographs, 52,* 19–56.

Juhnke, R., Barmann, B., Cunningham, M., & Smith, E. (1987). Effects of attractiveness and nature of request on helping behavior. *Journal of Social Psychology, 127,* 317–322.

Kaiser, S. B. (1997). *The social psychology of clothing: Symbolic appearances in context* (2nd ed.). New York: Fairchild.

Kupperbusch, C, Matsumoto. D., Kooken, K., Loewinger, S., Uchida, H., Wilson-Cohn, C., et al. (1999). Cultural influences on nonverbal expressions of emotion. In P. Philippot, R. S. Feldman. & E. J. Coats (Eds.), *The social context of nonverbal behavior* (pp. 17–44). Cambridge, England: Cambridge University Press.

Lamude, K. G., Daniels, T. D., & Smilowitz, M. (1995). Subordinates(satisfaction with communication and managers' relational messages. *Perceptual and Motor Skills, 81,* 467–471.

Lamude, K. G.. & Scudder, J. (1991). Hierarchical levels and type of relational messages. *Communication Research Reports, 8,* 149–157.

Lester, D. (1990). Overcrowding in prisons and rates of suicide and homocide. *Perceptual and Motor Skills, 71,* 274.

Lukavsky. J., Butler, S., & Harden, A. J. (1995). Perceptions of an instructor: Dress and students' characteristics. *Perceptual and Motor Skills, 81,* 231–240.

Lyman, S. 1VL, & Scott, M. B. (1967), Territoriality: A neglected sociological dimension. *Social Problems, 15,* 236–249.

Malatesta, C. Z., & Haviland, J. M. (1982). Learning display rules: The socialization of emotion expression in infancy. *Child Development, 53,* 991–1003.

Martel, L. F., & Biller, H. B. (1987). *Stature and stigma: The biopsychosocial development of short males.* Lexington, MA: Lexington.

Mazzella, R., & Feingold, A. (1994). The effects of physical attractiveness, race, socioeconomic status, and gender of defendants and victims on judgments of mock jurors: A meta-analysis. *Journal of Applied Social Psychology, 24,* 1315–1344.

Milgram, S. (1974). *Obedience to authority: An experimental view.* New York: Harper & Row.

Mills. J., & Aronson, E. (1965). Opinion change as a function of the communicator's attractiveness and desire to influence. *Journal of Personality and Social Psychology, 1,* 74–77.

Monsour, M. (2002). *Women and men as friends: Relationships across the life span in the 21st century.* Mahwah, NJ: Lawrence Erlbaum Associates, Inc.

Montagu, A. (1978). *Touching: The human significance of the skin* (2nd ed.). New York: Harper & Row.

Montepare, J. M., & Vega, C. (1988). Women's vocal reactions to intimate and casual male friends. *Personality and Social Psychology, 14,* 103–113.

Morris, D. (1971). *Intimate behavior.* New York: Random House.

Nussbaum, M. C. (2000). Emotions and social norms. In L. P. Nucci & G. B. Saxe (Eds.), *Culture, thought, and development* (pp. 41–63). Mahwah, NJ: Lawrence Erlbaum. Associates, Inc.

O'Hair, H. D., & Cody, M. J. (1994). Deception. In W. R. Cupach & B. H. Spitzberg (Eds.), *The dark side of interpersonal communication* (pp. 181–214). Hillsdale, NJ: Lawrence Erlbaum Associates, Inc.

O'Keefe, D. J. (1990). *Persuasion: Theory and research.* Newbury Park, CA: Sage.

Phillips, K. A. (1999). Body dysmorphic disorder and depression: Theoretical considerations and treatment strategies. *Psychiatric Quarterly, 70,* 313–331.

Rivano-Fischer, M. (1988). Micro territorial behavior in public transport vehicles: A field study on a bus route. *Psychological Research Bulletin, 28,* 18.

Robinson, J. D. (1998). Getting down to business: Talk, gaze, and body orientation during openings of doctor-patient consultations. *Human Communication Research, 25,* 97–123.

Rosenberg, S. W., Kahn. S., & Tran, T. (1991). Creating a political image: Shaping appearance and manipulating the vote. *Political Behavior, 13,* 345–367.

Schlenker, B. R., Britt, T. W., & Pennington, J. (1996). Impression regulation and management: Highlights of a theory of self-identification. In R. M. Sorrentino & E. T. Higgins (Eds.), *Handbook of motivation and cognition: The interpersonal context* (Vol. 3, pp. 118–147). New York: Guilford.

Segrin, C. (1999). The influence of nonverbal behaviors in compliance-gaining processes. In L. K. Guerrero, J. A. DeVito, & M. L. Hecht (Eds.), *The nonverbal communication reader: Classic and contemporary readings* (2nd ed., pp. 335–346). Prospect Heights, IL: Waveland.

Semic, B. (1999). Vocal attractiveness: What sounds beautiful is good. In L. K. Guerrero, J. A. DeVito, & M. L. Hecht (Eds.), *The nonverbal communication reader: Classic and contemporary readings* (2nd ed., pp. 149–155). Prospect Heights, IL: Waveland.

Sheppard, J. A., & Strathman, A. J. (1989). Attractiveness and height: The role of stature in dating preference, frequency of dating, and perceptions of attractiveness. *Personality and Social Psychology Bulletin, 15*, 617–627.

Sigelman, C. K., Thomas, D. B., Sigelman, L., & Ribich, F. D. (1986). Gender, physical attractiveness, and electability: An experimental investigation of voter biases. *Journal of Applied Social Psychology, 16*, 229–248.

Stice, E., Hayward, C, Cameron, R. P., Killen. J. D., & Taylor, C. B. (2000). Body-image and eating disturbances predict onset of depression among female adolescents: A longitudinal study. *Journal of Abnormal Psychology, 109*, 438–444.

Sundstrom, E., Bell, P. A.. Busby, P. L., & Asmus, C. (1996). Environmental psychology 1989–1994. *Annual Review of Psychology 47*, 482–512,

Tajfel, H., & Turner, J. C. (1979). An integrative theory of group conflict. In W. G. Austin & S. Worchel (Eds.), *The social psychology of intergroup relations* (pp. 33–47). Monterey, CA: Brooks-Cole.

Tracy. K. (1990). The many faces of facework. In H. Giles & W. P. Robinson (Eds.), *Handbook of language and social psychology* (pp. 209–226). Chichester, England: John "Wiley & Sons.

Wiemann. J. M., & Knapp, M. L. (1975). Turn-taking in conversation. *Journal of Communication, 25*, 75–92.

Worschel, S., & Austin, W. G. (Eds.). (1986). *The social psychology of intergroup relations*. Chicago: Nelson Hall.

QUESTIONS TO PONDER

1. Given the research reviewed in this selection, which code would you argue is the one that most affects our daily lives? Provide evidence for why the one you choose is significantly more important than other codes.

2. There were several studies discussed that had implications for people's performance on job interviews or other important interactions. What nonverbal behaviors would you recommend to someone going on a job interview? What nonverbal behaviors should this person avoid at all costs?

3. In this selection, nonverbal research was applied to a few theories and I argued that many other theories have been applied to explain nonverbal behaviors. Think of three theories discussed in the book (but not in this selection) and apply them to the nonverbal arena.

4. QVC and other home shopping channels make hundreds of millions of dollars by persuading viewers to make purchases they may otherwise not consider making. Nonverbal messages play a very important role in their success. Watch these channels carefully and review the ways they use nonverbal messages to influence viewers.

5. Watch Sunday morning political talk and interview shows. Closely examine how the nonverbal messages of both the interviewer and the person being interviewed affect their credibility. Pay especially close attention to kinesics, vocalics, and physical appearance. How does the interviewee recover from a possible threat to their credibility? What, does he or she do nonverbally in these cases?

Who Are You?

Understanding Others

1 These Things Called Empathy: Eight Related but Distinct Phenomena

C. Daniel Batson

Students of empathy can seem a cantankerous lot. Although they typically agree that empathy is important, they often disagree about why it is important, about what effects it has, about where it comes from, and even about what it is. The term *empathy* is currently applied to more than a half-dozen phenomena. These phenomena are related to one another, but they are not elements, aspects, facets, or components of a single thing that is empathy, as one might say that an attitude has cognitive, affective, and behavioral components. Rather, each is a conceptually distinct, stand-alone psychological state. Further, each of these states has been called by names other than empathy. Opportunities for disagreement abound.

In an attempt to sort out this disagreement, I wish first to identify two distinct questions that empathy is thought to answer. Then I wish to identify eight distinct phenomena that have been called empathy. Finally, I wish to relate these eight phenomena to the two questions.[1]

Empathy as an Answer to Two Different Questions

Application of the term *empathy* to so many distinct phenomena is, in part, a result of researchers invoking empathy to provide an answer to two quite different questions: How can one know what another person is thinking and feeling? What leads one person to respond with sensitivity and care to the suffering of another? For some students of empathy, answers to these two questions are related. However, many more seek to answer the first question without concern to answer the second, or vice versa.

The first question has been of particular interest to philosophers, cognitive scientists, neurophysiologists, primatologists, and developmental psychologists interested in the theory of mind. Both *theory theorists*, who suggest that we use our lay theories about the mind to infer the internal states of others, and *simulation theorists*, who suggest that we imagine ourselves in others' situations and read their internal states from our own, have invoked empathy to explain how we humans come to know what others are thinking and feeling.

The question of what leads us to respond with sensitive care to another's suffering has been of particular interest to philosophers and to developmental and social psychologists seeking to understand and promote prosocial action. The goal of these researchers is not to explain a particular form of knowledge but to explain a particular form of action: action by one person that effectively addresses the need of another. Those using empathy to answer this question are apt to say that empathic feelings *for* the other—feelings of sympathy, compassion, tenderness, and the like—produce motivation to relieve the suffering of the person for whom empathy is felt.

Eight Uses of the Term *Empathy*

An example may help clarify distinctions among different uses of the term *empathy*. Imagine that you meet a friend for lunch. She seems distracted, staring into space, not very talkative, a bit down. Gradually, she begins to speak, then to cry. She explains that she just learned that she is losing her job because of downsizing. She says that she is not angry but that she is hurt, and a bit scared. You feel very sorry for her, and say so. You are also reminded that there has been talk of job cuts where you work as well. Seeing your friend so upset makes you feel a bit anxious and uneasy. You also feel a brief flash of relief—"Thank God it wasn't me!" At least eight different psychological states you might experience in this interchange correspond to distinct concepts of empathy.

Concept 1: Knowing Another Person's Internal State, Including His or Her Thoughts and Feelings

Some clinicians and researchers have called knowing another person's internal state empathy (e.g., Preston & de Waal, 2002; Wispé, 1986). Others have called this knowledge "cognitive empathy" (Eslinger, 1998; Zahn-Waxler, Robinson, & Emde, 1992) or "empathic accuracy" (Ickes, 1993).

Sometimes, to ascertain what someone else is thinking and feeling can pose quite a problem, especially when one has only limited clues. But in our example, knowing your friend's internal state is relatively easy. Once she explains, you may be confident that you know what is on her mind: losing her job. From what she says, and perhaps even more from the way she acts, you may also think you know how she feels: she is hurt and scared. Of course, you could be wrong, at least about some nuances and details.

Concept 2: Adopting the Posture or Matching the Neural Responses of an Observed Other

Adopting the posture or expression of an observed other is a definition of empathy in many dictionaries. The philosopher Gordon (1995) speaks of this as "facial empathy." Among psychologists, adopting another's posture is more likely to be called "motor mimicry" (Dimberg, Thunberg, & Elmehed, 2000; Hoffman, 2000) or "imitation" (Lipps, 1903; Meltzoff & Moore, 1997; Titchener, 1909).

Preston and de Waal (2002) proposed what they claim is a unified theory of empathy that focuses on mimicked neural representations rather than mimicked motor activity. Their theory is based on a perception-action model. According to this model, perceiving another in a given situation automatically leads one to match the other's neural state because perception and action rely in part on the same neural circuits. As a result of the matched neural representation, which need not produce either matched motor activity or awareness, one comes to feel something of what the other feels, and thereby to understand the other's internal state.

To claim that either neural response matching or motor mimicry is the unifying source of all empathic feelings seems to be an overestimation of their role, especially among humans. Perceptual neural representations do not always and automatically lead to feelings, whether matched or unmatched. And at a motor level, neither humans nor other species mimic all actions of others. To find oneself tensing and twisting when watching someone balance on a tightrope is a familiar experience; it is hard to resist. Yet we may watch someone file papers with little inclination to mimic the action. Something more than automatic mimicry must be involved to select those actions that are mimicked and those that are not. Moreover, it has been found that mimicry itself may not be as reactive and automatic as has been assumed. Meltzoff and Moore (1997) present much evidence that mimicry or imitation is an active, goal-directed process even in infants. And in adults, mimicry often serves a higher-order communicative function (LaFrance & Ickes, 1981). In the words of Bavelas and colleagues (1986), "I show how you feel" in order to convey "fellow feeling" or support.

Rather than relying solely on response matching or mimicry to provide clues to the internal states of others, humans can also use memory and general knowledge to infer what others think and feel in various situations (Singer et al., 2004; Tomasello, 1999). Indeed, the problem of anthropomorphism arises precisely because we humans have the ability—and inclination—to make such inferences, even about other species. Equally important, humans can rely on direct communication from one another to learn about internal states. In our example, your friend told you what she was thinking and feeling.

Concept 3: Coming to Feel as Another Person Feels

Coming to feel the same emotion that another person feels is another common dictionary definition of empathy. It is also a definition used by some philosophers (e.g., Darwall, 1998; Sober & Wilson, 1998), neuroscientists (Damasio, 2003; Decety & Chaminade, 2003; Eslinger, 1998), and psychologists (Eisenberg & Strayer, 1987; Preston & de Waal, 2002). Often, those who use this definition qualify it by saying that the empathizer need not feel exactly the same emotion, only a similar one (e.g., Hoffman, 2000). However, what determines whether an emotion is similar enough is never made clear.

Key to this use of the term empathy is not only emotion matching but also emotion "catching" (Hatfield, Cacioppo, & Rapson, 1994). To know that one person has come to feel as another feels, it is necessary to know more than that the former has a physiological response of roughly the same magnitude at roughly the same time as the latter—what

Levenson and Ruef (1992) called "shared physiology." Shared physiology provides no clear evidence of either matching (the observer's arousal might be associated with a qualitatively different emotion) or catching (rather than being a response to the target's emotional state, the observer's arousal might be a parallel response to a shared situation, perhaps one to which the target's response drew attention).

Among philosophers, coming to feel as the other feels has often been called "sympathy," not empathy (Hume, 1740/1896; Smith, 1759/1853). Among psychologists, it has been called "emotional contagion" (Hatfield, Cacioppo, & Rapson, 1994), "affective empathy" (Zahn-Waxler, Robinson, & Emde, 1992), and "automatic emotional empathy" (Hodges & Wegner, 1997).

In one of the most frequently cited studies of the developmental origins of empathy, Sagi and Hoffman (1976) presented one- to two-day-old infants either with tape-recorded sounds of another infant crying, with sounds of a synthetic nonhuman cry, or with no sounds. Those infants presented with another infant's cry cried significantly more than those presented with a synthetic cry or with silence. Sagi and Hoffman (1976, p. 176), and many others since, interpreted this difference as evidence of an inborn "rudimentary empathic distress reaction," that is, as evidence of one newborn infant catching and matching another's affective state.

However, to interpret this research as evidence of an inborn rudimentary empathic reaction seems premature. There are alternative explanations for crying in response to another infant's cry, alternatives that to my knowledge have never been recognized in the literature. To give but one example, crying in response to another infant's cry may be a competitive response that increases the chances of getting food or comfort. (The infants in the Sagi and Hoffman study were tested 1 to 1½ hours before feeding time.) Imagine that we did a similar study using baby birds in a nest. We would not likely interpret the rapid spread of peeping and open-mouth straining once one baby bird starts peeping and straining as a rudimentary empathic reaction.

Concept 4: Intuiting or Projecting Oneself into Another's Situation

Listening to your friend, you might have asked yourself what it would be like to be a young woman just told she is losing her job. Imaginatively projecting oneself into another's situation is the psychological state referred to by Lipps (1903) as *Einfühlung* and for which Titchener (1909) first coined the English word *empathy*. Both were intrigued by the process whereby a writer or painter imagines what it would be like to be some specific person or some inanimate object, such as a gnarled, dead tree on a windswept hillside.

This original definition of empathy as aesthetic projection often appears in dictionaries, and it has appeared in recent philosophical discussions of simulation as an alternative to *theory theories* of mind. But such projection is rarely what is meant by empathy in contemporary psychology. Still, Wispé (1968) included such projection in his analysis of sympathy and empathy, calling it "aesthetic empathy."

Concept 5: Imagining How Another Is Thinking and Feeling

Rather than imagine how it would feel to be a young woman just told she is losing her job, you might imagine how your friend is thinking and feeling. Your imagining can be based both on what she says and does and on your knowledge of her character, values, and desires. Stotland (1969) spoke of this as a particular form of perspective taking, an "imagine him" perspective. More generally, it has been called an "imagine other" perspective (Batson, 1991).

Wispé (1968) called imagining how another is feeling "psychological empathy" to differentiate it from the aesthetic empathy of concept 4. Adolphs (1999) called it "empathy" or "projection"; Ruby and Decety (2004) called it "empathy" or "perspective taking."

In a perceptive analysis from a therapeutic perspective, Barrett-Lennard (1981) spoke of adopting an "empathic attentional set." This set involves "a process of feeling into, in which Person A opens him- or herself in a deeply responsive way to Person B's feelings and experiencing but without losing awareness that B is a distinct other self" (p. 92). At issue is not so much what one knows about the feelings and thoughts of the other but one's sensitivity to the way the other is affected by his or her situation.

Concept 6: Imagining How One Would Think and Feel in the Other's Place

Adam Smith (1759/1853) colorfully referred to the act of imagining how one would think and feel in another person's situation as "changing places in fancy." Mead (1934) sometimes called it "role taking" and sometimes "empathy"; Povinelli (1993) called it "cognitive empathy." Darwall (1998) spoke of "projective empathy" or "simulation." In the Piagetian tradition, imagining how one would think in the other's place has been called either "perspective taking" or "decentering" (Piaget, 1953).

Stotland (1969) called this an "imagine-self" perspective, distinguishing it from the imagine-other perspective of concept 5. The imagine-other and imagine-self forms of perspective taking have often been confused or equated with one another, despite empirical evidence suggesting that they should not be (Batson, Early, & Salvarani, 1997; Stotland, 1969).

To adopt an imagine-self perspective is in some ways similar to the act of projecting oneself into another's situation (concept 4). Yet these two concepts were developed independently in very different contexts, one aesthetic and the other interpersonal, and the self remains more focal here than in aesthetic projection, so it seems best to keep them separate.

Concept 7: Feeling Distress at Witnessing Another Person's Suffering

A state of distress evoked by witnessing another's distress—your feelings of anxiety and unease evoked by seeing how upset your friend was—has been given a variety of names, including "empathy" (Krebs, 1975), "empathic distress" (Hoffman, 1981), and "personal distress" (Batson, 1991).

This state does not involve feeling distressed *for* the other (see concept 8) or distressed *as* the other (concept 3). It involves feeling distressed *by* the state of the other.

Concept 8: Feeling for Another Person Who Is Suffering

In contemporary social psychology, the term "empathy" or "empathic concern" has often been used to refer to an other-oriented emotional response elicited by and congruent with the perceived welfare of someone else (e.g., Batson, 1991). *Other-oriented* here refers to the focus of the emotion; it is felt *for* the other. *Congruent* refers to the valence of the emotion—positive when the perceived welfare of the other is positive, negative when the perceived welfare is negative. To speak of congruence does not imply that the content of the emotion is the same or even similar, as in concept 3. You might, for example, feel sad or sorry for your friend, who is scared and upset.

Other-oriented emotion felt when another is perceived to be in need has not always been called empathy. It has also been called "pity" or "compassion" (Hume, 1740/1896; Smith, 1759/1853), "sympathetic distress" (Hoffman, 1981, 2000), and simply "sympathy" (Darwall, 1998; Eisenberg & Strayer, 1987; Preston & de Waal, 2002; Sober & Wilson, 1998; Wispé, 1986).

Implications

I have listed these eight phenomena to which the term empathy has been applied for two reasons. First, I hope to reduce confusion by recognizing complexity. Second, I wish to consider how each phenomenon fits into answers to the two questions raised at the outset.

It would simplify matters if empathy referred to a single object and if everyone agreed on what that object was. Unfortunately, as with many psychological terms, this is not the case. Both *empathy* and *sympathy* (the term with which empathy is most often contrasted) have been used in a variety of ways. Indeed, with remarkable consistency exactly the same state that some scholars have labeled empathy others have labeled sympathy. I have discerned no clear basis—either historical or logical—for favoring one labeling scheme over another. The best one can do is recognize the different phenomena, make clear the labeling scheme one is adopting, and use that scheme consistently.

Not all eight empathy phenomena are relevant to each of the two empathy-related questions. It is worth considering the relation of each phenomenon to each question in turn.

Question 1: How Do We Know Another's Thoughts and Feelings?

Knowing another person's internal state (concept 1) is the phenomenon for which the first question seeks an explanation. Five of the other phenomena have been offered as explanations. Adopting the posture or matching the neural responses of an observed other (concept

2), coming to feel as another person feels (concept 3), intuiting or projecting oneself into another's situation (concept 4), imagining how another is thinking and feeling (concept 5), and imagining how one would think and feel in the other's place (concept 6) have all been invoked to account for our knowledge of another person's thoughts and feelings.

Some accounts focus on only one of these phenomena. For example, a *theory theory* proponent might argue that we can successfully imagine another's internal state (concept 5) by drawing on our lay theories of what people in general, or people with the other's specific characteristics, are likely to think and feel. Other accounts combine several phenomena. A *simulation theory* proponent might argue that by intuiting and projecting oneself into the other's situation (concept 4) or by imagining how one would think and feel in the other's place (concept 6), one comes to feel as the other feels (concept 3), and knowledge of one's own feelings then enables one to know—or to believe one knows—how the other feels (concept 1). Alternatively, one might propose that by automatically adopting the posture or matching the neural responses of the other (concept 2), one comes to feel as the other feels (concept 3), which enables one to know how the other feels (concept 1).

The last two phenomena identified—feeling vicarious personal distress at witnessing another person's suffering (concept 7) and feeling for another who is suffering (concept 8)—are not sources of knowledge (or belief) about another's state; they are reactions to this knowledge. Thus, they are not likely to be invoked to explain how one knows what another is thinking and feeling. Instead, they figure prominently in answers to the second question.

Question 2: What Leads One Person to Respond with Sensitivity and Care to the Suffering of Another?

There is considerable evidence that feeling distress at witnessing another person in distress (concept 7) can produce motivation to help that person. This motivation does not, however, appear to be directed toward the ultimate goal of relieving the other's distress (i.e., altruistic motivation); the motivation appears to be directed toward the ultimate goal of relieving one's own distress (i.e., egoistic motivation; Batson, 1991). As a result, this distress may not lead one to respond with sensitivity to the suffering of another, especially if there is an opportunity to relieve one's own distress without having to relieve the other's distress. The importance of this motivational distinction is underscored by evidence that parents at high risk of abusing a child are the ones who more frequently report distress at seeing an infant cry (concept 7); those at low risk report increased other-oriented feelings—sympathy and compassion (concept 8)—rather than increased distress (Milner, Halsey, & Fultz, 1995).

Feeling for another person who is suffering (concept 8) is the form of empathy most often invoked to explain what leads one person to respond with sensitive care to the suffering of another. This feeling has, in turn, often been related to one or more of the other seven concepts as possible antecedents.

To feel for another, one must think one knows the other's internal state (concept 1) because feeling *for* is based on a perception of the other's welfare (e.g., that your friend is hurt and afraid). To feel for someone does not, however, require that this perception be accurate. It does not even require that this perception match the other's perception of his or her internal state, which is often the standard used in research to define empathic accuracy (e.g., Ickes, 1993). (In this research, the possibility that the other's perception of his or her internal state could be mistaken tends to be ignored. Is it really true, for example, that your friend is not angry?) Of course, action prompted by other-oriented feelings based on erroneous beliefs about the other's state is apt to be misguided, failing to reach the goal of providing sensitive care.

Matching neural representations or mimicking another's posture (concept 2) may facilitate understanding of, or belief about, another's state (concept 1) and thereby induce other-oriented feelings (concept 8). Still, it seems unlikely that either matching or mimicking is necessary or sufficient to produce such feelings. Your friend's tears may have caused you to cry too. But matching her neural state or mimicking her crying was probably not necessary for you to feel sorry for her. More likely, it was the reverse. Her tears made it clear to you how upset she was, and you cried because you felt sorry for her.

Coming to feel as the other feels (concept 3) may also be an important stepping-stone to understanding the other's state (concept 1) and thereby to other-oriented feelings (concept 8). Once again, however, research suggests that it is neither a necessary nor a sufficient precondition (Batson, Early, & Salvarani, 1997). To feel sorry for your friend you need not feel hurt and afraid too. It is enough to know that she is hurt and afraid (concept 1).

Feeling as the other feels may actually inhibit other-oriented feelings if it leads us to become focused on our own emotional state. Sensing the nervousness of other passengers on an airplane in rough weather, I too may become nervous. If I focus on my own nervousness, not theirs, I am likely to feel less for them, not more.

Intuiting or projecting oneself into another's situation (concept 4) may give one a lively sense of what the other is thinking and feeling (concept 1) and may thereby facilitate other-oriented feelings (concept 8). But when the state of the other is obvious because of what has happened or been said, intuition or projection is probably unnecessary. And when the other's state is not obvious, intuition or projection runs the risk of imposing an interpretation of the other's state that is inaccurate, especially if one does not have a precise understanding of relevant differences between oneself and the other.

Instructions to imagine how the other is feeling (concept 5) have often been used to induce other-oriented feelings for a person in need (concept 8) in participants in laboratory experiments (see Batson, 1991, for a review). Still, this imagine-other perspective should not be confused or equated with the other-oriented emotion it evokes (Coke, Batson, & McDavis, 1978).

When attending to another person in distress, imagining how you would think and feel in that situation (concept 6) may stimulate other-oriented feelings (concept 8). However, this imagine-self perspective is also likely to elicit self-oriented feelings of distress (concept 7; see Batson, Early, & Salvarani, 1997; Stotland, 1969). If the other's situation is unfamiliar or unclear, then imagining how you would think and feel in that situation may provide a useful, possibly essential, basis for perceiving the other's state (concept 1), a necessary precondition for experiencing other-oriented feelings. But once again, if the other differs from you, then focusing on how you would think and feel may prove misleading. And if the other's situation is familiar or clear, then to imagine how you would think and feel in that situation may actually inhibit other-oriented feelings (Nickerson, 1999). As you listened to your friend talk about losing her job, your thoughts about how you would feel if you lost your own job led you to become self-concerned, to feel anxious and uneasy—and lucky by comparison. These reactions likely dampened your other-oriented feelings of sorrow for her.

Because of prominence and popularity, I have dwelt on other-oriented feelings (concept 8) as a source of sensitive response to the suffering of others. But several of the other phenomena called empathy have been offered as sources of sensitive response, independent of mediation through other-oriented feelings for the sufferer. For example, it has been suggested that coming to feel as another person feels (concept 3)—perhaps combined with an imagine-other perspective (concept 5)—can lead us to respond directly to the other's suffering as we would to our own (Preston & de Waal, 2002). It has also been suggested that imagining how one would think and feel in the other's place (concept 6) can lead directly to a more sensitive response to the plight of members of stereotyped out-groups (Galinsky & Moskowitz, 2000).

For those whose profession commits them to helping others in need (such as clinicians, counselors, and physicians), accurate perception of the need—diagnosis—is of paramount importance because one is not likely to address a need effectively unless one recognizes it. Moreover, high emotional arousal, including arousal of other-oriented emotions, may interfere with one's ability to help effectively (MacLean, 1967). Accordingly, within the helping professions, emphasis is often placed on accurate knowledge of the client's or patient's internal state (concept 1), not on other-oriented feelings (concept 8), as the key source of effective response to need.

Conclusion

Distinctions among the various things called empathy are sometimes subtle, yet there seems little doubt that each exists. Most are familiar experiences. Their familiarity should not, however, lead us to ignore their significance. The processes whereby one person can come to know the internal state of another and can be motivated to respond with sensitive care are of enormous importance for our life together. Some great thinkers, such as the philosopher David Hume, have suggested that these processes are the basis for all social perception and interaction. They are certainly key elements of our social nature.

To recognize the distinctiveness of these eight things called empathy complicates matters. Still, it seems essential if we are to understand these phenomena and how they relate to one another. It also seems essential if we are to advance our understanding of how it is possible to know the internal states of others and to respond with sensitivity to their suffering. Fortunately, social neuroscience has already begun to recognize at least some of the distinctions, and has begun to identify their neural substrates (see, for example, Jackson, et al., 2006; Lamm, Batson, & Decety, 2007; Singer et al., 2004).

Acknowledgments

Thanks to Nadia Ahmad, Tobias Gschwendner, Jakob Eklund, Luis Oceja, Adam Powell, and Eric Stocks for helpful comments on a draft.

Note

1. I am certainly not the first to note a range of empathy-related concepts (see Becker, 1931; Reik, 1948; Scheler, 1913/1970). But as the intellectual landscape has changed, the relevant conceptual distinctions have also changed. Therefore, I shall not present earlier attempts at conceptual clarification.

References

Adolphs, R. (1999). Social cognition and the human brain. *Trends in Cognitive Sciences, 3*, 469–479.

Barrett-Lennard, G. T. (1981). The empathy cycle: Refinement of a nuclear concept. *Journal of Counseling Psychology, 28*, 91–100.

Batson, C. D. (1991). *The altruism question: Toward a social-psychological answer*. Hillsdale, NJ: Erlbaum.

Batson, C. D., Early, S., & Salvarani, G. (1997). Perspective taking: Imagining how another feels versus imagining how you would feel. *Personality and Social Psychology Bulletin, 23*, 751–758.

Bavelas, J. B., Black, A., Lemery, C. R., & Mullett, J. (1986). "I show you how you feel": Motor mimicry as a communicative act. *Journal of Personality and Social Psychology, 50*, 322–329.

Becker, H. (1931). Some forms of sympathy: A phenomenological analysis. *Journal of Abnormal and Social Psychology, 26*, 58–68.

Coke, J. S., Batson, C. D., & McDavis, K. (1978). Empathic mediation of helping: A two-stage model. *Journal of Personality and Social Psychology, 36*, 752–766.

Damasio, A. R. (2003). *Looking for Spinoza: Joy, sorrow, and the feeling brain*. Orlando, FL: Harcourt.

Darwall, S. (1998). Empathy, sympathy, care. *Philosophical Studies, 89*, 261–282.

Decety, J., & Chaminade, T. (2003). Neural correlates of feeling sympathy. *Neuropsychologia, 41,* 127–138.

Dimberg, U., Thunberg, M., & Elmehed, K. (2000). Unconscious facial reactions to emotional facial expressions. *Psychological Science, 11,* 86–89.

Eisenberg, N., & Strayer, J. (Eds.). (1987). *Empathy and its development.* New York: Cambridge University Press.

Eslinger, P. J. (1998). Neurological and neuropsychological bases of empathy. *European Neurology, 1998,* 193–199.

Galinsky, A. D., & Moskowitz, G. B. (2000). Perspective-taking: Decreasing stereotype expression, stereotype accessibility, and in-group favoritism. *Journal of Personality and Social Psychology, 78,* 708–724.

Gordon, R. M. (1995). Sympathy, simulation, and the impartial spectator. *Ethics, 105,* 727–742.

Hatfield, E., Cacioppo, J. T., & Rapson, R. L. (1994). *Emotional contagion.* New York: Cambridge University Press.

Hodges, S. D., & Wegner, D. M. (1997). Automatic and controlled empathy. In W. Ickes (Ed.), *Empathic accuracy* (pp. 311–339). New York: Guilford Press.

Hoffman, M. L. (1981). The development of empathy. In J. P. Rushton & R. M. Sorrentino (Eds.), *Altruism and helping behavior: Social, personality, and developmental perspectives* (pp. 41–63). Hillsdale, NJ: Erlbaum.

Hoffman, M. L. (2000). *Empathy and moral development: Implications for caring and justice.* New York: Cambridge University Press.

Hume, D. (1740/1896). *A treatise of human nature* (L. A. Selby-Bigge, Ed.). Oxford: Oxford University Press.

Ickes, W. (1993). Empathic accuracy. *Journal of Personality, 61,* 587–610.

Jackson, P. L., Brunet, E., Meltzoff, A. N., & Decety, J. (2006). Empathy examined through the neural mechanisms involved in imagining how I feel versus how you feel pain. *Neuropsychologia, 44,* 752–761.

Krebs, D. L. (1975). Empathy and altruism. *Journal of Personality and Social Psychology, 32,* 1134–1146.

LaFrance, M., & Ickes, W. (1981). Posture mirroring and interactional involvement: Sex and sex typing influences. *Journal of Nonverbal Behavior, 5,* 139–154.

Lamm, C., Batson, C. D., & Decety, J. (2007). The neural substrate of human empathy: Effects of perspective-taking and cognitive appraisal. *Journal of Cognitive Neuroscience, 19,* 1–17.

Levenson, R. W., & Ruef, A. M. (1992). Empathy: A physiological substrate. *Journal of Personality and Social Psychology, 63,* 234–246.

Lipps, T. (1903). Einfühlung, inner Nachahmung, und Organ-empfindungen. *Archiv für die gesamte Psychologie, 1*, 185–204.

MacLean, P. D. (1967). The brain in relation to empathy and medical education. *Journal of Nervous and Mental Disease, 144*, 374–382.

Mead, G. H. (1934). *Mind, self, and society*. Chicago: University of Chicago Press.

Meltzoff, A. N., & Moore, M. K. (1997). Explaining facial imitation: A theoretical model. *Early Development and Parenting, 6*, 179–192.

Milner, J. S., Halsey, L. B., & Fultz, J. (1995). Empathic responsiveness and affective reactivity to infant stimuli in high- and low-risk for physical child abuse mothers. *Child Abuse and Neglect, 19*, 767–780.

Nickerson, R. S. (1999). How we know—and sometimes misjudge—what others know: Imputing one's own knowledge to others. *Psychological Bulletin, 125*, 737–759.

Piaget, J. (1953). *The origins of intelligence in the child*. New York: International Universities Press.

Povinelli, D. J. (1993). Reconstructing the evolution of mind. *American Psychologist, 48*, 493–509.

Preston, S. D., & de Waal, F. B. M. (2002). Empathy: Its ultimate and proximate bases. *Behavioral and Brain Sciences, 25*, 1–72.

Reik, T. (1948). *Listening with the third ear: The inner experience of a psychoanalyst*. New York: Farrar, Straus.

Ruby, P., & Decety, J. (2004). How would you feel versus how do you think she would feel? A neuroimaging study of perspective taking with social emotions. *Journal of Cognitive Neuroscience, 16*, 988–999.

Sagi, A., & Hoffman, M. L. (1976). Empathic distress in the newborn. *Developmental Psychology, 12*, 175–176.

Scheler, M. (1913/1970). *The nature of sympathy* (P. Heath, Trans.). Hamden, CT: Archon Books.

Singer, T., Seymour, B., O'Doherty, J., Kaube, H., Dolan, R. J., & Frith, C. D. (2004). Empathy for pain involves the affective but not sensory components of pain. *Science, 303*, 1157–1162.

Smith, A. (1759/1853). *The theory of moral sentiments*. London: Alex Murray.

Sober, E., & Wilson, D. S. (1998). *Unto others: The evolution and psychology of unselfish behavior*. Cambridge, MA: Harvard University Press.

Stotland, E. (1969). Exploratory investigations of empathy. In L. Berkowitz (Ed.), *Advances in experimental social psychology* (Vol. 4, pp. 271–313). New York: Academic Press.

Titchener, E. B. (1909). *Lectures on the experimental psychology of the thought processes*. New York: Macmillan.

Tomasello, M. (1999). *The cultural origins of human cognition*. Cambridge, MA: Harvard University Press.

Wispé, L. (1968). Sympathy and empathy. In D. L. Sills (Ed.), *International encyclopedia of the social sciences* (Vol. 15, pp. 441–447). New York: Free Press.

Wispé, L. (1986). The distinction between sympathy and empathy: To call forth a concept a word is needed. *Journal of Personality and Social Psychology, 50*, 314–321.

Zahn-Waxler, C., Robinson, J. L., & Emde, R. N. (1992). The development of empathy in twins. *Developmental Psychology, 28*, 1038–1047.

Prejudice and Discrimination

If we were to wake up some morning and find that everyone was the same race, creed and color, we would find some other cause for prejudice by noon.

—*George Aiken*

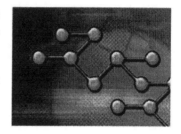

The seeds for conflict and prejudice were planted somewhere in the hills of Palmyra, New York, in 1830. There a young man named Joseph Smith, Jr., received a vision from the angel Moroni. Centuries before, Moroni, as a priest of the Nephites, wrote the history of his religion on a set of golden plates and buried them in the hills of Palmyra. When Moroni appeared to Smith, he revealed the location of the plates and gave him the ability to transcribe the ancient writings into English. This translated text became the *Book of Mormon*, the cornerstone of the Mormon religion. The *Book of Mormon* contained many discrepancies from the Bible. For example, it suggested that God and Jesus Christ were made of flesh and bone.

The conflicts between this newly emerging religion and established Christianity inevitably led to hostile feelings and attitudes between the two groups. Almost from the moment of Joseph Smith's revelations, the persecution of the Mormons began. Leaving Palmyra, the Mormons established a settlement in Kirtland, Ohio, in 1831, but it was a disaster. The Mormons didn't fit in well with the existing community. For example, the Mormons supported the Democratic Party, whereas most of the Christian population in Kirtland supported the Whigs. Mormonism also was a threat to the colonial idea of a single religion in a community. At a time when heresy was a serious crime, the Mormons were seen as outcast heretics. As a result, the Mormons were the targets of scathing newspaper articles that grossly distorted their religion. Mormons were socially ostracized, were denied jobs, became the targets of economic boycotts, and lived under constant threat of attack.

Because of the hostile environment in Kirtland, the Mormons moved on, splitting into two groups. One group began a settlement in Nauvoo, Illinois, and the other in Independence, Missouri. In neither place did the Mormons find peace. Near Nauvoo, for example, a Mormon settlement was burned to

Key Questions

As you read this chapter, find the answers to the following questions:

1. How are prejudice, stereotypes, and discrimination defined?

2. What is the relationship among prejudice, stereotypes, and discrimination?

3. What evidence is there for the prevalence of these three concepts from a historical perspective?

4. What are the personality roots of prejudice?

5. How does gender relate to prejudice?

6. What are the social roots of prejudice?

7. What is modern racism, and what are the criticisms of it?

8. What are the cognitive roots of prejudice?

9. How do cognitive biases contribute to prejudice?

the ground, and its inhabitants were forced to take cover in a rain-soaked woods until they could make it to Nauvoo. At the Independence settlement in 1833, Mormon Bishop Edward Partridge was tarred and feathered after refusing to close a store and print shop he supervised. The tensions in Missouri grew so bad that then Governor Lilburn W. Boggs issued the following order: "The Mormons must be treated as enemies and must be exterminated or driven from the State if necessary, for the public peace" (Arrington & Bitton, 1979).

As a result of the prejudice experienced by the Mormons, they became more clannish, trading among themselves and generally keeping to themselves. As you might imagine, this further enraged the Christian community that hoped to benefit economically from the Mormon presence. It was not uncommon for Mormons to become the targets of vicious physical attacks or even to be driven out of a territory. There was even talk of establishing an independent Mormon state, but eventually, the Mormons settled in Utah.

The fate of the Mormons during the 1800s eerily foreshadowed the treatment of other groups later in history (e.g., Armenians in Turkey, Jews in Europe, ethnic Albanians in Yugoslavia). How could the Mormons have been treated so badly in a country with a Constitution guaranteeing freedom of religion and founded on the premise of religious tolerance?

Attitudes provide us with a way of organizing information about objects and a way to attach an affective response to that object (e.g., like or dislike). Under the right circumstances, attitudes predict one's behavior. In this chapter, we explore a special type of attitude directed at groups of people: prejudice. We look for the underlying causes of incidents such as the Mormon experience and the other acts of prejudice outlined. We ask, How do prejudiced individuals arrive at their views? Is it something about their personalities that leads them to prejudice-based acts? Or do the causes lie more in the social situations? What cognitive processes cause them to have negative attitudes toward those they perceive to be different from themselves? How pervasive and unalterable are those processes in human beings? What are the effects of being a target of prejudice and discrimination? What can we do to reduce prejudice and bring our society closer to its ideals?

The Dynamics of Prejudice, Stereotypes, and Discrimination

When we consider prejudice we really must consider two other interrelated concepts: stereotyping and discrimination. Taken together, these three make up a triad of processes that contribute to negative attitudes, emotions, and behaviors directed at members of certain social groups. First, we define just what social psychologists mean by the term *prejudice* and the related concepts of stereotype and discrimination.

Prejudice

prejudice A biased attitude, positive or negative, based on insufficient information and directed at a group, which leads to prejudgment of members of that group.

The term **prejudice** refers to a biased, often negative, attitude toward a group of people. Prejudicial attitudes include belief structures, which contain information about a group of people, expectations concerning their behavior, and emotions directed at them. When negative prejudice is directed toward a group, it leads to prejudgment of the individual members of that group and negative emotions directed at them as well. It is important to note that the nature of the emotion directed at a group of people depends on the group to which they belong (Cottrell & Neuberg, 2005). In fact, Cottrell and Neuberg have constructed "profiles" characterizing the emotions directed at members of various groups. For example, African Americans (relative to European Americans) yield a profile showing anger/resentment, fear, disgust, and pity. In contrast, Native Americans mostly elicited pity with low levels of anger/resentment, disgust, and fear.

Prejudice also involves cognitive appraisals that are tied to different emotions directed at members of stigmatized groups (Nelson, 2002). For example, fear might be elicited if you find yourself stranded late at night in a neighborhood with a sizeable minority population. On the other hand, you might feel respect when at a professional meeting that includes members from that very same minority group. In short, we appraise (evaluate) a situation and experience an emotion consistent with that appraisal. This can account for the fact that we rarely exhibit prejudice toward all members of a stigmatized group (Nelson, 2002). We may display prejudice toward some members of a group, but not toward others in that group.

Of course, prejudice can be either positive or negative. Fans of a particular sports team, for example, are typically prejudiced in favor of their team. They often believe calls made against their team are unfair, even when the referees are being impartial. Social psychologists, however, have been more interested in prejudice that involves a negative bias—that is, when one group assumes the worst about another group and may base negative behaviors on these assumptions. It is this latter form of prejudice that is the subject of this chapter.

Different Forms of Prejudice

Prejudice comes in a variety of forms, the most visible of which are racism and sexism. *Racism* is the negative evaluation of others primarily because of their skin color. It includes the belief that one racial group is inherently superior to another. *Sexism* is the negative evaluation of others because of their gender (Lips, 1993). Of course, other forms of prejudice exist, such as religious and ethnic prejudice and heterosexism (negative attitudes toward gay men and lesbians), but racism and sexism are the two most widespread prejudices within U.S. society.

We must be very careful when we want to approach the issue of prejudice from a *scientific* perspective not to get caught up in the web of definitions of prejudice floating around in our culture. Partisan political groups and some media have propagated definitions for prejudice that encompass behaviors that a more scientific definition would not. For example, on the Web site of the Center for the Study of White American Culture (http://www.euroamerican.org/library/Racismdf.asp), we are offered the following definition of racism (actually, this is just the first among many principles defining racism):

> Racism is an ideological, structural, and historic stratification process by which the population of European descent, through its individual and institutional distress patterns, intentionally has been able to sustain, to its own best advantage, the dynamic mechanics of upward or downward mobility (of fluid status assignment) to the general disadvantage of the population designated as non-white (on a global scale), using skin color, gender, class, ethnicity or nonwestern nationality as the main indexical criteria used for enforcing differential resource allocation decisions that contribute to decisive changes in relative racial standing in ways most favoring the populations designated as "white."

Notice that this definition ties the notion of racism to the idea of keeping certain groups economically disadvantaged. What is interesting about the definition of racism offered on this site is how close it sounds to a socialist/Marxist manifesto. With only slight modifications, the definition sounds much like such a manifesto. For example, what follows is the same definition offered previously with a few strategic wording changes (shown in italics):

> *Capitalism* is an ideological, structural and historic stratification process by which the *ruling elite*, through its individual and institutional distress patterns, intentionally has been able to sustain, to its own best advantage, the dynamic mechanics of upward or downward mobility (of fluid status assignment) to the general disadvantage of *the proletariat* (on a global scale), *using social class* as the main criterion used for enforcing differential resource allocation decisions that contribute to decisive changes in relative racial standing *in ways most favoring the ruling elite.*

Another thing we need to be careful about is the overapplication of the term *racism* (or any other *–ism*) to behaviors not usually associated with prejudicial attitudes. Another trend in our culture by partisan political parties and the media is to apply the term *racism* to just about anything they see as opposing certain political ideas. Table 4.1 shows a list of such applications collected from the Internet. You could be branded as some kind of "-ist" if you adhere to one of the views listed. The point we wish to make is whether or not opposing some political idea or goals of a group makes you a racist.

What Exactly Does Race Mean?

An important note should be added here about the concept of race. Throughout U.S. history, racial categories have been used to distinguish groups of human beings from one another. However, biologically speaking, race is an elusive and problematic concept. A person's race is not something inherited as a package from his or her parents; nor are biological characteristics such as skin color, hair texture, eye shape, facial features, and so on valid indicators of one's ethnic or cultural background. Consider, for example, an individual whose mother is Japanese and father is African American, or a blond, blue-eyed person who is listed by the U.S. Census Bureau as Native American because her maternal grandmother was Cherokee. To attempt to define these individuals by race is inaccurate and inappropriate. Although many scientists maintain that race does not exist as a biological concept, it does exist as a social construct.

People perceive and categorize others as members of racial groups and often act toward them according to cultural prejudices. In this social sense, race and racism are very real and important factors in human relations. When we refer to race in this book, such as when we discuss race-related violence, it is this socially constructed concept, with its historical, societal, and cultural significance, that we mean.

Stereotypes

Prejudicial attitudes do not stem from perceived physical differences among people, such as skin color or gender. Rather, prejudice relates more directly to the characteristics we assume members of a different racial, ethnic, or other group have. In other words, it relates to the way we think about others.

People have a strong tendency to categorize objects based on perceptual features or uses. We categorize chairs, tables, desks, and lamps as *furniture*. We categorize love, hate, fear, and jealousy as *emotions*. And we categorize people on the basis of their

Table 4.1   Overapplications of the Concept of Prejudice

You might be a racist (or some kind of –ist) if:

1. You think that a state should decide whether its flag should display the Confederate battle flag.

2. You behave in ways that discriminate against minorities, even if discrimination was not intended.

3. You like a team's mascot that has a racial origin (e.g., Native American).

4. You "apply words like backward, primitive, uncivilized, savage, barbaric, or undeveloped to people whose technology [is less advanced]" (*http://fic.ic.org/ cmag/90/4490.html*).

5. You believe that monotheism is better than polytheism.

6. You believe that English should be the official language of the United States.

7. You DON'T believe that all "accents" and "dialects" are legitimate, proper, and equal in value."

8. You oppose affirmative action.

9. You oppose gay marriage.

---

race, gender, nationality, and other obvious features. Of course, categorization is adaptive in the sense that it allows us to direct similar behaviors toward an entire class of objects or people. We do not have to choose a new response each time we encounter a categorized object.

Categorization is not necessarily the same as prejudice, although the first process powerfully influences the second. We sometimes take our predisposition to categorize too far, developing rigid and overgeneralized images of groups. This rigid categorization—this rigid set of positive or negative beliefs about the characteristics or attributes of a group—is a **stereotype** (Judd & Park, 1993; Stangor & Lange, 1994). For example, we may believe that all lawyers are smart, a positive stereotype; or we may believe that all lawyers are devious, a negative stereotype. Many years ago, the political journalist Walter Lippmann (1922) aptly called stereotypes "pictures in our heads." When we encounter someone new who has a clear membership in one or another group, we reach back into our memory banks of stereotypes, find the appropriate picture, and fit the person to it.

In general, stereotyping is simply part of the way we do business cognitively every day. It is part of our cognitive "toolbox" (Gilbert & Hixon, 1991). We all have made judgments about individuals (Boy Scout leader, police officer, college student, feminist) based solely on their group membership. Stereotyping is a time saver; we look in our toolbox, find the appropriate utensil, and characterize the *college student*. It certainly takes less time and energy than trying to get to know that person (individuation; Macrae, Milne, & Bodenhausen, 1994). Again, this is an example of the cognitive miser at work. Of course, this means we will make some very unfair, even destructive judgments of individuals. All of us recoil at the idea that we are being judged solely on the basis of some notion that the evaluator has of group membership.

stereotype A set of beliefs, positive or negative, about the characteristics or attributes of a group, resulting in rigid and overgeneralized images of members of that group.

The Content of Stereotypes

What exactly constitutes a stereotype? Are all stereotypes essentially the same? What kinds of emotions do different stereotypes elicit? The answers to these questions can inform us on the very nature of stereotypes. Regardless of the actual beliefs and information that underlie a stereotype, there appear to be two dimensions underlying stereotypes: warmth (liking or disliking) and competence (respect or disrespect) (Fiske, Cuddy, Glick, & Xu, 2002). According to Fiske et al., these two dimensions combine to define different types of stereotypes. For example, high warmth and high competence yield a positive stereotype involving admiration and pride. Low warmth and low competence results in a negative stereotype involving resentment and anger. Finally, there can be mixed stereotypes involving high competence and low warmth or low competence and high warmth.

Explicit and Implicit Stereotypes

Stereotypes, like prejudicial attitudes, exist on the explicit and implicit level. Explicit stereotypes are those of which we are consciously aware, and they are under the influence of controlled processing. Implicit stereotypes operate on an unconscious level and are activated automatically when a member of a minority group is encountered in the right situation. The operation of implicit stereotypes was demonstrated in an interesting experiment conducted by Banaji, Harden, and Rothman (1993). Participants first performed a "priming task," which involved unscrambling sentences indicating either a male stereotype (aggressiveness), a female stereotype (dependence), or neutral sentences (neutral prime). Later, in a supposedly unrelated experiment, participants read a story depicting either a dependent (male or female) or an aggressive (male or female) target person. Participants then rated the target person in the story for the stereotypic or nonstereotypic trait.

The results of this experiment are shown in Figure 4.1. Notice that for both the male and female stereotypic traits, the trait was rated the same when the prime was neutral, regardless of the gender of the target. However, when the prime activated an implicit gender stereotype, the female stereotypic trait (dependence) was rated higher for female targets than for male targets. The opposite was true for the male stereotypic trait (aggressiveness). Here, aggressiveness was rated higher for male targets than for female targets. An incidental encounter with a stereotype (in this experiment, the prime) can affect evaluations of an individual who is a member of a given social category (e.g., male or female). Participants judged a stereotypic trait more extremely when the stereotype had been activated with a prime than when it had not. Thus, stereotyped information can influence how we judge members of a social group even if we are not consciously aware that it is happening (Banaji et al., 1993).

Explicit and implicit stereotypes operate on two separate levels (controlled processing or automatic processing) and affect judgments differently, depending on the type of judgment a person is required to make (Dovidio, Kawakami, Johnson, Johnson, & Howard, 1997). Dovidio and colleagues found that when a judgmental task required some cognitive effort (in this experiment, to determine whether a black defendant was guilty or not guilty of a crime), explicit racial attitudes correlated with judgments. However, implicit racial attitudes were not correlated with the outcome on the guilt-judgment task. Conversely, on a task requiring a more spontaneous, automatic response (in this experiment, a word-completion task on which an ambiguous incomplete word could be completed in a couple of ways—e.g., b_d could be completed as *bad* or *bed*), implicit attitudes correlated highly with outcome judgments. Thus, explicit and implicit racial attitudes relate to different tasks. Explicit attitudes related more closely to the guilt-innocence task, which required controlled processing. Implicit attitudes related more closely to the word-completion task, which was mediated by automatic processing.

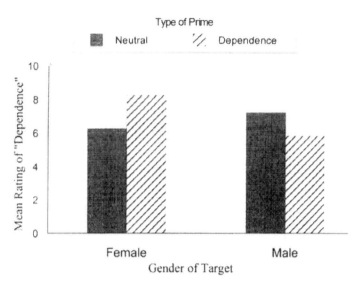

Figure 4.1   Results from an experiment on implicit stereotypes. When a prime activates an implicit female gender stereotype, a female stereotypic trait (dependence) was rated higher for female than for male targets. The opposite was true for the implicit male stereotypic trait (aggressiveness).

Based on data from Banaji, Harden, and Rothman (1993).

Can implicit stereotypes translate into overt differences in behavior directed at blacks and whites? In one experiment, Correll, Park, Judd, and Wittenbrink (2002) had college students play a simple video game. The task was for participants to shoot only armed suspects in the game. The race of the target varied between black and white, some of whom were armed and some unarmed. The results of their first experiment, shown in Figure 4.2, showed that white participants shot at a black armed target more quickly than a white armed target. They also decided NOT to shoot at an unarmed target more quickly if the target was white as compared to black. Correll et al. also provided evidence that the observed "shooter bias" was more related to an individual adhering to cultural biases about blacks as violent and dangerous rather than personally held prejudice or stereotypes.

The automatic activation of stereotypes has been characterized as being a normal part of our cognitive toolboxes that improves the efficiency of our cognitive lives (Sherman, 2001). However, as we have seen, this increased efficiency isn't always a good thing. Can this predisposition toward automatic activation of stereotypes be countered? Fortunately, the answer is yes. Automatic stereotypes can be inhibited under a variety of conditions (Sassenberg & Moskowitz, 2005), including thinking of a counter-stereotypic image or if stereotype activation is perceived to threaten one's self-esteem. Sassenberg and Moskowitz suggest that it is possible to train a person to inhibit automatic activation of stereotypes on a general level so that a wide variety of automatic stereotypes can be inhibited, not just specific ones.

Sassenberg and Moskowitz (2005) investigated the impact of inducing participants to "think different" when it comes to members of minority groups. Thinking different means "one has a mindset in which one is avoiding the typical associations with those groups—one's stereotypes" (p. 507). In their first experiment, Sassenberg and Moskowitz had participants adopt one of two mindsets. The first mindset was a "creative mindset" in which participants were told to think of two or three times that they were creative. The second mindset was a "thoughtful mindset" in which participants were told to think of two or three times they behaved in a thoughtful way.

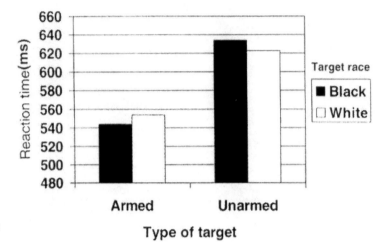

Figure 4.2 Reaction times to shoot armed or unarmed black or white suspects.

Based on data from Correll, Park, Judd, and Wittenbrink (2002).

After doing this, all participants completed a stereotype activation task. Sassenberg and Moskowitz found that stereotypes were inhibited when the "creative mindset" was activated, but not when the "thoughtful mindset" was activated. By encouraging participants to think creatively, the researchers were able to inhibit the activation of automatic stereotypes about African Americans. Sassenberg and Moskowitz suggest that encouraging people to "think differently" can help them inhibit a wide range of automatically activated stereotypes.

The "shooter bias" just discussed also can be modified with some work (Plant & Peruche, 2005). Plant and Peruche found that police officers showed the shooter bias during early trials with a computer game that presented armed or unarmed black or white suspects. However, after a number of trials, the bias was reduced. The average number of errors of shooting at an unarmed suspect was different for blacks and whites during early trials, but not during late trials. During the early trials the officers were more likely to shoot at an unarmed black suspect than an unarmed white suspect. During the later trials the rate of error was equivalent for the unarmed black and white suspects. Thus, police officers were able to modify their behavior in a way that significantly reduced the shooter bias.

Finally, two interesting questions center on when implicit stereotypes develop and when they become distinct from explicit stereotypes. One study sheds light on these two questions. Baron and Banaji (2005) conducted an experiment with 6-year-olds, 10-year-olds, and adults. Using a modified version of the Implicit Attitudes Test (IAT) for children, Baron and Banaji found evidence for anti-black implicit attitudes even among the 6-year-olds. Interestingly, the 6-year-olds also showed correspondingly high levels of explicit prejudice. However, whereas the 10-year-olds and adults showed evidence of implicit prejudice, they showed less explicit prejudice. Evidently, by the time a child is 10 years old, he or she has learned that it is not socially acceptable to express stereotypes and prejudice overtly. But, the implicit stereotypes and prejudice are there and are expressed in subtle ways.

Stereotypes as Judgmental Heuristics

Another way that implicit stereotypes manifest themselves is by acting as judgmental heuristics (Bodenhauser & Wyer, 1985). For example, if a person commits a crime that is stereotype consistent (compared to one that is not stereotype consistent), observers assign a higher penalty, recall fewer facts about the case, and use stereotype-based information to make a judgment (Bodenhauser & Wyer, 1985). Generally, when a negative behavior is stereotype consistent, observers attribute the negative behavior to internal, stable characteristics. Consequently, the crime or behavior is seen as an enduring character flaw likely to lead to the behavior again.

This effect of using stereotype-consistent information to make judgments is especially likely to occur when we are faced with a difficult cognitive task. Recall from Chapter 3 that many of us are cognitive misers, and we look for the path of least resistance when using information to make a decision. When faced with a situation in which we have both stereotype-consistent and stereotype-inconsistent information about a person, more stereotype-consistent information than inconsistent information is likely to be recalled (Macrae, Hewstone, & Griffiths, 1993). As Macrae and colleagues suggested, "when the information-processing gets tough, stereotypes (as heuristic structures) get going" (p. 79).

There are also individual differences in the extent to which stereotypes are formed and used. Levy, Stroessner, and Dweck (1998) suggested that individuals use implicit theories to make judgments about others. That is, individuals use their past experience to form a theory about what members of other groups are like. According to Levy and colleagues, there are two types of implicit theories: *entity theories* and *incremental theories*. Entity theorists adhere to the idea that another person's traits are fixed and will not vary according to the situation. Incremental theorists do not see traits as fixed. Rather, they see them as having the ability to change over time and situations (Levy et al., 1998). A central question addressed by Levy and colleagues was whether entity and incremental theorists would differ in their predisposition to form and use stereotypes. Based on the results of five experiments, Levy and colleagues concluded that compared to incremental theorists, entity theorists:

- Were more likely to use stereotypes.

- Were more likely to agree strongly with stereotypes.

- Were more likely to see stereotypes as representing inborn, inherent group differences.

- Tended to make more extreme judgments based on little information about the characteristics of members of a stereotyped group.

- Perceived a stereotyped group as having less intramember diversity.

- Were more likely to form stereotypes.

In addition to the cognitive functions of stereotypes, there is also an emotional component (Jussim, Nelson, Manis, & Soffin, 1995). According to Jussim and colleagues, once you stereotype a person, you attach a label to that person that is used to evaluate and judge members of that person's group. Typically, a label attached to a stereotyped group is negative. This negative label generates negative affect and mediates judgments of members of the stereotyped group. Jussim and colleagues pointed out that this emotional component of a stereotype is more important in judging others than is the cognitive function (information storage and categorization) of the stereotype.

Discrimination

discrimination Overt behavior—often negatively directed toward a particular group and often tied to prejudicial attitudes—which involves behaving in different ways toward members of different groups.

Discrimination is the behavioral component accompanying prejudice. Discrimination occurs when members of a particular group are subjected to behaviors that are different from the behaviors directed at other groups. For example, if members of a certain racial group are denied housing in a neighborhood open to other groups, that group is being discriminated against. Discrimination takes many forms. For example, it was not uncommon in the 19th through mid-20th centuries to see job advertisements that said "Irish need not apply" or "Jews need not apply." It was also fairly common practice to restrict access to public places, such as beaches, for Jews and blacks. And in the U.S. South, there were separate bathroom facilities, drinking fountains, and schools, and minorities were denied service at certain businesses. This separation of people based on racial, ethnic, religious, or gender groups is discrimination.

It is important to point out that discrimination often is a product of prejudice. Negative attitudes and assumptions about people based on their group affiliation have historically been at the root of prejudice. So, it is clear that many instances of discrimination can be traced directly to underlying prejudicial attitudes. However, discrimination can occur even in the absence of underlying prejudice. For example, imagine an owner of a small company who lives in a town where there are no minorities. This person hires all white employees. Now, the owner might be the most liberal-minded person in the world who would never discriminate based on race. However, his actions would technically be classified as discrimination. In this case the discrimination is not based on any underlying prejudice. Rather, it is based on the demographics of the area in which the company exists.

The Persistence and Recurrence of Prejudice and Stereotypes

Throughout history, members of *majority* groups (those in power) have held stereotypical images of members of *minority* groups (those not in power). These images supported prejudicial feelings, discriminatory behavior, and even wide-scale violence directed against minority-group members.

History teaches us that stereotypes and prejudicial attitudes are quite enduring. For example, some stereotypes of Jews and Africans are hundreds of years old. Prejudice appears to be an integral part of human existence. However, stereotypes and feelings may change, albeit slowly, as the context of our feelings toward other groups changes. For example, during and just after World War II, Americans had negative feelings toward the Japanese. For roughly the next 40 years, the two countries were at peace and had a harmonious relationship. This was rooted in the fact that the postwar American occupation of Japan (1945–1951) was benign. The Americans helped the Japanese rebuild their war-shattered factories, and the Japanese began to compete in world markets. But in the difficult economic times of the 1980s and early 1990s, many of the beliefs that characterized Japanese-American relations during World War II reemerged, although in somewhat modified form. Compared to how Japanese view Americans, Americans tend to see Japanese as more competitive, hard working, prejudiced, and crafty (see Figure 4.3). Japanese have a slight tendency to see Americans as undereducated, lazy, and not terribly hard working. Americans see Japanese as unfair, arrogant, and overdisciplined, as grinds who do nothing but work hard because of their conformity to group values (Weisman, 1991). Japanese, for their part, see Americans as arrogant

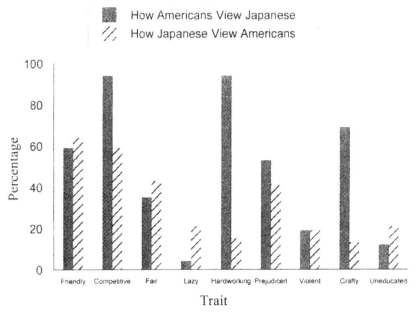

How Americans View Japanese
How Japanese View Americans

Figure 4.3 How the Americans and Japanese view one another. Both Americans and Japanese hold stereotypical views of the other group.

Based on data from a 1992 Times/CNN poll, cited in Holland (1992).

and lacking in racial purity, morality, and dedication (Weisman, 1991). The stereotypes on both sides have been altered and transformed by the passage of time, but like short skirts and wide ties, they tend to recycle. The periodicity of stereotypes suggests that they are based more on external factors such as economics and competition than on any stable characteristics of the group being categorized.

It is interesting to note that stereotypes and the cues used to categorize individuals change over time. Some historians of the ancient Mediterranean suggest that there was a time before color prejudice. The initial encounter of black Africans and white Mediterraneans is the oldest chapter in the chronicle of black-white relations. Snowden (1983) traced the images of Africans as seen by Mediterraneans from the Egyptians to Roman mercenaries. Mediterraneans knew that these black soldiers came from a powerful independent African state, Nubia, located in what today would be southern Egypt and northern Sudan. Nubians appear to have played an important role in the formation of Egyptian civilization (Wilford, 1992). Positive images of Africans appear in the artwork and writings of ancient Mediterranean peoples (Snowden, 1983)

The first encounters between blacks and whites were encounters between equals. The Africans were respected for their military skill and their political and cultural sophistication. Slavery existed in the ancient world but was not tied to skin color; anyone captured in war might be enslaved, whether white or black (Snowden, 1983). Prejudice, stereotyping, and discrimination existed too. Athenians may not have cared about skin color, but they cared deeply about national origin. Foreigners were excluded from citizenship. Women were also restricted and excluded. Only males above a certain age could be citizens and participate fully in society.

It is not clear when color prejudice came into existence. It may have been with the advent of the African–New World slave trade in the 16th century. Whenever it began, it is likely that race and prejudice were not linked until some real power or status differences arose between groups. Although slavery in the ancient world was not based exclusively on skin color, slaves were almost always of a different ethnic group, national origin, religion, or political unit than their owners. In the next sections, we explore the causes of prejudice, focusing first on its roots in personality and social life and then on its roots in human cognitive functioning.

Individual Differences and Prejudice: Personality and Gender

What are the causes of prejudice? In addressing this question, social psychologists have looked not only at our mental apparatus, our inclination to categorize, but also at characteristics of the individual. Is there such a thing as prejudiced personality? Are men or women more prone to prejudice? We explore the answers to these questions in this section.

authoritarianism
A personality characteristic that relates to a person's unquestioned acceptance of and respect for authority.

Social psychologists and sociologists have long suspected a relationship between personality characteristics and prejudice. One important personality dimension relating to prejudice, stereotyping, and discrimination is **authoritarianism**. Authoritarianism is a personality characteristic that relates to unquestioned acceptance of and respect for authority. Authoritarian individuals tend to identify closely with those in authority and also tend to be prejudiced.

The Authoritarian Personality

In the late 1940s, Adorno and other psychologists at the University of California at Berkeley studied people who might have been the prototypes of Archie Bunker (a character on the popular 1970s TV show *All in the Family*)—individuals who wanted different ethnic groups to be suppressed and degraded, preferably by an all-powerful government or state. Archie Bunker embodied many of the characteristics of the **authoritarian personality**, which is characterized by submissive feelings toward authority; rigid, unchangeable beliefs; and racism and sexism (Adorno, Frenkel-Brunswik, Levinson, & Sanford, 1950).

authoritarian personality
A personality dimension characterized by submissive feelings toward authority, rigid and unchangeable beliefs, and a tendency toward prejudicial attitudes.

Motivated by the tragedy of the murder of millions of Jews and other Eastern Europeans by the Nazis, Adorno and his colleagues conducted a massive study of the relationship between the authoritarian personality and the Nazi policy of *genocide*, the killing of an entire race or group of people. They speculated that the individuals who carried out the policy of mass murder were of a personality type that predisposed them to do whatever an authority figure ordered, no matter how vicious or monstrous.

The massive study produced by the Berkeley researchers, known as *The Authoritarian Personality*, was driven by the notion that there was a relationship, and interconnectedness, between the way a person was reared and various prejudices he or she later came to hold. The study surmised that prejudiced people were highly *ethnocentric*; that is, they believed in the superiority of their own group or race (Dunbar, 1987). The Berkeley researchers argued that individuals who were ethnocentric were likely to be prejudiced against a whole range of ethnic, racial, and religious groups in their culture. They found this to be true, that such people were indeed prejudiced against many or all groups that were different from themselves. A person who was anti-color tended to be anti-Semitic as well. These people seemed to embody a prejudiced personality type, the authoritarian personality.

The Berkeley researchers discovered that authoritarians had a particularly rigid and punishing upbringing. They were raised in homes in which children were not allowed to express any feelings or opinions except those considered correct by their parents and other authority figures. People in authority were not to be questioned and, in fact, were to be idolized. Children handled pent-up feelings of hostility toward these suppressive parents by becoming a kind of island, warding these feelings off by inventing very strict categories and standards. They became impatient with uncertainty and ambiguity and came to prefer clear-cut and simple answers. Authoritarians had very firm categories: This was good; that was bad. Any groups that violated their notions of right and wrong were rejected.

This rigid upbringing engendered frustration and a strong concealed rage, which could be expressed only against those less powerful. These children learned that those in authority had the power to do as they wished. If the authoritarian obtained power over someone, the suppressed rage came out in full fury. Authoritarians were at the feet of those in power and at the throats of those less powerful. The suppressed rage was usually expressed against a *scapegoat*, a relatively powerless person or group, and tended to occur most often during times of frustration, such as during an economic slump.

There is also evidence that parental attitudes relate to a child's implicit and explicit prejudice (Sinclair, Dunn, & Lowery, 2005). Sinclair et al. had parents of fifth and sixth graders complete a racial attitudes measure. The children completed measures of strength of identification with the parent and tests of implicit and explicit prejudice. The results showed that parental prejudice was significantly related to the child's implicit prejudice when the child's identification with the parent was high. So, it is children who have a strong desire to identify (take on the parent's characteristics) with the parent who are most likely to show implicit prejudice. A similar effect was found when the child's explicit prejudice was considered. When the child identified strongly with the parent, the parent's prejudice was positively associated with the child's explicit prejudice. This effect was the opposite for children who did not closely identify with the parents, perhaps indicating a rejection of parental prejudice among this latter group of children.

The authoritarian personality, the individual who is prejudiced against all groups perceived to be different, may gravitate toward hate groups. On July 2, 1999, Benjamin Smith went on a drive-by shooting rampage that killed two and injured several others. Smith took his own life while being chased by police. Smith had a history of prejudicial attitudes and acts. Smith came under the influence of the philosophy of Matt Hale, who became the leader of the World Church in 1996. Hale's philosophy was that the white race was the elite race in the world and that members of any other races or ethnic groups (which he called "inferior mud races") were the enemy. Smith himself believed that whites should take up arms against those inferior races. The early research on prejudice, then, emphasized the role of irrational emotions and thoughts that were part and parcel of the prejudiced personality. These irrational emotions, simmered in a pot of suppressed rage, were the stuff of prejudice, discrimination, and eventually, intergroup violence. The violence was usually set off by frustration, particularly when resources, such as jobs, were scarce.

Social psychologists have also looked at whether there is a prejudiced personality (Dunbar, 1995; Gough, 1951). An updated version of the older concept of authoritarianism is right-wing authoritarianism (RWA), a concept originated by Altemeyer (1981).

Right-wing authoritarianism is related to higher levels of prejudice. Gough developed a prejudiced scale (PR scale) using items from the Minnesota Multiphasic Personality Inventory. Gough (1951) reported that the PR scale correlated with anti-Semitic attitudes among midwestern high school students.

Dunbar (1995) administered the PR scale and two other measures of racism to white and Asian-American students. He also administered a measure of anti-Semitism to see if the PR scale still correlated with prejudiced attitudes. Dunbar found that Asian Americans had higher scores on both the PR scale and the measure of anti-Semitism than did whites, indicating greater anti-Semitism among Asians than whites. However, the only significant relationships on the PR scale between anti-Semitic and racist attitudes were among the white participants.

Social Dominance Orientation

social dominance orientation (SDO) Desire to have one's in-group in a position of dominance or superiority to out-groups. High social dominance orientation is correlated with higher levels of prejudice.

Another personality dimension that has been associated with prejudicial attitudes is the **social dominance orientation (SDO).** A social dominance orientation is defined as "the extent to which one desires that one's in-group dominate or be superior to out-groups" (Pratto, Sidanius, Stallworth, & Malle, 1994). In other words, individuals with a high SDO would like to see their group (e.g., racial or ethnic group) be in a dominant position over other groups.

Research also shows that one's SDO also correlates with prejudicial attitudes. For example, Pratto et al. (1994) found that a high SDO score was related to anti-black and anti-Arab prejudice. The higher the SDO score, the more prejudice was manifested. In a later study SDO was found to correlate with a wide range of prejudices, including a "generalized prejudice, and specific prejudices against homosexuals, the mentally disabled and with racism and sexism" (Ekehammar, Akrami, Gylje, & Zakrisson, 2004).

In an experiment (Kemmelmeier, 2005), white mock jurors were asked to judge a criminal case in which the defendant was black or white. The results showed no difference in how the white participants judged the black or white defendant. However, participants who scored high on a measure of social dominance showed more bias against the black defendant than participants who scored low on the social dominance measure. In fact, low SDO individuals showed a bias in favor of the black defendant.

Interestingly, measured differences between groups on the SDO dimension are related to the perceived status differences between the groups being tested (Levin, 2004). For example, Levin found that among American and Irish participants, individuals with high SDO scores saw a greater status difference between their group and an out-group (e.g., Irish Catholics versus Irish Protestants). In other words, an Irish Catholic person with a high SDO score saw a greater status difference between Irish Catholics and Irish Protestants than an Irish Catholic with a lower SDO score. A similar, but nonsignificant, trend was found for Israeli participants.

If we consider the SDO dimension along with authoritarianism, we can identify a pattern identifying highly prejudiced individuals. In a study by Altemeyer (2004), participants completed measures of SDO and right-wing authoritarianism (RWA). Altemeyer found modest correlations between the SDO scale and RWA scale and prejudice when the scales were considered separately. However, when the two scales were considered together (i.e., identifying individuals who were high on both SDO and RWA), stronger correlations were found with prejudice. Altemeyer concluded that individuals with both SDO and RWA are among the most prejudiced people you will find. Fortunately, Altemeyer points out, there are very few such individuals.

There is also evidence that SDO and RWA may relate differently to different forms of prejudice. Whitley (1999), for example, found that an SDO orientation was related to stereotyping, negative emotion, and negative attitudes directed toward African Americans and homosexuals. However, RWA was related to negative stereotypes and emotion directed at homosexuals, but not African Americans. In fact, RWA was related to positive emotions concerning African Americans.

Openness to New Experience and Agreeableness

A currently popular model of personality is the "big five" model of personality (McCrae & Costa, 1987). According to this approach there are five dimensions underlying personality: extroversion/introversion, agreeableness, conscientiousness, neuroticism, and openness to experience and culture. As we shall see, two of these dimensions (agreeableness and openness to experience) relate to prejudice. Briefly, agreeableness is a "friendliness dimension" including characteristics such as altruism, trust, and willingness to give support to others (Gerow & Bordens, 2005). Openness to experience includes curiosity, imagination, and creativity (Gerow & Bordens, 2005), along with a willingness to try new things and divergent thinking (Flynn, 2005).

Studies investigating the relationship between the big five personality dimensions and prejudice have shown that agreeableness and openness to experience correlate with prejudice. For example, Ekehammar and Akrami (2003) evaluated participants on the big five personality dimensions and measures of classic prejudice (overt, old-fashioned prejudice) and modern prejudice (prejudice expressed in subtle ways). Ekehammar and Akrami found that two of the big five personality dimensions correlated significantly with prejudice: agreeableness and openness to experience. Those participants high on the agreeableness and openness dimensions showed less prejudice. The remaining three dimensions did not correlate significantly with prejudice.

In another study, consisting of three experiments, Flynn (2005) also explored more fully the relationship between openness to experience and prejudice. The results of her three experiments confirmed that individuals who had high scores on openness to experience displayed less prejudice. For example, individuals who are open to new experiences rated a black interviewee as more intelligent, responsible, and honest than individuals who are less open to new experiences.

Gender and Prejudice

Another characteristic relating to prejudice is gender. Research shows that men tend to be higher than women on SDO (Dambrun, Duarte, & Guimond, 2004; Pratto et al., 1994). This gender difference appears to be rooted in different patterns of social identity orientations among men and women. Although men and women show in-group identification at equivalent levels (i.e., men identifying with the male in-group and women identifying with the female in-group), men more strongly identified with the male in-group than did women with the female in-group (Dambrun et al., 2004).

Research in this area has concentrated on male and female attitudes toward homosexuality. Generally, males tend to have more negative attitudes toward homosexuality than women (Kite, 1984; Kite & Whitley, 1998). Do men and women view gay men and lesbians differently? There is evidence that males have more negative attitudes toward gay men than toward lesbians (Gentry, 1987; Kite, 1984; Kite & Whitley, 1998). The findings for females are less clear. Kite and Whitley, for example, reported that women tend not to make distinctions between gay men and lesbians. Other research, however, shows that females show more negative attitudes toward lesbians than gay men (Gentry, 1987; Kite, 1984).

Baker and Fishbein (1998) investigated the development of gay and lesbian prejudice among a sample of 7th, 9th, and 11th graders. They found that males tended to be more prejudiced against gays and lesbians than females were, and male participants showed greater prejudice against gay males than against lesbians. Prejudice against gays and lesbians increased between 7th and 9th grade for both males and females; however, between the 9th and 11th grades, gay prejudice *decreased* for female participants, whereas it *increased* for male participants. Baker and Fishbein suggested that the increase in male antigay prejudice may be rooted in the male's increased defensive reactions to intimate relationships.

A central question emerging from this research is whether there are gender differences in other forms of prejudice. One study, for example, confirmed that males show more ethnic prejudice than females on measures concerning friendship and allowing an ethnic minority to live in one's neighborhood. Males and females did not differ when interethnic intimate relations were considered (Hoxter & Lester, 1994). There is relatively little research in this area, and clearly, more is needed to investigate the relationship between gender and prejudice for a wide range of prejudices.

The Social Roots of Prejudice

The research on the authoritarian personality and gender provides an important piece of the puzzle of prejudice and discrimination. However, it is only one piece. Prejudice and discrimination are far too complex and prevalent to be explained by a single, personality-based cause. Prejudice occurs in a social context, and another piece of the puzzle can be found in the evolution of feelings that form the basis of relations between dominant and other groups in a particular society.

To explore the social roots of prejudice, let's consider the situation of African Americans in the United States. During the years before the Civil War, black slaves were considered the property of white slave owners, and this arrangement was justified by the notion that blacks were in some way less human than whites. Their degraded condition was used as proof of their inferiority.

In 1863, in the middle of the Civil War, President Lincoln issued the Emancipation Proclamation, setting slaves free. But abolition did little to end prejudice and negative attitudes toward blacks. The Massachusetts 54th Regiment, for example, was an all-black Union Army unit—led by an all-white officer corps. Blacks were said to lack the ability to lead; thus no black officers were allowed. Because of these stereotypes and prejudices, members of the 54th were also paid less than their white counterparts in other regiments. Initially also, they were not allowed in combat roles; they were used instead for manual labor, such as for building roads.

Despite prejudice, some blacks did rise to positions of prominence. Frederick Douglass, who escaped from slavery and became a leader and spokesperson for African Americans, was instrumental in convincing President Lincoln to issue the Emancipation Proclamation and to allow black troops to fight in the Civil War. Toward the end of the war, over 100,000 black troops were fighting for the North, and some historians maintain that without these troops, the result of the Civil War may have been different.

Over the course of the next hundred years, African Americans made strides in improving their economic and social status. The U.S. Supreme Court ruled in *Brown v. Board of Education* that segregated (separate but equal) schools violated the Constitution and mandated that schools and other public facilities be integrated. Since then, the feelings of white Americans toward African Americans have become more positive (Goleman, 1991). This change in attitude and behavior reflects the importance of social norms in influencing and regulating the expression of feelings and beliefs.

Yet there is a curious nature to these feelings. White Americans almost unanimously endorse such general principles as integration and equality, but they are generally opposed to steps designed to actualize these principles, such as mandatory busing or affirmative action (Katz, Wackenhut, & Hass, 1986). It may be that white Americans pay lip service to the principle of racial equality. They perceive African Americans as being *both* disadvantaged by the system *and* deviant. In other words, white Americans are aware that African Americans may have gotten a raw deal, but they also see them as responsible for their own plight (Katz et al., 1986). Remember that the human tendency to attribute behavior to internal rather than external causes makes it more likely that people will ascribe the reasons for achievement or lack of it to the character of an individual or group.

Although we may no longer have tarring and feathering of members of different groups, prejudice still exists in more subtle forms. If acquired early enough, prejudice seems to become part of one's deepest feelings:

> Many southerners have confessed to me, for instance, that even though in their minds they no longer feel prejudice toward African Americans, they still feel squeamish when they shake hands with an African American. These feelings are left over from what they learned in their families as children. (Pettigrew, 1986, p. 20)

Given the importance of racial issues in U.S. history and given the way people process information in a categorical and automatic way, some observers assume that racist feelings are the rule for Americans (Gaertner & Dovidio, 1986).

Incidents from daily life seem to bear out this conclusion. In 2003 conservative commentator Rush Limbaugh was called to task for comments he made in his role as an ESPN sports commentator. Limbaugh speculated that the sportswriters were pulling for black quarterback Donovan McNabb to succeed because McNabb was black. Most pundits viewed Limbaugh's comments as racist even though Limbaugh denied his comments were racist. In any event, Limbaugh resigned his ESPN position because of the uproar about his comments.

In July 2006, the Sony Corporation was accused of using a racist advertisement in the Netherlands for its new "White PlayStation Portable" game unit. The advertisement showed a white woman grabbing the face of a black woman aggressively. The slogan on the advertisement read "PlayStation Portable White Is Coming." Despite the accusations, Sony was sticking by the advertisement. A spokesperson for Sony denied that the advertisement was racist, adding that the women depicted were intended to contrast the new white gaming system with its existing black system (Gibson, 2006).

Even our politicians are not exempt from letting racially charged statements slip out. In 2002, Senate Majority Leader Trent Lott made questionable statements at the 100th birthday celebration of Senator Strom Thurmond. Thurmond was one of the so-called "Dixiecrats" in the 1940s. The Dixiecrats comprised a group of Democrats who split off from the main party because of the insertion of a civil rights plank in the Democratic Party platform. In 1948 Thurmond ran as a third-party candidate for president on the Dixiecrat ticket. At his 100th birthday celebration, Lott said "I want to say this about my state: When Strom Thurmond ran for president, we voted for him. We're proud of it. And if the rest of the country had followed our lead, we wouldn't have had all these problems over all these years, either." Once again these statements were labeled as racist. Lott denied any racist intent and apologized for his statements (NPR, 2002). Regardless, he was forced to resign his post as Senate majority leader (although he remained a senator).

Modern Racism

Although racist beliefs and prejudicial attitudes still exist, they have certainly become less prevalent than they once were. For example, according to data from the General Social Survey (1999), attitudes toward blacks improved between 1972 and 1996. Figure 4.4 shows some of the data from this survey. As shown in Figure 4.4, responses reflecting more positive racial attitudes can be seen in questions concerning whether whites have a right to keep blacks out of their neighborhood (blacks out), whether one would vote for a black presidential candidate (black president), whether whites would send their children to a school where more than 50% of the children were black (send children), whether they would vote to change a rule excluding blacks from a social club (change rule), and whether they would support a law preventing housing discrimination (housing law).

Despite these gains, prejudice still exists. Why this contradiction? Since the study of the authoritarian personality was published several decades ago, it has become more difficult (socially and legally) to overtly express prejudice against individuals from particular racial groups. It is not unusual, for example, for an individual to be removed from his or her job because of a racist statement. For example, in 1996, WABC (a New York) radio station fired Bob Grant, one of its most popular on-air personalities because of a history of racist statements. Even calling a racist a racist can get you fired. Alan Dershowitz, a prominent attorney, was fired from his talk show after calling Grant despicable and racist. Even if racism was not the intent, one can still be fired for

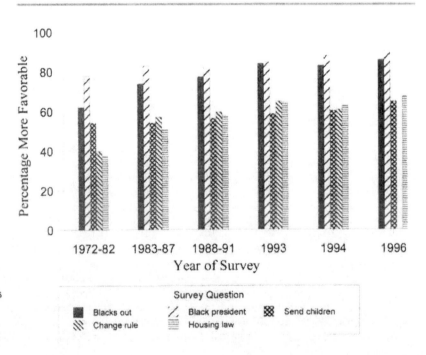

Figure 4.4 The changing face of racial prejudice. Between the years 1972 and 1996, whites have shown more favorable attitudes towards blacks.

Based on data from General Social Survey (1999).

using racial (or other ethnic) slurs. Even the appearance of prejudice from someone in an official position is unacceptable today.

Some social psychologists believe that many white Americans currently are **aversive racists**, people who truly believe they are unprejudiced, who want to do the right thing but, in fact, feel very uneasy and uncomfortable in the presence of someone from a different racial group (Gaertner & Dovidio, 1986). When they are with members of other groups, they smile too much, are overly friendly, and are sometimes very fearful. These feelings do not lead the aversive racist to behave in a negative way toward members of other groups; rather, they lead him or her to avoid them.

This more subtle prejudice is marked by an uncertainty in feeling and action toward people from different racial groups. McConahay (1986) referred to this configuration of feelings and beliefs as **modern racism**, also known as *symbolic racism*. Modern racists moderate their responses to individuals from different racial groups to avoid showing obvious prejudice; they express racism but in a less open manner than was formerly common. Modern racists would say that yes, racism is a bad thing and a thing of the past; still, it is a fact that African Americans "are pushing too hard, too fast, and into places where they are not wanted" (p. 93).

McConahay devised a scale to measure modern racism. In contrast to older scales, the modern racism scale presents items in a less racially charged manner. For example, an item from the modern racism scale might ask participants whether African Americans have received more economically than they deserve. On an old-fashioned scale, an item might ask how much you would mind if an African American family moved in next door to you. According to McConahay, modern racists would be more likely to be detected with the less racist items on an old-fashioned scale. McConahay found that the modern racism scale is sensitive enough to pick up more subtle differences in an individual's racial feelings and behaviors than the older scales. The modern racism scale tends to reveal a more elusive and indirect form of racism than the older scales.

In one of McConahay's experiments, participants (all of whom were white) were asked to play the role of a personnel director of a major company. All had taken a version of the modern racism scale. The "personnel director" received a resume of a graduating college senior who was a very ordinary job candidate. The race of the candidate was manipulated: for half of the participants, a photograph of an African American was attached, and for the other half, a photograph of a white person was attached.

Another variable was added to the experiment in addition to the race of the applicant. Half of each group of participants were told that there were no other qualified candidates for the job. This was called the *no anchor* condition, because the personnel directors had no basis for judgment, no other candidate against which to evaluate the ordinary candidate. The other half of each group saw the resumes of two other candidates, both white, who were far superior to the ordinary candidate, white or African American. This was called the *anchor* condition, because the personnel directors now had a basis for comparison.

Personnel directors in all four groups were asked to make a decision about the candidate on a scale ranging from "definitely would hire" to "definitely would not hire." McConahay's findings revealed that individuals who have high scores on the modern racism scale (indicating that they are prejudiced) do not treat white candidates any differently than their nonprejudiced counterparts.

Whether they scored 0 or 25 or somewhere in between on the scale, all participants rated the white candidates in both the anchor and the no-anchor condition in a similar way. Participants with low scores (near 0) rated white candidates about the same, whereas high scorers (closer to 25) rated the white no-anchor candidate a little higher than the white anchor candidate.

aversive racist Person who believes he or she is unprejudiced, but feels uneasy and uncomfortable in the presence of someone from a different racial group.

modern racism Subtle racial prejudice, expressed in a less open manner than is traditional overt racial prejudice and characterized by an uncertainty in feeling and action toward minorities.

More interesting are the ratings of African American candidates. For nonprejudiced participants, African Americans, anchored or not, were rated precisely the same. But there was a very large difference between candidates for the prejudiced participants. An unanchored African American candidate was absolutely dismissed, whereas the anchored African American candidate, compared to more qualified whites, was given the highest rating.

Why these differences? Recall that modern racists are rather uncertain about how to feel or act in situations with members of different racial or ethnic groups. They particularly do not want to discriminate when others will find out about it and can label what they did as racist (Donnerstein & Donnerstein, 1973). To reject a very ordinary African American candidate when there were no other candidates probably would not be seen as prejudiced, because the candidate was not qualified. Note how much more favorably the modern racist judged the white candidate in the same anchor circumstances.

But when there is a chance that his or her behavior might be termed racist, the modern racist overvalues African Americans. This is seen when there were qualified white candidates (anchor condition). The modern racist goes out of his or her way to appear unprejudiced and therefore gives the ordinary African American candidate the highest rating. Participants who scored low on the modern racism scale felt confident about how to feel and act in racial situations. People from different racial groups do not make them uncomfortable; they "call it like they see it" (Hass, Katz, Rizzo, Bailey, & Eisenstadt, 1991).

The concept of modern racism is not without its critics. Some suggest that it is illogical to equate opposition to an African American candidate or affirmative action programs with racism (Sykes, 1992). Other critics point out that modern racism researchers have not adequately defined and measured modern racism (Tetlock, 1986). They also point out that high correlations exist (ranging from about $r = .6$ to $.7$) between old-fashioned racism and modern racism. That is, if a person is a modern racist, he or she also is likely to be an old-fashioned racist. According to these critics, there simply may not be two forms of racism.

The fact is that race is a complex issue and contains many facets. In the past, according to public opinion surveys, whites were essentially either favorable or unfavorable to the cause of African Americans. But racial feelings are more subtle now. Someone might be against busing of schoolchildren but not opposed to having an African American neighbor (Sniderman & Piazza, 1994). Additionally, a person's racial attitudes are often affected by his or her politics. Individuals who have favorable attitudes toward African Americans but who perceive affirmative action policies to be unfair may come to dislike African Americans as a consequence (Sniderman & Piazza, 1994).

Changing Social Norms

What accounts for the changes we see in the expression of racist sentiments and for the appearance of modern racism? Our society, primarily through its laws, has made the obvious expression of racism undesirable. Over the past 30 years, social norms have increasingly dictated the acceptance of members of different racial and ethnic groups into mainstream society. Overt racism has become socially unacceptable. But for many individuals, deeply held racist sentiments remain unchanged. Their racism has been driven underground by society's expectations and standards.

Because of changed social norms, charges of prejudice and discrimination are taken seriously by those against whom they are made. In 2002, the Cracker Barrel restaurant chain was sued by the Justice Department on behalf of several patrons who claimed they had been discriminated against because of their race. In the lawsuit, the plaintiffs alleged that Cracker Barrel showed a pattern of discrimination against African Americans by refusing them service, allowing white waitstaffers not to serve blacks, seating black patrons in a segregated area, and making black patrons wait longer than white patrons to be seated (NAACP, 2002). In 2004 Cracker Barrel settled the suit with the Justice Department. Cracker Barrel agreed to overhaul its manager and employee training (Litchblau, 2004).

Despite such cases, it appears that societal norms have been altered, allowing racial and ethnic animosities and prejudices to be expressed. One good example of these shifting norms is the proliferation of hate on the Internet. It is nearly impossible to get an accurate count of the number of hate sites on the Internet. However, according to the Antidefamation League (1999), hate groups such as Neo-Nazis, Skinheads, and the Ku Klux Klan are using the Internet to spread their message of hate. The Internet has allowed hate speech and the advocacy of violence against minorities to cross national boundaries. For example, on one Web site, one can peruse a variety of racist cartoons and purchase hate-related products. Hate-based "educational materials" are also easily obtained on the Internet. One program called *The Jew Rats* portrays Jews as rats who are indoctrinated to hate others and take over the world. Racist video games are also readily available. One game called *Bloodbath in Niggeria* involves shooting caricatures of Africans who pop up in huts. Yet another called *Border Patrol* allows gamers to shoot illegal Mexican immigrants running across the U.S. border. In addition, the Internet provides a medium that can help hate groups organize more easily. In addition to organizing on a local level, hate sites can now easily link hate groups across land and ocean, making the spread of hate and prejudice much easier.

On the other hand, there is evidence that attitudes, although not necessarily behavior, toward specific groups have become more positive. For example, gender stereotypes seem to have lessened recently at least among college students, if not among older individuals (Swim, 1994). In this case, social norms in favor of greater equality seem to be holding. Finally, it is worth noting that social norms operate on a number of levels simultaneously. It is generally true that societal norms have turned against the overt expression of prejudice, and this has reduced prejudice. However, norms also operate on a more "local" level. Not only are we affected by societal norms, but we are also influenced by the norms of those closest to us (e.g., family and friends). If it is normative within your immediate group of family and friends not to be prejudiced or express prejudices, then odds are you won't. If, however, your immediate family and friends are prejudiced and express prejudices, then you will probably do the same. Generally, we strive to be "good group" members, which often means following the norms established by that group, whether positive or negative (Crandall, Eshleman, & O'Brien, 2002).

The Cognitive Roots of Prejudice: From Categories to Stereotypes

Cognitive social psychologists believe that one of the best ways to understand how stereotypes form and persist is to look at how humans process information. As we saw in Chapters 2 and 3, human beings tend to be cognitive misers, preferring the least effortful means of processing social information (Taylor, 1981). We have a limited capacity to deal with social information and therefore can deal with only relatively small amounts at any one time (Fiske & Taylor, 1991).

Given these limitations, people try to simplify problems by using shortcuts, primarily involving category-based processes (Bodenhausen & Wyer, 1985; Brewer, 1988). In other words, it is easier to pay attention to the group to which someone belongs than to the individual traits of the person. It takes less effort and less time for someone to use category-based (group-based) information than to try to deal with people on an individual basis (Macrae et al., 1994). For example, in June 1998 when James Byrd was dragged to death in Texas, he was chosen as a victim purely because of his race. Byrd, a black man, was hitchhiking home from a party when three white men stopped to pick him up. The three men beat Byrd and then chained him to their truck and dragged him to death—all because he was black and in the wrong place at the wrong time. Research studies of the cognitive miser demonstrate that when people's ability or motivation to process information is diminished, they tend to fall back on available stereotypes. For example, in one study, when a juror's task was complex, he or she recalled more negative things about a defendant if the defendant was Hispanic than if the defendant did not belong to an identifiable group. When the juror's task was simple, no differences in judgment were found between a Hispanic and a non-Hispanic defendant (Bodenhausen & Lichtenstein, 1987). When the situation gets more complicated, individuals tend to rely on these stereotypes.

Individuals are more likely to fall back on stereotypes when they are not at the peak of their cognitive abilities (Bodenhausen, 1990). Bodenhausen tested participants to determine if they were "night people"—individuals who function better in the evening and at night—or "day people"—individuals who function better in the morning. He then had participants make judgments about a student's misconduct. Sometimes the student was described in nonstereotypic terms (his name was "Robert Garner"), and in other situations he was portrayed as Hispanic ("Roberto Garcia"), as African American, or as an athlete.

The experiment showed that when people are not at their peak (morning people at night or night people in the morning), they tend to solve problems by using stereotypes. As shown in Figure 4.5, morning types relied on the stereotype to judge the student when presented with the case in the evening; evening types fell back on stereotypes in the morning. These findings suggest that category-based judgments take place when we do not have the capacity, the motivation, or the energy to pay attention to the target, and these lead human beings into a variety of cognitive misconceptions and errors.

Figure 4.5
Ratings of perceived guilt as a function of time of day, personality type, and stereotype activation. When individuals are not at their cognitive peak, they are more likely to rely on stereotypes when making judgments.

Based on data from Bodenhausen, 1990

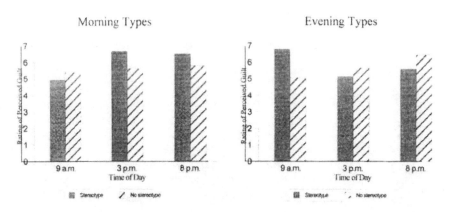

Identification with the In-Group

One of the principal cognitive processes common to all human beings seems to be the tendency to categorize people either as belonging to an in-group (us) or an out-group (them). This tendency has implications beyond simple categorization. We tend to identify with and prefer members of the in-group. We also tend to ascribe more uniquely "human emotions" (e.g., affection, admiration, and pride) to the in-group than the out-group (Leyens et al., 2000). Taken together, these tendencies comprise the **in-group bias**. This tendency to favor the in-group is accompanied by a simultaneous tendency to identify "different" others as belonging to a less favored out-group, which we do not favor.

in-group bias The powerful tendency of humans to favor over other groups the group to which they belong.

Our tendency to favor the in-group and vilify the out-group is related to the type of emotions we experience about those groups. When we feel good about something that the in-group does or is associated with and feel anger over what the out-group does, then we are most likely to strongly identify with the in-group (Kessler & Hollbach, 2005). So, for example, if our country is associated with something good (e.g., winning an Olympic medal) and another country is associated with something bad (e.g., a judging scandal at the Olympics), we feel the most in-group pride and are likely to strongly identify with the in-group. Conversely, we are less likely to identify with the in-group when it is associated with something bad and the out-group is associated with something good (Kessler & Hollbach, 2005). In other words, we are likely to bask in reflected glory (BIRG) when the in-group does something good and cut off reflected failure (CORF) when the in-group does something bad (Kessler & Hollbach, 2005). This might explain why so many people change attitudes quickly (e.g., about the 2003 Iraq War) when news is bad (CORFing). However, when things are going well (e.g., the early stages of the Iraq War), we experience a sense of national pride and are happy with our BIRGing.

How we perceive and judge members of an out-group depends, at least in part, on how we perceive the in-group. The in-group is normally used as a standard by which the behavior of out-group members is judged (Gawronski, Bodenhausen, & Banse, 2005). In fact, a contrast effect occurs when in-group and out-group members are compared on the same traits. For example, if members of an in-group perceive that their group possesses a trait, they are likely to perceive that out-group members do not (Gawronski et al., 2005). In short, the way we perceive our own group (the in-group) has a lot to do with how we perceive the out-group.

Henri Tajfel, a social psychologist, studied the phenomenon of in-group favoritism as a way of exploring out-group hostility. He was preoccupied with the issue of genocide, the systematic killing of an entire national or ethnic group. As a survivor of Nazi genocide of European Jews from 1939 to 1945, Tajfel had a personal as well as a professional interest in this issue (Brown, 1986).

Unlike earlier researchers, who emphasized the irrational thoughts and emotions of the prejudiced personality as the source of intergroup violence, Tajfel believed that cognitive processes were involved. He believed that the process of categorizing people into different groups led to loyalty to the in-group, which includes those people one perceives to be similar to oneself in meaningful ways. Inevitably, as in-group solidarity forms, those who are perceived to be different are identified as members of the out-group (Allport, 1954; Billig, 1992).

Tajfel was searching for the minimal social conditions needed for prejudice to emerge. In his experiments with British school boys, he found that there was no situation so minimal that some form of in-group solidarity did not take shape. He concluded that the need to favor the in-group, known as the in-group bias, was a basic component of human nature. What are the reasons for this powerful bias?

As noted in Chapter 2, we derive important aspects of our self-concepts from our membership in groups (Turner, 1987). These memberships help us establish a sense of positive social identity. Think of what appears to be a fairly inconsequential case of group membership: being a fan of a sports team. When your team wins a big game, you experience a boost, however temporary, to your sense of well-being (by BIRGing). You don't just root for the team; you become part of the team. You say, "We beat the heck out of them." Think for a moment about the celebrations that have taken place in Detroit, New York, Boston, and elsewhere after home teams won professional sports championships. It is almost as if it wasn't the Tigers or the Mets or the Celtics who won, but the fans themselves.

When your team loses the big game, on the other hand, you feel terrible. You're tempted to jump ship. It is hard to read the newspapers or listen to sportscasts the next day. When your team wins, you say, "We won." When your team loses, you say, "They lost" (Cialdini, 1988). It appears that both BIRGing and jumping ship serve to protect the individual fan's self-esteem. The team becomes part of the person's identity.

Social Identity Theory

Tajfel's (1982) social identity theory assumes that human beings are motivated to positively evaluate their own groups and value them over other groups, in order to maintain and enhance self-esteem. The group confers on the individual a social identity, that part of a person's self-concept that comes from her membership in social groups and from her emotional connection with those groups (Tajfel, 1981).

social identity theory (SIT) An assumption that we all need to have a positive self-concept, part of which is conferred on us through identification with certain groups.

Fundamental to **social identity theory (SIT)** is the notion of categorizing the other groups, pigeonholing them, by the use of stereotypes—those general beliefs that most people have about members of particular social groups (Turner, 1987). People are motivated to hold negative, stereotypes of out-groups; by doing so, they can maintain the superiority of their own group and thereby maintain their positive social (and self) identity.

Generally, any threat to the in-group, whether economic, military, or social, tends to heighten in-group bias. Additionally, anything that makes a person's membership in a group more salient, more noticeable, will increase in-group favoritism. One series of experiments showed that when people were alone, they were likely to judge an out-group member on an individual basis, but when they were made aware of their in-group membership by the presence of other members of their group, they were likely to judge the out-group person solely on the basis of stereotypes of the out-group (Wilder & Shapiro, 1984, 1991). The increase of in-group feelings promoted judgments of other people on the basis of social stereotypes. When group membership gets switched on, as it does, for example, when you are watching the Olympics or voting for a political candidate, then group values and social stereotypes play a larger role in how you react.

Self-Categorization Theory

Increase in self-esteem as a result of group membership is central to SIT (Grieve & Hogg, 1999). To increase members' self-esteem, the in-group needs to show that it is distinct from other groups in positive ways (Mummenday & Wenzel, 1999). Central to an extension of SIT, **self-categorization theory (SCT)** is the notion that self-categorization is also motivated by the need to reduce uncertainty (Hogg & Mullin, 1999). The basic idea is that people need to feel that their perceptions of the world are correct, and this correctness is defined by people—fellow group members—who are similar to oneself in important ways. In a study by Haslam, Oakes, Reynolds, and Turner (1999), when the category Australian was made salient for a group of Australian students, it tended to reduce uncertainty about the characteristics that comprise one's social group.

self-categorization theory (SCT) A theory suggesting that people need to reduce uncertainty about whether their perceptions of the world are "correct" and seek affirmation of their beliefs from fellow group members.

Consequently, it regulated and structured the members' social cognition. This is consistent with SCT. When reminded of their common category or group membership, the Australian students were more likely to agree on what it meant to be Australian.

What are the consequences of uncertainty? Grieve and Hogg (1999) showed that when uncertainty is high (i.e., when group members did not know if their performance was adequate or would be successful in achieving group goals), groups were more likely to downgrade or discriminate against other groups. In other words, uncertainty is a threat. Uncertainty was also accompanied by increased group identification. So threat creates a kind of rally-round-the-flag mentality. Self-categorization theory suggests, then, that only when the world is uncertain does self-categorization lead to discrimination against other groups (Grieve & Hogg, 1999). Self-categorization theory adds a bit of optimism to its parent theory's (SIT) outlook by suggesting that categorization does not always lead to discrimination, and if threat can be managed or alleviated, little discrimination or intergroup antagonism need occur.

A Biological Perspective on the In-Group Bias

Tajfel's research has shown us that the formation of an in-group bias serves basic social and self needs primarily by maintaining personal self-esteem. Some scientists, specifically sociobiologists—scientists who take a biological approach to social behavior—believe that ethnocentrism (the increased valuation of the in-group and the devaluation of out-groups) has a foundation in human biological evolution. They point out that for the longest part of their history, humans lived in small groups ranging from 40 to 100 members (Flohr, 1987). People had to rely on the in-group and gain acceptance by its members; it was the only way to survive. It would make sense, then, that a strong group orientation would be part of our human heritage: Those who lacked this orientation would not have survived to pass their traits on to us.

Sociobiologists also point out that people in all cultures seem to show a naturally occurring *xenophobia,* or fear of strangers. This fear may also be part of our genetic heritage. Because early populations were isolated from one another (Irwin, 1987), people may have used similar physical appearance as a marker of blood relationship (Tonnesmann, 1987). Clearly, there was always the possibility that people who looked different could be a threat to the food supply or other necessities of survival. Sociobiologists argue that it is reasonable to expect that people would be willing to cooperate only with humans of similar appearance and biological heritage and that they would distrust strangers (Barkow, 1980).

In modern times, as Tajfel showed, we still derive much of our identity from group membership; we fear being excluded from groups (Baumeister & Tice, 1990). High respect for our own groups often means a devaluing of other groups. This is not necessarily a big problem until groups have to compete for resources. Because the world does not appear to offer a surplus of resources, competition among groups is inevitable. Of particular interest to sociobiologists is a study by Tajfel (1982) and his coworkers in which it was demonstrated that children show a preference for their own national group long before they have a concept of country or nation. Children ranging in age from 6 to 12 years old were shown photographs of young men and were asked how much they liked those men. Two weeks later, the children were shown the same photographs again. They were also told that some of the men belonged to their nation and others did not. The children had to decide which young men were "theirs" (belonged to their country) and which were not. The researchers found that the children were more likely to assign the photographs they liked to their own nation. Therefore, liking and in-group feelings go together at an age when children cannot really comprehend fully the idea of a nation (Flohr, 1987).

In sum, those who offer a biological perspective on intergroup prejudice say that strong in-group identification can be understood as an evolutionary survival mechanism. We can find examples throughout human history of particular ethnic, racial, and religious groups that have strengthened in-group bonds in response to threats from the dominant group (Eitzen, 1973; Myrdal, 1962). Strengthening of these in-group bonds may help the group survive, but this is only one way of looking at the in-group bias. Acceptance of this notion does not require us to neglect our social psychological theories; it simply gives us some idea of the complexity of the issue (Flohr, 1987).

The Role of Language in Maintaining Bias

Categorization is, generally, an automatic process. It is the first step in the impression formation process. As mentioned earlier, it is not the same as stereotyping and prejudice, but it powerfully affects these other processes. One way in which categorizing can lead to prejudice is through language. The way we sculpt our world via the words and labels we use to describe people connects the category to prejudice. Social psychologist Charles Perdue and his colleagues tested the hypothesis that the use of words describing in-groups and out-groups unconsciously forms our biases and stereotypes (Perdue, Dovidio, Gurtman, & Tyler, 1990).

Perdue suggested that the use of collective pronouns—we, us, ours, they, their, theirs—is very influential in how we think about people and groups. We use these terms to assign people to in-groups and out-groups. In one study, Perdue and his colleagues showed participants a series of nonsense syllables (*xeh, yof, laj*) paired with pronouns designating in-group or out-group status (*we, they*). Participants were then asked to rate each of the nonsense syllables they had just seen in terms of the pleasantness or unpleasantness of the feelings they evoked. As shown in Figure 4.6, nonsense words paired with in-group pronouns were rated much more favorably than the same nonsense words paired with out-group pronouns or with control stimuli. Out-group pronouns gave negative meaning to previously unencountered and neutral nonsense syllables.

In a second experiment, these investigators demonstrated that in-group and out-group pronouns bias the processing of information about those groups. Participants saw a series of positive- and negative-trait words, such as *helpful, clever, competent, irresponsible, sloppy,* and *irritable*. Now, a positive trait ought to be positive under any circumstances, and the same should hold true for negative traits, wouldn't you agree? *Skillful* is generally positive; *sloppy* is generally negative. But as Figure 4.7 shows, it took participants longer to describe a negative trait as negative when that trait had been associated with an in-group pronoun. Similarly, it took participants longer to describe a positive trait as positive when it had been associated with an out-group pronoun. It took them little time to respond to a positive trait associated with an in-group pronoun and to a negative trait associated with an out-group pronoun.

These findings suggest that we have a nonconscious tendency (after all, the participants were not aware of the associations) to connect in-group labels with positive attributes rather than negative ones and out-group labels with negative attributes rather than positive ones. These associations are so strong that they shape the way we process subsequent information. They also seem to be deep and long lasting, a fact that may help explain why stereotypes remain so tenacious.

illusory correlation
An error in judgment about the relationship between two variables in which two unrelated events are believed to covary.

Illusory Correlations

The tendency to associate negative traits with out-groups is explained by one of the fundamental cognitive bases of stereotyping, the illusory correlation. An **illusory correlation** is an error in judgment about the relationship between two variables or, in other

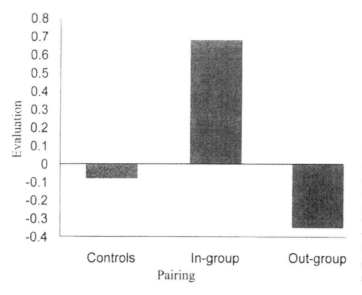

Figure 4.6
Standardized ratings
of target syllables as
a function of pronoun
pairing. Syllables paired
with in-group pronouns
were judged more pleasant
those those paired with out-
group pronouns.

From Perdue, Dovidio, and Tyler.

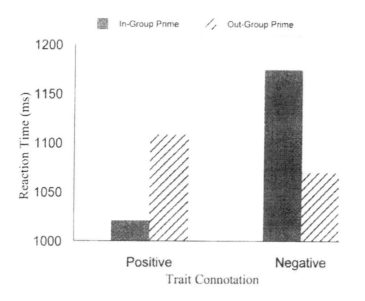

Figure 4.7   Reaction
times to positive and
negative trait descriptors as
a function of pronoun type
(in-group or out-group).
Information processing is
affected by in-group and
out-group thinking.

From Perdue, Dovidio, and Tyler (1990)

words, a belief that two unrelated events covary (are systematically related) (Hamilton & Sherman, 1989). For example, a person may notice that each time he wears his old high school bowling shirt when he goes bowling, he bowls very well. He may come to believe that there is a connection between the two events. Similarly, if you think that members of a minority group are more likely than members of a majority group to have a negative trait, then you perceive a correlation between group membership and behavior relating to that trait (Schaller, 1991).

Sometimes this cognitive bias crops up even among trained professionals. For example, a physician diagnosed a young, married African American woman with chronic pelvic inflammatory disease, an ailment related to a previous history of sexually transmitted disease. This diagnosis was made despite the fact that there was no indication in her medical history that she had ever had such a disease. As it turned out, she actually had endometriosis, a condition unrelated to sexually transmitted diseases (*Time*, June 1, 1992). The physician's beliefs about young black women, that they are sexually promiscuous, led to a diagnosis consistent with those beliefs. Research supports this anecdote. For example, participants have been found to ascribe different abilities to a girl depending on whether she is portrayed as having a lower or higher socioeconomic-status background (Darley & Gross, 1983).

These examples illustrate the human tendency to overestimate the co-occurrence of pairs of distinctive stimuli (Sherman, Hamilton, & Roskos-Ewoldsen, 1989). In the case of the misdiagnosis, the presence of two distinctive stimuli—a young black woman and a particular symptom pattern—led the physician to conclude that the woman's disorder was related to her sexual history. The tendency to fall prey to this illusion has been verified in other experiments (Chapman & Chapman, 1967).

The illusory correlation helps explain how stereotypes form. The reasoning goes like this: Minority groups are distinctive because they are encountered relatively infrequently. Negative behavior is also distinctive because it is, in general, encountered less frequently than positive behavior. Because both are distinctive, there is a tendency for people to overestimate the frequency with which they occur together, that is, the frequency with which minority group members do undesirable things (Sherman et al., 1989).

Research shows that if people are presented with information about a majority group and a minority group and these groups are paired with either rare or common traits, people associate the smaller group with the rarer trait (Hamilton & Sherman, 1989). If both a minority and majority group have the same negative trait, say a tendency toward criminal behavior, the negative behavior will be more distinctive when paired with the minority as compared to the majority group. Our cognitive apparatus seems to lead us to make an automatic association between negative behavior and minority-group membership.

Distinctive characteristics are also likely to play a critical role in the formation of category-based responses. In any gathering of people, we pay more attention to those who appear to be different from others, such as a white in an otherwise all-black group, or a man in an all-woman group. Skin color, gender, and ethnicity are salient characteristics.

One function of automatic evaluation is to point to events that may endanger the perceiver (Pratto & John, 1991). Certainly, sociobiologists would agree with that notion. The human ability to recognize friend from foe, safety from danger, would have fundamental survival value (Ike, 1987). For example, people automatically responded to an angry (salient) face in a happy crowd (Hansen & Hansen, 1988). An angry person among friends is dangerous. Another study demonstrated that individuals automatically turn their attention from a task to words, pictures, or events that might be threatening (Pratte & John, 1991). Participants attended more rapidly to salient negative traits than to positive ones. This automatic vigilance may lead people to weigh undesirable attributes in those around them differently than positive attributes.

When we encounter other groups, then, it is not surprising that we pay more attention to the bad things about them than the good. Negative social information grabs our attention. This greater attention to negative information may protect us from immediate harm, but it also helps perpetuate stereotypes and may contribute to conflict between groups (Pratto & John, 1991).

From Illusory Correlations to Negative Stereotypes via the Fundamental Attribution Error   The fact that a negative bit of information about a different group has grabbed our attention does not necessarily lead to discrimination against that group. There must be a link between the salience of negative information and prejudiced behavior. The fundamental attribution error—the tendency to overestimate internal attributes and underestimate the effect of the situation—supplies this link and plays a role in the formation of discriminatory stereotypes. This is particularly true when perceivers do not take into account the roles assigned to people. Recall the quiz show study described in Chapter 3 in which participants thought that the quiz show questioners were smarter than the contestants (Ross, Arnabile, & Steinmetz, 1977), even though roles had been randomly assigned.

This confusion between internal dispositions and external roles has led to punishing negative stereotypes of different groups. Let's consider just one example, the experience of the Jews in Europe over the past several hundred years (Ross & Nisbitt, 1991). Historically, Jews had many restrictions imposed on them in the countries where they resided. They were prevented from owning land; they often had to be in certain designated areas; they could not enter politics; and many professions were closed to them.

This exclusion from the greater society left the Jews with two options: either convert to Christianity or maintain their own distinctive culture. Most Jews opted for the latter, living within the walls of the ghetto (in fact, the word *ghetto* is derived from the Venetian word *Gheto*, which referred to a section of the city where iron slag was cooled and Jews were forced to live) assigned to them by the Christian majority and having little to do with non-Jews. Exclusion and persecution strengthened their in-group ties and also led the majority to perceive them as clannish. However, one segment of the Jewish population was highly visible to the mainstream society—the money lenders. Money lending was a profession forbidden to Christians and open to Jews (Ross & Nisbett, 1991). Although it was held in contempt, it was an essential function in national and international business, especially as capitalism began to develop. Jewish money lenders became important behind-the-scenes figures in the affairs of Europe. Thus, the most distinctive members of the group—distinctive for their visibility, their economic success, and their political importance—were invariably money lenders.

The distinctive negative role of money lending, although restricted to only a few Jews, began to be correlated with Jews in general. Jews were also seen as distinctive because of their minority status, their way of life, their unique dress, and their in-group solidarity. All of these characteristics were a function of the situation and roles thrust on the Jews by the majority, but they came to be seen, via the fundamental attribution error, as inherent traits of Jewish people in general. These traits were then used as a justification for discrimination, based on the rationale that Jews were different, clannish, and money grubbing.

Jews have been depicted in negative ways throughout history. For example, in Shakespeare's *The Merchant of Venice*, the Jewish money lender, Shylock, is depicted as a bloodthirsty person who will stop at nothing to extract his pound of flesh for repayment of a defaulted debt. However, do these stereotypes still crop up today in "enlightened" American communities? Movie director Steven Speilberg grew up in New Jersey and Arizona but never experienced anti-Semitism until his family moved to Saratoga, California, during his senior year in high school:

> He encountered kids who would cough the word *Jew* in their hands when they
> passed him, beat him up, and throw pennies at him in study hall. "It was my
> six months of personal horror. And to this day I haven't gotten over it nor have I
> forgiven any of them." *(Newsweek,* December 20, 1993, p. 115)

Historically, Jews were not the only group to suffer from majority exclusion and the fundamental attribution error (Ross & Nisbett, 1991). The Armenians in Turkey, the Indians in Uganda, and the Vietnamese boat people were all money middlemen who took on that role because no other positions were open to them. All of these groups suffered terrible fates.

The Confirmation Bias

People dealing with Jews in the 18th century in Europe or with Armenians in Turkey at the turn of the 20th century found it easy to confirm their expectancies about these groups; perceivers could recall the money lenders, the strange dress, the different customs. Stereotypes are both self-confirming and resistant to change.

Numerous studies show that stereotypes can influence social interactions in ways that lead to their confirmation. In one study, some participants were told that a person with whom they would soon talk was in psychotherapy; other participants were told nothing about the person (Sibicky & Dovidio, 1986). In actuality, the individuals they talked to were randomly chosen students from basic psychology courses; none were in therapy. After the interviews, participants were asked to evaluate the person with whom they had interacted. Those individuals identified as therapy clients were rated less confident, less attractive, and less likable than the individuals not described as being in therapy.

We can see from this study that once people have a stereotype, they evaluate information within the context of that stereotype. After all, none of the people being interviewed in the experiment were in fact in therapy. The differences between the ratings had to be due to the participants' stereotypical view of what somebody in therapy must be like. Describing a person as being in therapy seems to lead to a negative perception of that person. People who hold negative stereotypes about certain groups may behave so that group members act in a way that confirms the stereotype (Crocker & Major, 1989). The confirmation bias contributes in many instances to self-fulfilling prophecies. If you expect a person to be hostile, your very expectation and the manner in which you behave may bring on that hostility. In the study just described, participants who thought they were interacting with someone in therapy probably held a stereotypical view of all people with psychological problems. It is likely that they behaved in a way that made those individuals uneasy and caused them to act in a less confident manner.

The Out-Group Homogeneity Bias

An initial effect of categorization is that members of the category are thought to be more similar to each other than is the case when people are viewed as individuals. Because we have a fair amount of information about the members of our own group (the in-group), we are able to differentiate among them. But we tend to view members of other groups (out-groups) as being very similar to one another (Wilder, 1986). This phenomenon of perceiving members of the out-group as all alike is called the **out-group homogeneity** bias (Linville, Fischer, & Salovey, 1989).

out-group homogeneity bias The predisposition to see members of an out-group as having similar characteristics or being all alike.

194

The out-group homogeneity hypothesis was tested in one study involving students from Princeton and Rutgers Universities (Quattrone & Jones, 1980). Participants, who were either Rutgers or Princeton students, saw a videotape of a student supposedly from the other school. The videotaped person had to decide whether he wanted to wait alone or with other people before being a participant in a psychological experiment. The actual participant then had to predict what the average student at the target university (Rutgers for Princeton students and Princeton for Rutgers students) would do in a similar situation.

Would the participants see students at the other university as similar to the student they had viewed? Would they predict that most Princeton students (or Rutgers students) would make the same choice as the Princeton student (or Rutgers student) in the film clip? These questions get at the issue of whether people see out-group members as more similar to one another than to the in-group members. In fact, this is pretty much what the study showed, although there was a greater tendency to stereotype Princeton students than Rutgers students. That seems logical, because it is probably easier to conjure up a stereotype of Princeton student. In general, however, results supported the notion that the out-group homogeneity bias leads us to think that members of out-groups are more similar to one another than to members of in-groups.

A second outcome of out-group homogeneity bias is the assumption that any behavior of an out-group member reflects the characteristics of all group members. If a member of an out-group does something bad, we tend to conclude, "That's the way those people are." In contrast, when an in-group member does something equally negative, we tend to make a dispositional attribution, blaming the person rather than our own in-group for the negative behavior. This has been referred to as the **ultimate attribution error**: We are more likely to give in-group members the benefit of the doubt than out-group members (Pettigrew, 1979).

ultimate attribution error
The tendency to give in-group, but not out-group, members the benefit of the doubt for negative behaviors.

Once we construct our categories, we tend to hold on to them tenaciously, which may be both innocent and destructive. It is innocent because the process is likely to be automatic and nonconscious. It is destructive because stereotypes are inaccurate and often damaging; individuals cannot be adequately described by reference to the groups to which they belong.

In general, social psychologists have not made a consistent attempt to determine the accuracy of stereotypes. Much of the early research on stereotypes assumed that stereotypes were inaccurate by definition. More recently, the issue of stereotype accuracy has been addressed by Judd and Park (1993). They suggested several technical standards against which the accuracy of a stereotype can be measured. For example, consider the notion that Germans are efficient. One standard that Judd and Park suggested to measure the accuracy of that stereotype is to find data that answers the questions: Are Germans in reality more or less efficient than the stereotype? Is the group attribute (efficiency) exaggerated?

Of course, to apply these standards, we need some objective data about groups. We need to know how groups truly behave with respect to various characteristics. For some attributes, say, kindness or sensitivity, it is probably impossible to obtain such information. For others, there may be readily available data.

In McCauley and Stitt's 1978 study of the accuracy of stereotypes, white participants' estimates of certain attributes of the African American population were compared with public records (as cited in Judd & Park, 1993). The attributes estimated were percentage of high school graduates, number of crime victims, and number of people on the welfare rolls. This study showed that whites underestimated the differences between

African Americans and themselves with respect to these attributes. In other words, whites thought more African Americans graduated from high school than was true, and they thought fewer African Americans were victims of crime than the data showed.

Is it important to know if a stereotype is accurate? Technically it is, because many of the earlier definitions of stereotypes assume that inaccuracy is part of the definition of the concept (Stangor & Lange, 1994). Most stereotypes are unjustified generalizations; that is, they are not accurate. But, even if they are accurate, stereotypes still have a damaging effect on our perception of others. None of us would wish to be judged as an individual by the worst examples of the group(s) to which we belong.

In previous chapters, we have seen how automatic and controlled processing enter into the social cognition process. Some people use controlled processing to readjust initial impressions of others in instances where new information conflicts with existing categorization (Fiske & Neuberg, 1990; Trope, 1986). Automatic and controlled processing again come into play when we consider how stereotypes are maintained and how prejudiced and nonprejudiced individuals differ.

The Difference between Prejudiced and Nonprejudiced Individuals

Devine (1989) contends that stereotypes are automatically activated when we encounter a member of a particular social group. According to Devine, some people are able to consciously alter their prejudiced responses, whereas others are not. Devine found that those interested in being nonprejudiced think differently from those who are not. For example, prejudiced individuals are more willing to indulge in negative thoughts and behaviors toward members of different racial and ethnic groups than nonprejudiced individuals. Devine also found that both high- and low-prejudiced whites hold almost the same stereotypes of African Americans. However, nonprejudiced individuals think those stereotypes are wrong.

Devine also found that the main difference between prejudiced and nonprejudiced whites was that nonprejudiced whites are sensitive to and carefully monitor their stereotypes. The nonprejudiced person wants his or her behavior to be consistent with his or her true beliefs rather than his or her stereotypes. When given a chance to use controlled processing, nonprejudiced individuals show behavior that is more consistent with nonprejudiced true beliefs than stereotyped beliefs. In contrast, the behavior of prejudiced individuals is more likely to be guided by stereotypes. In another study, nonprejudiced individuals were more likely than prejudiced individuals to feel bad when they had thoughts about gay men and lesbians that ran counter to their beliefs (Monteith, Devine, & Zuwerink, 1993). When nonprejudiced individuals express prejudicial thoughts and feelings, they feel guilty about doing so (Devine, Montieth, Zuwerink, & Elliot, 1991).

What happens if automatic processing takes over? According to Devine, activating a stereotype puts a person into automatic mode when confronting a person from the stereotyped group. The automatically activated stereotype will be acted on by both prejudiced and nonprejudiced individuals unless there is an opportunity to use controlled processing (Devine, 1989). Devine found that when participants in an experiment were prevented from switching to controlled processing, both prejudiced and nonprejudiced individuals evaluated the behavior of an African American negatively.

We can draw several conclusions from Devine's research. First, prejudiced individuals are less inhibited about expressing their prejudice than nonprejudiced individuals. Second, no differences exist between prejudiced and nonprejudiced individuals when stereotype activation is beyond conscious control. Third, nonprejudiced people work hard to inhibit the expression of negative stereotypes when they have the opportunity to monitor behavior and bring stereotypes under conscious control. Fourth, nonprejudiced individuals realize that there is a gap between their stereotypes and their general beliefs about equality, and they work continually to change their stereotyped thinking.

How easy is it to identify a prejudiced person? If you see a person in a Ku Klux Klan outfit distributing hate propaganda or burning a cross on someone's lawn, that's pretty easy. However, many people do not express prejudices in such obvious ways. When we encounter someone who makes racist or sexist comments, we can pretty easily identify that person as prejudiced (Mae & Carlston, 2005). Further, we will express dislike for that person, even if he or she is expressing ideas with which we agree (Mae & Carlston, 2005). So, it seems we are pretty adept at identifying individuals who express negative prejudices. However, when it comes to detecting positive prejudices, we are less adept. Speakers who espouse negative prejudices are more likely to be identified as prejudiced than those who espouse positive prejudices (Mae & Carlston, 2005).

The Consequences of Being a Target of Prejudice

Imagine being awakened several times each night by a telephone caller who inundates you with racial or religious slurs. Imagine being a second-generation Japanese American soldier on December 8, 1941 (the day after the Pearl Harbor attack), and being told you are no longer trusted to carry a gun in defense of your country. Imagine being an acknowledged war hero who is denied the Medal of Honor because of race-related suspicions of your loyalty to the country for which you had just fought. In each of these instances, a person becomes the target of prejudicial attitudes, stereotypes, and discriminatory behavior directed at him or her. What effect does being the target of such prejudice have on an individual? To be sure, being a target of discrimination generates a great deal of negative affect and has serious emotional consequences for the target (Dion & Earn, 1975). Next, we explore some of the effects that prejudice has on those who are its targets.

Ways Prejudice Can Be Expressed

In his monumental work on prejudice called *The Nature of Prejudice*, Gordon Allport (1954) suggested that there are five ways that prejudice can be expressed. These are *antilocution*, talking in terms of prejudice or making jokes about an out-group; *avoidance*, avoiding contact with members of an out-group; *discrimination*, actively doing something to deny members of an out-group something they desire; *physical attack*, beatings, lynchings, and the like; and *extermination*, an attempt to eliminate an entire group. One issue we must address is the reaction shown by members of an out-group when they are targeted with prejudice. It is fairly obvious that those faced with overt discrimination, physical attack, and extermination will respond negatively. But what about reactions to more subtle forms of prejudice? What toll do they take on a member of a minority group?

Swim, Cohen, and Hyers (1998) characterized some forms of prejudice as *everyday prejudice*: "recurrent and familiar events that can be considered commonplace" (p. 37). These include short-term interaction such as remarks and stares, and incidents that can be directed at an individual or an entire group. According to Swim and colleagues, such incidents can be initiated either by strangers or by those with intimate relationships with the target and have a cumulative effect and contribute to the target's experience with and knowledge of prejudice.

Prejudice-Based Jokes

How do encounters with everyday prejudice affect the target? Let's start by looking at one form of antilocution discussed by Allport that most people see as harmless: prejudice-based jokes. Most of us have heard (and laughed at) jokes that make members of a group the butt of the joke. Many of us may have even told such jokes, assuming that they do no harm. But how do those on the receiving end feel? Women, for example, find sexist jokes less funny and less amusing than nonsexist jokes (LaFrance & Woodzicka, 1998). They also tend to report feeling more disgusted, angry, hostile, and surprised by sexist versus nonsexist jokes. They also tend to roll their eyes (indicating disgust) and touch their faces (indicating embarassment) more in response to sexist than to nonsexist jokes (LaFrance & Woodzicka, 1998).

Ryan and Kanjorski (1998) directly compared the reactions of men and women to sexist jokes. They found that compared to men, women enjoyed sexist humor less and found it less acceptable and more offensive. Interestingly, men and women did not differ in terms of telling sexist jokes. A more ominous finding was that for men, there were significant positive correlations between enjoyment of sexist humor and rape myth acceptance, adversarial sexual beliefs, acceptance of interpersonal violence, likelihood of engaging in forced sex, and sexual aggression. In another study, the exposure of men with sexist attitudes to sexist jokes was related to tolerance for sexism and fewer negative feelings about behaving in a sexist manner (Ford, Wentzel, & Lorion, 2001). These findings may lend some credence to Allport's (1954) idea that antilocution, once accepted, sets the stage for more serious expressions of prejudice.

A study reported by Thomas and Esses (2004) confirms the relationship between sexist attitudes and enjoyment of sexist humor. Male participants completed measures of sexism and authoritarianism. They then evaluated two types of sexist jokes. Half of the jokes were degrading to women and half degrading to men. The results showed that male participants who scored highly on the sexism scale found the jokes degrading females funnier and were more likely to repeat them than male participants who were low on the sexism measure. Sexism did not relate to the evaluation of the jokes that degraded men.

Stereotype Threat

As noted earlier, affiliation with groups often contributes to a positive social identity. What about membership in a group that does not confer a positive social identity? Not all social groups have the same social status and perceived value. What happens when an individual is faced with doing a task for which a negative stereotype exists for that person's group? For example, it is well-established that blacks tend to do more poorly academically than whites. What happens when a black individual is faced with a task that will indicate academic aptitude?

One intriguing hypothesis about why blacks might not score well on standard tests of IQ comes from an experiment conducted by Steele and Aronson (1995). According to Steele and Aronson, when a person is asked to perform a task for which there is a negative stereotype attached to their group, that person will perform poorly because the task is threatening. They called this idea a **stereotype threat**. To test the hypothesis that members of a group perform more poorly on tasks that relate to prevailing negative stereotypes, Steele and Aronson conducted the following experiment. Black and white participants took a test comprising items from the verbal section of the Graduate Record Exam. One-third of the participants were told that the test was diagnostic of their intellectual ability (diagnostic condition). One-third were told that the test was a laboratory

stereotype threat
The condition that exists when a person is asked to perform a task for which there is a negative stereotype attached to their group and performs poorly because the task is threatening.

tool for studying problem solving (nondiagnostic condition). The final third were told that the test was of problem solving and would present a challenge to the participants (nondiagnostic—challenge condition). Steele and Aronson then determined the average number of items answered correctly within each group.

The results of this experiment showed that when the test was said to be diagnostic of one's intellectual abilities, black and white participants differed significantly, with black participants performing more poorly than white participants. However, when the *same* test was presented as nondiagnostic, black and white participants did equally well. There was no significant difference between blacks and whites in the nondiagnostic-challenge condition. Overall across the three conditions, blacks performed most poorly in the diagnostic condition. In a second experiment, Steele and Aronson (1995) produced results that were even more pronounced than in their first. They also found that black participants in the diagnostic condition finished fewer items and worked more slowly than black participants in the nondiagnostic condition. Steele and Aronson pointed out that this is a pattern consistent with impairments caused by test anxiety, evaluation apprehension, and competitive pressure.

In a final experiment, Steele and Aronson (1995) had participants perform word-completion tasks (e.g., — — ce; la — —; or — — ack that could be completed in a racially stereotyped way (e.g., race; lazy; black) or a nonstereotyped way (e.g., pace; lace; track). This was done to test if stereotypes are activated when participants were told that a test was either diagnostic or nondiagnostic. Steele and Aronson found that there was greater stereotype activation among blacks in the diagnostic condition compared to the nondiagnostic condition. They also found that in the diagnostic condition, blacks were more likely than whites to engage in self-handicapping strategies (i.e., developing behavior patterns that actually interfere with performance, such as losing sleep the night before a test). Blacks and whites did not differ on self-handicapping behaviors in the nondiagnostic condition.

These findings help us understand why blacks consistently perform more poorly than whites on intelligence tests. Intelligence tests by their very nature and purpose are diagnostic of one's intellectual abilities. According to Steele and Aronson's (1995) analysis, when a black person is faced with the prospect of taking a test that is diagnostic of intellectual ability, it activates the common stereotype threat that blacks are not supposed to perform well on tests of intellectual ability. According to Steele and Aronson, the stereotype threat impairs performance by generating evaluative pressures. Recall that participants who were under stereotype threat in the diagnostic condition spent more time doing fewer items. As they became more frustrated, performance was impaired. It may also impair future performance, because more self-handicapping strategies are used by blacks facing diagnostic tests. In short, the stereotype threat creates an impairment in the ability to cognitively process information adequately, which in turn inhibits performance. So, lower scores on IQ tests by blacks may relate more to the activation of the stereotype threat than to any genetic differences between blacks and whites.

Steele and his colleagues extended the notion of the stereotype threat to other groups. For example, Spencer, Steele, and Quinn (cited in Aronson, Quinn, & Spencer, 1998) found that men and women equated for math ability performed differently on a math test, depending on whether they were told that there were past results showing no gender differences in performance on the test (alleviating the stereotype threat) or given no information about gender differences (allowing the stereotype threat to be activated). Specifically, when the "no gender differences" information was given, men and women performed equally well on the test. However, when the stereotype threat was allowed to be activated (i.e., that women perform more poorly on math tests than do men), men scored significantly higher than women. Aronson and Alainas reported similar effects for Latino versus white participants and white males versus Asian males (cited in Aronson et al., 1998).

In a more direct test of the relationship between gender, stereotype threat, and math performance, Brown and Josephs (1999) told male and female students that they would be taking a math test. One-half of the participants of each gender were told that the test would identify exceptionally strong math abilities, whereas the other half were told that the test would uncover especially weak math skills. Brown and Josephs reasoned that for males the test for strong math skills would be more threatening, because it plays into the stereotype that males are strong in math. On the other hand, the test for weakness would be more threatening to females, because females stereotypically are viewed as being weak in math. Their results were consistent with Steele and Aronson's stereotype threat notion. Males performed poorly on the test that supposedly measured exceptional math skills. Conversely, females performed poorly on the test that was said to identify weak math skills. In both cases, a stereotype was activated that was relevant to gender, which inhibited performance. According to Brown and Josephs, the stereotype threat for math performance is experienced differently for males and females. Males feel more threatened when faced with having to prove themselves worthy of the label of being strong in math skills, whereas females feel more threatened when they face a situation that may prove a stereotype to be true.

Stereotype threat also operates by reducing positive expectations a person has going into a situation. For example, based on a person's previous experience, he or she may feel confident about doing well on the SATs, having a positive expectation about his or her performance on the exam. Now, let's say that a stereotype of this person's group is activated prior to taking the exam. The resulting stereotype threat may lower that person's expectations about the test, and as a consequence, the person does not do well.

The fact that this scenario can happen was verified in an experiment by Stangor, Carr, and Kiang (1998). Female participants in this experiment all performed an initial task of identifying words. Afterward, some participants were told that their performance on the task provided clear evidence that they had an aptitude for college-level work. Other participants were told that the evidence concerning college performance was unclear. Next, participants were told that there was either strong evidence that men did better than women on the second test (stereotype threat) or that there were no sex differences (no stereotype threat). Before working on the second task, participants were asked to rate their ability to perform the second task successfully. The results of this experiment, shown in Figure 4.8, were clear. When a stereotype threat was not activated, performance was affected by the feedback given after the first task. Those participants who believed that there was clear, positive evidence of college aptitude had higher expectations of success than those given unclear feedback. In the stereotype threat condition, the two groups did not differ in their expectations concerning the second task.

Thus, in addition to arousing anxiety about testing situations, stereotype threats also lower one's expectations about one's performance. Once these negative expectations develop, a self-fulfilling prophecy is most likely developed that "Because I am a female, I am not expected to do well on this task." Poor performance then confirms that prophecy.

Whether the arousal related to a stereotype threat adversely affects performance depends, in part, on the nature of the task individuals must perform. A consistent finding in social psychology is that arousal enhances performance on a simple task but inhibits performance on a more difficult task (we discuss this effect in detail in Chapter 8). Ben Zeev,

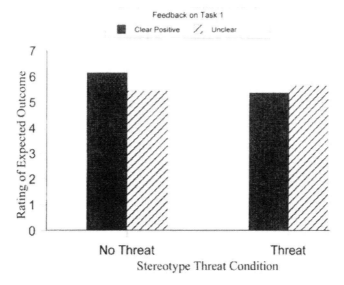

Feedback on Task 1

■ Clear Positive   ╱ Unclear

Figure 4.8 Task performance as a function of feedback about prior performance and activation of a stereotype threat. When no threat was activated, participants used performance on a prior task to form expectations about further performance. When a threat was activated, performance was affected by what was expected based on the stereotype.

From Charles Stangor, Christine Carr, and Lisa Kiang (1998).

Fein, and Inzlicht (2005) conducted a study to investigate this effect. Participants performed either a simple task (writing their names in cursive several times) or difficult task (writing their names in cursive backwards) under stereotype threat or no threat. Ben Zeev et al. found that the arousal associated with the stereotype threat enhanced performance on the simple task and inhibited performance on the difficult task.

In a second experiment Ben Zeev et al. found that how participants attributed the cause for their arousal affected performance. Once again, participants were exposed to either a stereotype threat condition or no-threat condition. Participants were told that one purpose of the study was to investigate performance while being exposed to subliminal noise. Participants in the misattribution condition were told that the subliminal noise would produce physical symptoms such as arousal and nervousness. Participants in the control group were told that the subliminal noise would have no physical side effects. All participants completed a moderately difficult math test while being exposed to the noise. The results showed that participants in the control group showed the usual stereotype threat effect (poorer performance under threat versus no threat). However, in the misattribution condition there was no significant threat effect on performance. Hence, if you can attribute your arousal to something other than a stereotype, you will perform well. Arousal related to stereotype threat appears to be an important mediator of performance, as is how the source of the arousal is attributed.

Finally, activating a stereotype threat does not always lead to a decrement in performance. In one experiment, Keller and Bless (2005) manipulated the ease of activating stereotype information (easy versus difficult) along with whether a stereotype threat was activated. Participants completed a questionnaire that they believed tested "emotional intelligence" but actually measured verbal ability. Keller and Bless found the typical stereotype threat effect when activation of stereotype information was easy. That is, when activation was easy, participants who experienced stereotype threat performed more poorly on the test of verbal ability than participants who did not experience stereotype threat. However, when activation was difficult, there was no significant difference in performance between the two stereotype threat groups. In fact, the results showed a slight reversal of the effect. Keller and Bless suggest that when a stereotype can be easily activated, it may reinforce the validity of the stereotype in the mind of the individual. The stereotype that is presumed to be valid is then more likely to inhibit performance than one that is harder (and presumably less valid) to activate.

The impact of a stereotype threat also is mediated by one's locus of control. Locus of control is a personality characteristic relating to whether a person believes he or she controls his or her outcomes (internal locus of control) or external events control outcomes (external locus of control). Cadinu, Maass, Lombardo, and Frigerio (2006) report that individuals with an internal locus of control exhibited a greater decrease in performance under stereotype threat than individuals with an external locus of control.

Collective Threat

The preceding studies show how being the target of a stereotype can affect individual behavior in a very specific context (i.e., testing). Stereotypes can also have a broader, more general effect by making members of stereotyped groups sensitive to the stigmatizing effects of the stereotype. In other words, a person from a stereotyped group may become overly concerned that a transgression by a member of one's group may reflect badly on him or her as an individual (Cohen & Garcia, 2005). Cohen and Garcia refer to this as **collective threat**. Collective threat flows from "the awareness that the poor performance of a single individual in one's group may be viewed through the lens of a stereotype and may be generalized into a negative judgment of one's group" (Cohen & Garcia, 2005, p. 566).

Cohen and Garcia conducted a series of studies to assess the effects of collective threat. In their first study junior and senior high school students completed a questionnaire that included measures of collective threat (concern that behavior of other members of one's group will reflect badly on the group as a whole), stereotype threat (concern that one's own behavior will reflect badly on one's group), and a more generalized threat of being stereotyped (concern that people will judge the participant based on what they think of the participant's racial group). Cohen and Garcia (2005) compared the responses from students representing three racial/ethnic groups: blacks, whites, and Latinos. Garcia and Cohen found that minority students (blacks and Latinos) were more likely to experience each of the three types of threats than white students. They also found that experiencing collective threat was negatively related to self-esteem. The more a student experienced collective threat, the lower the student's self-esteem, regardless of the race of the student. Collective threat was also related to a drop in student grade point averages. High levels of perceived collective threat were related to significant drops in grade point average.

A series of follow-up experiments confirmed the results from the questionnaire study. Black students who were randomly assigned to a condition that created collective threat (compared to control students) experienced lower self-esteem and also performed more poorly on a standardized test. Additionally, the students tended to distance themselves from a group member who caused the collective threat. Finally, Cohen and Garcia (2005) found that the effects of collective threat were not limited to racial groups. In their last experiment reported, the effects of collective threat were replicated using gender stereotypes (lower math ability than men) rather than racial stereotypes. Women distanced themselves (sat further way from) another woman who confirmed the math inability stereotype.

collective threat
The awareness that the poor performance of a member of one's group may be evaluated with a stereotype and may be generalized into a negative judgment of one's entire group.

Expecting to Be a Target of Prejudice

Another way that being the target of prejudice can affect behavior occurs when people enter into a situation in which they expect to find prejudice. Imagine, for example, that you are a minority student who will be meeting his white roommate for the first time. Could your behavior be affected by your belief that your white roommate might harbor prejudices and negative stereotypes about your group? The answer to this question is that it certainly could.

Research reported by Shelton, Richeson, and Salvatore (2005) confirmed this very effect. They found a relationship between the expectation of encountering prejudice and how they perceived interracial interactions. Specifically, Shelton et al. found that the more a minority student expected prejudice from another white student, the more negative they viewed interaction with that person. This relationship was found in a diary study (students kept a diary of their experiences with their white roommates) and in a laboratory experiment in which prejudice was induced. Shelton et al. also assessed the perceptions of the white students in their studies. Interestingly, they found that the more the minority student expected the white student to be prejudiced, the more *positive* the encounter was seen by the white student. This latter finding suggests a major disconnect between the perceptions of the minority and white students. Minority students who expect prejudice (and probably experienced it in the past) may misinterpret white students' behaviors as indicative of prejudice, making the interaction seem more negative than it actually is. White students who do not have the history of experiencing prejudice may be operating in a state of ignorant bliss, not realizing that innocent behaviors may be misconstrued by their minority counterparts.

Coping with Prejudice

It should be obvious from our previous discussion that being a target of prejudice has a variety of negative consequences. Individuals facing instance after instance of everyday prejudice must find ways to deal with its effects. How, for example, can an overweight person who is constantly the target of prejudice effectively manage its consequences? In this section, we explore some strategies that individuals use to cope with being a target of prejudice.

Raising the Value of a Stigmatized Group

One method of coping with prejudice when your group is stigmatized, oppressed, or less valued than other groups is to raise its value. This is done by first convincing group members of their own self-worth and then convincing the rest of society of the group's worth. The function of all consciousness-raising efforts and positive in-group slogans is to persuade the members of scorned or less-valued groups that they are beautiful or smart or worthy or competent. This first step, maintaining and increasing self-esteem, can be approached in at least two ways (Crocker & Major, 1989; Crocker, Voelkl, Testa, & Major, 1991): attributing negative events to prejudice of the majority and comparing oneself to members of one's own group.

First, for example, supposed that an African American woman is denied a job or a promotion. She can better maintain her self-esteem if she attributes this outcome to the prejudice of the person evaluating her. Of course, people are usually uncertain about the true motives of other people in situations like this. Although a rejection by a majority group member can be attributed to the evaluator's prejudice, the effects on the self-esteem of the minority person are complex.

Some of these effects were investigated in a study in which African American participants were evaluated by white evaluators (Crocker & Major, 1989). When participants thought that evaluators were uninfluenced by their race, positive evaluations increased their self-esteem. But when participants knew that evaluators were influenced by their race, positive evaluations decreased their self-esteem. Compared to whites, African Americans were more likely to attribute both positive and negative evaluations to prejudice. Any judgment, positive or negative, that the recipient thought was based on racism led to a decrease in self-esteem (Crocker et al., 1991).

Uncertainty about such evaluations thus has important consequences for self-esteem. In our society, African Americans are often evaluated primarily by whites, which suggests that they may always feel uncertain about their evaluators' motives (Crocker et al., 1991). This uncertainty may be exacerbated for African American females who are evaluated by white males (Coleman, Jussim, & Isaac, 1991).

Even when race (or some other characteristic) works in one's favor, uncertainty or *attributional ambiguity* may be aroused. For example, a minority group member who receives a job where an affirmative action program is in effect may never know for certain whether he or she was hired based on qualifications or race. This attributional ambiguity generates negative affect and motivation (Blaine, Crocker, & Major, 1995). In one study participants who believed that they received a job due to sympathy over a stigma experienced lower self-esteem, negative emotion, and reduced work motivation than those who believed they received the job based on qualifications (Blaine et al., 1995).

Making In-Group Comparisons

Second, members of less-favored groups can maintain self-esteem by comparing themselves with members of their own group, rather than with members of the more favored or fortunate groups. In-group comparisons may be less painful and more rewarding for members of stigmatized groups. Research supports this hypothesis in a number of areas, including pay, abilities, and physical attractiveness (Crocker & Major, 1989). Once group members have raised their value in their own eyes, the group is better placed to assert itself in society.

As the feelings of cohesiveness and belonging of the in-group increase, there is often an escalation in hostility directed toward the out-group (Allport, 1954). History teaches us that self-identifying with an in-group and identifying others with an out-group underlies many instances of prejudice and intergroup hostility.

Anticipating and Confronting Prejudice

Swim, Cohen, and Hyers (1998) suggested that another strategy for individuals from a stigmatized group is to try to anticipate situations in which prejudice will be encountered. By doing this, the individual can decide how to best react or to minimize the impact of prejudice. The individual may decide to alter his or her demeanor, manner of dress, or even where he or she goes to school or lives in an effort to minimize the likelihood of encountering prejudice (Swim et al., 1998).

Once a person has made an assessment of a situation for anticipated prejudice, that person must next decide what course of action to take. The individual could choose to confront the prejudice and move toward the original goal or choose to avoid the prejudiced situation and find some alternative (Swim et al., 1998). Confronting prejudice means "a volitional process aimed at expressing one's dissatisfaction with discriminatory treatment to a person or group of people who are responsible for engaging in a discriminatory event" (Kaiser & Miller, 2004, p. 168). For example, a woman who has just been told a nasty, sexist joke can confront the joke teller and point out the inappropriateness of the joke. Although it may be noble to confront prejudice and discrimination, the reality is that many of us don't do it. In one experiment, for example, in which women were subjected to sexist comments, only 45% of the women confronted the offender. However, privately, a vast majority of the women expressed private distaste for the comments and the person who made them (Swim & Hyers, 1999). Why would the women who experienced sexism be reluctant to confront it? Unfortunately, there is not a lot of research on this issue. One study (Kaiser & Miller, 2004), however, did look into this question. Women were asked to recall instances of sexism that they had encountered in their lives (e.g., sexism in the workplace, experiencing demeaning comments, or exposure to stereotyped sex role concepts). The women also completed measures of optimism and cognitive appraisals of confronting sexism. The results showed that women who perceived confronting prejudice as cognitively difficult (e.g., not worth the effort, anxiety producing) were less likely to have reported confronting the sexism they had experienced. Kaiser and Miller also found a relationship between optimism and cognitive appraisals. Women with a more optimistic outlook viewed confrontation as less threatening than women with a pessimistic outlook. In short, women with optimistic outlooks are more likely to confront prejudice than those with a pessimistic outlook. Thus, both personality characteristics and cognitive evaluations are involved in the decision to confront prejudice. Of course, this conclusion is tentative at this time, and we don't know if similar psychological mechanisms apply to coping with other forms of prejudice.

Compensating for Prejudice

Members of a stigmatized group can also engage in *compensation* to cope with prejudice (Miller & Myers, 1998). According to Miller and Myers, there are two modes of compensation in which a person can engage. When **secondary compensation** is used, individuals attempt to change their mode of thinking about situations to psychologically protect themselves against the outcomes of prejudice. For example, a person who wants to obtain a college degree but faces prejudice that may prevent reaching the goal would be using secondary compensation if he or she devalued the goal (a college education is not all that important) or disidentified with the goal (members of my group usually don't go to college). On the other hand, **primary compensation** reduces the actual threats posed by prejudice. Coping strategies are developed that allow the targets of prejudice to achieve their goals. For example, the person in the example could increase his or her effort (study harder in school), use latent skills (become more persistent), or develop new skills to help achieve goals that are blocked by prejudice. When primary compensation is used, it reduces the need for secondary compensation (Miller & Myers, 1998).

Interestingly, coping with prejudice is different if you are talking about individual coping as opposed to group coping. Mummendey, Kessler, Klink, and Mielke (1999) tested coping strategies tied to two theories relating to being a target of prejudice: social identity theory and relative deprivation theory. As you read earlier, social identity theory proposes that individuals derive part of their self-concept from affiliation with a group. If the group with which you affiliate has negative stereotypes attached to it, the social identity will be negative. According to *relative deprivation theory,* members of

secondary compensation
A method of handling prejudice involving attempts to change one's mode of thinking about situations to psychologically protect oneself against the outcomes of prejudice.

primary compensation
A method by targets of prejudice that reduces threats posed by using coping strategies that allow the targets of prejudice to achieve their goals.

a stereotyped group recognize that they are undervalued and reap fewer benefits from society than more preferred groups. In theory, negative social identity should lead to individually based coping strategies, whereas perceived relative deprivation should lead to group-based coping (Mummendey et al., 1999).

To test this hypothesis, residents of former East Germany were administered a questionnaire concerning social identity and relative deprivation. The questionnaire also measured several identity management strategies. Mummendey and colleagues (1999) found that social identity issues were handled with management strategies (e.g., mobility and recategorization of the self to a higher level in the group) that stressed one's individual attachment with an in-group. Management techniques relating to relative deprivation were more group based, focusing on group-based strategies such as collective action to reduce relative deprivation. In addition, social identity issues were tied closely with cognitive aspects of group affiliation, whereas relative deprivation was mediated strongly by emotions such as anger.

Reducing Prejudice

A rather gloomy conclusion that may be drawn from the research on the cognitive processing of social information is that normal cognitive functioning leads inevitably to the development and maintenance of social stereotypes (Mackie, Allison, Vorth, & Asuncion, 1992). Social psychologists have investigated the strategies that people can use to reduce prejudice and intergroup hostility. In the following sections, we explore some of these actions.

Contact between Groups

contact hypothesis

A hypothesis that contact between groups will reduce hostility, which is most effective when members of different groups have equal status and a mutual goal.

In his classic book *The Nature of Prejudice* (1954), Gordon Allport proposed the **contact hypothesis.** According to this hypothesis, contact between groups will reduce hostility when the participants have equal status and a mutual goal. However, evidence for the contact hypothesis is mixed. On the one hand, some research does not support the contact hypothesis (Miller & Brewer, 1984). Even if there is friendly contact, people still manage to defend their stereotypes. Friendly interaction between individual members of different racial groups may have little effect on their prejudices, because the person they are interacting with may be seen as exceptional and not representative of the out-group (Horwitz & Rabbie, 1989). On the other hand, some research does support the contact hypothesis (Van Laar, Levin, Sinclair, & Sidanius, 2005). Van Laar et al. looked at the effects of living with a roommate from a different racial or ethnic group. They found that students who were randomly assigned to live with an out-group roommate showed increasingly positive feelings as the academic year progressed. The most positive effect of contact was found when the out-group roommate was African American. Even better, the increasing positive attitudes toward African Americans were found to generalize to Latinos. Interestingly, however, both white and black participants showed increasingly *negative* attitudes toward Asian roommates as the year progressed.

In one early study, two groups of boys at a summer camp were made to be competitive and then hostile toward each other (Sherif, Harvey, White, Hood, & Sherif, 1961). At the end of the camp experience, when the researchers tried to reduce the intergroup hostility, they found that contact between the groups and among the boys was not sufficient to reduce hostility. In fact, contact only made the situation worse. It was only when the groups had to work together in pulling a vehicle out of the mud so that they could continue on a long-awaited trip that hostility was reduced. This cooperation on a goal that was important to both groups is called a *superordinate goal,* which is essentially the same as Allport's notion of a mutual goal.

Further evidence that under certain circumstances contact does lead to a positive change in the image of an out-group member comes from other research. In one study, for example, college students were asked to interact with another student described as a former patient at a mental hospital (Desforges et al., 1991). Students were led to expect that the former patient would behave in a manner similar to a typical mental patient. Some of the participants were initially prejudiced toward mental patients, and others were not. After working with the former mental patient in a 1-hour-long cooperative task, the initially prejudiced participants showed a positive change in their feelings about the former patient.

As shown in Figure 4.9, participants experienced a three-stage alteration. At first, they formed a category-based impression: "This is a former mental patient, and this is the way mental patients behave." But equal status and the necessity for cooperation (Allport's two conditions) compelled the participants to make an adjustment in their initial automatically formed impression (Fiske & Neuberg, 1990). This is the second stage. Finally, once the adjustment was made, participants generalized the change in feelings to other mental patients (although they might have concluded, as tends to be more common, that this patient was different from other former mental patients). Note that the readjustment of the participants' feelings toward the former mental patient was driven by paying attention to the personal characteristics of that individual.

In another setting (a schoolroom), Eliot Aronson found that the use of tasks that require each person to solve some part of the whole problem reduces prejudice among schoolchildren (Aronson, Blaney, Stephan, Sikes, & Snapp, 1978). This approach, called the *jigsaw classroom,* requires that each group member be assigned responsibility for a part of the problem. Group members then share their knowledge with everyone else. The concept works because the problem cannot be solved without the efforts of all members; thus each person is valued. This technique also tends to increase the self-esteem of members of different ethnic groups because their efforts are valued.

Does the contact hypothesis work? Yes, but with very definite limits. It seems that both parties have to have a goal they both want and cannot achieve without the other. This superordinate goal also has to compel both to attend to each other's individual characteristics. It also seems to be important that they be successful in obtaining that goal. A recent meta-analysis confirms that contact strategies that conform to the optimal conditions have a greater effect on prejudice than those that do not (Tropp & Pettigrew, 2005a). Additinally Tropp and Pettigrew (2005a) found that the prejudice-reducing effects of contact were stronger for majority-status groups than minority-status groups.

Figure 4.9 Three stages in the alternation of characteristics attributed to the typical group member and general attitudes toward the group through structured contact with a group member.

From Desforges (1991).

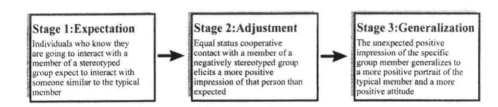

207

Even when all these conditions are met, individuals may revert to their prior beliefs when they leave the interaction. Palestinians and Israelis meeting in Egypt to resolve differences and negotiate peace may find their stereotypes of the other side lessening as they engage in face-to-face, equal, and (perhaps) mutually rewarding contact. But when they go home, pressure from other members of their groups may compel them to take up their prior beliefs again.

Finally, research has investigated how contact reduces prejudice. Recent evidence suggests that intergroup contact mediates prejudice through emotional channels rather than directly reducing stereotypes and other cognitive aspects of prejudice (Tropp & Pettigrew, 2005b).

Personalizing Out-Group Members

According to Henri Tajfel (1982), the Nazis attempted to deny Jews and others their individuality, their identity, by defining them as outside the category of human beings, as *Untermenschen,* subhumans. This dehumanization made it easy for even humane individuals to brutalize and kill because they did not see the individual men, women, and children who were their victims (Horwitz & Rabbie, 1989).

If dehumanizing people makes it easier to be prejudiced, even to carry out the worst atrocities, then perhaps humanizing people, personalizing them, can reduce stereotyping and prejudice. People are less likely to use gender stereotypes, for example, when they have the time to process information that tells them about the distinctive traits of individual males and females (Pratto & Bargh, 1991). Humanizing members of a group does not necessarily mean that we must know or understand each individual in that group (Bodenhausen, 1993). It means we understand that we and they have a shared humanity and that we all feel the same joys and pains. Overall, although personalization is not always successful, especially if the individual is disliked, it does make it more difficult for people to act in a prejudiced manner (Fiske & Neuberg, 1990).

In the 1993 movie *Schindler's List,* an event occurs that illustrates the notion of humanizing the other group. Schindler has managed to save 1,200 Jews otherwise destined for the gas chambers by employing them in his factory. Schindler knows that the German guards have orders to kill all the Jews should the war end. When news comes that the war is over, the guards stand on a balcony overlooking the factory floor, their weapons pointed at the workers. But these Germans have had contact with the Jews; they have seen Schindler treat them humanely, and they have heard them praying and celebrating the Sabbath. Schindler, desperate to save his charges, challenges the Germans: "Do you want to go home as men or as murderers?" The guards hesitate and then slowly leave. Did the Germans put up their weapons out of a sense of shared humanity, or were they simply tired of killing people? In any event, the Jews survived.

Reducing the Expression of Prejudice through Social Norms

In the spring of 1989, four African American students at Smith College received anonymous notes containing racial slurs. The incident led to campus-wide protests. It also inspired an experiment designed to determine the most effective way to deter such expressions of hatred (Blanchard, Lilly, & Vaughn, 1991). The answer? Attack the behaviors—the acts of hatred themselves—not people's feelings about racial issues.

In one experiment, students were asked how they felt the college should respond to these anonymous notes. Some participants then "overheard" a confederate of the experimenters express the opinion that the letter writer, if discovered, should be expelled. Other participants "overheard" the confederate justify the letters by saying the African

American students probably did something to deserve it. The study showed that clear antiracist statements (the person should be expelled) set a tone for other students that discouraged the expression of racial sentiment. Because, as we have seen, racial stereotypes are automatically activated and resistant to change, the best way to discourage racial behavior is through the strong expression of social norms—disapproval from students, campus leaders, and the whole college community (Cook, 1984).

Another kind of prejudice, *heterosexism*, has been deflected in recent years by appeal to social norms as well as by the threat of social sanctions. The Gay and Lesbian Alliance Against Defamation (GLAAD), increasingly supported by public opinion, has targeted pop musicians who sing antigay lyrics and make antigay statements. In 2004, GLAAD issued a statement denouncing singer Beenie Man for his antigay lyrics. One of Man's songs included lyrics such as "I'm dreaming of a new Jamaica; we've come to execute all the gays" (Testone, 2004). As a result of pressure from gay rights groups, MTV cancelled an appearance by Man on its music awards show in 2005.

Reducing Prejudice through Training

Another strategy employed to reduce prejudice is training individuals to associate positive characteristics to out-group members or to dissociate negative traits from those members. This strategy has been adopted in many contexts. Industries, colleges and universities, and even elementary and high school programs emphasize diversity and attempt to improve intergroup relations and reduce prejudice and stereotyping. In this section we will see if such strategies are effective.

Evidence for the effectiveness of training against stereotypes was found in an experiment by Kawakami, Dovidio, Moll, Hermsen, and Russin (2000). Kawakami et al. had participants respond to photographs of black and white individuals associated with stereotypic and nonstereotypic traits associated with the photographs. Half of the participants received training to help them suppress automatic activation of stereotypes. These participants were trained to respond "No" to a white photograph associated with stereotypical white characteristics and "No" to a black photograph associated with stereotypical black characteristics. They were also trained to respond "Yes" when a photograph (black or white) was associated with a nonstereotypic trait. The other half of the participants were provided with training that was just the opposite. The results showed that after extensive training participants who were given stereotype suppression training were able to suppress stereotypes that were usually activated automatically.

In a similar experiment, Kawakami, Dovidio, and van Kamp (2005) investigated whether such training effects extended to gender stereotypes. During the training phase of the experiment, some participants were told that they would see a photograph of a face along with two traits at the bottom of the photograph. Participants were instructed to indicate which of the two traits was *not* culturally associated with the person depicted. So, for example, a face of a female was shown with the traits "sensitive" (a trait stereotypically associated with females) and "strong" (a trait not stereotypically associated with females). The correct answer for this trial would be to select "strong." Participants in the "no training" condition did not go through this procedure. All participants then evaluated four potential job candidates (all equally qualified). Two of the applicants were male and two were female. Participants were told to pick the best candidate for a job that involved leadership and supervising doctors. Half of the participants in the training condition did the applicant rating task immediately after the training, whereas the other half completed a filler task before completing the applicant rating task (this introduced a delay between the training and rating task).

Kawakami et al. (2005) found that participants in the no training and the training with no delay before the rating task were more likely to pick a male candidate than female candidate for the leadership position. These participants displayed sexist preferences. However, when the training and application-rating task were separated by a filler task, sexist preferences were significantly reduced. Kawakami et al. (2005) suggest that when there was no filler task, participants may have felt unduly influenced to pick a female applicant. Because of psychological reactance (i.e., not liking it when we are told to do something), these participants selected the male applicants. Reactance was less likely to be aroused when the training and task were separated.

How about more realistic training exercises? In one study, Stewart et al. (2003) exposed participants to a classic racial sensitivity exercise. This exercise involves using eye color as a basis for discrimination. For example, blue-eyed individuals are set up as the preferred group and brown-eyed individuals in the subordinate group. During the exercise the blue-eyed individuals are treated better, given more privileges, and given preferential treatment. Participants in a control group did not go through this exercise. The results showed that participants in the exercise group showed more positive attitudes toward Asians and Latinos than participants in the control group (the exercise produced only marginally better attitudes toward African Americans). Participants in the exercise group also expressed more displeasure with themselves when they caught themselves thinking prejudicial thoughts.

Hogan and Mallot (2005) assessed whether students enrolled in a course on race and gender experienced a reduction in prejudice (measured by the Modern Racism Scale). Participants in the study were students who were either currently enrolled in the course, had taken the course in the past, or had not taken the course. Hogan and Miller found that participants who were currently enrolled in the class showed less racial prejudice than participants in the other two groups. The fact that the participants who had completed the course showed more prejudice than those currently enrolled suggested to Hogan and Miller that the effects of the race/gender course were temporary.

What is clear from these studies is that there is no simple, consistent effect of training on racial prejudice. Of course, this conclusion is based on only a few studies. More research is needed to determine the extent to which diversity or racial sensitivity training will reduce prejudice.

A Success Story: The Disarming of Racism in the U.S. Army

During the Vietnam War, race relations in the U.S. Army were abysmal (Moskos, 1991). Fights between white and African American soldiers were commonplace in army life in the 1970s. By the early 1980s, the army was making an organized and determined effort to eliminate racial prejudice and animosities. It appears to have succeeded admirably. Many of the strategies the army used are based on principles discussed in this chapter. Let's consider what they were.

One important strategy used by the army was the *level playing field* (Moskos, 1990, 1991). This means that from basic training onward, everyone is treated the same—the same haircuts, the same uniforms, the same rules and regulations. This helps to reduce advantages and handicaps and make everyone equal. The army also has a basic remedial education program that is beneficial for those with leadership qualities but deficits in schooling.

A second factor is a rigid no-discrimination policy. Any expression of racist sentiments results in an unfavorable rating and an end to a military career. This is not to say that officers are free of racist sentiments; it merely means that officers jeopardize their careers if they express or act on such sentiments. A racial insult can lead to a charge of incitement to riot and is punishable by time in the brig. The army uses social scientists to monitor the state of racial relations. It also runs training programs for equal-opportunity instructors, whose function is to see that the playing field remains level.

The army's ability to enforce a nonracist environment is supported enormously by the *hierarchy* that exists both within the officer corps and among the noncommissioned officers. The social barriers that exist in the army reflect rank rather than race. A sergeant must have a stronger identification with his or her peer sergeants than with members of the same race in lower ranks.

Finally, the army's nondiscriminatory environment is visible in its leadership. Many African Americans have leadership roles in the army, including General Colin Powell, the former chairman of the Joint Chiefs of Staff.

What lessons can we learn from the U.S. Army's experience? First, a fair implementation of the contact hypothesis is a good starting point for reducing prejudice. Equal-status interaction and clear mutual goals, even superordinate goals, are essential ingredients of effective contact. Clear and forceful support of the program by leadership is another ingredient. Anyone who violates the policy suffers. At the same time, positive action is taken to level prior inequalities. The army's special programs ensure that everyone has an equal chance.

Some of these lessons cannot be transferred from the army setting. Civilian society does not have the army's strict hierarchy, its control over its members, or its system of rewards and punishments. But the fundamental lesson may be that race relations can best be served by strengthening positive social norms. When social norms are very clear, and when there is a clear commitment to nondiscrimination by leadership—employers, politicians, and national leaders—individual members of society have the opportunity to transcend their prejudices and act on their shared humanity.

The Mormon Experience Revisited

We opened this chapter with a discussion of the experience of the Mormons in the 1800s. The Mormons were the victims of stereotyping (branded as heretics), prejudice (negative attitudes directed at them by the population and the press), and discrimination (economic boycotts). They were viewed as the out-group by Christians (the in-group) to the extent that they began living in their own homogeneous enclaves and even became the target of an extermination order. Once the "us" versus "them" mentality set in, it was easy enough for the Christian majority to pigeonhole Mormons and act toward individual Mormons based on what was believed about them as a group. This is what we would expect based on social identity theory and self-categorization theory. By perceiving the Mormons as evil and themselves as the protectors of all that is sacred, the Christian majority undoubtedly was able to enhance the self-esteem of its members.

The reaction of the Mormons to the prejudice also fits nicely with what we know about how prejudice affects people. Under conditions of threat, we tend to band more closely together as a protection mechanism. The Mormons became more clannish and isolated from mainstream society. This is an example of using primary compensation to cope with the prejudice. The Mormons decided to keep to themselves and tried not to antagonize the Christian majority. Unfortunately, this increased isolation was viewed by the majority as further evidence for the stereotypes about the Mormons. Ultimately, the cycle of prejudice continued until the Mormons were driven to settle in Utah.

Chapter Review

1. How are prejudice, stereotypes, and discrimination defined?

   Prejudice is defined as a biased, often negative, attitude about a group of people. Prejudicial attitudes include belief structures housing information about a group and expectations concerning the behavior of members of that group. Prejudice can be positive or negative, with negative prejudice—dislike for a group—being the focus of research and theory. A stereotype is a rigid set of positive or negative beliefs about the characteristics of a group. A stereotype represents pictures we keep in our heads. When a prejudiced person encounters a member of a group, he or she will activate the stereotype and fit it to the individual. Stereotypes are not abnormal ways of thinking. Rather, they relate to the natural tendency for humans to categorize. Categorization becomes problematic when categories become rigid and overgeneralized. Stereotypes may also form the basis for judgmental heuristics about the behavior of members of a group. Discrimination is the behavioral component of a prejudicial attitude. Discrimination occurs when prejudicial feelings are turned into behavior. Like stereotyping, discrimination is an extension of a natural tendency to discriminate among stimuli. Discrimination becomes a problem when it is directed toward people simply because they are members of a group. It is important to note that discrimination can occur in the absence of prejudice, and prejudice can exist without discrimination.

2. What is the relationship among prejudice, stereotypes, and discrimination?

   Prejudice, stereotypes, and discrimination are related phenomena that help us understand why we treat members of certain groups with hostility. Prejudice comes in a variety of forms, with sexism (negative feelings based on gender category) and racism (negative feelings based on apparent racial category) being most common. Stereotyped beliefs about members of a group often give rise to prejudicial feelings, which may give rise to discriminatory behavior.

   Stereotypes also may serve as judgmental heuristics and affect the way we interpret the behavior of members of a group. Behavior that is seen as stereotype-consistent is likely to be attributed internally and judged more harshly than behavior that is not stereotype-consistent.

3. What evidence is there for the prevalence of these concepts from a historical perspective?

   History tells us that stereotyping, prejudice, and discrimination have been with human beings for a long time. Once formed, stereotypes and prejudices endure over time. Stereotyped views of Japanese by Americans (and vice versa) endured from the World War II era through the present. Prejudicial feelings also led to religious persecution in the United States against groups such as the Mormons.

4. What are the personality roots of prejudice?

One personality dimension identified with prejudice is authoritarianism. People with authoritarian personalities tend to feel submissive toward authority figures and hostile toward different ethnic groups. They have rigid beliefs and tend to be racist and sexist. Social psychologists have also explored how members of different groups, such as whites and blacks, perceive each other. An updated version of the authoritarian personality is right-wing authoritarianism (RWA), which also relates to prejudice. Social dominance orientation (SDO) is another personality dimension that has been studied. People high on social dominance want their group to be superior to others. SDO is also related to prejudice. When SDO and RWA are considered together, they are associated with the highest levels of prejudice. Finally, two dimensions of the "big five" approach to personality (agreeableness and openness) are negatively related to prejudice. There is also evidence that SDO and RWA may relate differently to different forms of prejudice. SDO is related to stereotyping, negative emotion, and negative attitudes directed toward African Americans and homosexuals, and RWA is related to negative stereotypes and emotion directed at homosexuals, but not African Americans.

5. How does gender relate to prejudice?

Research shows that males are higher on SDO than females and tend to be more prejudiced than females. Research on male and female attitudes about homosexuality generally shows that males demonstrate a more prejudiced attitude toward homosexuals than do females. Males tend to have more negative feelings toward gay men than toward lesbians. Whether females show more prejudice against lesbians than against gay men is not clear. Some research shows that women don't make a distinction between gays and lesbians, whereas other research suggests greater prejudice against lesbians than against gay men. Other research shows that males tend to show more ethnic prejudices than females.

6. What are the social roots of prejudice?

Prejudice must be considered within the social context within which it exists. Historically, dominant groups have directed prejudice at less dominant groups. Although most Americans adhere to the notion of equity and justice toward minorities such as African Americans, they tend to oppose steps to reach those goals and only pay lip service to the notion of equity.

7. What is modern racism, and what are the criticisms of it?

In modern culture, it is no longer acceptable to express prejudices overtly, as it was in the past. However, prejudice is still expressed in a more subtle form: modern racism. Adherents of the notion of modern racism suggest that opposing civil rights legislation or voting for a candidate who opposes affirmative action are manifestations of modern racism.

Critics of modern racism point out that equating opposition to political ideas with racism is illogical and that the concept of modern racism has not been clearly defined or measured. Additionally, the correlation between modern racism and old-fashioned racism is high. Thus, modern and old-fashioned racism may be indistinguishable.

8. What are the cognitive roots of prejudice?

Cognitive social psychologists have focused on stereotypes and intergroup perceptions when attempting to understand prejudice. As humans, we have a strong predisposition to categorize people into groups. We do this even when we have only the most minimal basis on which to make categorizations. We classify ourselves and those we perceive to be like us in the in-group, and others whom we perceive to be different from us we classify in the out-group. As a result of this categorization, we tend to display an in-group bias: favoring members of the in-group over members of the out-group.

Tajfel proposed his social identity theory to help explain in-group bias. According to this theory, individuals are motivated to maintain a positive self-concept, part of which comes from membership in groups. Identification with the in-group confers us with a social identity. Categorizing dissimilar others as members of the out-group is another aspect of the social identity process. When we feel threatened, in-group bias increases, thereby enhancing our self-concept. Self-categorization theory suggests that self-esteem is most likely to be enhanced when members of the in-group distinguish themselves from other groups in positive ways.

The in-group bias may also have biological roots. We have a strong wariness of the unfamiliar, called xenophobia, which sociobiologists think is a natural part of our genetic heritage. It may have helped us survive as a species. It is biologically adaptive, for example, for a child to be wary of potentially dangerous strangers. The in-group bias may serve a similar purpose. Throughout history there are examples of various groups increasing solidarity in response to hostility from the dominant group to ensure group survival. Prejudice, then, may be seen as an unfortunate by-product of natural, biologically based behavior patterns.

Because it is less taxing to deal with a person by relying on group-based stereotypes than to find out about that individual, categorizing people using stereotypes helps us economize our cognitive processing effort. Quick categorization of individuals via stereotypes contributes to prejudicial feelings and discrimination. Automatic language associations, by which we link positive words with the in-group and negative words with the out-group, contribute to these negative feelings.

9. How do cognitive biases contribute to prejudice?

Cognitive biases and errors that lead to prejudice include the illusory correlation, the fundamental attribution error, the confirmation bias, the out-group homogeneity bias, and the ultimate attribution error. An illusory correlation is the tendency to believe that two unrelated events are connected if they are systematically related. If you have a tendency to believe that members of a minority group have a negative characteristic, then you will perceive a relationship between group membership and a behavior related to that trait. Additionally, illusory correlations help form and maintain stereotypes. A prejudiced person will overestimate the degree of relationship between a negative trait and a negative behavior. The fundamental attribution error (the tendency to overestimate the role of internal characteristics in the behavior of others) also helps maintain stereotypes and prejudice. Because of this error, individuals tend to attribute negative behaviors of a minority group to internal predispositions rather than to situational factors. The confirmation bias maintains prejudice because individuals who hold negative stereotypes about a group look for evidence to confirm those stereotypes. If one expects a minority-group member to behave in a negative way, evidence will be sought to confirm that expectation. The out-group homogeneity bias is the tendency to see less diversity among members of an out-group than among members of an in-group. As a consequence, a negative behavior of one member of an out-group is likely to be seen as representative of the group as a whole. The ultimate attribution error occurs when we attribute a negative behavior of a minority group to the general characteristics of individuals who make up that group, whereas we attribute the same behavior of an in-group member to situational factors.

10. Are stereotypes ever accurate, and can they be overcome?

There are studies that show that some stereotypes sometimes are accurate. However, accurate or not, stereotypes are still harmful, because they give us a damaging perception of others. There is a tendency to judge individuals according to the worst example of a group represented by a stereotype. Stereotypes can be overcome if one uses controlled processing rather than automatic processing when thinking about others.

11. How do prejudiced and nonprejudiced individuals differ?

One important way in which more- and less-prejudiced individuals differ is that the latter are aware of their prejudices and carefully monitor them. Less-prejudiced persons tend not to believe the stereotypes they hold and act accordingly. Prejudiced individuals are more likely to use automatic processing and energize stereotypes than are less-prejudiced individuals who use controlled processing. However, even nonprejudiced persons will fall prey to stereotyping if stereotypes are activated beyond their conscious control.

12. What is the impact of prejudice on those who are its target?

There are many ways that prejudice can be expressed, some more serious than others. However, it is safe to say that even the lowest level of expression (antilocution) can have detectable emotional and cognitive consequences for targets of prejudice. Everyday prejudice has a cumulative effect on a person and contributes to the target's knowledge and experience with prejudice. Targets of prejudice-based jokes report feelings of disgust, anger, and hostility in response to those jokes.

Another way that targets of prejudice are affected is through the mechanism of the stereotype threat. Once a stereotype is activated about one's group, a member of that group may perform poorly on a task related to that threat, a fact confirmed by research. Another form of threat is collective threat, which occurs when a person from a stereotyped group becomes overly concerned that a transgression by a member of one's group may reflect badly on him or her as an individual. Collective threat comes from a concern that poor performance by one member of one's group may be viewed as a stereotype and generalized to all members of that group.

13. How can a person who is the target of prejudice cope with being a target?

Usually, individuals faced with everyday prejudice must find ways of effectively managing it. If one's group is devalued, stigmatized, or oppressed relative to other groups, prejudice can be countered by raising the value of the devalued group. This is done by first convincing group members of their own self-worth and then by convincing the rest of society of the worth of the group. Another strategy used by individuals from a stigmatized group is to try to anticipate situations in which prejudice will be encountered. Individuals can then decide how to best react to or minimize the impact of prejudice, for example, by modifying their behavior, the way they dress, or the neighborhood in which they live. A third way to cope with stress is through the use of compensation. There are two modes of compensation in which a person can engage. When secondary compensation is used, an individual attempts to change his or her mode of thinking about situations to psychologically protect him- or herself against the outcomes of prejudice. For example, a person who wants to obtain a college degree but faces prejudice that may prevent reaching the goal would be using secondary compensation if he or she devalued the goal (a college education is not all that important) or disidentified with the goal (members of my group usually don't go to college). On the other hand, primary compensation reduces the actual threats posed by prejudice. Coping strategies are developed that allow the target of prejudice to achieve his or her goals.

14. What can be done about prejudice?

Although prejudice has plagued humans throughout their history, there may be ways to reduce it. The contact hypothesis suggests that increased contact between groups should increase positive feelings. However, mere contact may not be enough. Positive feelings are enhanced when there is a superordinate goal toward which groups work cooperatively. Another strategy is to personalize out-group members; this prevents falling back on stereotypes. It is also beneficial to increase the frequency of antiracist statements that people hear, a form of strengthening social norms. A strong expression of social norms, disapproval of prejudice in all of its variations, is probably the best way to discourage and reduce prejudiced acts. Prejudice may also be reduced through training programs that seek to dissociate negative traits from minority group members. Although these programs have met with some success, there is no simple, consistent effect of training on racial prejudice.

2

ABOUT PRIVILEGED GROUPS

In any educational context, it is helpful to know your audience, to understand with whom you're working. Being a member of a privileged group affects one's world view, assumptions, and behavior. In this chapter, I'll explore what it means to be part of a privileged group and the significance of this for our educational efforts. Specifically, I'll discuss some common characteristics of dominant groups and dominant group members, multiple identities and the experience of privilege, and the resistance to acknowledging one's privilege.

Characteristics of Privileged Groups

There are several key attributes of privileged groups. In the first part of the discussion, I will focus on what characterizes a dominant group. I will then consider the implications of these qualities for members of privileged groups. While I will focus on what is generally true for dominant groups, it is important to keep in mind that there are also significant variations among forms of oppression and among individuals.

Normalcy

The dominant cultural and societal norms are based on the characteristics of the privileged group (Wildman, 1996). The dominant group becomes the point of reference against which other groups are judged. It becomes "normal". This standard of normalcy is also used to define what is good and right. These cultural norms become institutionalized and establish policy and practice. Catherine MacKinnon (1989) illustrates how this is true about males.

> Men's physiology defines most sports, their health needs largely define insurance coverage, their socially designed biographies define workplace expectations and successful career patterns, their perspectives and concerns define quality in scholarship, their experiences and obsessions define merit, their military service defines citizenship, their presence defines family, their inability to get along with each other—their wars and rulerships—defines history, their image defines god, and their genitals define sex. (p. 224)

White, Christian, middle class, heterosexual norms pervade our culture. Schools are one place where this is evident. The communication patterns and cultural styles used in most educational settings are more typical of White, upper middle class families. There is an emphasis on individualistic learning, competition, and quiet and controlled classrooms, as opposed to collectivist values, oral traditions, and more active behavior, which are more common in other cultural groups (Delpit, 1995; Greenfield & Cocking, 1996; Viadro, 1996). The structure and content of standardized tests have been based on White, middle class males, giving rise to concerns about gender and racial bias (Sadker, Sadker, & Zittleman, 2009; Santelices & Wilson, 2010). The conformity, or lack thereof, to these norms has significant impact on educational success and achievement. For example, one study (Morris, 2007) found that teachers tend to view the behavior of Black girls as not "ladylike" and discourage behaviors and characteristics that lead to their class involvement and academic achievement.

This is also true in the workplace. Consider the style of speech and dress required for success in the business world. "Proper English", suits or other "professional attire", and a refined interpersonal style are the accepted standards. A study of the experiences of women, Jews, Blacks, Asians, Latinos, and gay men and lesbians in positions of corporate leadership found that while the faces may be more diverse, the behaviors and values remain the same (Domhoff & Zweigenhaft, 1998a). To be successful, these groups must conform to the norms and expectations of the dominant group. "Hedging against traditional stereotypes, Jewish and Black executives must be properly reserved, Asian executives properly assertive, gay executives traditionally masculine, and lesbian executives traditionally feminine" (Domhoff & Zweigenhaft, 1998b, p. 44). People cannot be "too Jewish", "too Black", or "too gay".

The image of a "good family" (still) consists of a mother who is home raising children and a father who is earning the money. When I recently bought a house, I got a strong dose of these cultural norms. I made many calls about hiring someone to do work in the house, saying only that I recently bought it and my full name (first and last). With a few exceptions, people referred to me as Mrs Goodman, assumed that I had a "handy husband" and that I would be home during the day. The possibility that I might be single or a lesbian was not part of most people's thinking.

Other cultural norms are also widespread. I became painfully aware that I was not part of the norm when I attended a huge educational conference in a major hotel in San Francisco during the week of Passover and there was not a matzoh in sight. (Matzoh is unleavened cracker like bread eaten by Jews during Passover as a substitute for leavened bread which is not allowed.) Look in most mainstream card stores and notice how often you see a person with a disability, a person of color or a gay couple on the front, unless the card is targeted for that particular population. Whiteness as the norm in skin tone was revealed in reports about the color of a gown worn by First Lady Michelle Obama which described it as "nude" or "flesh tone" (later, revised to "champagne") (Critchell, 2010). It is particularly ironic since Mrs Obama is African American and the dress hardly matched her skin tone, clearly evident in all the pictures.

We often become aware of the norms when we are exposed to the reverse or an exception. Try switching to all female pronouns when reading something using the generic "he". When I visited Atlanta, I was struck the first time I saw brown mannequins throughout a department store, despite having lived around New York City and other urban areas of the Northeast. Guided fantasies which reverse the norms, such as ones where homosexuality is the most common and accepted form of sexual orientation also illustrate what we take for granted as standard and appropriate.

Moreover, we tend to indicate the identity of individuals only when they are not what we consider the norm, otherwise their social identity is assumed and unnamed. People are likely to refer to the "woman doctor", "Arab store owner", "Latino businessman", "lesbian teacher" or "disabled lawyer", even when their social identity is not significant to the story. Yet how often would someone use the terms "male", "White", "able bodied," or "heterosexual" to refer to indi viduals in similar positions? Sometimes, only through exposure to difference can we begin to see what we have become accustomed to and take to be "normal".

An example of how notions of normalcy get internalized is illustrated in a conversation I had with my daughter when she was eight. She was describing how a friend of hers who is bi racial—Chinese and White, was being teased because of the shape of her eyes. In the course of this conversation, Halle said, "But my eyes are just. … " She paused to search for the right word. She finished her sentence by hesitantly saying "normal." I used this teachable moment to offer her other lan guage to describe her eyes (oval) and to discuss how what is "normal" depends on the context (in China, her friend's eyes would be considered "normal") and that things can be different without having to be considered "normal" or not.

When a group is part of the norm, they also get seen and see themselves as "objective" and "neutral". Other groups have biases and agendas. This was evident in the confirmation hearing of Judge Sonia Sotomayor to the Supreme Court. There was much discussion (and concern) about how her being a woman and Latina would shape her decisions, but virtually no discussion about how being male and White influences the decisions of the other Justices.

Superiority

This sense of normalcy also leads to a sense of superiority. Not only is it normal, it's better. Differences get converted into "better or worse" with the attributes of the dominant group the winners. For example, not only is "standard English" more socially accepted, it is considered "better" than other cultural dialects. Not only are heterosexual nuclear families considered more "common" than gay or lesbian families, they are considered the "best" family structure. White (European) culture, as expressed in music, art, dance, and literature is considered more sophisticated than and superior to the cultures of other racial/ethnic groups (which may be considered interesting but "primitive").

The conversion of differences into notions of superiority/inferiority, is seen in a study to assess children's attitudes, beliefs, and social preferences about children with different skin tones. (http://cnn.com, May 2010). Children in early childhood and middle school were asked various questions to see which skin tones (ranging from light to dark) they associated with positive and negative traits (e.g. smart, dumb, nice, mean, etc). The children, as a whole, revealed a "White bias", associating lighter skin with positive attributes and darker skin with negative attributes, though White children expressed a far greater bias.

Even the same traits may be named and valued differently depending on whether they are associated with a privileged or an oppressed group. Christians are "thrifty" while Jews are "cheap"; heterosexual men are "studs" while gay men are "promiscuous"; men are "leaders" while women are "bitches"; Whites are "shrewd" while Asians are "sneaky". Privileged groups uphold their own attributes as preferable while distorting and disparaging the qualities of others.

Superiority is not always conveyed in blatant and intentional ways. It is the expectation (often unconscious) that people of color should assimilate to White norms in order to be acceptable and accepted. A similar process occurs when women are expected to adopt "male" styles of leadership and communication in order to be viewed as competent and effective in the workplace (though, they can't be too "masculine" either). Trying to get people from disadvantaged groups to be "more like us" is usually a sign of supremacy at work, carrying the implicit message that "our way" is better.

This sense of superiority extends from the characteristics and culture of the dominant group to the individuals themselves. Oppression is commonly defined, in part, as the belief in the inherent superiority of one group over another. This influences how people are viewed and treated. People in professional positions are considered worthier of respect than people in working class jobs. There is usually more public outcry when a White woman is raped or a White child is killed than when this occurs to a woman or child of color. People with developmental disabilities have been seen as appropriate guinea pigs for dangerous medical experiments. Even at the level of the Supreme Court, Judge Ruth Bader Ginsberg related an experience familiar to many women when she discussed how in conferences with the other Supreme Court judges, her points were often ignored until they were made by one of the male judges (Lewis, 2009).

People from disadvantaged groups are generally labeled as substandard or aber rant. They are assumed to be less capable due to innate defects or deficiencies (Miller, 1976). For example, women are too emotional, Blacks are less intelligent, gays are morally deviant, and people with disabilities are defective. Not only are people from subordinated groups somehow inferior, but by logical extension, people from dominant groups are superior. This reasoning allows privileged groups to rationalize the systematic unfair treatment of people from oppressed groups and to feel entitled to power and privilege.

Cultural and Institutional Power and Domination

Oppression involves unequal social power—access and control of resources, goods, and rewards/punishments that enhance one's capacity to get what one needs and influence others. This allows for domination, the ability for one social group to systematically subjugate, control, manipulate, and use other people for its own ends. Social power and domination is created and maintained through interpersonal, institutional, and cultural forces. The privileged group creates systems and structures that reflect its values, embodies its characteristics, and advances its interests. A structural perspective on inequality recognizes the role of public policies and institutional practices, not simply individual attitudes, in developing and perpetuat ing societal inequality. People are increasingly using the term "White supremacy", not to refer to racial extremists, but to describe how notions of White superiority are embedded in our institutions and ideology. Unequal power systems are sus tained by shaping people's worldviews, controlling resources, and constraining opportunities.

Since social oppression has both ideological and structural dimensions, it can take many forms. At times, it is blatant and coercive and the advantages to the privileged group are clear, such as with Jim Crow laws or forced (uninformed) sterilization. Often, however, it is more subtle and insidious, with less obvious benefits to the privileged group, such as media images that portray women as sex objects, or eco nomic policies that maintain some unemployment to ensure a pool of cheap, surplus labor.

Privileged groups define the mainstream culture—behavior patterns, symbols, institutions, values, and other human made components of society (Banks, 1991). They determine what is acceptable and unacceptable, what is valued and ignored. Other groups are relegated as "subcultures". For example, the dominant cultural norms are reflected in our standards of beauty. The image of a beautiful woman is someone who is young, extremely thin, tall, light skinned, with Anglo features, and finely textured hair, and often blond and blue eyed. According to mainstream time norms, people should be ruled by the clock. People are expected to be prompt and to end meetings according to pre arranged times. Other cultural groups are more relaxed about time, and begin and complete activities when they feel ready to do so. Often, this is seen as lazy and undisciplined.

Advantaged groups also establish the dominant ideology—a pervasive set of ideas and ways of looking at reality. The dominant ideology forms individual conscious ness and both justifies and conceals domination (Kreisberg, 1992, p. 15). The con cept of "hegemony" (Gramsci & Forgacs, 2000) describes the ways in which the privileged group imposes their conception of reality in a manner accepted as common sense, as "normal" and as universal. As Jean Baker Miller (1976) explains,

"A dominant group has the greatest influence in determining a culture's overall outlook—its philosophy, morality, social theory and even its science. The dominant group, thus, legitimizes the unequal relationship and incorporates it into society's guiding concepts"(p. 8). This dominant ideology, which I discuss in more depth in Chapter 4, is embedded in institutional structures and practices that shape our consciousness and experiences. What we learn (and don't learn) in school, what we see (and don't see) in the media, how we are expected to act at work, how our economy is structured, who are held up as role models, and what research gets funded and validated, reflects and reinforces the dominant ideology. This informs our sense of what is important, true, and real about ourselves, others, and the world. This power to define reality is labeled "true power" by Derald Sue (2010a). He explains, "When a clash of realities occur, mainstream groups have the tools—education, mass media, peer social groups and institutions to define and impose realities upon other groups" (p. 46).

When privileged groups have greater institutional power, it allows them to establish policies and procedures that can provide, deny or limit opportunities and access to resources and social power. In 2007, the top 1% of the population owned almost 35% of the privately held wealth in the US; the top 20% controlled approximately 85% of the wealth in this country (Wolff, 2010); in 2010, only about 3% of CEOs of the Fortune 500 companies were women (Catalyst, 2010); and women and people of color are still grossly underrepresented in Congress. They exercise control over access to health care, housing, education, employment, political representation, fair judicial treatment, and legal rights.

Privileged groups also define acceptable roles for people in subordinated groups. These roles usually involve providing services that people from advantaged groups do not want to do or do not highly value. This social manipulation impedes human dignity and self determination. Conversely, people from privileged groups can provide benefits to others from their own social group—by sharing information, providing jobs, creating laws and policies, contributing money, making appointments to boards and committees, and facilitating social and political connections.

The control of the dominant belief system and major institutions results in psycho logical domination as well. People from both privileged and marginalized groups often begin to accept the messages from the dominant culture of dominant group superiority and subordinated group inferiority. When this is absorbed by people from the privileged group, it is sometimes called "internalized superiority/supremacy."

Sometimes it is conscious, but often "it is the unconscious, internalized values and attitudes that maintain domination, even when people do not support or display overt discrimination or prejudice" (hooks, 1989, p. 13). For people from oppressed groups, "internalized oppression" or "internalized inferiority" undermines their self esteem, sense of empowerment, and intragroup solidarity. It encourages unhealthy, dysfunctional behavior. In addition, people from oppressed groups are encouraged to develop personal and psychological characteristics that are pleasing to the privi leged group—being submissive, dependent, docile (Miller, 1976). As long as people believe that they are inferior or deserve their situation, consider their treatment fair or for their own benefit, or are constrained in their self development, they will not effectively challenge the current system.

Since the dominant ideology is embedded in our institutional practices and individual consciousness, for oppression to continue, we just need to act "nor mally", to go along with the status quo. It does not require malice or bad intentions to perpetuate systems of domination. We have been conditioned to see our social systems as normal and natural, even if some societal inequities are recognized.

Since only privileged groups have institutional power and the ability to system atically enforce their views, only they may be "oppressive" (e.g. racist, sexist, ableist, etc). Certainly, people from *all* social groups (advantaged and disadvantaged) have prejudices and may act in discriminatory ways. Women may stereotype men, gays may deride heterosexuals, and Latinos may favor other Latinos for jobs. However, I, like many others, make the distinction between oppression and other terms such as prejudice, bigotry or bias. None of the oppressed groups has the societal power to systematically disadvantage the corresponding privileged group. Consequently, from this line of thinking, there is no "reverse racism" even though people of color can act in hurtful, unfair ways toward White people. The shorthand definition "prejudice + social power = oppression" is useful to capture this distinction.

Privilege

Oppression involves both systematic disadvantage *and* advantage. This "system of advantage" (Wellman, 1977) bestows on people from privileged groups greater access to power, resources, and opportunities that are denied to others and usually gained at their expense. Most discussions of social injustice focus on the subjugation of oppressed groups—the ways in which they are discriminated against, margin alized, exploited, manipulated, demeaned, and physically and emotionally attacked. Less attention is given to the other part of the dynamic—the privileging of the dominant group.

Social oppression creates privilege systems—benefits or unearned advantages sys tematically afforded people from dominant groups simply because of their social group membership. " ... What makes something a privilege is the unequal way in which it is distributed and the effect it has on elevating some people over others"

(Johnson, 2005, p. 175). It includes what we are able to take for granted or not have to think about simply because we are part of an advantaged group; people from disadvantaged groups cannot make the same assumptions. Peggy McIntosh (1988) describes White privilege as "an invisible weightless knapsack of special provisions, maps, passports, codebooks, visas, clothes, tools and blank checks" (p. 71). Privileges can be both material and psychological; they can include concrete benefits as well as psychological freedoms; often these are interrelated. McIntosh lists numerous privileges for Whites that reflect these two interconnected dimensions. She writes,

> I can go home from most meetings of the organizations I belong to feeling somewhat tied in, rather than isolated, out of place, outnumbered, unheard, feared or hated; I can arrange to protect my children most of the time from people who might not like them; I can go into a supermarket and find the food I grew up with, into a hairdresser's shop and find someone who can deal with my hair; I can be pretty sure that if I ask to talk to 'the person in charge' I will be facing a person of my race; I can be pretty sure that my children will be given curricular materials that testify to the existence of their race; I can take a job with an affirmative action employer without having co workers on the job suspect that I got it because of my race; I can do well in a challenging situation without being called a credit to my race; I can swear, or dress in second hand clothes, or not answer letters, or be late to meetings without having people attribute these behaviors to the bad morals, the poverty, or the illiteracy of my race; I can think over many options, social, political, imagi native or professional, without asking whether a person of my race would be accepted or allowed to do what I want to do. (pp. 5–9)

(Using her work as a template, there are now lists of privileges for many other groups.)

Male privilege is evident in an exercise I do with groups of university men and women.[1] I ask them to describe what they do on a daily basis to ensure their safety. The men have a hard time coming up with a list. On the other hand, the women quickly cite numerous efforts: locking doors, walking with buddies, getting rides, avoiding certain areas, checking their cars, staying inside during late hours. Men have the privilege of being able to move about with less thought, worry, and con straint. (For men facing other forms of oppression—racism, classism, heterosexism, ableism—the privilege of safety may be significantly limited).

People with class privilege have access to the best medical care; to leisure and vacations; to good housing, food, and clothing; and to governmental financial advantages (e.g. tax breaks, write offs for mortgages). They feel entitled to be trea ted respectfully, to be taken seriously, and to have opportunities to use their talents. They can choose work that may be meaningful, though not well compensated, knowing they have a safety net—other marketable skills, opportunities for education, or financial resources. They can use connections to get jobs or to be admitted to college. It's interesting to note that when opportunities are gained due to connections, there is not the outcry about merit. On the other hand, affirmative action is constantly attacked (cf. Larew, 2010).

Able bodied people do not have to think about access to buildings—for education, cultural events, employment, socializing; about travel—around one's own town, vacation areas, conference sites; or about needing assistance to do basic daily tasks. They do not fear that people will assume them to be less intelligent or less productive solely because of a (possibly irrelevant) disability. My privilege as a hearing person became starkly apparent at a conference I attended. One of the participants in a session I was facilitating was a woman who was deaf. The con ference provided interpreters during the workshop. At one of the social events, she motioned me over to say hello to a colleague who was also deaf, but there was no interpreter. We were unable to communicate effectively since I didn't know sign language. Not only did I feel frustrated and disappointed that I was missing out on getting to know some interesting people, I realized how much I enjoyed and gained from being able to socialize and network with so many people at the conference while they sat by themselves, unable to interact with the rest of the participants.

People with Christian privilege do not have to take personal days to observe their religious holidays or worry whether institutional dining halls and cafeterias will have foods that meet their religious dietary needs. They can travel around the country and find churches they can attend and hear music on the radio or programs on TV that reflect their religion. Prayers at public occasions will usually be based on Christianity (even if they're intended to be non denominational) and their holy day (Sunday) is taken into account when scheduling work, school, or public events (Blumenfeld, Joshi, & Fairchild, 2008; Schlosser, 2003; Seifert, 2007).

Heterosexuals can freely display public affection, talk openly about their partner, have their relationship publicly acknowledged and celebrated, and be protected from discrimination. They don't need to worry if it's all right to bring their partner to events (and then, if they can dance together); if they'll lose their job if they're "out"; if they'll be accepted by their neighbors, or if their partner will be considered "family" under hospital guidelines and thus be able to visit or make medical decisions.

I became aware of another aspect of heterosexual privilege when I worked on a committee against homophobia on a university campus. When I was hired to do human relations education, it was clear that few people on campus were willing to publicly deal with issues of heterosexism, despite the often stated need and some very active (though essentially closeted) gay and lesbian faculty and staff. I quickly formed a committee (open to everyone) to address gay, lesbian, and bisexual issues on campus (transgender issues weren't in people's consciousness then). There was a lot of interest and a strong representation of lesbians, gay men, and bisexuals. While we worked very collaboratively, I was the "chair" and "contact person"—regularly sending out notices of our meetings and events, being called by the student news paper to report on our activities. On a campus that felt unsafe to most gays, I rea lized that as a heterosexual, I had more freedom to be public about working against homophobia than my lesbian and gay colleagues. I had the safety of not being "found out", despite assumptions that I was a lesbian. It felt like a privilege to be visible around this issue. (This is not to deny the fact that people from privileged groups do face risks when being allies.)

Promoting identification with superiority and privilege helps to prevent people from an advantaged group from allying with people from one of their disadvantaged groups. White poor and working class men have often used (and have been encouraged to use) their "whiteness" to feel privileged while rejecting an alliance with men of color in a similar class position (Roediger, 1991). They rely on racism and their sense of White privilege to create separation, instead of forging a common struggle against classism and economic exploitation.

Moreover, oppression is maintained not just by taking actions *against* dis advantaged groups but by increasing privileges *for* advantaged groups. "Inequality gets reproduced through advantages to Whites as much or more so than it does through discrimination against minorities" (DiTomaso, 2003). We need to examine both parts of the dynamic. For example, even when White women and people of color (and others from subordinated groups) are not actively denied jobs, unless they are included in the informal social network, mentored, encouraged to take on new responsibilities, and provided opportunities for professional development, the net effect will be that they will not advance at the same rate as White men. White men are being privileged even though White women and people of color may not be facing overt discrimination.

There is a growing recognition of how the history and cumulative effect of interlocking benefits for the dominant group affect current inequities, particularly related to race (California Newsreel, 2003; Katznelson, 2006; Lipsitz, 1998; Lui, Robles, Leondar Wright, Brewer, & Adamson, 2006). There has been a legacy of institutional (including government) policies, as well as more informal practices, that have unfairly privileged people from dominant groups. "Histories of unearned advantages, unequal distribution of resources, the effects of housing segregation, access to job connections—these are the factors that reproduce the unequal outcomes that we see" (DiTomaso, 2003).

Moreover, people from dominant group receive privileges regardless of their individual attitudes. They neither have to be aware of the advantages nor want them to receive them.

> In the same way that men benefit from a patriarchal system by the way resources are distributed, even if they don't have antipathy toward women, white people are given the spoils of a racist system even if they're not personally racist. (Powell, 2003)

McIntosh also makes distinctions among privileges. She suggests that some are advantages that everyone is entitled to and should be a right; these need to be extended to all. Examples include having your neighbors be decent to you, not having your race work against you in employment, or not being followed or har assed in stores. Other privileges confer dominance and reinforce our present hier archies, such as being able to ignore less powerful people, to manipulate our legal system to avoid punishment, to withhold information or resources, or to advance your interests to the detriment of others. These need to be rejected and eliminated. Therefore, as we examine privilege systems, we need to consider how privileges are constructed, how they are used to further systemic and structural inequality, and how to ensure that everyone has access to the privileges that should be human rights.

Individuals from Privileged Groups

Individuals are affected by being part of a privileged group and the dominant cul ture. Their experiences and perspectives are shaped by their social position. The effects of being dominant group members are reflected in people's attitudes, think ing, and behavior. I'll discuss several of the most common traits. Again, these vary according to the individual and their other social identities.

Lack of Consciousness

People from privileged groups tend to have little awareness of their own dominant identity, of the privileges it affords them, of the oppression suffered by the corre sponding disadvantaged group, and of how they perpetuate it. In the first place, people from privileged groups generally do not think about their dominant group identity.

I conduct a couple of activities that highlight this point. At the beginning of a class or workshop, I'll ask people to introduce themselves by choosing words to describe who they are. People of color will virtually always refer to their racial/ cultural identity, while someone who is White rarely will (Wildman, 1996 and Tatum, 1997 report similar findings).

In another activity, I list common social categories: race, sex, religion, sexual identity, ability/disability, class, age, and ethnicity, and ask people to choose the two or three that are most important to who they are, to their sense of identity. I later ask them to choose the three that feel least important. Again, most people include in their three most important identities subordinated ones (though depending on the group, people are less likely to reveal their sexual orientation if they are gay, lesbian, or bisexual). The three least important are dominant iden tities. The one consistent exception is sex; both females and males often include it in their top three. This is not surprising since sex is such a salient and referenced social category.

When these results are pointed out to people in the class, I ask them why they think this occurs and why they chose the identities they did. People who choose a subordinated identity as most important talk about feeling very aware of that identity—it makes them feel different, others make them aware of it, it has created obstacles to overcome, or it is where they get mistreated. On the other hand, they recognize that their dominant identity is something to which they generally do not need to pay attention.

Even though we are most exposed to information about privileged groups, people from these groups tend to have the least self awareness about that aspect of their identity and its social significance. This absence of consciousness about their social identity, seems to, in part, reflect unequal power relationships. Miller (1976) maintains that people from dominant groups are deprived of feedback about their behavior from people from subordinated groups (since it's unsafe to tell), and therefore don't learn about their impact on others. Nor do mainstream institutions (media, schools) provide this kind of perspective. (I also think that most people from privileged groups are not interested in or are afraid of knowing anyway, a point discussed later.) Nonetheless, people from advantaged groups are allowed, in fact encouraged, to remain unaware. In contrast, people from disadvantaged groups become highly attuned to and knowledgeable about the dominant group since their survival depends on it.

This lack of awareness relates to being the norm, and therefore not needing to think about one's social identity. It's like being a fish in water—when you're surrounded by water as part of your natural environment, it's hard to be aware of it. And, this water has been filtered through the dominant ideology. People from privileged groups are surrounded by their culture and therefore don't notice it. This allows them to see themselves as individuals, not as part of a group that has social power and privilege. While members of other social groups may be lumped together, obliterating individual and intragroup differences, people from privileged groups tend to see themselves as unique individuals who succeed or fail based on their own merit.

Moreover, this "fish in water" phenomenon contributes to the lack of awareness people from dominant groups have about their privileges. Because the norm or reality is perceived as including these benefits, the privileges are not visible to the dominant group (Wildman, 1996). As I stated earlier, since privileges are things we usually take for granted and assume to exist, they therefore tend to be invisible. Frequently, we do not realize that something is a privilege until we compare it with the experience of the disadvantaged group. Several examples illustrate this occurrence.

One Sunday morning I was in New York City saying goodby to my then boy friend. As we stood on the curb next to my car kissing, I heard some people down the block behind me clapping. We stopped, and as I slowly turned around, I saw four men sitting on the back of a truck laughing and applauding. I felt mortified. As I was recounting this episode to a lesbian friend of mine, it suddenly occurred to me how this was about heterosexual privilege. I could blithely and obliviously kiss on the street, and then be applauded for my action. I doubt that my gay or lesbian friends would so unconsciously kiss their lover in public, or that they would likely get such a positive reaction. I had the luxury of just worrying about being embarrassed.

I am usually unaware of my privilege as an able bodied person until I am with a person who has a disability. For several days of a conference I was attending, I wandered about the large hotels looking for the sessions, joined friends for meals, and explored the city. I then met a colleague who used a wheelchair. She generally limited herself to the sessions that were being held in one hotel since navigating it was difficult enough. Trying to get out of the hotel, cross the streets, and move about other hotels was too time consuming and exhausting. Finding an accessible place to have dinner became another issue. After spending most of the day together, we arrived back at our hotel and found that the elevator in the lobby that stopped at our floor was closed for the evening. Since the suggested alternative was up an escalator (which was impossible to do in a wheelchair), we ended up taking the freight elevator. Technically, the hotel and the conference were wheelchair acces sible. However, it made me realize how much I take my mobility, and what it affords me, for granted.

In these previous examples, the privilege is clear if we try to become conscious of it. In other cases, the privilege is more hidden. In an effort to explore sex discrimina tion, the television show *Prime Time* matched a White man and a White woman on all variables except sex (e.g. overall appearance, education). (*The Fairer Sex*, 1993). They went out separately to look for jobs, buy a car, etc. Both applied for a job as a territory manager for a landscape business that was advertised in the newspaper. Even though based on their resumes she was better qualified for the job, when the man was interviewed he took an aptitude test and was told about managerial pos sibilities; when the woman was interviewed, she took a typing test and was asked about her secretarial skills.

They conducted a similar experiment with a White man and a Black man to examine racism (*True Colors*, 1992). In one situation, they both responded to an ad for an apartment to rent. The Black man was told that the apartment was rented, while the White man, who went in later, was told that the apartment was still available. In both of these situations, not only did the White man receive better treatment and more opportunities than the woman or Black man, but those options and advancements were gained at their expense. The White man had these chances because others were denied the same opportunity. If there weren't hidden cameras, the White man never would have known that the woman or Black man were not treated as he was. He was just being treated nicely. Unfortunately, this kind of treatment becomes a privilege, an unearned advantage.

While these segments are becoming dated, personal stories and more recent research indicate that these same dynamics continue to exist (cf. Bertrand and Mullainathan, 2004; U.S. Housing Scholars and Research and Advocacy

Organizations, 2008). Dominant group members may be unaware that they are the recipients of privileged treatment and that it is at the expense of others. They therefore believe that their achievements are based on their own merit, not on systematic advantage. (See Hawkesworth, 1993, Chapter 2, for a review of the research that documents how sexist bias privileges men at women's expense.) They are less likely to realize how "business as usual" could still cause injustice.

Lastly, because the privileges are sometimes hidden and the discrimination subtle, people from privileged groups don't realize the pervasiveness of oppression. They assume their experiences and treatment are "normal". This assumption, coupled with little knowledge of the injustices that people from disadvantaged groups face, allows them to remain unconscious. People from advantaged groups are taught to notice neither inequalities nor privileges. They are "privileged to remain innocent" (Lazarre, 1996).

This lack of consciousness allows for the unintentional perpetuation of injustice. People do not realize that what they are doing is biased or discriminatory. Gaertner and Dovidio (1986) coined the term *aversive racism* to refer to when White people espouse egalitarian values but unconsciously hold negative feelings and beliefs about people of color. This leads them to engage in racist acts without being aware of it and to deny that racism is affecting their behavior (Dovidio & Gaertner, 2005). More broadly, the unconscious and unintentional expressions of bias and prejudice toward socially devalued groups are often called microaggressions (Sue, 2010a, 2010b). There are innumerable examples of these, yet one situation captures this well. A photo in a local newspaper featured a White boy and an African American boy, with the White boy in the foreground. The title was announcing the winner of the "geography bee". The caption began with the name of the White boy and the fact that he finished in second place. It then explained that the other boy was the winner, and gave his name. Even when the African American deserved the spotlight, from looking at the photo (and the order of the information in the cap tion), it appeared that the White boy was the winner. A positive image of an African American male was diminished, yet newspapers have no difficulty high lighting African American males when they are involved in illegal activity. While some people may intentionally promote racist or other oppressive images, I doubt whether the photographer of the picture or the editor of the newspaper intended to convey such a distorted and implicitly racist message. Yet, they colluded with institutional racism. Since people do not have to act in overtly discriminatory ways, but just behave "normally" or "unconsciously" to perpetuate oppression, it is easy to remain unaware of the impact of their own actions or of their institution's practices.

Denial and Avoidance of Oppression

There is a fine line between recognizing that some privileges may be less obvious and therefore easy to overlook, and choosing not to see or look for them. Similarly, there is a difference between lacking an awareness of the extent of social injustice and deciding not to acknowledge it. People from privileged groups have the options to deny the existence of oppression and to avoid dealing with it. Lazarre (1996) refers to this as "willful innocence." (See Kivel, 2002 for a discussion of the tactics people from privileged group use to retain their benefits and avoid their responsibility.)

For the reasons cited earlier, people from privileged groups tend to be less con scious of oppression and more likely to deny that it exists. In their reality, they are generally unhampered by their social identity and ignorant of the mistreatment of others. Along with a sense of superiority, it becomes easy to proclaim that if it is not an issue from their perspective, then it's not an issue. Since their life can proceed rather well under the current circumstances, they do not need to bother to explore or listen to the complaints of others. They can ignore claims of discrimination and label those who raise issues as oversensitive or troublemakers. Denying that there is oppression also allows the system of domination to remain in place *and* to be justified.

This is exacerbated by the fact that people from advantaged and disadvantaged groups tend to define oppression differently. In the case of racism, Whites are more likely to see racism as "individual acts of meanness" (McIntosh, 1988. p. 5), indivi dual acts of prejudice and discrimination, or as extreme actions that are the excep tion rather than the norm. Blacks are more likely to see it as daily indignities and as a system of institutionalized practices and policies that work to their disadvantage (Duke, 1992; Shipler, 1997). Therefore, if people only recognize injustice when it is blatantly expressed by individuals, they will never understand the depth and breadth of social oppression.

Admitting that there is oppression and that one participates in it opens up the possibility of personal discomfort. As Allan Johnson (2005) explains, people from privileged groups feel they should be exempt from such an experience.

> Dominant groups typically show the least tolerance for allowing themselves to feel guilt and shame. Privilege, after all, should exempt one from having to feel such things. They experience reminders of their potential for feeling guilt as an affront that infringes on their sense of entitlement to a life unplagued by concern for how their privilege affects other people. The right to deny that privilege exists is an integral part of privilege itself. So men can be quick to complain about "being made to feel guilty" without actually *feeling* guilty. (p. 62, italics in the original)

This privilege is sometimes referred to as "the right to comfort". This was expressed very directly at a training I conducted with a group of university students. The first several activities highlighted the groups' diversity and clearly made the point that we need to value our differences and create equality for all groups. After participating in an exercise that physically demonstrated White privilege and institutional racism, a White male said that he didn't like the activity because it made him feel uncomfortable and bad about being White. He understood that the point of the activity was to demonstrate inequities and knew that the purpose was not to make White people feel guilty. Nevertheless, he still insisted that his discomfort made him not want to engage, and therefore the activity was counterproductive. He felt entitled to the privilege of not having to be uncomfortable, and therefore had the privilege of choosing not to confront issues of racism.

People from privileged groups can also choose to remain silent when they are aware of injustice. The impact on people from disadvantaged groups in usually more profound and immediate, and thus more likely to elicit a greater need to respond. Since people from privileged groups are usually less directly affected, they can decide not to take action. In fact, there is incentive not to do so. First, people from advantaged groups who point out inequities and challenge the status quo often put themselves at risk. They may face retaliation at work or school, ostracism, harassment, or violence. Second, it disrupts a system that largely works to their benefit. People from privileged groups tend to have more to lose, at least in the short run, if they make waves. (However, in Chapter 5, I'll discuss the extensive costs of oppression to people from dominant groups as well.)

Sense of Superiority and Entitlement

Being part of the norm, a member of the dominant group, and the beneficiary of (invisible) privileges often leads to a sense of superiority and entitlement or internalized superiority/supremacy. Even though this sense of identity is false and unearned, people from dominant groups come to expect certain treatment and opportunities. They feel they *deserve* the privileges they have come to assume will be theirs. This attitude is beyond a healthy sense of self respect or pride in one's cultural group; it can be arrogance and snobbery. They not only expect their needs to get met, but often believe that their needs should supersede others' needs.

People with class privilege (money or status) expect their phone calls to be returned promptly and their work to receive priority. I notice that students who are upper middle class, especially males, feel more entitled to my time and attention as a professor. They expect individual attention and accommodations to meet their needs. In general, men expect their wants and desires to take precedence over a woman's. Sometimes, people have a clear sense of entitlement and consciously believe that they deserve special treatment. Many times, people who are acting entitled rarely see their behavior in this light. They are just doing what they think anyone would or should do.

This sense of superiority often becomes evident when people from an advantaged group encounter someone from a disadvantaged group in a position of expertise or authority over them. Men may balk at having a woman boss or Whites may be uncomfortable with a person of color as the doctor or consultant. People from privileged groups are often suspect of the ability, knowledge, or right to such status of people from oppressed groups. This may reflect more than just stereotypes and bias. This arrangement calls into question the implicit superiority of people from the dominant group and what they assume is the appropriate social order. Some of the personal and political attacks on President Obama could be viewed in this way.

Multiple Identities and Experiences of Privilege

In my description of common characteristics of people from privileged groups, I have narrowly focused on a single aspect of one's identity. However, that is only one strand of a whole tapestry. Individuals' other social identities color their experience of that dominant identity, and more broadly, affect one's overall experience of both privilege and oppression. Not everyone benefits equally; privi leges are mediated by one's other social positions. Other social statuses affect the degree to which an individual experiences the advantages of privilege.

Privileges gained through a dominant identity may be mitigated or reduced because of a subordinated identity. Class privilege certainly provides many advan tages, yet it may be limited by racism, sexism or heterosexism. Even middle and upper class Black men get stopped by police and suspected for criminal activity; in fact, being in a "nice neighborhood" or driving an expensive car will often bring on this suspicion. Women in high level positions still do not command the same respect or influence as men in similar positions. Openly gay men do not have the same access to corporate or political power (or membership in the "Old Boys Network") as heterosexual men. (As described earlier in this chapter, people from various oppressed groups rarely have the same access to high level institutional power, and when they do, it is at a cost.)

Nor does privilege in one area prevent subordination in another. Wealthy women are still subject to sexual violence even though they have greater opportu nities to protect their safety. Being able bodied, heterosexual, and White does not exempt a working class person from class oppression. A White man in his 30s who has the benefits of race, sex, and age may still face employment discrimination because he has a disability. In extreme cases, other dominant identities or privileges are irrelevant. No aspect of privilege could protect the Japanese from internment, Native Americans from removal, or Jews from extermination.

On the other hand, the experience of oppression in one aspect generally does not eradicate the experience of privilege in another. Some feminists feel that because they are all women and experience sexism their experiences are similar. White women, able bodied women or heterosexual women may ignore the way they have privileges in other parts of their lives. Some Jews may be subject to anti Semitism, yet still have white skin privilege. Men of color confront racism, yet still benefit from sexism and patriarchy.

Moreover, one's other intersecting identities not only affect one's degree of pri vilege but also shape that privileged identity. For example, a Black man's experience and identity as a man is different than a White man's; a Jewish person's experience and identity as a White person is different than a White Anglo Saxon Protestant's.

Though not absolute, our particular mix of identities does shape our experiences. Privilege can help alleviate experiences of oppression. The more dominant identities one has, the more one can draw on those privileges to deal with the discrimination and disempowerment faced in his/her subordinated roles. The more subordinated identities one has, the more likely the privilege one does have is eroded. However, this is not simply an additive game; our social identities are not a balance sheet where one can just compare the number of identities on the dominant side and the number on the subordinated side and know how much power, privilege, or freedom one has. Individuals and the dynamics of oppression are much more complicated than that. Some people argue that certain oppressions are worse than others or have greater impact. As noted in the previous chapter, Young (1990) points out there may be different "faces" or manifestations of oppression which are experienced to greater or lesser degrees by different oppressed groups. Oppressions may be linked but not comparable. As Audre Lorde (1983) asserts, "there is no hierarchy of oppressions".

Resistance to Seeing Oneself as Privileged

Many people have reactions to considering themselves privileged or dominant. Some people have difficulty thinking in those terms about themselves; others can do it, but just don't like the idea. There are several reasons for these types of responses.

First, being "privileged", "dominant", or an "oppressor" has negative connotations. Many people assume it means that individuals willfully discriminate against or mistreat others. It seems to refer to the "bad guys". Most people don't see themselves, or want to see themselves, in that light. They consider themselves nice people who try to treat people fairly.

Second, most people do not even realize that they are privileged or part of groups with greater social power. As I have described, most people from dominant groups don't think about that identity; they are simply "normal". They also do not realize the extent of systemic inequalities and the ways they are advantaged. It is hard to accept being privileged when you are unaware of your privileges or feel you have earned them.

Even if people from dominant groups are aware of their social status, they don't *feel* privileged or powerful. Most people are struggling to live their lives. They worry about their jobs, their families, and their health. They personally do not have access to great amounts of resources or make decisions that affect the nation. More people feel controlled rather than in control. Given the individualistic and competitive nature of our society, few people feel secure. The fact that most people think of themselves as individuals, rather than as members of a social group exacerbates the difficulty of seeing themselves as privileged. Since individuals themselves do not alone create and maintain dominant ideologies and oppressive structures, it is understandable that an individual would not feel that they have had much of a role in societal oppression. Since they *personally* don't feel advantaged, it is difficult to acknowledge that they are part of a group that is. A White woman expresses this realization:

> I never thought about it before, but there are many privileges to being White. In my personal life, I cannot say that I have ever felt that I had the advantage over a Black person, but I am aware that my race has the advan tage. (Tatum, 1997, p. 102)

Alternatively, some people from dominant groups feel that they are the ones at a disadvantage. This is particularly true for Whites who feel that people of color are now the ones getting the benefits, especially in the job market. However, when conducting exercises where White people are asked if they would rather be a person of color, virtually no Whites indicate that they would like to switch.

Moreover, the sense of privilege is relative. First, Johnson (2005) contends that people tend to assess their relative standing in comparison to people like themselves (looking sideways) or to people more advantaged than themselves (looking up). Rarely do we judge ourselves in relation to people worse off than ourselves (downwards). Therefore, if our "peers" or those "above" us seem better off than we do, it is of little comfort or consequence that others are in worse positions. There fore, people are usually quite aware of their relative deprivation but refuse to acknowledge their relative privilege.

Second, not all people in a particular advantaged group are similarly situated. Certainly the experience of class privilege of someone in the top 1% of wealth in this country is quite different from someone who is comfortably middle class. Third, other subordinated identities erode one's sense of privilege. Some people from a targeted group claim that their oppression undermines any privileges they may receive from their dominant identity. Rather, I would say that other social positions affect the *degree* to which someone is advantaged in one's dominant identity. An individual can recognize privileges due to one's dominant identities while also acknowledging how those identities are affected by one's other targeted identities. Privilege and oppression are not mutually exclusive, even if there is a dynamic between them.

As noted before, people tend to focus on their subordinated identities. For people who are part of a privileged group, their targeted identity(ies) will usually have greater significance than their dominant identity(ies). This makes it more dif ficult for them to identify as someone from a privileged group and to acknowledge that status. Most people will tend to see themselves as someone from a dis advantaged group, ignoring their privileges in other aspects of their lives. In the models of social identity development I will describe in the following chapter, there is a stage where people are very invested in their subordinated identity. At this point, it is particularly challenging for individuals to examine their privilege from a dominant identity.

Conclusion

This chapter broadly describes privileged groups and offers perspectives to appreciate how they might see themselves and the world. The dominant culture, both overtly and covertly, promotes the normalcy and superiority of the advantaged group, and their right to power and privilege. People from advantaged groups therefore tend to be less aware and less sensitive to oppression and feel entitled to privileges (which they don't see and believe are deserved). There is generally little opportunity, support or incentive for people from privileged groups to explore their identity and examine its social implications. Thus, this provides a social imperative and challenge for social justice educators. In the following chapter, I will discuss ways to approach facilitating an educational process toward awareness and change.

7

THE JOY OF UNLEARNING PRIVILEGE/ OPPRESSION

> Unlearning racism and other "isms" has been one of the best things I've done in my life. I've spent many years working on these issues. I've attended countless workshops, classes, and groups. Sometimes it's been really hard and uncomfortable. I've had my share of tears, guilt, and anger but it's been worth it. It's been such a liberating experience.

At this point, people in my diversity classes or workshops are usually looking at me with a mixture of mild disbelief and curiosity, but almost all with rapt attention. Mine is a perspective they rarely hear. Typically, when a White person thinks about unlearning racism or a man has the opportunity to examine sexism, their first response is usually negative: "It will make me feel bad", "I'll just feel guilty", "I'll just be bashed and blamed for all the problems in the world." These common reactions led me to believe that something was missing. People from privileged groups needed to understand the benefits of engaging in meaningful, ongoing unlearning privilege/oppression work. They needed a vision of what they had to gain, if they overcame their preconceptions and opened their hearts and minds.

I knew my view of unlearning privilege/oppression as valuable and transformative was not unique. As I discussed this with others, people quickly offered their own metaphors and adjectives for how this work has been deeply gratifying. Most often people spoke of it as *healing, freeing,* and *liberating.* Quite the contrary to the negative associations, people who have actually participated in a process to unlearn privilege and oppression have found it to be an overwhelmingly positive and profound experience. I could see there was a bigger story to tell.

I struggled with finding words to capture what I meant by *unlearning privilege/ oppression.* I wanted to convey that it is a *multifaceted and comprehensive process which includes both self reflection and social analysis.* Unlearning privilege/oppression includes examining one's biases, socialization, attitudes, behaviors, and worldview. It also entails understanding 1) the historical and contemporary manifestations of the oppression, 2) how inequality is systemic and institutionalized, and 3) the privilege and oppression experienced by the dominant and subordinated groups. It means learning how to be an ally and challenge injustice. In addition, I wanted a term that was inclusive of different forms of social inequality. I decided to expand on the more commonly used term *unlearning racism* and use *unlearing privilege/oppression*. I wanted to use both the terms *privilege* and *oppression* since for people from domi nant groups, it was particularly important to be looking at privilege in addition to the oppression more generally. At the moment, this is the best word or phrase I could find to capture this complex process.

I also grappled with using the word *joy*. I chose the title *The Joy of Unlearning Privilege/Oppression* as a play on *The Joy of Sex* or *The Joy of Cooking*. I wanted to capture the irony of connecting unlearning privilege/oppression with something joyful. While not everyone got the joke, the term *joy* actually did speak to many people's experiences. I do not intend for this language to be flip or trivializing of the hard work involved in unlearning privilege/oppression or of the oppression suffered by people from marginalized groups. I do hope it captures people's attention and helps them think about what this work can mean in their lives.

Theories of racial/social identity development, discussed earlier in Chapter 3, describe changes in how people perceive themselves, others, and social issues. They capture both a sense of process and a state of more complex awareness. These fra meworks describe movement through different levels of consciousness or schemas related to one's racial or social identity, implying an unlearning process. For exam ple, Helms (2007) refers to the evolution from a racist to a non racist White iden tity. While none of these theories suggests that one reaches a final, discrete "stage", they do describe perspectives that indicate greater consciousness and complexity. Yet, they say little about how people feel about themselves and their lives once they achieve this level of consciousness. My research on the joy of unlearning privilege/ oppression described in this chapter can be seen as building and elaborating on these theories by offering illustrations of how people experience the capacity to live with this greater awareness.

I solicited people's experiences of unlearning privilege/oppression when they are in the privileged group through workshops, conferences, and list serves, collecting dozens of verbal and written responses. In addition, I conducted in depth interviews with people from various privileged groups. Responses were primarily in relation to sexism, racism, and/or heterosexism though other "isms" were referenced as well. Most people focused on one form of oppression as their basis for discussion and then added thoughts about unlearning others. In many cases, people had a deeper passion about one "ism" even though they clearly recognized and cared about other forms of inequality, and injustice in general. The quotations in this chapter are the words of the respondents.

As I analyzed people's responses, I noticed an interesting relationship between the main benefits of unlearning privilege/oppression and the results of my study on the costs of oppression to people from privileged groups described in the earlier chapter. Even though I conducted the research for these two studies years apart, with completely different people, the themes strongly correlate. The main costs of oppression identified are: the loss of mental health and authentic sense of self, the loss and diminishment of relationships, the loss of developing a full range of knowledge, the loss of moral and spiritual integrity, and the loss of safety and quality of life. These very same qualities are what people felt they had gained or reclaimed as a result of their unlearning process. The joys of unlearning privilege/oppression seem to mitigate the costs of oppression, at least on a personal level; they were able to remediate many of the negative affects on themselves and their relationships. The costs of oppression provide a useful context and backdrop when reading about the joys of unlearning privilege/oppression.

In this chapter, I will first discuss the benefits of unlearning privilege/oppression identified by people from privileged groups, which are grouped into five main themes: knowledge and clarity; an enriched life; greater authenticity and humanity; empowerment, confidence, and competence; and liberation and healing. There is overlap among the themes since the benefits gained are clearly interrelated and mutually reinforcing. As people discuss their present experiences, their comparisons are to their lives before they seriously undertook unlearning privilege/oppression. Later in the chapter, I describe what the respondents identify as the key factors that have helped them unlearn oppression and that help them stay on this journey.

Knowledge and Clarity

Unlearning privilege/oppression provides information and perspectives that give people new lenses for viewing themselves and the world. This enables individuals from privileged groups to be more conscious, informed, and insightful. As a result, they develop not only intellectual knowledge about how society operates but personal knowledge as well. People expand their ability to analyze and understand the dynamics of oppression as they manifest in society and in their own psyche. One person considers unlearning privilege/oppression a "sociological and personal study."

By its very nature, systems of oppression misrepresent and ignore wide realms of knowledge about people, cultures, history, and social realities. Gaining information and frameworks for analysis is a compelling part of the unlearning process. "Nothing is more interesting, thought provoking or rewarding." Respondents refer to unlearning privilege/oppression as "a mystery to unpack" and "deeply fascinating." "I think more complexly and ask what am I missing or not seeing?" a person explains.

Very often, systems of oppression feel confusing and irrational. People know something is wrong but cannot necessarily name it or articulate it. A greater understanding of oppression helps people figure out the world in which they live and their role in it. It "creates meaning in a system that doesn't make sense" and "intellectually connects the dots." As one woman expresses, "I feel more humane and sane in a culture that often does not feel sane to me."

One aspect of intellectual growth involves rethinking what one has accepted as true and considering perspectives one has never considered before. As people from privileged groups unlearn oppression, they recognize how much they have missed and how limited their world and thinking has been. As one person puts it, "I busted out of my own head." Unlearning privilege/oppression also encourages people from dominant groups to reexamine their notions of who and what is to be valued.

> Whole groups of people were unknown to me. I was taught not to see them as offering valuable perspectives. I had a narrow, hierarchical view—a sense of superiority. But now those people, that information and those perspectives are available to me.

Understanding different forms of oppression and how they manifest allows me to feel less "stupid". I can follow and respond appropriately to conversations about personal experiences or current events. I can appreciate political analyses and offer my perspective. I much prefer feeling like I "get it" to feeling "clueless." I'm sure this is preferable to the people I'm talking with as well.

Intellectual understanding is only one facet of deepening one's knowledge and clarity. Unlearning privilege/oppression also enhances self understanding. It offers opportunities and tools for self examination. As people unlearn oppression, they investigate and uncover aspects of themselves previously hidden, distorted, or ignored. One respondent explains that it "gave me a way to examine my experiences with more consciousness and capacity to understand things." Another adds, "I'm a more whole person psychologically. I better understand my personal experiences and history." Individuals can explore their personal traits, socialization, and life path in the context of the larger dynamics of privilege and oppression.

A critical component of examining one's identity is looking at how one has internalized the messages of the dominant culture. Unlearning privilege/oppression is becoming aware of one's biases, attitudes, beliefs, and behaviors that reflect and perpetuate systems of oppression. Respondents realize that denying that they have prejudices or that they are unscathed by living under systems of inequality precludes the possibility of working toward greater personal consciousness and liberation for all. As the respondents make clear, acknowledging their biases is not simply accepting and justifying them, but bringing them to light so they can be worked through. This allows them to dispel their stereotypes and correct their erroneous thinking.

Increased self knowledge and clarity also helps people realize that despite their biases and internalized superiority, they are not bad people. They, therefore, feel less mired in guilt or shame. People from privileged groups can be deeply and genuinely committed to social justice but still embody oppressive conditioning, regardless of whether it is conscious or intentional. One woman describes being able to "accept myself as being both a racist and anti racist. That those two aspects co exist together in me." People who are unlearning privilege/oppression acknowledge that they will never be completely enlightened and thus, must live with themselves in their imperfect state while they strive to become their best selves and create greater justice.

These insights into themselves are not only personally helpful, they also allow people to be clearer when dealing with others. The better they can separate their issues or biases from those of others, the better they can take responsibility for their thoughts and feelings. "I don't project my own stuff and judge others, especially others from dominant groups." Individuals can more quickly recognize their "bag gage" and how it affects their reactions and interactions. "I know there are uncon scious ways I get triggered, but I can stop them and not act them out as much." They are more conscious of how their attitudes or assumptions may impact their behavior. People become increasingly adept at recognizing ways they enact and reinforce dynamics of superiority/inferiority. "The more open one is to one's racism, the less it gets acted out."

Some respondents particularly note that they can take things less personally. They can better discern when reactions or situations are about them in particular or more generally about people from their social group. This is heard most frequently from White people in relation to people of color or about White people's role in racism. For example, a White woman can hear the anger from a woman of color and not assume it's directed at her personally. Another White woman tries to explain how she feels a collective responsibility for historical racism and the benefits she derives from it, but recognizes that she is not responsible for every act committed by every White person. "I can listen to stories from people of color or Whites and not feel personally responsible for past history as much as I don't feel responsible for the invention of the telephone."

Awareness of different social realities also helps people from privileged groups develop perspective on their own lives. They take less for granted and have greater appreciation for what they have. Several mention that they realize that "other people's plights can be worse than yours. It helps you to step back and gain per spective." Despite the focus on their own development as they unlearn oppression, understanding others' subjugation helps them become less self absorbed.

An Enriched Life

People who have been unlearning privilege/oppression feel their lives are richer and more fulfilling in numerous ways. One is living with greater meaning and purpose. They have found issues they feel passionately about and engage in efforts that feel significant. Work for social justice gives their life depth and direction.

Their process of unlearning privilege/oppression has also introduced them to new relationships and new worlds. Several people highlight this point:

If you have true, genuine interest in others and value them, it opens you to enriching experiences and relationships with a broader range of people.

It [unlearning privilege/oppression] exposed me to other ways of being, an awareness of other oppressions and the different ways people are in the world. I'm more open to everyone and everything.

Respondents have been able to make connections with a greater array of people, particularly with whom they previously had limited relationships. Their expanding relationships are usually due to being in a wider range of places and engaging in more varied activities that bring them into meaningful contact with others. As a result, they have a more diverse community of friends and acquaintances. "Because of this work, people have come into my life and my children's lives." In addition, as people become more aware and comfortable, they find they can more easily engage in situations they may have avoided before. A man explains, "Unlearning privilege/oppression expands the relationships and people I can be comfortable with. I can be in spaces where I'm the 'only one' and be comfortable." In return, respondents find other people are more interested in them as well. "I have an 'enriched community'. I'm more open to others, others are more open to having me as a friend."

Openness to new experiences and relationships gives people from privileged groups exposure to the cultures and wisdom of marginalized peoples. They increasingly explore and learn from others' worldviews, literature, history, art, philosophy, music, theater, and spirituality. For example, men discuss being enriched by learning about women's spirituality and more collaborative ways of engaging; White people find value in more collectivist worldviews and the histories of people of color. While there can be concerns about appropriation and exploitation, there are also appropriate ways to embrace other cultural contributions and perspectives.

Relationships with people from their dominant group often improve as well. On the one hand, people who have developed greater awareness sometimes have less interest or patience with people from their privileged group, if those others are also not raising their consciousness about social justice. On the other hand, many find that their unlearning process allows them to develop more compassion and connection with others from their dominant group. One White person explains, "I feel less judgmental. I don't judge other Whites, I don't project my own stuff." Another adds, "I used to have a White identity in opposition to other Whites. Divide and conquer, racist or not. I came to a place of deep love for White people and see myself as part of White people."

Moreover, when people engage with others from their privileged group in unlearning privilege/oppression, it can deepen their relationships. Men are often part of a men's group while White people often meet with other Whites to work on their racism. These shared experiences require openness, trust, and support, moving people beyond a superficial level of interaction. Several people mention that when they and their partner are both involved in unlearning the same oppression, it brings them closer together.

These more diverse networks of connections and deeper relationships can reduce feelings of isolation. In the process of unlearning privilege/oppression, people often need to reevaluate their current friendships and sometimes let go of relationships as their attitudes, behaviors, and priorities change. They may feel alone or worry about losing their social network. This may remain true for some, however most of these respondents ultimately feel more connected, not less. One man explains it this way:

> People often fear the loss of family and connection. Rather than feel more isolated, I feel less isolated. I have an extended sense of family and community, like we're all in this together. Often we feel like we're on the fringe when we're part of the social justice community, but I'm part of a community.

Since my life, like many others, is often segregated along racial and class lines, it is often through social justice work that I can develop relationships with a broader diversity of people. It is a context where we can come together with some shared interests and values and work together toward common goals. When I don't have these relationships, my life feels sterile. Being with people who share my dominant group identities can have its comforts, but this homogeneity lacks the vibrancy that makes me feel more stimulated and engaged. For many respondents, a wider range of relationships and greater sense of community is something that most enriches their lives. They cherish having connections with more diverse people and feeling part of a larger human community as well as part of a group of people committed to social justice.

Authenticity and Greater Humanity

Respondents repeatedly discuss a deep desire to feel more authentic within themselves, in their relationships, and in their lives. Being authentic refers to feeling more genuine and true to oneself. They want to know who they are without the limitations of their conditioning and to have meaningful connections with others. Individuals describe "gaining a sense of wholeness and feeling more complete" and "connecting at a deeper level and living closer to my core values."

Unlearning privilege/oppression clearly enables greater authenticity. Because of his work unlearning privilege/oppression, one man reports, "I am authentic now in ALL relationships. I am who I am wherever I am and now stand up for my beliefs." Another person explains,

> I wished to live "authentically" within my own shell. Upon deeper examination, at age 45, much of what I was, had accumulated and been provided felt inauthentic. Admitting that inauthentic feeling was a *huge* but crucial step. Pursuing my own unlearning process these past 12 years has allowed me to

see privilege when it's presented, and to question myself in ways that I have never needed to question before. The result is an inner calmness with my self perception, but it is coupled with a persistent desire to educate and keep the process of awareness raising alive in myself and for others.

Some respondents find they can be more truly themselves, regardless of how their identity is usually socially constructed. People are more able to reevaluate societal expectations, refuse to fit into the prescribed boxes, and make choices about how they want to be. One woman describes her experience:

As a heterosexual woman athlete, I was not the stereotypical female. I had to deal with my own fear that if I act outside the traditional gender norms, people would think I was a lesbian. I developed the confidence to be myself: confident, loud, strong physically. I could live with myself easier, feel better in my own skin.

A heterosexual male explains how he came to terms with his male identity and embraced different aspects of himself. "I now see that everything is a spectrum. I don't have to put myself in a category; I don't have to pigeonhole myself."

The authenticity of people from privileged groups is hindered by internalizing beliefs about their group's superiority and the other group's inferiority. This is the foundation upon which oppression is built. A significant piece of unlearning privilege/oppression work for people from dominant groups is understanding and rejecting this ideology. As people are able to do this, they no longer need to elevate themselves and their social group while diminishing the oppressed group. They can experience a truer sense of their own humanity, as well as that of others. "Learning to let go of the clearly erroneous but often covert sense of one's own superiority helped me feel more fully human."

Becoming more authentic and more human also entails reclaiming one's full emotional capacities. Living in unfair and unequal societies encourages people to suppress and deny their feelings in order to dull the effects of oppression. "Privilege requires us to shut down emotionally, to shut down from other people. I can now be in touch with feelings." Unlearning privilege/oppression helps people regain their ability to feel and be empathic.

Feelings for and about other people grow as one's knowledge of systemic inequality increases. "The deeper my understanding of oppression, the wider my capacity for compassion, care, presence and generosity." People can better appreciate how everyone is trapped in dysfunctional and harmful social systems. Having a systemic, rather than just an individual focus, helps people feel more empathy. It shifts away from blaming the victim or blaming individuals from privileged groups for their oppressive behavior by considering the larger social context and conditioning. One woman found, "I am more able to forgive others from dominant groups when I'm in the oppressed group."

In addition, several people note that they have become more focused on being true to themselves and their ideals, and less concerned with being liked or appreciated by people from the oppressed group. "I've shifted from wanting to be thought well of by people of the subordinate group to being accountable to them. I'm striving for internal consistency. I want to be authentic and consistent—to see myself and have others see me that way." While relationships and accountability are important, seeking "approval" from others is not the driving force.

Overwhelmingly, respondents focus on how much they long for and value authentic relationships across differences. As individuals feel more authentic themselves, they can be more authentic with others. Not only do people have a broader range of relationships, those relationships are also more genuine and fulfilling. People maintain that these more meaningful relationships are a direct result of their unlearning privilege/oppression. One man more pointedly says, "A fulfilling relationship with my partner is only possible because of the work I did on sexism." People from the privileged group are able to engage in more honest, conscious, and caring ways, and feel more trusted by people from the oppressed group. This creates a stronger relational foundation that allows both parties to be more vulnerable. Some respondents tell how humbling and moving it is when people from the oppressed group openly share their experiences and struggles with oppression. In discussing her relationships with friends of color, a White woman notices, "I can be authentic—warts and all—and I will still be liked." She did not have to worry about being perfect or fear that making mistakes would undermine the friendships.

Unlearning privilege/oppression allows individuals to experience their own humanity and see the full humanity of other people. Often, when White people say, "I don't see color, I just see people" or "I've transcended race", they are expressing a discomfort with acknowledging race or an ignorance of the significance of racial differences. (This can also occur in relation to other social identities.) One of the benefits of the unlearning process is being able to relate to others as "just people", while simultaneously recognizing the importance of social identities and the complexities of who people are. One of the greatest joys I experience is when I can be with someone from a subordinated group and connect unself consciously as two human beings, while still being mindful of our various social identities and their relevance. There is neither the anxious focus on a particular identity nor the erasure of it.

In general, people from privileged groups describe feeling less guarded and more spontaneous in their relationships with people from the subordinated group. They do not have to constantly self monitor. For myself, humor (and gentle sarcasm) is part of my cultural style. If I don't feel comfortable enough to joke around, I cannot be fully myself and I feel stilted. I love being able to use my humor freely feeling comfortable enough to trust what will come out of my mouth and that it will be received as intended.

As a result of unlearning privilege/oppression, many people feel they can live more authentic lives and feel more inner peace. There is greater congruence with who they want to be, what they do, and how they live. Respondents repeatedly express sentiments such as, "I know I'm doing the right thing. I'm closer to who I want to become." Many specifically talk about how this moral/spiritual alignment allows them a sense of spiritual integrity. "I can sleep well at night, knowing I did the best I could to challenge injustice and raise awareness in others." "I could meet my maker and hold my head up—that's priceless." People feel more serenity within themselves and with the way they can be in the world. "As a result of this work, I no longer feel inauthentic and have a genuine peacefulness with who I am, what I stand for and where I am making a difference." Another echoes, "I have an inner peace knowing I'm not acting in ways that harm others and I'm less likely to perpetuate racism." This inner calm has wider implications. As one person recognizes, "The more internal peace I have with who I am, the more peace I can extend to others."

Often respondents report experiencing spiritual growth and strength as well. "My spirit is more whole, more nourished." For some people, their moral/spiritual values are a driving force from the beginning. Others suggest that these became more central as they became increasingly involved with social justice issues. In either case, the desire to live in a way consistent with their vision of themselves and the world they want to see is a strong component of many people's unlearning work.

Empowerment, Confidence, and Competence

A deeper understanding of oppression, a clearer sense of themselves, and more diverse relationships builds empowerment, confidence, and competence to address social justice issues. One person labels unlearning privilege/oppression as "agency enhancing." Another person notes, "Doing this work has provided me with a fearlessness and a feeling of strength in what I do." Rather than feeling overwhelmed and hopeless about creating change, many people report quite the opposite.

> "Understanding privilege is a powerful antidote to the immobilization of guilt because it enhances your ability to take concrete action."

> "I feel more powerful, not powerless—to do what I can do."

> "It frees up a lot of energy to take action. I'm not in constant conflict internally."

Respondents' increased confidence and trust in themselves makes them more willing to acknowledge their limitations and mistakes. They are not as fearful of being imperfect. It is easier to admit their errors, learn from them, and keep going. As one man explains,

> I am no longer afraid of making mistakes. Trust me, I make plenty of them, but I know more about how to own them and I'm willing to look at their origins, which helps me to avoid them the next time around.

Most respondents highlight that they have become less defensive. As one person puts it, "I have enough confidence in myself and my commitment to take in feedback and move on." They can listen to critical feedback from others and not just shut down or push back. "I am willing to take risks, learn from mistakes, hear criticisms as constructive feedback and not be devastated." This is a key quality since I do not know anyone involved with social justice work who has not struggled at times with feeling defensive when they said or did something offensive or ignorant.

As a teacher and trainer, I have many opportunities to make mistakes and be challenged by participants from the subordinated group regarding oppression issues. As I continue to unlearn oppression and feel more confidence in my knowledge and skills, I find it easier to stay present and try to understand what those individuals are saying rather than immediately to defend myself or feel overwhelmed. When I do get defensive or mess up and feel demoralized, it is easier to recover. I can remind myself of all the times I have been effective and use my support network to help me learn from mistakes and keep them in perspective.

Whether formally or informally, most respondents are educating others about social justice issues. Their own unlearning privilege/oppression is inextricably tied to their competence and effectiveness in doing so. As one person puts it "steps for self, become steps for the work." The more knowledge and experience one has in dealing with oppression issues, the more one has to draw from when engaging others. "I've been in circles I wouldn't have otherwise been in which gives me access to information, perspectives, and experiences that I can then share with others." As people are clearer about how systematic inequality operates, they can be more articulate when teaching others. The more grounded they feel in the content, the better they can explain it and respond to questions and challenges. Increased knowledge not only leads to greater clarity but also lets people feel more self assured and comfortable. "A deeper grasp of the material gives me more confidence in dealing with it and helping others see it."

Many people describe feeling better able to work with and serve people from marginalized groups. Several different facets of this are mentioned. One aspect is being able to connect more effectively with them. "When you're able to truly see people from subordinated groups as equal, you can better build relationships and be flexible." Moreover, people can be more conscious of how they unintentionally may be enacting oppressive dynamics and how someone from the marginalized group might view them. They can better understand the initial distrust or anger directed at them because of their dominant identity and professional role.

Another facet is appreciating and adapting to other ways of being and doing. People are not as limited in their thinking or behavior. "As I was able to overcome some of my male conditioning, able to be less adversarial, more collaborative, I could build relationships and problem solve with women I worked with." Con sciousness and flexibility enhance any kind of working relationship with people from other social groups.

The third way is recognizing how the problems of clients/students/employees are related to the oppression they experience. It allows practitioners to appreciate that individual issues are often reflections of larger social/political dynamics and structures. This helps alleviate the tendency to "blame the victim" or focus solely at an individual level, without also addressing the greater context.

As people do their own consciousness raising work as a member of a privileged group, they are usually better at working with others from dominant groups, whe ther the same or different from their own. They can connect with more patience and empathy. Some of this compassion comes from realizing that, like themselves, other people from privileged groups are shaped by the conditioning of the larger society. This perspective can also help them understand and address the resistance they encounter. They can see themselves in others.

Many people find that they can now be a positive example for individuals from privileged groups. "It feels good to be able to be a role model, to do anti heterosexism work and be a resource for other heterosexuals." When people from a privileged groups work with people from the oppressed group as co trainers, they can model equitable, respectful relationships which value each other's styles and perspectives. They can also illustrate that all of us have internalized biases and make mistakes but can learn from them and grow. "The more I can laugh at myself (about my own mistakes), the more disarming and more able I am to help others take risks." By sharing their process of unlearning, they can make it feel safer for others to do their own self exploration.

Another important component is being able to show others from privileged groups how to be an ally. They can talk about how they have worked against oppression and some of their experiences doing so. "I try to share both my successes and mistakes in trying to be an ally. I want people to realize that there are ways they can be helpful but also realize some of the pitfalls." As people unlearn oppression and increase their effectiveness being an ally, they can pass this wisdom onto others and support their involvement with social change.

Liberation and Healing

In the broadest sense, unlearning privilege/oppression is liberating and healing for people from privileged groups. It is a transformative process that infuses their whole being and permeates their entire life. "Generally, I'm a better person—happier, with a more interesting life, better mental health, and smarter."

It is liberating to let go of beliefs, feelings, and patterns of behavior that have been limiting or destructive. It's like a burden has been lifted or a constriction has been loosened. "I feel so much lighter" one woman reports. Another states, "It's a way to freedom." Overcoming fears is central to this experience of liberation. They no longer feel preoccupied with worries about what they'll find out about them selves, engaging with those who are different, doing or saying the wrong thing, offending others, or how their life would change for the worse.

This sense of freedom is in contrast to the negative effects of living under systems of oppression. As one respondent puts it, "White supremacy depends on so many things that are bad for us—numbing, violence, silence." Another similarly expresses,

"Privilege looks like it makes life easier but really it increases fear, stress, and soul death."

Individuals who are unlearning privilege/oppression strive to break free from this deadening, unaware state:

> I think White privilege and White supremacy for so long have placed us all in a trance, and doing this work, studying our history and better understanding the nature of this work and the need for it helps me get out of the trance. I continue to read and study history and it feels like layers are peeling away, like I'm waking up. Slowly.

Many respondents discuss how unlearning privilege/oppression is a means to heal from the myriad ways people from privileged groups are damaged psychologically, emotionally, intellectually, socially, and spiritually. Healing occurs when they let go of guilt and fears, when they gain a clearer understanding of the world, when they become more authentic in themselves and with others, when they live their lives in morally consistent ways, when they have meaningful relationships across differences, and when they can take action to foster social justice.

For myself and the other respondents, the benefits of unlearning privilege/oppression undoubtedly outweigh the risks or costs. The joy of reclaiming one's humanity, living an enriched life, and creating a better world is a satisfying and motivating force. In the following sections, I explore what assists people on their journey of unlearning privilege/oppression.

Key Unlearning Experiences

When I asked people what was most helpful or significant in their process of unlearning privilege/oppression, a range of influences were cited. These include experiences with different people, opportunities for self reflection, information and frameworks for analysis, and mentors. The most influential factors may change throughout their lives. What may have stimulated them early in their journey is different from what may have most impact later on.

Not surprisingly, access to theories and information prove particularly valuable. All respondents have done readings or attended classes or workshops on issues of oppression. Sometimes, personal experiences occurred first and the theory came later. "Trainings offered frameworks and analysis for what I was already seeing and experiencing." Other times, learning about privilege and oppression motivated fur ther exploration. A class or workshop prompts the interest in these issues and the desire to seek out more knowledge and contacts. Regardless of which occurs first, respondents recognize the value of both first hand experiences and relationships, and theory, analysis, and information.

Overwhelmingly, people talk about relationships with people from oppressed groups as critical in their unlearning process. Most salient is the opportunity to have meaningful conversations over time, which include talking about privilege and oppression. These conversations may occur in the context of a professional rela tionship, a friendship, or a family relationship. They all allow for a deepening con nection, a growing trust, and the sharing of feelings, experiences, and perspectives in an increasingly open way. They permit people from the privileged group to gain an intimate understanding of the experiences of the marginalized group.

Another aspect is being able to be in the places and spaces of people from the oppressed group. So often, people from privileged groups meet people from mar ginalized groups in places that are defined by the dominant culture. It can be very different to be with people from subordinated groups in the spaces in which they are most comfortable or in which they are the majority. It is not that people from privileged groups just insert themselves into places where they are not welcome or in voyeuristic ways. They are invited into spaces because of a relationship or because of a mutually beneficial collaboration.

These contacts and relationships lead to growth in several ways. It forces people to acknowledge their biases, either due to their own awareness or by being con fronted by the person from the oppressed group. It allows people to see the strug gles first hand, to appreciate what living with that oppression is like. It also lets someone be known enough to see them first as their friend, as a whole human being, not first as a person from a subordinated group. In addition, people can make connections with their own oppressions. They can draw similarities between the oppression they face in another aspect of their identity and what this group experiences. As one person realized, "I wanted to be recognized as a Black woman. I realized gays wanted to be recognized too."

In addition, experience with one oppressed group helps in understanding other "isms". While there are great differences in how people experience subordination, there are also many commonalities. As people intellectually understand one form of oppression and develop caring relationships with people from that oppressed group, they can transfer some of that knowledge and concern to other forms of inequality. Furthermore, the openness required to unlearn oppression can carry over into other situations. As one person says, "Unlearning heterosexism made me generally more tolerant of other things and people."

Several people describe being called on their oppressive attitudes and behaviors as significant moments in their unlearning process. Even when they are deeply humi liated or angered when they are confronted, it spurs growth. Generally, when the challenge comes from people they value, it is easier to take it in. "Some of my key learning experiences were from people who were willing to confront me, who cared about me, and loved me enough to do so."

In some instances, respondents are confronted by people from their own privi leged group. In referring to his experience in a men's group, " I wasn't attacked, but my defenses crumbled. It was harder to discount what they were saying." Other times, it is from individuals from the oppressed group. As one White woman recalls, "I was confronted by the people of color I was training with. I was playing out my internalized dominance in my attitudes and behavior. I had to own my past and current behaviors." In the moment, people have different feelings about being challenged, but ultimately they recognize it as a valuable experience.

None of these experiences or information would have been as significant to the respondents' unlearning process, if there were not the willingness to engage in deep self exploration. Individuals recognize that the way out is through; we need to acknowledge and accept all parts of ourselves in order to be and act differently. If we try to disown or disengage from these "negative" aspects, they never get addressed or keep us locked in destructive feelings. "Coming to terms with my own history allowed me to move out of shame and guilt." Another person elaborates on this point.

> I found that acknowledging racist or sexist thoughts loosened the shame. It allowed the letting go of shame—of thinking, "I'm bad for having objecti fying or bigoted thoughts." I realized it's part of cultural conditioning—"normal". It was better not keeping it hidden—that's unhealthy, it gives it power, it keeps it alive, digging inside.

Several people stress the importance of self compassion as they do this personal work. "It's like meditation. It got easier when I let go of self judgment which just compounds fears and bad feelings." This is echoed by another:

> I see this path as a Buddhist path. We need to mindfully look at and con template who we are. With loving compassion, we need to come to accep tance of who we are with all our faults. … The more open one is to one's own racism, the less it gets acted out. In trying not to be that, we are more that.

The value of looking honestly at oneself is especially important to recognize. Many people resist self examination as part of unlearning privilege/oppression since they fear what it will reveal. They may fear getting stuck in the pain, guilt, or negative feelings about themselves. Yet, delving into these feelings is what allows people not to get trapped in them.

Staying on the Journey—Then and Now

People from privileged groups can more easily make the choice not to think about or unlearn oppression. So, why and how have people stayed on this journey—in the past and in the present? Respondents are quick to note that there is always more that they could do and more they need to know. They are aware of contradictions in their lives. Yet, they have stayed committed to continuing this process and to living in greater congruence with social justice.

One response to why they have stayed on the journey stood out. It is that it feels good. Again, this is in stark contrast with people's assumptions that there will only be pain. There are a wide variety of experiences that give people positive feelings. A sampling of responses are listed below:

"The times I 'get' it."
"My relationships and friends."
"Meeting my own expectations for how I want to be. I set the bar and the closer I get to it is rewarding."
"When I feel more clarity and integrity."
"I continue to be enriched."
"I get a high when I see people shift."
"I am re energized when I effectively confront and negotiate my biases."
"The passionate feeling I have is hard to stay away from."

As seen in the other sections, when people feel more powerful, more aligned with their values, smarter, more passionate, more effective, and more authentically con nected to themselves and others, they naturally want to continue on this path.

For many people, unlearning privilege/oppression addresses their personal needs. Overwhelmingly they crave authentic relationships with all people, but especially with those from the oppressed group. Many describe an intrinsic "zest for growth" and need for continual personal and spiritual development. Some are motivated by a desire to deal with their own pain and discomfort or to make amends for past mistakes. "I felt bad much of the time when I wasn't dealing with it (racism). I had much more fear. Denial and fear of judgment just led to wasted energy and pain."

There are also more concrete needs as well. Several mention the need to keep their job (usually as a trainer or educator). Others talk about their desire to keep their friends and to continue to expand their social connections. A number of people recognize that their privilege allows them the time or money to pursue opportunities to unlearn their oppression. They could more easily follow their desire for growth or connection. "'I didn't have to worry about my survival—other privileges make it easier to focus on doing this work."

Support from others is critical for staying on this journey. It comes from a number of sources in a variety of ways. It is not always warm and fuzzy, but ulti mately people feel cared for and encouraged. Being connected to others who share their commitment to social justice is mentioned often. Respondents are sustained by "other allies and by being part of caring communities." One person explains, "I stay engaged by actively seeking and maintaining communities of support and account ability with people who share my identities and people who have different iden tities." A number of people have families or partners with whom they can share the journey or mutually encourage each other's growth. Some find support from being part of groups or organizations that address social justice issues. At times, people actively need to seek out like minded others so they do not feel alienated or alone.

Relationships with both people from the subordinated group and people from their privileged group are needed. Having other allies to talk with and process with is salient for many respondents. This gives them a space to figure things out or deal with their feelings, apart from people from the oppressed group. They can share common experiences and struggles. Many also refer to the support from individuals from the subordinated group who are willing to challenge and hang in there with them. The trust bestowed on them from people from the marginalized group enhances their confidence and desire to continue their learning.

In addition, role models from the past and present are frequently helpful. It allows people to feel connected to a larger movement and history, to learn from the risks others took, to find examples of how to be an ally, and to have a vision of how they want to be. Role models offer inspiration and build courage.

Respondents clearly feel a commitment and responsibility to continue their unlearning process and to create social justice. This may be derived from their religious or spiritual teachings, political principles, personal beliefs, and/or inner calling. Several people indicate that their relationships with individuals from the oppressed group are central. They feel an increased responsibility to continually earn their trust, not to be hurtful, and to work to alleviate the suffering and inequality people face. "I can't forget the people I love and they won't let me forget." Another person adds, "I feel a responsibility to show up and be more useful."

A number of people who are also members of oppressed groups make the connection between their own oppression and that faced by other people. They know what it's like to be oppressed and they do not want to inflict that on others. "I have an acute understanding of being oppressed. I *do not* want to participate in another's oppression." Another adds, "I connect to my own struggle as a Black woman and being marginalized."

Those who are parents or have close relationships with children express the desire to leave them a better world. They also feel the responsibility to educate their children to be less biased and to understand injustice. People want to be able to effectively talk with their children about oppression, so they can notice, analyze, and intervene when there is inequity.

Moreover, it's important to be able to support children to be who they are, particularly if they are part of an oppressed group, so they can feel empowered and self accepting.

> You don't know who your kids will be. I want to be there for my kids or the kids of friends and neighbors. If you don't do the work, you'll just be part of a system that makes them feel bad or creates obstacles, and contributes to them being someone who they're not.

Being able to be on and stay on the journey of unlearning privilege/oppression seems to require that people can value discomfort and trust that it will bring them to a better place. They see discomfort not as an enemy to be destroyed, but a teacher to be embraced. Being uncomfortable means that there is growth. They accept that they will be uneasy, but "discomfort is not such a bad thing. Change requires discomfort." Others state, "Comfort can mean complacency, not being alive." "Discomfort keeps me motivated. Racism isn't comfortable and shouldn't be. If there is no discomfort, it's a red flag I'm getting complacent."

Not only is discomfort unavoidable and welcomed, it is tolerable and worth it. This is clearly counter to those who try to avoid feeling uncomfortable and fear that it will be unbearable and destructive. "Yes, it can be painful and incriminating at first … but the results of getting 'unstuck' are well worth the messiness." Another explains,

> There is a profound freedom in getting honest and talking about these things (talking about racism and her family's involvement with it). Despite the fact that it makes my ancestors and people of my race look and feel awful. So what. It's all about healing. And healing hurts sometimes. So I guess you could call all anti racism work and White privilege/White supremacy awareness work "joyful pain."

In addition to accepting discomfort, a number of people speak about needing to trust the process, to believe that this will be worth it. You need to be "willing to surrender, to let go, to trust that you're going to get to another place." When discussing how to engage others, one woman says, you need to "help them see the promise of going to an uncomfortable place". Unlearning privilege/oppression can be uncomfortable, but people survive and thrive as a result.

None of the respondents feels like there is an option of turning back, of undoing or stopping this journey. It is part of who they are and how they live their lives. People describe it as: "I'm beyond the point of no return—I can't close that 'third eye'". "Not being part of social justice is just not an option".

Respondents recognize that they are continually a work in progress. People are quick to add that they still have much to learn, that they make mistakes and that they see this as ongoing. "This isn't an end product; it's a process. The highs and lows of the work are constant. I continually disappoint myself and others." No one wants to give the impression, that despite all they have learned, that they are "done".

> I recognize that being an ally is an everyday endeavor, and each day I need to turn in and subsequently re earn my ally identity. Being an ally is like being funny. You should not need to tell people that you are it, it should be apparent.

Others express, "There is no final place of Nirvana." "I'm keenly aware that it takes constant vigilance, self reflection, and analysis." I can concur. No matter how long I do this work, I'm always finding new issues to learn about, ways to understand myself, and avenues to challenge inequality.

Conclusion

What is striking from all these stories is the overwhelming sense of how valuable and significant this work has been—how liberating it is, how much better people feel about themselves, how their lives have been enhanced, how good it feels. While I initiallychose the word "joy" as ironic, it fits much better than I expected. These feelings challenge two main reasons people resist engaging in unlearning privilege/oppression: 1) that I'm fine, and there's no purpose in subjecting myself to this and 2) that it is just going to hurt and not be worth it. As one woman explains, "It's hard to know what's missing or how life could be different until one experiences it."

In some ways, this process is like psychotherapy or counseling. (I am not saying as educators we should be doing therapy with our students or that our classes/work shops are counseling sessions!) There are some issues or some dis ease impeding our life that draws us into therapy. Therapy can be painful and uncomfortable at times; it can reveal things that are hard to acknowledge about ourselves, the people we're close to, and the situations we're in. But its goal is not destructive, it's restorative. It is not meant to harm but to heal. It's about becoming healthier and more whole. Ultimately, we come out the other side with a clearer view of ourselves and others and an enhanced capacity to deal with life. It is not that we are now the model of mental health and that we live our lives with perfect clarity and balance. But we have changed in significant ways. Like unlearning privilege/oppression, hard work and discomfort are part of a healing process that brings us to a better place from which we keep evolving. We are more equipped to continue to learn from mis takes and new situations. We are better able to take more risks, to become the person we want to be, and to help create the world we want to live in.

There seems to be a point in the unlearning privilege/oppression process where people get "over the hump"—where the scale tips toward feelings of growth and healing and less toward discomfort and guilt. Sometimes, people are overwhelmed with reevaluating previous beliefs and integrating new perspectives. Someone described it as feeling like standing in quicksand or in shifting sand. Eventually, people find more of a foundation from which to progress. It may also be harder in earlier phases to appreciate how this effort will be beneficial. The costs and struggles are most salient. Consistent with social/racial identity development theories, there may be times in the beginning and middle of the process where one is more likely to feel guilt, shame, anger, or pain rather than joy or liberation. I was doing a workshop on the "Joy of Unlearning Privilege/Oppression" where I asked people to identify how they had benefited from unlearning privilege/oppression and one woman responded, "I'm not feeling much joy!" One interviewee shared that feeling but now feels differently, "I felt a lot of guilt before it felt liberating. The liberating part comes from the work we do for justice, that I'm doing the right thing." It can be helpful for people to see that staying with the process will be worth it.

Unlearning privilege/oppression reminds me of a mountain climbing adventure. A mountain guide is telling you how great it is, but like most of the people you know, you enjoy the comfort and security of your couch. You don't know where this journey is leading. You worry there is too much risk, that it's going to be too taxing and not much fun. Yet, on some level you realize that you may be missing an opportunity, that there is something exciting out there and that sitting on the couch may not be the best way to live your life. It helps that the guide is skilled and supportive. It's hard to resist her enthusiasm and reassurance. You trust her enough to take the first steps.

You find you're not alone on this journey, that there are other travelers on this path with your guide. Some start out slowly like you. Others are eager to bound ahead, feeling more sure footed. As you start out, you're tentative and out of shape; it's hard. There aren't any views. People suffer to varying degrees from blisters and sore muscles. You think about turning back. But there is something about the mountain air and the nature around you that feels stimulating and healing. With the guide's support, you keep putting one foot in front of the other. You have the camaraderie of the other hikers who trudge along with different amounts of enthusiasm but you help keep each other going. You observe other hikers far ahead of you who seem to be enjoying the outing.

Gradually you notice the beauty around you. You get glimpses of views. Eventually, it gets easier as you get in better shape and feel more comfortable on the terrain. You hike higher and higher, seeing beautiful vistas and wildlife. You feel healthier than before and begin to appreciate why the effort was worth it. You reach a top of a mountain and get a rush of the wonder of nature. But the hike still continues over the endless range of mountains. People continue on different paths over the ridges. You find other hikers to join on this ongoing adventure. While there are always new vistas and beauty to experience, there are also the ups and downs of the trail, descents into valleys, stumbles, blisters, and bug bites. You realize that those too are part of the journey that continues to lead you to new levels of fitness, greater competencies, and breathtaking panoramas. There is no turning back.

As educators, people need to trust us as their guides. We can offer them challenge and support in their unlearning process. They need to hear that there is something meaningful to be gained that is worth the effort. As one respondent says, "I was closed off, but didn't know it because I didn't know differently." Through these stories about the joy of unlearning privilege/oppression, we can help people know differently. We can hold out the vision of greater humanity and liberation.

How Do We Get Along?

Creating Dialogue

LIVING WITH OTHERS
THE INEVITABLE CONFLICT

✑

"In order to be free one has to reach a measure of independence. However, the complexity of our societies traps human
beings in a network of relations that render their independence
utterly vulnerable."

Abraham Joshua Heschel (1958)

"Whatever increase in social intelligence and moral goodwill may
be achieved in human history, may serve to mitigate the brutalities
of social conflict, but they cannot abolish the conflict itself."

Langdon B. Gilkey (2001)

OTHERS AND CONFLICTS

We live with others. We are trapped in networks of mutual dependen-
cies with those others. These relations to others are, according to Freud
(1984, p. 98), a source of human suffering that we experience as more
grievous than the pain that is caused by the destructive forces of our
bodies and nature.

Human existence binds us to each other and, as Sartre wrote (1947), the others can be hell (*"L'enfer c'est les autres"*). In *Huis Clos,* he tells us that to experience living in hell, it is sufficient to spend time with others in an enclosed space. We are strangers to each other, anxious about each other, uncertain about where we are heading and whether we are getting anywhere anyway. We are dependent on each other, and all of us are extremely vulnerable in deep existential ways. We know from the historical record that even in this fragile situation, human beings have a tremendous talent to make hellish life even worse. We have many tricks in our box to make our adversaries into our enemies and to let incompatibilities escalate into violent hostilities.

Living with others is difficult because human interdependence implies that the judgment about who we are—what our significance is—is lodged with others. It is a fundamental feature of human existence that these others are perceived as our adversaries. This perception becomes ever more critical as the communities in which we live—through changes in global demographics—evolve into multicultural and multireligious spaces where we experience increasing density with increasingly more people who are strangers: people of different origin, religious values, cultural practices, and languages. The encounters between "us" and "them" all too often escalate into deadly conflicts. But can these encounters be avoided? Should we ignore each other with "civil inattention" (Goffmann, 1963, p. 84) as many city dwellers do: strangers in the night who avoid eye contact? Or should we opt for living in voluntary "ghettoization" and erect walls between different communities that cannot live in peace? Should we seriously accept the historical possibility that the liberal dream about peaceful, multiethnic, multireligious societies is a dream indeed (Dahrendorf, 2002)?

Human life is impossible without the relations we develop on global, local, and personal levels. These relations are never without conflict. There are always opposing positions, differences, incompatibilities, and disagreements. Conflict is a constitutive element of human life. If we accept this, it seems odd that so much time and energy is invested worldwide in the prevention and resolution of conflict. We should rather direct our efforts to understanding and preventing conflicts from escalating into irreparable damage.

An essential element of the effort to resolve conflict is the Cartesian position that assumes that reality-out-there is a stable given that is cognizable provided we use the correct ways of perception. This means that if our perception is not corrupted by all kinds of societal and personal influences, we can see reality as it is. In order to achieve this objective perception of reality, we need to develop shared values and beliefs. However, as long as people have different values and beliefs, they will see things differently. Thus, it is at this point that the Cartesian position turns out to be a misleading illusion. There is no homogeneity in human perception. In fact, we all live in different universes. Our distinct physiological features and our different personal experiences ensure that we do not live in the same world. Even within the same culture or even the same community, the general experience is that "every man speaks a language somewhat of his own" (Boulding, 1962, p. 295). As a consequence, disagreements and disputes are basic to human existence. Conflict is a central part of living with others. In parent-child relations, it is rare that children and parents do not have different positions. In fact, adolescence is often a time of increased parent-child conflict, when parents and adolescents tend to have different interpretations of the conflict. Parents see disagreements arising from morality, personal safety, and conformity concerns, and adolescents view them as issues of personal choice (Smetana, 1989). What's more, the parent-child conflict does not end at adolescence. Research indicates that many adults continue to have conflicts with their parents. Clarke, Preston, Raskin, and Bengtson (1999) found that intergenerational conflicts can occur regarding styles of interaction, lifestyle choices, child-rearing practices, political and religious values, work habits, and household standards. Thus, conflict is a feature of family life. Sprey (1969, pp. 703–704) noted that families can be viewed as systems in conflict: They consist of "ongoing confrontation between its members, a confrontation between individuals with conflicting interests in their common situation." Relative to other types of relationships, adults report that they experience the greatest degree of criticism and emotional conflict in their marriage, even in happy marriages, followed closely by their relationships with siblings, adolescent children, and parents (Argyle & Furnham, 1983).

Accepting the inevitability of conflict may help us to discover that conflict can even be desirable. Marital conflict may be the best way to discover you made the wrong choice. As Canary, Cupach, and Messman observed (1995, p. 124), "Perhaps more than any other type of interaction, conflict acts as a catalyst for personal development." Even babies learn from the conflicts with their parents how to deal with the conduct of the parental others. As a result, their attempts to resolve these confrontations at all costs may seriously obstruct the independent development of children toward success in reaching maturity.

However, conflict can also be a positive force for change. It can act as an agent of reform, adaptation, and development. Karen Horney (1945, p. 27) stated that "To experience conflicts knowingly, though it may be distressing, can be an invaluable asset." Thus, conflict does not necessarily stand in the way of satisfactory human relations. The frequency of conflict says relatively little about the quality of relationships (Canary, Cupach, & Messman, 1995, p. 126). Instead, conflict can be a source of creativity and growth.

Without conflict, there are no innovations in arts and technology. Without conflict, there can be no science. The basis of scientific investigation is that scientists disagree on almost everything. Thus, when the scientific community claims to have a consensus, one needs to be suspicious about the quality of the scientific work. The claim made by Al Gore and the UN Intergovernmental Panel on Climate Change that the science about global warming is settled is a stunningly unscientific statement. It is inherent to scientific work that there can be no consensus on global warming as the doomsday authorities suggest.

If there had been no confrontations about the validity of theoretical constructs, science would have never moved beyond Aristotelian insights. Scientific progress is a constant process of controversies that lead to the temporary acceptance of paradigms that are then contested by fundamentally new theories and facts. The paradigm that seems better than its competitors will be adopted as the prevailing body of scientific thought until it is contested by even better insights.

Inevitable in the scientific process is that scientists see different things and draw different conclusions even if they make the same observation. Thomas Kuhn gives many telling examples of this in his book on the structure of scientific revolutions (1962).

Without conflict, societies could not be democratically organized. The essence of politics is conflict. Political practice is about the distribution and execution of power and inevitably involves opposite positions. Therefore, disagreement and tension are part of the political process. Expressing these frictions is more productive for democracy than seeking consensus, as consensus politics always tends to exclude people. We have to accept that every consensus exists as a temporary result of a provisional hegemony, as a stabilization of power, and that it always entails some form of exclusion. Pluralist political systems may demand some level of consensual agreement, but this should be a "conflictual consensus" (Mouffe, 2000). A well-functioning democracy calls for a vibrant clash of political positions. Pluralism is inherently an ongoing conflictual process rather than a smooth and rational process. Chantal Mouffe (2000) pleaded for "agonistic" politics, arguing that whereas antagonism is a struggle between enemies, agonism refers to the struggle between adversaries. In politics, there will always be opponents and, thus, conflicts. Particularly among liberal politicians, there is a tendency to obscure this truism, proposing that conflicts can always be resolved through negotiation. Living within a democratic arrangement, however, implies learning to live with fundamental conflicts. The way in which some multicultural societies, like the Netherlands, use the political discourse of "integration" suggest that it is desirable and possible to ignore basic social contradictions and conflicts. This avoidance behavior can be fatal for the development of a strong democracy. In a strong democracy (Barber, 1984), interests and insights will inevitably clash and social conflict never ends.

Conflict is intrinsic to human society and pervades our lives in many different ways, at various levels, and with differing degrees of intensity and various outcomes. This can be described as *a situation in which interdependent human actors engage in verbal or non-verbal disputes about the perceived incompatibility of positions on issues that are relevant to them.* The argumentation for this choice of words runs as follows:

- "Situation" implies the possibility that disputes may be episodic and incidental (fleeting) or permanent and structural.
- The interdependence between actors can be of unequal magnitude and scope. Interdependent relationships can be skewed or balanced in terms of power structure. In the course of interactions, power is essential in the sense of the capacity to set the agenda of a dispute (e.g., by leaving certain issues out) and to influence the outcome of the dispute.
- The reference to perception is pertinent because incompatible positions can be based on delusions or upon empirical observations. The crucial question is whether actors perceive that there are incompatibilities rather than whether these are real.
- Real or imagined incompatibilities can be shallow and of marginal importance or deep and of fundamental significance.
- Issues that people take different positions on cover a wide range and can be almost anything: a claim to ownership of an object, an expectation of affection, a violation of relationship rules, personal preferences, lifestyles, appearances, or modes of communication.

- Positions that actors (individuals, groups, or states) take imply claims to objects of want, which can be material or immaterial and can range from territories to lifestyles, money, love, obedience, or attention. The legitimacy of such claims may be contested by other actors who refuse to comply. Positions may be negotiable because disputes may result from partial information and failed communication. Positions may also be nonnegotiable because the actors are in radical disagreement. If people are in radical disagreement, modes of coexistence must be found that, although they may not resolve the conflict, may tame its escalation toward irreparable damage. After the events of 9/11, many UN member states and religious organizations called for interreligious and intercultural dialogues. The UN 2001 Year of Dialogue between Civilizations put the urgent need for such dialogue on the global political agenda. However, although the proponents of dialogue often assume the readiness to conduct dialogue as a given (Apel, 1988; Habermas, 1993), they ignore the possibility of radical disagreement and irreconcilable differences. Whereas any serious dialogue presupposes that the participants are open to transforming their own prejudices, assertions, and assumptions into questions, those who are locked into their preferred absolutist worldviews are incapable of doing just that.

In both literature and practice, a great deal of attention is paid to preventing and/or resolving conflicts. This attention finds expression in an impressive volume of publications (from scholarly treatises to "for Dummies" pamphlets), an endless series of expensive seminars (with engaging keynote speakers and lavish lunches), and international conferences such as the Deutsche Welle Global Medium Forum in 2008 on "Media in Peacebuilding and Conflict Prevention." All this activity suggests that conflicts can and should be prevented and that they can and should be resolved. However, if indeed conflict is a constitutive element of the human condition and inherent to human life, it cannot be prevented. Moreover, conflicts cannot always be resolved, and sometimes it is even undesirable to want them resolved. Some conflicts are irresolvable because they result from fundamental personality, cultural, or religious differences or from essential and mutually exclusive needs of parties. Conflicts may be insoluble because there is no reasonable answer to the clash of positions. There are situations in life that demand choices between two or more fundamental moral principles that are equally valid but demand different and conflicting courses of action. These are called dilemmas because any course of action violates a basic value. If we violate principle "A" by doing "X," we commit a wrong. Equally, if we violate principle "B" by doing "Y," we also commit a wrong. Thus, we have to decide between two wrongs. The ultimate choice, as presented in the motion picture *Sophie's Choice*, is a confrontation with an insoluble conflict. The movie features Meryl Streep as Sophie, a mother who, in Nazi Germany, faces a choice without a morally satisfying solution when a German soldier gives her the choice to save either her young son or her daughter from deportation and subsequent death. Sophie has to save both her children yet can save only one. No trick from the book can help her to resolve this conflict.

Rather than relying on the conflict resolution gurus, parties should find ways to live with such disputes without irreparably damaging their relationship. People may have disputes about non-negotiable wants that cannot be de-escalated and will have to accept that history just takes its bloody route.

Conflicts have both overt and silent dimensions. If there is no conflict, this may mean the peaceful family is simply between hostilities, in a suspension of warfare. But the mere cessation of hostilities does not mean that a conflict has been resolved. Parties often mull over conflicts long after the confrontational situation has ended, so the silent dispute may continue. Thus, conflicts do not disappear when parties have forgiven each other; they may reappear in different forms. The ending of a conflict may almost immediately lead to another conflict, possibly less violent but still very disturbing for those involved. At the level of family life, an illustration comes from the solution of marital conflicts through divorce, after which the separation may lead the children into conflicts with their parents, their teachers, and other authorities. Although the verbal abuse between the parents is gone, now feelings of guilt and uncertainty afflict the kids and the use of drugs seems the only way out. The core conflict that is caused by a lack of stability and trust in family relations was not resolved.

An illustration at the international level could be the postgenocidal situation in Cambodia. After the unimaginable massacres by Pol Pot and the Khmer Rouge, the liberation arrived, establishing a ruthless "free" market economy that caused enormous gaps between the privileged elite and disenfranchised majorities: a new conflict with its own losers and victims. The core conflict that is caused by the reality of a dangerously divided population was not resolved.

Very real conflicts may be downsized by compromises, but these are not the same as solutions. Compromises often create artificial harmony. Compromise solutions may be accepted even though none of the actors is particularly content with this and the confrontation of positions could—in the end—have yielded a more beneficial outcome (Pruitt & Kim, 2004, p. 97).

Conflicting self-interests between social groups can never be fully resolved. A temporary accommodation may be achieved, usually based upon the physical power that one group is able to wield over the other group. As soon as the other group feels strong enough to challenge this power, however, it will try to change the accommodation toward serving its own collective egoism.

Withdrawing from and avoiding conflict can be constructive in the short term but is often very dysfunctional in the longer term. Real issues and real positions on these issues will not disappear because of avoidance behavior. If one party really wants to address an issue and the other withdraws, this does not lessen the interest the first party has in the dispute and does not improve relational quality.

Often conflicts remain latent and are kept under control by normative rules of conduct that people have formally accepted or internalized for the governance of their behavior in the family, at work, or on the road. Most societies have developed mechanisms to deal with conflict and prevent it from turning violent. Every society has rules, etiquettes, and rituals to cope with conflict in ways that seek to limit the damage done to fellow human beings. In the higher-developed animals, we find a great deal of rituals to avoid such damage. If nonhuman animals kill their own species, they usually kill only a small number. Conversely, human animals are capable of killing vast numbers of their own species in relatively short periods. Thus, human rituals to tame aggression are poorly developed. A partial explanation for this may be that humans throughout history are confronted with strong external disturbances, such as rapid technological developments that create ever-larger distances between points of acting and the consequences thereof. Technology creates "moral distance" between bomber pilots and their victims. In modern warfare, such as in Afghanistan, enemies are killed from great distances: In the Afghan-Pakistan border region, unmanned Predator and Reaper planes are used to fire missiles at enemy targets. Those unmanned aerial vehicles are directed to their targets by Air Force staff in Nevada, United States. Fighters and civilians are destroyed by remote control, and after the killing, the shooters have dinner at home.

The behavior of nonhuman animals that restrains conflict through acts of submission (such as a wolf that offers its bare neck to a stronger contender) may be very rational but tends to be seen by humans as weak behavior. Moreover, human beings are able to kill each other thinking this is what they should do. Humans have an extraordinary capacity of self-justification for extremely cruel behavior.

At the same time, people have also developed ritualizations of aggression and violence that make it possible to compete with others without killing each other. Although sports may illustrate such a ritualization, these activities risk losing their capacity for controlling escalation when professionalization and commercialization transform them into excessive and obsessive competition.

Escalation is difficult to control when there is too much at stake in winning versus losing and when we label the losers as a negative category. In competitive processes, inevitably there are "losers," and our societies are not particularly friendly to those who lose. Recognizing the dignity of the losers is difficult in highly competitive environments.

THE DYNAMICS OF CONFLICT: THE ESCALATION SPIRAL

Martii Ahtisaari, the 2008 Nobel Peace Prize laureate, stated in a press interview, "Every conflict can be resolved" (*International Herald Tribune*, October 11–12, 2008). One can only hope that the interviewer inaccurately quoted the global mediator, as some conflicts cannot be resolved due to the radical disagreement of parties to the dispute. Actually, in most of Ahtisaari's mediation successes, it is likely that conflicts were not fundamentally resolved but instead hostilities were temporarily suspended and may come back with a vengeance.

Some secessionist conflicts ended (e.g., Northern Ireland), but other "old" conflicts erupted again in 2005–2006 (e.g., Sri Lanka). New generations take up old fights, as in Kashmir or in Myanmar. There may be a cease-fire agreement in an ethnic conflict, but the danger of violence remains if this is not yet fully implemented (e.g., Burundi). Or there may be a peace accord in a Muslim-Christian confrontation (e.g., Chad) that is still contested. Hostilities may be over, but parties are ready to resume fighting if final settlements are not achieved or not implemented, as with the Armenians in Azerbaijan, the Kurds in Iraq, and the Dimasas, Garos, Karbis, and Nagas in India. Agreements may be contested, as in the case of the Chittagong Hill Tribes in Bangladesh, the Bougainvilleans in Papua New Guinea, and the Malaitans and Guadalcanalese in the Solomon Islands. In at least fifteen currently active conflicts over self-determination, parties may take up violent tactics again. According to the 2008 Peace and Conflict study,

> in late 2005, for example, violence broke out in Sri Lanka, rupturing a 2002 cease-fire agreement between the government and the Liberation Tigers of Tamil Eelam (LTTE). In Azerbaijan, sporadic clashes broke out over the disputed region of Nagorno-Karabakh, intensifying hostilities that had been relatively quiet for a number of years.... Old adversaries are the most significant source of today's active conflicts.... Most of these conflicts began many years ago. (Hewitt, Wilkenfeld, & Gurr, 2008, p. 23)

The tribal bloodbath in Kenya (2008) is over, but on April 10, 2009, a leading Kenyan newspaper pleaded on its front page: "Don't lead us back to war." All the explosive material for another violent outburst is still in place.

Hewitt, Wilkenfeld, and Gurr refer to this phenomenon as "conflict recurrence." Such terminology suggests that the conflict goes away and then recurs. However, in most of the "conflict recurrences" cited above, the core conflict never stopped; rather, its root causes were not effectively dealt with in conflict mediation efforts (Hewitt et al., 2008, p. 3).

If one concludes that important types of conflict cannot be prevented, cannot really be resolved, and, in some cases, should not be resolved as they are essential to human life and its development, the core problem is not to prevent or to resolve conflicts, but instead to understand the dynamics of conflict. This is particularly important in the serious areas of risk that will be discussed in chapter 6. It is essential to understand how disagreements cross an "invisible line" and develop into lethal confrontations. How do disputes escalate from safety zones to danger zones? Conflicts become dangerous when the invisible line, which has no clear demarcation, is crossed, and there are different invisible lines in different situations. Once they are crossed, conflicts escalate and may have very damaging, even lethal outcomes. Even at festive occasions such as a family Christmas dinner, escalating disputes can be readily observed. Many dinner conversations take the form of disputes, in which opposite positions are expressed. They may end in different ways: They can spiral into violence or finish with a compromise, standoff, stonewalling, or withdrawal. They quickly take a detrimental turn when the tone gets combative. This can happen because of criticizing personal characteristics, making sarcastic remarks, or expressing contempt. A succession of claims and counterclaims in the dispute transforms the family dinner table into a battlefield.

Although human beings have an impressive capacity to cope with serious incompatibilities in creative and constructive ways, sometimes it goes wrong and they move toward destructive aggression. Conflicts may lead parties (nations, groups, individuals) from dispute toward hostility, where the other is no longer an adversary (as in courtrooms or on sports fields) but now an enemy (as in warfare). Escalation implies that incompatible positions move from disputes to violent hostilities—even to warfare. In the process, lighter tools are replaced by heavier tools: Shouting progresses to throwing rocks and then to using firearms. While disputes are escalating, actors shift from looking at an insignificant issue to focusing on an all-encompassing problem with their relationship. They go from arguing to win to the deliberate hurting of the other.

Escalating spirals are often hard to stop once they get started because each side feels that failing to retaliate will be seen as a sign of weakness, inviting further annoying behavior from the other side. In addition, neither side is willing to make conciliatory moves that might break the cycle. One reason for this is that the other is not trusted to reciprocate such assuaging moves: The other is the aggressor and, thus, the one to blame. In the escalation process, the parties become increasingly involved in and committed to the issue at stake.

In escalatory processes, people's environments may provide strong forms of physiological and emotional arousal (Pruitt & Kim, 2004, p. 126), including noise, sexual excitement, alcohol, frustration, anger, time pressure, or air pollution. Such factors diminish the capacity for rational choice making and make people vulnerable to inflammatory encouragements to use violence.

Escalation may be driven by perceptions or experiences of injustice that may originate in events that happened in the past. When victims exaggerate the damage done to them, they are likely to seek revenge. The negative experiences with the adversary strengthen biased perceptions about the other party, and through the mechanism of selective perception, only those characteristics of the adversary that confirm its evil nature are seen. This confirmation justifies hostile attitudes and the use of violence. In the process, the differences between "us" and "them" grow bigger, and interactions between the parties subside, thus giving more space to fake stories, misinformation, and plain lies. Violent action born out of revenge often contributes to a circular process that spirals with every turn into more violence. Once the conflict spirals into the direction of open hostilities, the opponent is—often through propaganda—de-individuated and dehumanized.

In the process of escalation, the cohesiveness of groups tends to become stronger and the readiness to act in extreme ways grows among the individual members of the group. In the escalation process, groups seek strong leaders who are willing to engage in extreme hostile action and to endorse such action. Leaders who come to power because of their forceful and violent performance have an interest in perpetuating the conflict.

In conflict escalation, emotional factors are essential variables, as actors involved in a dispute may want to win their substantial claim but also have fears about losing face or being seen as a loser.[1] In processes of escalation, emotions such as anger, fear, jealousy, grief, greed, shame, sadness, panic, humiliation, or vengeance play a crucial role and have an enormous impact on human behavior. Conflicts are never merely about objective conditions but instead involve subjective feelings. In preventing conflict escalation, focusing on mere substance is insufficient because in disputes, there is both content and context, and the latter is often loaded with emotions. The emotional context may even hinder one from being able to see the rational content of a conflict. For instance, people may be so afraid of terrorism that they are unable to see that terrorists may have substantial and rational political demands. What's more, people's emotional responses to terrorist threats may also obscure that what people perceive as an incomprehensible and sudden outburst of outrage may in fact be the perpetrator's rational response to an undesirable situation. Large-scale murder can be a very rational process executed with conscious intentions and through established organizational structures.

In another example, in the workplace people may have a substantial dispute about getting a salary raise but also worry (the contextual emotion) about not getting this raise. Although the way in which the disputing actors communicate says something about what they substantially want, it also says something about how they feel about each other. In the dispute, a remark by one person of nonconsequential substance may be experienced by another as hostile, thus evoking an antagonistic response that will, in turn, evoke even more hostility.

Because conflicts have both substantive and emotional components, the balance between cognitive capacity and emotional sensitivity is crucial to prevent escalation. When people approach their disputes largely from a cognitive angle and focus on the substance of disagreements, the emotional dimension may get insufficient attention. If they ignore that the conflict may also be about emotions, such as hurt feelings or a sense of betrayal, the rational solution is likely to be temporary only. Alternatively, when the emotional approach fails to discover the rational content of the dispute, the rejection of the (perceived) rationality of demands leads the protagonists into escalation.

It is useful to observe how well in most day-to-day encounters people are capable of maintaining the equilibrium of their cognitive capacity and their emotional sensitivity. This is very fortunate because otherwise we would be permanently involved in civil warfare. However, the risk of escalation is always present, and under certain circumstances, the balance breaks down and disputing parties fail to stop the escalatory process.

People often develop emotional attitudes toward others on the basis of their own actions and, thus, may have hostile attitudes toward those others who they hurt. Such attitudes may endure and escalate because of the human capacity to reduce cognitive dissonance—the discrepancy between what we know (or think we know about ourselves/our self-perceptions) and what we do. We believe we are quite decent and well-tempered people, and yet we scream at others who we see as being the cause of our behavior. Once we establish a negative image of others, we tend to be selective with the information we receive about these people and filter away anything that does not serve our judgment. People are great artists when coping with evidence that undermines their initial impressions. Once the other is seen as evil, whatever he does or does not do only confirms our position. We selectively inform ourselves and selectively evaluate the information. Moreover, we tend to seek information that confirms our position.

Playing on power differences in conflict situations may easily escalate the dispute. Discounting the needs of the weaker actors can cause feelings of humiliation that then lead to hostility and even to violence. When the less powerful perceive that they will lose in the dispute, they may turn to violent action.

As fleeting conflicts shift to low-intensity conflicts, the options for escalation or de-escalation are still open to the actors. When these low-intensity conflicts shift to high-intensity conflicts, the use of violence becomes a realistic option.

The spiral of conflict escalation moves from disagreement through aggression to destruction. The four key drivers of this spiral are: anxiety, agitation, alienation, and accusation in a mirror.

Chapter 1

Anxiety[2]

On the basis of historical, social-psychological, and clinical observations, the first phase of the spiral is, arguably, a state of anxiety. I use the concept of anxiety to describe a mixed bag of emotions, including primarily fear, anger, and humiliation. Here, I use anxiety to mean more than simply concern, as there may be nothing wrong with people being concerned about health or climate issues among others. It also indicates more than alertness, as it may be a good thing to be aware of impending dangers. Rather, here I use the concept to denote a condition of "emotional strain" that leads people to feel that they have lost not only control over their lives but also a sense of meaning.

Anxiety is inherent to the human condition. Ontologically, humans live in the permanent tension between Being and Non-Being, between life and death, love and abandonment, success and failure. In a diffuse ("subjective") way, we are aware of uncertainties and threats that are not necessarily connected with "objective" events. We are conscious of gaps between expectation and reality. This existential basic layer finds expression in emotions connected to concrete experiences like illness, unemployment, divorce, or bankruptcy—emotions such as fear, anger, humiliation, shame, and grief.

Although societies have probably always known times of anxiety, a general "state of anxiety" is arguably a prominent feature of modern societies. As opinion polls in European countries, conducted through the Eurobarometer,[3] and in the United States show, people in these countries experience a great deal of anxiety that political, economic, and environmental circumstances will soon get a lot worse. There is a shared anxiety about economics, focusing on inflation, unemployment, and food prices. People are also anxious about the threat of epidemic diseases, credit crises, food shortages, rising prices of oil, terrorism, the danger of Islam, bird flu, genetically modified food, and global warming. Then there is urban anxiety, and its manifestations include locked cars, closed doors, gated communities, and ubiquitous surveillance.

An overall feeling of anxiety means that the world is seen as a dangerous place. This perception has inspired the large-scale manufacturing of surveillance systems, the mushrooming of private security services, and the empty streets at night in many metropolitan centers. Many people are continually anxious about their lives, health, families, relations, money, possessions, or status in society.

Anxiety not only relates to basic human needs such as food, security, and identity, but also to territorial integrity. Like most animals, humans are very concerned about controlling their territory, and they may extend this to include a range of physical objects or even their partners. People are particularly prone to develop these anxieties in competitive environments: Competition breeds anxiety!

Human beings are forever competing, either with one another or with themselves. Competition pervades all human relationships—at work, in school, in the family ("the kids have to win medals in contests") and even in friendships and love. This compulsive competitiveness constrains the human potential for spiritual and moral growth. Its exclusive emphasis on "more, bigger, and better" gives preferential treatment to all those human achievements that can be quantified and, as such, may even constrain human life. Competition aims to extinguish or subjugate one's competitor. Its logical conclusion is the absurdity of leaving no one to compete with: the dictator without people to dictate. But even short of this absurdity, competition leads to irrational behavior, such as crowds competing to get out of a building on fire or a person persistently competing with him/herself and, as a result, becoming a neurotic wreck. Human beings have been competitive throughout history, but necessarily on a limited scale. This competitive nature never mattered so much as it does today. The scale of competition used to be limited because there was only a limited notion of how many potential contenders there were; physical and technical constraints limited the number of competitors that could be eliminated. The environment was perceived as a finite system because the human being was the final point in the evolution and the globe was considered a closed system. Today the scale of competition has dramatically increased because there are more people (population growth), they all want more, and there are more competitors for the same resources. Most physical restraints have been removed in technological development: We can now kill the competitor many times over. The environment is now seen as an infinite system: Competition has no limits and can now also be extended into outer space.

As a result, we are confronted with the unprecedented pervasiveness of competition in practically all social fields. In addition, even our better-intentioned endeavors use such competitive metaphors as "war on poverty," "combat of racism," or "fight against illiteracy." Finally, deceptively as well as perversely, the jargon of economists suggests the ideal of perfect competition. Because our competitive efforts are no longer physically restrained, we need to rely on moral restraint lest we carry our natural instincts to absurd degrees.

Modern capitalism tends to isolate people from each other and creates the lonely, anxious individual as a result of relentless competition (Fromm, 1964). Rollo May suggested that "competitive individualism militates against the experience of community, and that lack of community is a centrally important factor in contemporaneous anxiety" (1977, p. 166). He argued that individualism and the loss of community mean insecurity and a feeling of helplessness (p. 168). This means that in modern capitalism, persons are in fact devalued; we are all for sale. The question "what is my worth?" is a source of constant anxiety, and we persistently worry about success (p. 170). You are worth more if you defeat others—they stand potentially in the way of your success.

Competitiveness implies societal hostility. This hostility leads to more anxiety, which leads to more competition, which leads to more hostility and to more anxiety—and the loop continues.

In many countries where conflicts escalated toward mass violence, there were—before the escalation—states of serious societal anxiety. In Turkey, there was a great deal of anxiety because the Armenians—although for a long time a persecuted and discriminated minority—managed to modernize and make social and economic progress that might in future threaten the Turkish majority. Many Turks felt anxious about threats to Turkish identity as well as feared external aggression (Chalk & Jonassohn, 1990, p. 19). Likewise, there was a general state of anxiety in Germany before World War II, as there was among populations in the Balkan countries before the civil wars. In Rwandan society—before the genocide—Hutus were anxious about what might happen to them in the future, fearing that Tutsis would come to dominate and humiliate them and, as a result, feeling their survival to be threatened. This enabled the political leaders to make people obey their genocidal instructions.

The use of anxiety was very visible as part of the politics of the George W. Bush administration during the post–9/11 period, but it was also exploited in Britain as political instrument. Frank Furedi (2005, p. 126) stated that "Since 9/11, politicians, business, advocacy organizations and special interest groups have sought to further their narrow agendas by manipulating public anxiety about terror." He went on to state that politicians do "regard fear as an important resource for gaining a hearing for their message" (p. 123). Politicians and social movements from different ideological beliefs use people's anxieties to achieve certain goals. He wrote, "political elites, public figures, sections of the media and campaigners are directly culpable for using fear to promote their agenda" (p. 123). Thus, manipulating feelings of helplessness helps to muzzle dissent and calls for unity. This research suggests that in moments of pending disaster, we have to stick together.

Worldwide, environmentalists and health campaigners rouse anxiety. A basic tenet of their scare stories—whether those be about abrupt climate change or genetically modified food—is an alleged and perceived threat that usually is disproportional compared to the real danger. According to Furedi,

> The belief that social solidarity is far more likely to be forged around a reaction to the bad than around the aspiration for the good exercises a strong influence over politicians, opinion makers and academics. Instead of being concerned about the destructive consequences of the mood of anxiety and fear that afflicts the public, many social theorists regard these as sentiments that can be harnessed for the purpose of forging social cohesion. (2005, p. 136)

Sociologists Ulrich Beck (2002) and Anthony Giddens (1994) are among the social theorists who have argued that creating anxiety (particularly fear) functions to positively contribute to societal consensus on crucial issues and to solidarity. Focusing on evil things to come motivates people to act. In fact, Giddens proposed the mobilization of people around a "negative utopia" (1994, p. 223). Fear of the future is idealized as the essential instrument to people's awareness, alertness, and readiness to act. Such visions enjoy wide political and popular support and ignore in a cavalier way that shared anxiety reinforces an in-group identification, the demand for a strong leader, and, thus, exacerbates the fear of the out-group threat that needs to be eliminated. The in-group begins to believe that in order to achieve a good society, the out-group needs to be destroyed. Leaders offer utopian visions that imply the exclusion of the others.

Anxiety increases people's susceptibility to agitation. As a collective state of mind, it makes people vulnerable to manipulation, undermines their autonomous thought and choice, inspires the call for strong leadership, and makes people distrustful of each other. The collective experience of anxiety reinforces group coherence, diminishes and erodes independent thought and autonomous choice, and makes people vulnerable to manipulation, and in their experience of helplessness and uncertainty, the search for strong leadership becomes increasingly important. Anxiety is an unpleasant experience, and the anxious person seeks a scapegoat for his feelings of helplessness and threat. Seeing the world within an "anxiety frame" increases feelings of helplessness, feeds social distrust, and diminishes people's agency (May, 1977, p. 135). For example, in the Balkan conflict, psychiatrists Jovan Raskovic and Radovan Karadzic to a large extent manufactured anxiety about the other. They used the eugenic doctrines developed by German psychiatrists before and during the Holocaust and made them the cornerstones of the politics of "ethnic cleansing."[4] As Raskovic stated, "If I hadn't created this emotional strain in the Serbian people, nothing would have happened" (Citizen's Commission on Human Rights, 2006) Anxiety is a social construction that is probably significantly mediated through a pervasive media discourse about anxiety that has little synchronicity with real-life events.

Agitation

For the second phase of the spiral of escalation, people need to be aroused to collective destructive action. Their anxiety needs to be transformed into aggressive behavior. This requires manipulative leadership. Their anxiety needs the angry political leader (the "capo") who manages to focus the state of anxiety (by identifying the target groups as scapegoats) and who justifies destructive feelings. "Capospeech" is often characterized by inflammatory, divisive, exclusionary, utopian rhetoric, and it is filled with references to past victories or past tragedies (Volkan, 2004, pp. 48–49). In the escalating spiral of the Kosovo conflict, Serb leaders—both political and intellectual—used a historical emotion of martyrdom to incite ordinary Serbs to deeply hate Albanians in Kosovo. Serbs felt societal anxiety because they feared that the expansion of the Albanian Muslim population in Kosovo would outnumber them. Albanians were referred to as a group—and as "terrorists."

Albanians were de-individuated and portrayed as dangerous threats. The leadership propaganda—given a broad public platform in state-controlled Serbian broadcasting—repeatedly suggested that the Serbs were at risk, under threat, and likely to be victims in the near future.

Furthermore, in former Yugoslavia, before the outbreak of the Serb/Croat War, most people felt anxious about the future, a general anxiety that could be manipulated by both Serb and Croat leaders. In their agitation, they used references to historical events and to past injustice to justify and nurture their anxiety. In 1989, at the 600th commemoration of the Battle of Kosovo Polje, Serb leader Slobodan Milosevic assured his followers that Muslims would never again defeat the Serbs, and he referred to deep cultural differences between Serbs and Croats. Alternatively, Croat leader Franjo Tudjman often spoke in his public speeches about the fundamental cultural rift between Croats and Serbs, stating that "Croats belong to a different culture—a different civilization from the Serbs" (Gallagher, 1997, p. 55). Agitation means that the leader expresses anger, identifies the object of anger (the others), and uses inflammatory rhetoric that activates anger and aggression in the followers, who in turn pressure the leader further toward destructive aggression that should lead to the elimination of the object of their anxiety (Volkan, 2004, p. 13). Emphasizing and legitimizing cultural difference makes it easier to target the different others as scapegoats and as the sources of anxiety, whether those different others be Jews (Nazi Germany), peasants (Stalin), people who wear glasses (Cambodia), or the bourgeois (Mao).

The war chant may begin with the "capo," but soon others join the chorus. The capo needs a supportive act—it is never the leader alone! War is not merely a personal initiative but rather a systemic process. Power needs an audience. Imagine that you delete from pictures of agitators such as Adolf Hitler the cheering masses. Power would simply evaporate. What if, in the run-up to the First World War, people had stayed home in Berlin, Paris, St. Petersburg, Vienna and London?

Angry political leaders know how to manipulate people's anxiety to their benefit. They provide a target for people's anger. Hostility needs direction and the leader identifies the targets. He also provides the justification for people's hostile feelings. Essential to this phase of the spiral is that people rally around the leader and collectively create mythical enemies and cleansing rituals. The angry leaders exaggerate people's need to have enemies and lead large groups into a mental regression in which individuality gets lost and collective identity wins over individual identity (Volkan, 2004, p. 159). In this process, basic social trust is replaced with "blind trust" (Volkan, 2004, p. 14). When angry leaders manipulate the sense of collective identity and collective enmity, they prepare the ground for the collective destruction of human dignity.

Alienation

Exposing people to anxiety and agitation does not automatically imply that that they are then ready to humiliate or murder the individual members of the targeted scapegoats. Humans may be a nasty species, but most people do not easily destroy others. Some help is required!

In order to actively or passively participate in collective destructive action, a third phase is essential, in which ordinary people engage in collective humiliation and mass slaughter. This third stage is difficult because even when people are collectively fearsome, angry, and aggressive, they still resist truly and seriously harming other members of the species. Compared to animals, we may kill more easily and more massively, but we should not exaggerate our murderous activities: Most people find it difficult to kill a fellow human being. In most cultures, there are strong taboos against killing the innocent; important moral rules tell people not to kill; and there is the eternal fear of retaliation and punishment. All these factors need to be removed through a process that disinhibits the obstacles to mass murder.

Studies in military history (e.g., Holmes, 1986) suggest that soldiers in combat have often fired over their enemies' heads, and many even did not fire at all. World Wars I and II provide much evidence of soldiers not being able to kill. Dave Grossman (1995, p. 31) stated that "Looking another human being in the eye, making an independent decision to kill him, and watching as he dies due to your action combine to form the single most basic, important, primal, and potentially traumatic occurrence of war." Modern armies focus a great deal of training on techniques of psychological conditioning in order to overcome soldiers' resistance to killing. In these techniques, an essential element is obedience to the leader because very few people kill when they are not ordered to do so: "Many factors are at play on the battlefield, but one of the most powerful is the influence of the leader" (Grossman, 1995, p. 144). Other factors are the role of group pressure (few people kill without the support of their group) and the fear of letting others down (few people can live with the guilt of betraying those with whom one bonded during dangerous situations) (Grossman, 1995, p. 90).

Because only a minority of human beings have no capacity for empathy and cannot feel the pain they cause, the mind management techniques to ease the difficulty of killing are intended primarily to remove empathy by increasing the emotional distance between aggressor and victim. This implies teaching that the victim is inferior, different, and does not deserve the same moral standards as we do. As Helen Fein proposed, through these techniques, the victim is recategorized "outside the universe of moral obligation" (in Benesch, 2004, p. 500). To treat other humans as totally different from us, modern military training requires a process of alienation that disconnects people from one another. Disconnectedness facilitates the de-individuation and dehumanization of the enemy. We are no longer killing human beings but rather demons and animals.

Because effective elimination requires that the object is de-individuated and dehumanized, the perpetrator has to be disconnected from the victim, who is no longer a victim with a face and a unique personality. Human empathy needs to be locked out. This happened, for example, in pre–World War II programs in which the Japanese military trained their troops to kill people who did not attack them. Diary reports of Japanese soldiers reflect the belief that the Chinese were a subhuman species. Thus, the role of dehumanization is likely to be essential in collective violence. Research findings (e.g., the Milgram experiment, 1963) seem to indicate that aggression against an anonymous victim is more likely than against a visible victim.[5]

Accusation in a Mirror

The last decisive step in the spiral of escalation is that the dehumanized others (thought of as cockroaches and vermin) must be seen as real dangers so that killing them can be justified as self-defense. This can be achieved through the reversal of accusations. We accuse them of threatening us. Because most people will kill if their lives are threatened, when they feel their own lives (and those of their loved ones) are endangered if they do not kill the other. When we see the other is guilty of what the aggressor plans to do, he deserves to be punished for intending to exterminate us. Killing then becomes an act of self-defense, and this constitutes—worldwide—the legally and morally acceptable justification for homicide!

CONCLUSION

Life is conflict, and like other animals, people have developed all kinds of rituals to ward off violent confrontations. They are often sufficiently creative in dealing with disputes in constructive—or at least nondestructive—ways. However, quarrels within and between groups can spiral toward forms of collective destructive action and lethal confrontation.

In this escalation of conflict, the first driver is anxiety. This represents a mixed bag of experiences such as fear, anger, grief, humiliation, and shame. Then, for these emotions to become "agents" in the escalation process, they need the drive of external agitation. The "angry" leader exploits these anxious emotions in his inciting rhetoric, and the followers—in a state of arousal—will, in turn, incite the leader to pursue aggressive action. Anxiety and the inclination to solve problems through force are essential to the human condition. If manipulated by unscrupulous leaders, these emotions form a lethal explosive that can transform ordinary people into assassins. The third driver of the spiral encourages people to perceive others as "aliens," as outsiders. Alienation means there is no feeling of solidarity and fellowship: The others are strangers who cannot be trusted; they are members of an out-group who are denied the recognition of their humanity. They are no longer seen as unique individuals, as people like ourselves.

What happens in the escalation process is that the initial difficult problem of serious incompatibility of positions expands and its proportions grow. The adversarial tone becomes hostile as adversaries are increasingly seen as enemies. The tools change from verbal abuse to physical violence. People develop the belief that the enemy (the out-group) must be destroyed and that, eventually, the physical elimination of the enemy will be realized. The aggressor will justify this final deed by reversing accusations: The others posed a lethal threat to our group and we killed them in an act of legitimate self-defense.

These four major drivers in the spiral of escalation are social constructs that, therefore, need to be mediated by social institutions. Among these institutions, the mass media are particularly important channels of mediation. They are the main sources of people's knowledge about conflicts and the key sources of people's frames of thought about conflicts. In the following chapter how far the performance of mass media facilitates the matrix of these four drivers—anxiety, agitation, alienation, and accusation in a mirror—which is basic to the collective destruction of human dignity, needs to be explored.

Nonviolent Communication: A Language of Compassion

by Marshall B. Rosenberg, Ph.D.

Chapter One: Giving from the Heart, the Heart of Nonviolent Communication

> "What I want in my life is compassion, a flow between myself and others based on a mutual giving from the heart."
> —Marshall B. Rosenberg

Introduction

Believing that it is our nature to enjoy giving and receiving in a compassionate manner, I have been preoccupied most of my life with two questions. What happens to disconnect us from our compassionate nature, leading us to behave violently and exploitatively? And conversely, what allows some people to stay connected to their compassionate nature under even the most trying circumstances?

My preoccupation with these questions began in childhood, around the summer of 1943, when our family moved to Detroit, Michigan. The second week after we arrived, a race war erupted over an incident at a public park. More than forty people were killed in the next few days. Our neighborhood was situated in the center of the violence, and we spent three days locked in the house.

When the race riot ended and school began, I discovered that a name could be as dangerous as any skin color. When the teacher called my name during attendance, two boys glared at me and hissed, "Are you a kike?" I had never heard the word before and didn't know it was used by some people in a derogatory way to refer to Jews. After school, the two were waiting for me: they threw me to the ground, kicked and beat me.

Since that summer in 1943, I have been examining the two questions I mentioned. What empowers us, for example, to stay connected to our compassionate nature even under the worst circumstances? I am thinking of people like Etty Hillesum, who remained compassionate even while subjected to the grotesque conditions of a German concentration camp. As she wrote in her journal at the time,

> "I am not easily frightened. Not because I am brave but because I know that I am dealing with human beings, and that I must try as hard as I can to understand everything that anyone ever does. And that was the real import of this morning: not that a disgruntled young Gestapo officer yelled at me, but that I felt no indignation, rather a real compassion, and would have liked to ask, 'Did you have a very unhappy childhood, has your girlfriend let you down?' Yes, he looked harassed and driven, sullen and weak. I should have liked to start treating him there and then, for I know that pitiful young men like that are

dangerous as soon as they are let loose on mankind."
—Etty Hillesum: A Memoir

While studying the factors that affect our ability to stay compassionate, I was struck by the crucial role of language and our use of words. I have since identified a specific approach to communicating—speaking and listening—that leads us to give from the heart, connecting us with ourselves and with each other in a way that allows our natural compassion to flourish. I call this approach Nonviolent Communication, using the term "nonviolence" as Gandhi used it—to refer to our natural state of compassion when violence has subsided from the heart. While we may not consider the way we talk to be "violent," our words often lead to hurt and

NVC: a way of communicating that leads us to give from the heart

pain, whether for ourselves or others. In some communities, the process I am describing is known as Compassionate Communication; the abbreviation "NVC" is used throughout this book to refer to Nonviolent or Compassionate Communication.

a way to focus attention

NVC is founded on language and communication skills that strengthen our ability to remain human, even under trying conditions. It contains nothing new; all that has been integrated into NVC has been known for centuries. The intent is to remind us about what we already know—about how we humans were meant to relate to one another—and to assist us in living in a way that concretely manifests this knowledge.

NVC guides us in reframing how we express ourselves and hear others. Instead of being habitual, automatic reactions, our words become conscious responses based firmly on an awareness of what we are perceiving, feeling, and wanting. We are led to express ourselves with honesty and clarity, while simultaneously paying others a respectful and empathic attention. In any exchange, we come to hear our own deeper needs and those of others. NVC trains us to observe carefully, and to be able to specify behaviors and conditions that are affecting us. We learn to identify and clearly articulate what we are concretely wanting in a given situation.

We perceive relationships in a new light when we use NVC to hear our own deeper needs and those of others.

The form is simple, yet powerfully transformative.

As NVC replaces our old patterns of defending, withdrawing, or attacking in the face of judgment and criticism, we come to perceive ourselves and others, as well as our intentions and relationships, in a new light. Resistance, defensiveness, and violent reactions are minimized. When we focus on clarifying what is being observed, felt, and needed rather than on diagnosing and judging, we discover the depth of our own compassion. Through its emphasis on deep listening—to ourselves as well as others—NVC fosters respect, attentiveness, and empathy, and engenders a mutual desire to give from the heart.

Although I refer to it as "a process of communication" or a "language of compassion," NVC is more than a process or a language. On a deeper level, it is an ongoing reminder to keep our attention focused on a place where we are more likely to get what we are seeking.

There is a story of a man under a street lamp searching for something on all fours. A policeman passing by asked what he was doing. "Looking for my car keys," replied the man, who appeared slightly drunk. "Did you drop them here?" inquired the officer. "No," answered the man, "I dropped them in the alley." Seeing the policeman's baffled expression, the man hastened to explain, "But the light is much better here."

Let's shine the light of consciousness on places where we can hope to find what we are seeking.

I find that my cultural conditioning leads me to focus attention on places where I am unlikely to get what I want. I developed NVC as a way to train my attention—to shine the light of consciousness—on places that have the potential to yield what I am seeking. What I want in my life is compassion, a flow between myself and others based on a mutual giving from the heart.

This quality of compassion, which I refer to as "giving from the heart," is expressed in the following lyrics by my friend, Ruth Bebermeyer:

> I never feel more given to
> than when you take from me —
> when you understand the joy I feel
> giving to you.
> And you know my giving isn't done
> to put you in my debt,
> but because I want to live the love
> I feel for you.
>
> To receive with grace
> may be the greatest giving.
> There's no way I can separate
> the two.
> When you give to me,
> I give you my receiving.
> When you take from me, I feel so
> given to.
>
> Song "Given To" (1978) by Ruth Bebermeyer from the album, "Given To."

When we give from the heart, we do so out of a joy that springs forth whenever we willingly enrich another person's life. This kind of giving benefits both the giver and the receiver. The receiver enjoys the gift without worrying about the consequences that accompany gifts given out of fear, guilt, shame, or desire for gain. The giver benefits from the enhanced self-esteem that results when we see our efforts contributing to someone's well-being.

The use of NVC does not require that the persons with whom we are communicating be literate in NVC or even motivated to relate to us compassionately. If we stay with the principles of NVC, motivated solely to give and receive compassionately, and do everything we can to let others know this is our only motive, they will join us in the process and eventually we will be able to respond compassionately to one another. I'm not saying that this always happens quickly. I do maintain, however, that compassion inevitably blossoms when we stay true to the principles and process of NVC.

the nvc process

To arrive at a mutual desire to give from the heart, we focus the light of consciousness on four areas—referred to as the four components of the NVC model.

First, we observe what is actually happening in a situation: what are we observing others saying or doing that is either enriching or not enriching our life? The trick is to be able to articulate this observation without introducing any judgment or evaluation—to simply say what people are doing that we either like or don't like.

Four components of NVC:
1. observation
2. feeling
3. needs
4. request

Next, we state how we feel when we observe this action: are we hurt, scared, joyful, amused, irritated, etc.? And thirdly, we say what needs of ours are connected to the feelings we have identified. An awareness of these three components is present when we use NVC to clearly and honestly express how we are.

For example, a mother might express these three pieces to her teenage son by saying, "Felix, when I see two balls of soiled socks under the coffee table and another three next to the TV, I feel irritated because I am needing more order in the rooms which we share in common."

She would follow immediately with the fourth component—a very specific request: "Would you be willing to put your socks in your room or in the washing machine?" This fourth component addresses what we are wanting from the other person that would enrich our lives or make life more wonderful for us.

Thus, part of NVC is to express these four pieces of information very clearly, whether verbally or by other means. The other aspect of this communication consists of receiving the same four pieces of information from others. We connect with them by first sensing what they are observing, feeling, and needing, and then discover what would enrich their lives by receiving the fourth piece, their request. As we keep our attention focused on the areas mentioned, and help others do likewise, we establish a flow of communication, back and forth, until compassion manifests naturally: what I am observing, feeling, and needing; what I am requesting to enrich my life; what you are observing, feeling, and needing; what you are requesting to enrich your life....

NVC Process

The concrete actions we are **observing** that are affecting our well-being

How we are **feeling** in relation to what we are observing

The **needs,** values, desires, etc. that are creating our feelings

The concrete actions we **request** in order to enrich our lives

> Two parts of NVC:
> 1. expressing honesty through the four components
> 2. receiving empathically through the four components

When we use this model, we may begin either by expressing ourselves or by empathically receiving these four pieces of information from others. Although we will learn to listen for and verbally express each of these components in Chapters 3–6, it is important to keep in mind that NVC does not consist of a set formula, but adapts to various situations as well as personal and cultural styles. While I conveniently refer to NVC as a "process" or "language," it is possible to express all four pieces of the model without uttering a single word. The essence of NVC is to be found in our consciousness of these four components, not in the actual words that are exchanged.

applying nvc in our lives and world

When we use NVC in our interactions, with ourselves, with another person, or in a group, we become grounded in our natural state of compassion. It is therefore an approach that can be effectively applied at all levels of communication and in diverse situations:

intimate relationships
families
schools
organizations and institutions
therapy and counseling
diplomatic and business negotiations
disputes and conflicts of any nature.

Some people use NVC to create greater depth and caring in their intimate relationships:

"When I learned how I can receive (hear), as well as give (express), through using NVC, I went beyond feeling attacked and 'door mattish' to really listening to words and extracting their underlying feelings. I discovered a very hurting man to whom I had been married for 28 years. He had asked me for a divorce the weekend before the [NVC] workshop. To make a long story short, we are here today, together, and I appreciate the contribution [it has] made to our happy ending. . . . I learned to listen for feelings, to express my needs, to accept answers that I didn't always want to hear. He is not here to make me happy, nor am I here to create happiness for him. We have both learned to grow, to accept, and to love, so that we can each be fulfilled."
—workshop participant in San Diego

Others use it to build more effective relationships at work. A teacher writes:

"I have been using NVC in my special education classroom for about one year. It can work even with children who have language delays, learning difficulties, and behavior problems. One student in our classroom spits, swears, screams, and stabs other students with pencils when they get near his desk. I cue him with, 'Please say that another way. Use your giraffe talk.' [Giraffe puppets are used in some workshops as a teaching aid to demonstrate NVC.] He immediately stands up straight, looks at the person towards whom his anger is directed, and says calmly, 'Would you please move away from my desk? I feel angry when you stand so close to me.' The other students might respond with something like 'Sorry! I forgot it bothers you.'

I began to think about my frustration with this child and to try to discover what I was needing from him (besides harmony and order). I realized how much time I had put into lesson planning and how my need for creativity and contribution were being short-circuited in order to manage behavior. Also, I felt I was not meeting the educational needs of the other students. When he was acting out in class, I began to say, 'I need you to share my attention.' It might take a hundred cues a day, but he got the message and would usually get involved in the lesson."
—teacher, Evanston, Illinois

A doctor writes:

"I use NVC more and more in my medical practice. Some patients ask me whether I am a psychologist, saying that usually their doctors are not interested in the way they live their lives or deal with their diseases. NVC helps me understand what the patients' needs are and what they are needing to hear at a given moment. I find this particularly helpful in relating to patients with hemophilia and AIDS because there is so much anger and pain that the patient/healthcare-provider relationship is often seriously impaired. Recently a woman with AIDS, whom I have been treating for the past five years, told me that what has helped her the most have been my attempts to find ways for her to enjoy her daily life. My use of NVC helps me a lot in this respect. Often in the past, when I knew that a patient had a fatal disease, I myself would get caught in the prognosis, and it was hard for me to sincerely encourage them to live their lives. With NVC, I have developed a new consciousness as well as a new language. I am amazed to see how much it fits in with my medical practice. I feel more energy and joy in my work as I become increasingly engaged in the dance of NVC."

—physician in Paris

Still others use this process in the political arena. A French cabinet member visiting her sister remarked how differently the sister and her husband were communicating and responding to each other. Encouraged by their descriptions of NVC, she mentioned that she was scheduled the following week to negotiate some sensitive issues between France and Algeria regarding adoption procedures. Though time was limited, we dispatched a French-speaking trainer to Paris to work with the cabinet minister. She later attributed much of the success of her negotiations in Algeria to her newly acquired communication techniques.

In Jerusalem, during a workshop attended by Israelis of varying political persuasions, participants used NVC to express themselves regarding the highly contested issue of the West Bank. Many of the Israeli settlers who have established themselves on the West Bank believe that they are fulfilling a religious mandate by doing so, and they are locked in conflict not only with Palestinians but with other Israelis who recognize the Palestinian hope for national sovereignty in this region. During a session, one of my trainers and I modeled empathic hearing through NVC, and then invited participants to take turns role-playing each others' position. After twenty minutes, a settler announced her willingness to consider relinquishing her land claims and moving out of the West Bank into internationally recognized Israeli territory if her political opponents were able to listen to her in the way she had just been listened to.

Worldwide, NVC now serves as a valuable resource for communities facing violent conflicts and severe ethnic, religious, or political tensions. The spread of NVC training and its use in mediation by people in conflict in Israel, the Palestinian Authority, Nigeria, Rwanda, Sierra Leone, and elsewhere have been a source of particular gratification for me. My associates and I were recently in Belgrade over three highly charged days training citizens working for peace. When we first arrived, expressions of despair were visibly etched on the trainees' faces, for their country was enmeshed in a brutal war in Bosnia and Croatia. As the training progressed, we heard the ring of laughter in their voices as they shared their profound gratitude and joy for having found the empowerment they were seeking. Over the next two weeks, during trainings in Croatia, Israel, and Palestine, we again saw desperate citizens in war-torn countries regaining their spirits and confidence from the NVC training they received.

I feel blessed to be able to travel throughout the world teaching people a process of communication that gives them power and joy. Now, with this book, I am pleased and excited to be able to share the richness of Nonviolent Communication with you.

summary

NVC helps us connect with ourselves and each other in a way that allows our natural compassion to flourish. It guides us to reframe the way we express ourselves and listen to others by focusing our consciousness on four areas: what we are observing, feeling, and needing and what we are requesting to enrich our lives. NVC fosters deep listening, respect, and empathy and engenders a mutual desire to give from the heart. Some people use NVC to respond compassionately to themselves, some to create greater depth in their personal relationships, and still others to build effective relationships at work or in the political arena. Worldwide, NVC is used to mediate disputes and conflicts at all levels.

nvc in action

Interspersed throughout the book are dialogues entitled "NVC in Action." These dialogues intend to impart the flavor of an actual exchange where a speaker is applying the principles of Nonviolent Communication. However, NVC is not simply a language or a set of techniques for using words; the consciousness and intent which it embraces may be expressed through silence, a quality of presence, as well as through facial expressions and body language. The NVC in Action dialogues you will be reading are necessarily distilled and abridged versions of real-life exchanges, where moments of silent empathy, stories, humor, gestures, etc. would all contribute to a more natural flow of connection between the two parties than might be apparent when dialogues are condensed in print.

I was presenting Nonviolent Communication in a mosque at Deheisha Refugee Camp in Bethlehem to about 170 Palestinian Moslem men. Attitudes toward Americans at that time were not favorable. As I was speaking, I suddenly noticed a wave of muffled commotion fluttering through the audience. "They're whispering that you are American!" my translator alerted me, just as a gentleman in the audience leapt to his feet. Facing me squarely, he hollered at the top of his lungs, "Murderer!" Immediately a dozen other voices joined him in chorus: "Assassin!" "Child-killer!" "Murderer!"

Fortunately, I was able to focus my attention on what the man was feeling and needing. In this case, I had some cues. On the way into the refugee camp, I had seen several empty tear gas canisters that had been shot into the camp the night before. Clearly marked on each canister were the words "Made in U.S.A." I knew that the refugees harbored a lot of anger toward the U.S. for supplying tear gas and other weapons to Israel.

I addressed the man who had called me a murderer:

I: Are you angry because you would like my government to use its resources differently? (I didn't know whether my guess was correct, but what is critical is my sincere effort to connect with his feeling and need.)

He: Damn right I'm angry! You think we need tear gas? We need sewers, not your tear gas! We need housing! We need to have our own country!

I: So you're furious and would appreciate some support in improving your living conditions and gaining political independence?

He: Do you know what it's like to live here for twenty-seven years the way I have with my family—children and all? Have you got the faintest idea what that's been like for us?

I: Sounds like you're feeling very desperate and you're wondering whether I or anybody else can really understand what it's like to be living under these conditions.

He: You want to understand? Tell me, do you have children? Do they go to school? Do they have playgrounds? My son is sick! He plays in open sewage! His classroom has no books! Have you seen a school that has no books?

I: I hear how painful it is for you to raise your children here; you'd like me to know that what you want is what all parents want for their children—a good education, opportunity to play and grow in a healthy environment.

He: That's right, the basics! Human rights—isn't that what you Americans call it? Why don't more of you come here and see what kind of human rights you're bringing here!

I: You'd like more Americans to be aware of the enormity of the suffering here and to look more deeply at the consequences of our political actions?

Our dialogue continued, with him expressing his pain for nearly twenty more minutes, and I listening for the feeling and need behind each statement. I didn't agree or disagree. I received his words, not as attacks, but as gifts from a fellow human willing to share his soul and deep vulnerabilities with me.

Once the gentleman felt understood, he was able to hear me as I explained my purpose for being at the camp. An hour later, the same man who had called me a murderer was inviting me to his home for a Ramadan dinner.

Nonviolent Communication (NVC) is sometimes referred to as compassionate communication.

By Marshall B. Rosenberg, Ph.D.

Its purpose is to:

1. create human connections that empower compassionate giving and receiving
2. create governmental and corporate structures that support compassionate giving and receiving.

NVC involves both communication skills that foster compassionate relating and consciousness of the interdependence of our well being and using power with others to work together to meet the needs of all concerned.

This approach to communication emphasizes compassion as the motivation for action rather than fear, guilt, shame, blame, coercion, threat or justification for punishment. In other words, it is about getting what you want for reasons you will not regret later. NVC is NOT about getting people to do what we want. It is about creating a quality of connection that gets everyone's needs met through compassionate giving.

The process of NVC encourages us to focus on what we and others are observing separate from our interpretations and judgments, to connect our thoughts and feelings to underlying human needs/values (e.g. protection, support, love), and to be clear about what we would like towards meeting those needs. These skills give the ability to translate from a language of criticism, blame, and demand into a language of human needs - - a language of life that consciously connects us to the universal qualities "alive in us" that sustain and enrich our well being, and focuses our attention on what actions we could take to manifest these qualities.

Nonviolent Communication skills will assist you in dealing with major blocks to communication such as demands, diagnoses and blaming. In CNVC trainings you will learn to express yourself honestly without attacking. This will help minimize the likelihood of facing defensive reactions in others. The skills will help you make clear requests. They will help you receive critical and hostile messages without taking them personally, giving in, or losing self-esteem. These skills are useful with family, friends, students, subordinates, supervisors, co-workers and clients, as well as with your own internal dialogues.

Nonviolent Communication Skills

NVC offers practical, concrete skills for manifesting the purpose of creating connections of compassionate giving and receiving based in a consciousness of interdependence and power with others. These skills include:

1. Differentiating observation from evaluation, being able to carefully observe what is happening free of evaluation, and to specify behaviors and conditions that are affecting us;

2. Differentiating feeling from thinking, being able to identify and express internal feeling states in a way that does not imply judgment, criticism, or blame/punishment;
3. Connecting with the universal human needs/values (e.g. sustenance, trust, understanding) in us that are being met or not met in relation to what is happening and how we are feeling; and
4. Requesting what we would like in a way that clearly and specifically states what we do want (rather than what we don't want), and that is truly a request and not a demand (i.e. attempting to motivate, however subtly, out of fear, guilt, shame, obligation, etc. rather than out of willingness and compassionate giving).

These skills emphasize personal responsibility for our actions and the choices we make when we respond to others, as well as how to contribute to relationships based in cooperation and collaboration.

With NVC we learn to hear our own deeper needs and those of others, and to identify and clearly articulate what "is alive in us". When we focus on clarifying what is being observed, felt, needed, and wanted, rather than on diagnosing and judging, we discover the depth of our own compassion. Through its emphasis on deep listening—to ourselves as well as others—NVC fosters respect, attentiveness and empathy, and engenders a mutual desire to give from the heart. The form is simple, yet powerfully transformative.

Founded on consciousness, language, communication skills, and use of power that enable us to remain human, even under trying conditions, Nonviolent Communication contains nothing new: all that has been integrated into NVC has been known for centuries. The intent is to remind us about what we already know—about how we humans were meant to relate to one another—and to assist us in living in a way that concretely manifests this knowledge.

The use of NVC does not require that the persons with whom we are communicating be literate in NVC or even motivated to relate to us compassionately. If we stay with the principles of NVC, with the sole intention to give and receive compassionately, and do everything we can to let others know this is our only motive, they will join us in the process and eventually we will be able to respond compassionately to one another. While this may not happen quickly, it is our experience that compassion inevitably blossoms when we stay true to the principles and process of Nonviolent Communication.

NVC is a clear and effective **model** for communicating in a way that is cooperative conscious, and compassionate.

The NVC Model |

by Marshall B. Rosenberg, Ph.D.

The 2 Parts and 4 Components of NVC

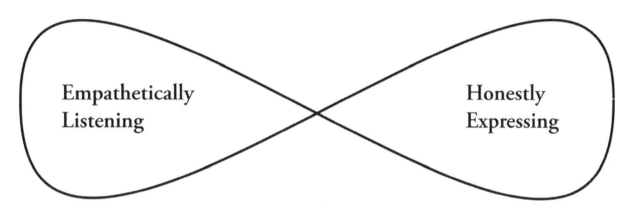

empathetically listening:

    observations

    feelings

    needs

    requests

honestly expressing:

    observations

    feelings

    needs

    requests

Both sides of the NVC model: empathetically listening and honestly expressing, use the four steps of the model: observations, feelings, needs, requests.

Feelings Inventory |

by Marshall B. Rosenberg, Ph.D.

The following are words we use when we want to express a combination of emotional states and physical sensations. This list is neither exhaustive nor definitive. It is meant as a starting place to support anyone who wishes to engage in a process of deepening self-discovery and to facilitate greater understanding and connection between people.

There are two parts to this list: feelings we may have when our needs are being met and feelings we may have when our needs are not being met.

We also have **a list of needs.**

Feelings when your needs are satisfied

AFFECTIONATE

compassionate
friendly
loving
open hearted
sympathetic
tender
warm

ENGAGED

absorbed
alert
curious
engrossed
enchanted
entranced
fascinated
interested
intrigued
involved
spellbound
stimulated

HOPEFUL

expectant

CONFIDENT

empowered
open
proud
safe
secure

EXCITED

amazed
animated
ardent
aroused
astonished
dazzled
eager
energetic
enthusiastic
giddy
invigorated
lively
passionate
surprised
vibrant

GRATEFUL

appreciative
moved
thankful
touched

INSPIRED

amazed
awed
wonder

JOYFUL

amused
delighted
glad
happy
jubilant
pleased
tickled

EXHILARATED

blissful
ecstatic
elated
enthralled

PEACEFUL

calm
clear headed
comfortable
centered
content
equanimous
fulfilled
mellow
quiet
relaxed
relieved
satisfied
serene
still
tranquil
trusting

REFRESHED

enlivened
rejuvenated
renewed
rested
restored

encouraged
optimistic

exuberant
radiant
rapturous
thrilled

revived

Feelings when your needs are not satisfied

AFRAID
apprehensive
dread
foreboding
frightened
mistrustful
panicked
petrified
scared
suspicious
terrified
wary
worried

ANNOYED
aggravated
dismayed
disgruntled
displeased
exasperated
frustrated
impatient
irritated
irked

ANGRY
enraged
furious
incensed
indignant
irate
livid

CONFUSED
ambivalent
baffled
bewildered
dazed
hesitant
lost
mystified
perplexed
puzzled
torn

DISCONNECTED
alienated
aloof
apathetic
bored
cold
detached
distant
distracted
indifferent
numb
removed
uninterested
withdrawn

DISQUIET
agitated
alarmed
discombobulated
disconcerted

EMBARRASSED
ashamed
chagrined
flustered
guilty
mortified
self-conscious

FATIGUE
beat
burnt out
depleted
exhausted
lethargic
listless
sleepy
tired
weary
worn out

PAIN
agony
anguished
bereaved
devastated
grief
heartbroken
hurt
lonely
miserable
regretful
remorseful

TENSE
anxious
cranky
distressed
distraught
edgy
fidgety
frazzled
irritable
jittery
nervous
overwhelmed
restless
stressed out

VULNERABLE
fragile
guarded
helpless
insecure
leery
reserved
sensitive
shaky

YEARNING
envious
jealous
longing
nostalgic
pining
wistful

outraged

resentful

AVERSION

animosity

appalled

contempt

disgusted

dislike

hate

horrified

hostile

repulsed

disturbed

perturbed

rattled

restless

shocked

startled

surprised

troubled

turbulent

turmoil

uncomfortable

uneasy

unnerved

unsettled

upset

SAD

depressed

dejected

despair

despondent

disappointed

discouraged

disheartened

forlorn

gloomy

heavy hearted

hopeless

melancholy

unhappy

wretched

Needs Inventory |

by Marshall B. Rosenberg

The following list of needs is neither exhaustive nor definitive. It is meant as a starting place to support anyone who wishes to engage in a process of deepening self-discovery and to facilitate greater understanding and connection between people.

We have another list that might also be of interest to you: **a list of feelings.**

CONNECTION	**CONNECTION** continued	**HONESTY**	**MEANING**
acceptance	safety	authenticity	awareness
affection	security	integrity	celebration of
appreciation	stability	presence	life
belonging	support		challenge
cooperation	to know and be known	**PLAY**	clarity
communication	to see and be seen	joy	competence
closeness	to understand and	humor	consciousness
community	be understood		contribution
companionship	trust	**PEACE**	creativity
compassion	warmth	beauty	discovery
consideration		communion	efficacy
consistency	**PHYSICAL WELL-BEING**	ease	effectiveness
empathy	air	equality	growth
inclusion	food	harmony	hope
intimacy	movement/exercise	inspiration	learning
love	rest/sleep	order	mourning
mutuality	sexual expression		participation
nurturing	safety	**AUTONOMY**	purpose
respect/self-respect	shelter	choice	self-expression
	touch	freedom	stimulation
	water	independence	to matter
		space	understanding
		spontaneity	